Robert O'Harrow, Jr.

No Place

TO HIDE

FREE PRESS
NEW YORK LONDON TORONTO SYDNEY

P

FREE PRESS

A Division of Simon & Schuster, Inc.
1230 Avenue of the Americas
New York, NY 10020

Copyright © 2005 by Robert O'Harrow, Jr.

FREE PRESS and colophon are
trademarks of Simon & Schuster, Inc.

For information about special discounts for bulk purchases,
please contact Simon & Schuster Special Sales:
1-800-456-6798 or business@simonandschuster.com

Designed by Karolina Harris

Manufactured in the United States of America

1   3   5   7   9   10   8   6   4   2

Library of Congress Cataloging-in-Publication Data
O'Harrow, Robert
No place to hide / Robert O'Harrow, Jr.
p. cm.
Includes bibliographical references and index.
1. Information technology—Social aspects. 2. Information society. 3. Electronic surveillance. 4. Privacy, Right of. I. Title.
HM851.04   2005
303.48'33'0973—dc22   2004056397

ISBN 0-7432-5480-5

AUTHOR'S NOTE

No Place to Hide would have gone nowhere without the intellectual and financial support of the Center for Investigative Reporting. The center is a stronghold of journalistic idealism. It exemplifies Brandeis's idea that sunlight "is said to be the best of disinfectants" through its support of an array of muckraking projects. The center's financial backing gave me the time to figure out a direction for the book, write a proposal, and travel extensively for original reporting at the project's core. Some of that money came from philanthropic groups, including the Ford Foundation, the Deer Creek Foundation, and the Carnegie Corporation of New York.

As important as the money was the enthusiasm of the center's director, Burt Glass, who thrashed through ideas with me during innumerable phone calls. Burt never wasted a chance to express his confidence in our endeavor.

To Christina

Men born to freedom are naturally alert to repel invasion of their liberty by evil-minded rulers. The greatest dangers to liberty lurk in insidious encroachment by men of zeal, well-meaning but without understanding.

—SUPREME COURT JUSTICE LOUIS D. BRANDEIS

CONTENTS

No Place
to Hide

INTRODUCTION:
NO PLACE TO HIDE

THE PENNSYLVANIA CONVENTION CENTER fills two long blocks in downtown Philadelphia. With more than 400,000 square feet of exhibition space, the main hall has enough room inside to hold a track meet, or six football fields, or some rather large parties. The center is known as the home of the city's annual flower and car shows. Organizations from around the country also gather there for the proximity to the city's historic sites: the nearby Liberty Bell, Independence Hall, and other landmarks from the nation's birth seem to convey a certain integrity to their activities. It's where the International Association of Chiefs of Police had its technology conference in October 2003.

For several days, thousands of law enforcement officials from the United States and abroad wandered through the exhibits. Some lingered at booths featuring dull black handguns. Others inspected a mini-tank designed for riots. They eyed crisp blue uniforms and tried on bulletproof vests. They formed a long line for the virtual shooting range, a training system that came complete with a life-sized culprit projected on a video screen. The *pop, pop, pop* of their practice sessions filled the air. But the great majority of police came to Philadelphia to

look at a different sort of gear. They wanted the stuff of homeland security: databases and dossiers, surveillance cameras, and computer tools
for intelligence analysts. And in greater numbers than ever before, the
information industry was there to oblige them.

The center was abuzz with an atmosphere that could be described as
part carnival, part science fiction. Row after row of pitch men and women
touted their companies' ability to preserve life and liberty by helping police watch everything more closely. One contractor, Raytheon Communications Infrared, displayed a car with a night-vision camera mounted on
the roof. The FBI promoted its growing use of DNA to identify people,
while Treasury agents touted their growing access to reports about suspicious bank accounts. PricewaterhouseCoopers, the accounting and consulting firm, was among those offering a slick handbook describing how
best to seize computers, email, and telephone calls. There was even a
group, partly funded by the Justice Department, giving away a CD showing local police how to become intelligence agencies, not just crime-
busters. "Turn-Key Intelligence: Unlocking Your Agency's Intelligence
Capabilities," the CD was labeled. "Today's emphasis on intelligence
makes it a must-do for most agencies in the United States."

Near the entrance was information giant ChoicePoint, a Georgia
company marketing its ability to deliver billions of records about Americans online to police in every state. Names, addresses, jobs, cars, family, criminal records. ChoicePoint collects, analyzes, and sells it all. Next
to its booth were firms that help law enforcement manage the Choice-
Point files. One of them showed how it delivers the reports to cell
phones, PalmPilots, and laptop computers. Another, Orion Scientific
Systems, claimed to help police use the data to identify and track troublemakers who might be criminals or terrorists. "Orion develops and
implements all-source automated collection and analytical tools designed for intelligence, law enforcement and global security analysis,"
the company's brochure said.

Not far away was a LexisNexis display. A salesman dressed in a golf
shirt showed how the company's own collection of personal records,
legal cases, and billions of news articles can help track someone down.
"We have a lot of derogatory information on people. Judgments, liens,
bankruptcies . . . ," the salesman said to a police chief from a little town
in Kansas. Across the aisle was one of the LexisNexis partners, a tech-

nology company called I2, which does something called data mining. Data mining is a computer process that helps reduce the amount of time it takes to discover a nugget of information gold in a giant database from weeks or months to an instant or two. The I2 software spits out graphic displays about a person's activities and associates that look like colorful spiderwebs. The company's aim echoes the futuristic law enforcement world in the science fiction movie *Minority Report,* where one group of police specializes in rooting out actual crimes before they occur. "We are," said I2 president John J. Reis, "principally a company whose focus is all about converting large volumes of information into actionable intelligence, to help the law enforcement and intelligence communities resolve crimes faster and through predictive analysis help to thwart crimes before they occur."

There was a company called Identix whose salesman cheerfully demonstrated the workings of a small machine called IBIS. Though it looked like a handheld vacuum cleaner, it was actually an identity tool. The IBIS had a small hole in the front to electronically capture fingerprints. Above that was a dime-size lens that takes digital photos of a suspect's face. The Identix salesman explained that the device was meant to improve police efficiency by enabling them to wire the finger- and face prints back to headquarters for verification. Identix also markets one of the nation's most sophisticated face recognition programs.

In the back of the great hall was Verint Systems, a company whose name is derived from "verifiable intelligence." Verint works closely with marketers, who use the company's technology to track and assess customers. But it was there to promote its catalogue of surveillance gear. Verint had important contracts with the Defense and Justice departments, but it wanted to expand its market to state and local police. The company displayed eavesdropping equipment that could listen in on telephone calls, capture email from the Web, and sift through digital video recordings for suspicious behavior.

Generating its own buzz was a firm called Seisint, short for seismic intelligence. Seisint's main product is Accurint, an information service that holds out the promise of giving police entry into society's every nook and cranny. "Instantly FIND people, their assets, their relatives, their associates, and more," the marketing material said. "Search the entire country for less than the cost of a phone call—a quarter."

What made Seisint stand out, though, was a new service called the Multi-state Anti-Terrorism Information Exchange. Whimsically dubbed the Matrix, in a nod to the popular dystopian movie, the system combines commercially available details about American adults with millions of criminal and government records. That had never been done before, at least not publicly. The company wasn't shy about what it could mean for regular cops. The "invisible become visible," its leaflets said. (Police who had used Matrix gave it rave reviews. "It's scary," one said. "I mean, I can call up everything about you, your pictures and pictures of your neighbors.")

Many at the expo knew that Justice Department and Homeland Security officials had budgeted millions of dollars for Matrix, possibly for use as an anchor in a national intelligence- and information-sharing system. Now police at the conference could see the fabled Matrix firsthand. All they had to do was sign up for a "law enforcement only" demonstration in the center's Liberty Ballroom, which they did with enthusiasm. For some police, the power of it was irresistible.

AFTER THE TERROR ATTACKS on September 11, 2001, our government leaders could not resist the promise that information technology would make us safe again. Even as the fires burned where almost three thousand people had died, they turned to computers, surveillance gear, and mountains of information about Americans as part of their nascent war on terror. This was an earnest impulse, shared by small-town police and G-men alike. If we could only know more about everyone, they reasoned, we would be able to discern the lethal few from the many good.

That fantasy had been brewing in the law enforcement world for a long time. It took a data revolution to make it feasible on an epic scale. Suddenly, after the terror attacks, the government was wedded as never before to the revolutionaries: the many information brokers, database marketers, and technology makers who had quietly amassed vast reservoirs of information about us and created tools to track, assess, and predict our behavior.

The collection of personal information has long been a part of American culture. The sweep and depth and pace of that collection took on dramatic new dimensions in the 1990s, thanks in large part to profound improvements in computing and the advent of the Internet. Much of this took place out of the public's view, and largely without the public's direct consent. In some cases, data entrepreneurs sold their services to police as a way to streamline law enforcement. In many others, marketers simply wanted to know their customers better. They wanted to automate the process of customer relationships. They asked questions that could only be answered with more data. Who is someone really? What motivates people? How are they likely to behave? How can we get them to open their wallets? How do we separate the relatively few very profitable customers from the rest?

These questions are a lot harder than they might seem at first glance. To answer them, companies of all stripes went on a data collection binge, gathering, parsing, and shaping more information about more people than ever before in history. It wasn't just the credit bureaus or banks or those people who called incessantly at dinnertime. It was the Safeway or Vons groceries where you bought your steaks and beer and diapers. It was the CVS Pharmacy where you filled your Valium prescription. It was US Airways or American Airlines. The politicians to whom you donated money. The company that issued your Visa card. The publishers of *Vogue* and *The New Yorker* and the other magazines you read. The direct mailer who sold you sex toys. It was the company that gave you a toll-free number to make life more convenient, the electronic toll operator, countless World Wide Web sites and companies you've never heard about, who harvest data from surveys, public records, credit card applications, warranty cards, and so many other forms, like giant combines harvesting wheat.

That was only the beginning. New devices emerged that enabled mobile phone companies to say precisely where you stood on the planet. Grocery stores and banks began using electronic fingerprint readers to authenticate who you were—or give you the discounts you wanted. Tiny radio frequency identification devices, some as small as fleas, could be embedded in product packages, clothing, or even money, enabling another sort of tracking that was impossible before. Computer processors monitored the location and activity of cars. And computer software enabled individual banks to watch and assess every one of millions of transactions on a given day, looking for signs that you might be a criminal, a tax cheat, or have questionable ties to unsavory people.

Cities and businesses and schools installed more and more cameras, some loaded with automated face recognition programs.

Almost everyone you do business with collected information about you, sold it to someone else, or sifted it for their own mercantile ends. In some cases, you eagerly sought out the benefits and conveniences they offered in exchange for your information. By now those bargains are being transformed, usually without your input, into a public-private security infrastructure, the likes of which the world has never seen.

THE GOVERNMENT'S TURN TO SURVEILLANCE was almost reflexive. Within hours of the 9/11 attacks, officials everywhere sought out private companies: Could they help track down the terrorists and bolster homeland security? Not since Pearl Harbor had the nation faced as devastating an attack. In 1941 and 1942, heavy industry responded with a massive boost in production of trucks, tanks, bullets, and shells. Now the government was asking Information Age businesses for a different sort of materiel. Swept away by a patriotic fervor, information technology specialists flung open giant computer systems across the country to help law enforcement and intelligence agencies search for clues about the nineteen hijackers and their accomplices.

Financial institutions gave access to credit card activity. Banks pored through customer accounts. Internet service providers helped trace email and account details. Data giants such as Acxiom Corp., ChoicePoint, and Seisint searched through billions of demographic and marketing records on behalf of investigators, often using thin threads of information about suspects to pull together hefty dossiers about their time in the United States. Northwest, JetBlue, American, and other airlines handed over manifests about passengers from across the country. Never mind the carefully crafted privacy promises, issued over the years to soothe customers.

At the same time, hundreds of companies followed through on a wartime tradition: they swamped Washington's bureaucracy with profitable proposals. Data mines. National IDs. Fingerprint readers. Sensors that can remotely replicate an agent's "sixth sense" of imminent trouble. The list goes on and on. Even in a nation long anxious about the specter of Big Brother, all this seemed to make sense to many people, at least at the time. No one knew where the next attack would occur. Much of the country braced itself for atomic bomb explosions or the spread of anthrax. The White House said it needed to fight an unorthodox war. Counterterrorism authorities charged with keeping us safe said, over and over, that meant more data and more intelligence. The USA Patriot Act dramatically expanded the government's ability to eavesdrop and snoop with little public oversight. It is only one of many powers the government has invoked to collect information in the war on terror. The Defense Advanced Research Projects Agency even created an ominous new branch, the Information Awareness Office, which began work on a global surveillance system. "I'd be happy to trade off some of my freedom for security" became a common refrain. So intent was the push for security that few people contemplated, let alone questioned, the consequences of the government's aggressive acquisition of personal information and the sudden, fearful acquiescence of American citizens.

There's no disputing that expanded use of surveillance and datavcillance has helped the government in important ways. And it's no stretch to say information technology will be a crucial part of the war on terror for the rest of our lives. Authorities have detained scores of suspected terrorists, based on evidence they collected surreptitiously. They also are sharing information and intelligence far more readily, from small-town agencies to the CIA. That's due in part to pathbreaking networks and information systems, such as the Matrix, as well as to changes in law enforcement culture. But few people understand the true scope of these efforts, and for good reasons. Our leaders have often invoked national security concerns to cloak their activities in secrecy. White House and Justice Department officials declined to spell out publicly all the measures they're taking, even to Congress in some cases. Attorney General John Ashcroft, meanwhile, urged agencies to narrowly interpret requests made under federal Freedom of Information laws. The evidence is there, though. Many documents and interviews with business and government officials show that authorities have ripped through old restraints on government surveillance, often with the best intentions, certainly with new legal authorities. To be sure, there have been setbacks for the government along the way. Privacy advocates have hindered some projects, such as the Defense Department's Total Information Awareness initiative and the Matrix, both of which came under intense criticism after becoming public. This resistance cut across ideological lines, but it is episodic and ad hoc. The drive for more monitoring, data collection, and analysis is relentless and entrepreneurial. Where one effort ends, another begins, often with the same technology and aims. Total Information Awareness may be gone, but it's not forgotten. Other kinds of Matrix systems are already in the works. And since the approval of the USA Patriot Act in October 2001, the Justice Department has never stopped seeking ever broader authorities, whether through a Patriot Act II or, as in the spring of 2004, demands for unprecedented access to communication online.

The government's ability to examine our lives is only going to increase in coming years, as the National Commission on Terrorist Attacks Upon the United States made clear in a landmark report in the summer of 2004. After analyzing the intelligence and security failures that preceded the terror attacks, the group, better known as the 9/11 Commission, called for standardized identification, widespread use of fingerprints and other biometrics, far greater information sharing, and a consolidated intelligence system. Such measures are crucial to our security, the Commission concluded, even though they will raise profound new questions about our civil liberties. "Even without the changes we recommend," the report said, "the American public has vested enormous authority in the U.S. government" [p. 394].

Surveillance comes with a price. It dulls the edge of public debate, imposes a sense of conformity, introduces the uneasy feeling of being watched. It chills culture and stifles dissent. By definition, it is often secret and hard to hold to account. That is why in the 1970s Congress shut down domestic intelligence operations that had led to so many abuses by the FBI, CIA, the U.S. Army, and others. It's also why it passed information and privacy laws. These not only restricted how the government could collect and use information about citizens. They required agencies to be more open. The new legal authorities and the government's partnership with private information companies now pose a direct threat to this three-decade-old effort toward openness. It's a simple fact that private companies can collect information about people in ways the government can't. At the same time, they can't be held accountable for their behavior or their mistakes the way government agencies can. Their capabilities have raced far ahead of the nation's understanding and laws. The legacy of these efforts will be with us for many years.

Peter Swire, who served as the nation's first privacy counselor in the Clinton administration, has warned that we're heading toward the creation of a "security-industrial complex." He intentionally echoed a famous phrase in the prophetic speech that President Dwight Eisenhower gave on the occasion of his departure from the White House in 1961. "In the councils of government, we must guard against the acquisition of unwarranted influence, whether sought or unsought, by the military-industrial complex. The potential for the disastrous rise of misplaced power exists and will persist," Eisenhower said. "We must never let the weight of this combination endanger our liberties or democratic processes. We should take nothing for granted. Only an alert and knowledgeable citizenry can compel the proper meshing of the huge industrial and military machinery of defense with our peaceful methods and goals, so that security and liberty may prosper together."

Swire, a business law professor at the Moritz College of Law of the Ohio State University, contends that national security is being invoked to justify measures that threaten some of the traditions—of individual privacy, autonomy, and civil liberties—that help define our national character. Behind these measures are self-interested companies—increasingly powerful private contractors to which the government is outsourcing many of the exigencies of surveillance and security. "You have government on a holy mission to ramp up information gathering and you have an information technology industry desperate for new markets," Swire said. "Once this is done, you will have unprecedented snooping abilities. What will happen to our private lives if we're under constant surveillance?"

ON MARCH 15, 2002, at a coliseum in Fayetteville, North Carolina, President George W. Bush beamed as the soldiers from Fort Bragg and their families chanted: "U.S.A.! U.S.A.! U.S.A!"

The memories of the attacks six months before were fresh. The president was there to spell out his plans for a long, relentless war on terror. "We want every terrorist to be made to live like an international fugitive, on the road, with no place to settle, no place to organize, no place to hide."

It was a powerful moment. It also was an ironic echo to a warning from Senator Frank Church three decades before. Church had served as head of a commission formed to examine the nation's history of domestic surveillance. He had seen firsthand what can happen when law enforcement and intelligence agencies amass too much secret influence. In the late 1960s and early 1970s, some worked outside the rules, targeting innocent people and groups for their political views, or because someone mistakenly assumed an individual posed a threat. Church was especially concerned about the government's use of computers and eavesdropping technology. Such equipment, he said, could serve as a powerful weapon abroad. The use of it could also spin out of control, especially in the hands of tyrannical leaders.

"That capability at any time could be turned around on the American people and no American would have any privacy left, such is the capability to monitor everything—telephone conversations, telegrams, it doesn't matter," he said on a television news program in 1975. "There would be no place to hide."

Like it or not, the technology is now being turned on American citizens and foreigners alike. It is being deployed at every level of law enforcement and intelligence. It's vastly more powerful, varied, and sophisticated than Church ever contemplated those many years ago. As a consequence, the president's wish may come true, and the terrorist will have no place to hide. But then, there's a chance that neither will we.

1

SIX WEEKS IN AUTUMN

———————

ASSISTANT ATTORNEY GENERAL VIET DINH took his seat in La Colline restaurant on Capitol Hill and signaled for a cup of coffee. It was one of those standard Washington breakfasts, where politicos mix schmoozing and big ideas to start their days.

An intense foot soldier for Attorney General Ashcroft, Dinh had been in his job for only a few months. He wanted to make a good impression on others at the session and craved the caffeine to keep his edge. As he sipped his fourth cup and listened to the patter of White House and Hill staffers, a young man darted up to the table. "A plane has crashed," he said. "It hit the World Trade Center."

Dinh and the rest of the voluble group went silent. Then their beepers began chirping in unison. At another time, it might have seemed funny, a Type-A Washington moment. Now they looked at one another and rushed out of the restaurant. It was about 9:30 am on September 11, 2001.

Dinh hurried back to the Justice Department, where the building was being evacuated. Like countless other Americans, he was already consumed with a desire to strike back. Unlike most, however, he had an inkling of how: by doing whatever was necessary to strengthen the government's legal hand against terrorists.

JIM DEMPSEY WAS SIFTING THROUGH EMAILS at his office at the Center for Democracy and Technology on Farragut Square when his boss, Jerry Berman, rushed in. "Turn on the TV," Berman said. Dempsey reached for the remote, and images came rushing at him. Crisp sunshine. Lower Manhattan glinting in the brilliance. A jetliner cutting through the scene.

Dempsey was a lanky and slow-speaking former Hill staffer who combined a meticulous attention to detail with an aw-shucks demeanor. Since the early 1990s, he has been one of the leading watchdogs of FBI surveillance initiatives, a reasoned and respected civil liberties advocate routinely summoned to the Hill by both political parties to advise lawmakers about technology and privacy issues.

As he watched the smoke and flames engulf the World Trade Center, he knew it was the work of terrorists, and the FBI was foremost in his mind. "They have screwed up so bad," he said to himself. "With all the powers and resources that they have, they should have caught these guys."

At the same moment, it dawned on him that his work—and the work of many civil liberties activists over the years to check the increasingly aggressive use of technology by law enforcement officials—was about to be undone.

THE CAR ARRIVED at Senator Patrick Leahy's house in northern Virginia shortly after 9 am. The Vermont Democrat took his place in the front seat and, as the car coursed toward the Potomac, he read through some notes about the pending nomination of a new drug czar and thought about a meeting that morning at the Supreme Court.

Half-listening to the radio, Leahy heard something about an explosion and the World Trade Center. He asked the driver to turn it up, then called some friends in New York. They told him what they were seeing on television. It sounded ominous. The car continued toward the Supreme Court and the conference he was to attend with Chief Justice

William Rehnquist and circuit court judges from around the country. Leahy headed to the Court's conference room, with its thickly carpeted floors and oak-paneled walls lined with portraits of the first eight chief justices. When Rehnquist arrived, Leahy leaned toward him and whispered, "Bill, before we start, I believe we have a terrorist attack."

As if on cue, a muffled boom echoed through the room. Smoke began rising across the Potomac from the Pentagon.

Leahy chaired the Senate Judiciary Committee, putting him at the center of an inevitable debate about how to fight back. Leahy was one of Congress's most liberal members, a longtime proponent of civil liberties who had always worked to keep the government from trampling individual rights. But Leahy was also a former prosecutor, a pragmatist who understood what investigators were up against in trying to identify and bring down terrorists.

He knew that conservatives were going to press him for more police powers while civil libertarians would look to him as their standard-bearer. Leahy wanted to strike the right balance. But after watching an F-16 roar over the Mall that afternoon, he resolved to do whatever he could, as a patriot and a Democrat, to give law enforcement officials more tools to stop future attacks.

THE ATTACKS ON THE WORLD TRADE CENTER and the Pentagon didn't just set off a national wave of mourning and ire. They reignited and re-shaped a smoldering debate over the proper use of government power to peer into the lives of ordinary people.

The argument boiled down to this: In an age of high-tech terror, what is the proper balance between national security and the privacy of millions of Americans, whose personal information is already more widely available than ever before? Telephone records, emails, oceans of detail about individuals' lives—the government wanted access to all of it to hunt down terrorists before they struck.

For six weeks that fall, behind a veneer of national solidarity and bi-partisanship, Washington leaders engaged in pitched, closed-door arguments over how much new power the government should have in the name of national security. They were grappling not only with the specter of more terrorist attacks but also with the chilling memories of

Cold War Red-baiting, J. Edgar Hoover's smear campaigns, and Water-gate-era wiretaps.

At the core of the dispute was a body of little known laws and rules that, over the last half century, defined and limited the government's ability to snoop: Title III of the Omnibus Crime Control and Safe Streets Act governed electronic eavesdropping. The "pen register, trap and trace" rules covered the use of devices to track the origin and destination of telephone calls. The Foreign Intelligence Surveillance Act, or FISA, regulated the power to spy domestically when seeking foreign intelligence information.

The White House, the Justice Department, and their allies in Congress now wanted to ease those restraints, and they wanted to do it as quickly as possible. Though put into place to protect individuals and political groups from past abuses by the FBI, CIA, and others, the restrictions were partly to blame for the intelligence gaps on September 11, the government said. Implicit in that wish list was the desire to tap into the data revolution. In the previous decade, the world had watched the power of computers increase at an extraordinary pace. At the same time, the price of data storage plummeted, while new software tools enabled analysts to tap into giant reservoirs of names, addresses, purchases, and other details, and make sense of it all. It was a kind of surveillance that didn't rely only on cameras and eavesdropping. This was the age of behavioral profiling and at the front were the marketers who wanted you to open your wallet. Now the government wanted their help.

The administration also wanted new authority to secretly detain individuals suspected of terrorism and to enlist banks and other financial services companies in the search for terrorist financing. Law enforcement sought broad access to business databases filled with information about the lives of ordinary citizens. All this detail could help investigators search for links among plotters.

Jim Dempsey and other civil libertarians agreed that the existing laws were outdated, but for precisely the opposite reason—because they already gave the government access to immense amounts of information unavailable a decade ago. Handing investigators even more power, they warned, would lead to privacy invasions and abuses.

• • •

THEY STARED AT A TELEVISION in the bright sunroom of Dinh's Chevy Chase home, a handful of policy specialists from the Justice Department who wondered what to do next. Only hours before, they had fled their offices, cringing as fighter jets patrolled Washington's skies. Now, as news programs replayed the destruction, they talked about their friend Barbara Olson, conservative commentator and wife of Solicitor General Ted Olson. She was aboard American Airlines Flight 77 when it crashed into the Pentagon.

Dinh couldn't believe Barbara was gone. He'd just had dinner at the Olsons' house two nights before, and she had been in rare form. Her humor was irrepressible. Dinh passed around a book of photography she had signed and given to him and the other dinner guests, *Washington, D.C.: Then and Now.*

It was hard to process so much death amid so much sunshine. Dinh and his colleagues tried to focus on the work ahead. They agreed they faced a monumental, even historic task: a long-overdue reworking of anti-terrorism laws to prevent something like this from happening again on American soil. Their marching orders came the next morning, as they reconvened in a conference room in Dinh's suite of offices on the fourth floor of Justice. Ashcroft wasn't there—he was in hiding along with other senior government officials. Just before the meeting, Dinh had spoken to Adam Ciongoli, Ashcroft's counselor, who conveyed the attorney general's desires.

"Beginning immediately," Dinh told the half dozen policy advisers and lawyers, "we will work on a package of authorities"—sweeping, dramatic, and based on practical recommendations from FBI agents and Justice Department lawyers in the field. "The charge [from Ashcroft] was very, very clear: 'all that is necessary for law enforcement, within the bounds of the Constitution, to discharge the obligation to fight this war against terror,'" he said.

Dinh's enthusiasm for the task was evident. At thirty-four, he seemed perpetually jazzed up, smiled often and spoke quickly, as though his words, inflected with the accent of his native Vietnam, couldn't keep up with his ideas. A graduate of Harvard Law School, he had learned his way around Washington as an associate special counsel to the Senate Whitewater committee, and as a special counsel to Senator Pete Domenici (R-N.M.) during the Clinton impeachment trial. "What are the problems?" Dinh asked the group around the table.

For the next several hours—indeed, over the next several days—Dinh's colleagues catalogued gripes about the legal restraints on detective and intelligence work. Some of the complaints had been bouncing around the FBI and Justice Department for years. Because of the law's peculiarities, it was unclear if investigators were allowed to track the destination and origin of email the same way they could phone calls. They could obtain search warrants more easily for a telephone tape machine than for commercial voice-mail services. And the amount of information that intelligence agents and criminal investigators were permitted to share was limited, making it much harder to target and jail terrorists.

All of this, the lawyers agreed, had to change. Now.

JIM DEMPSEY WAS SWAMPED. Reporters, other activists, congressional staffers—everyone wanted his take on how far the Justice Department and Congress would go in reaction to the attacks. "We were getting fifty calls a day," he recalled. Dempsey knew Congress would not have the will to resist granting dramatic new powers to law enforcement. It was a classic dynamic: Something terrible happens. Legislators rush to respond. They don't have time to investigate the policy implications thoroughly, so they reach for what's available and push it through.

That was a nightmare for Dempsey. Looking for signs of hope that the legislative process could be slowed, even if it could not be stopped, he made his own calls around town. "A crisis mentality emerges, and there was clearly a crisis. . . . The push for action, the appearance of action, becomes so great."

Within days of the attack, a handful of lawmakers took to the Senate floor with legislation that had been proposed and shot down in recent years because of civil liberties concerns. Many of the proposals had originally had nothing to do with terrorism. One bill, called the Combating Terrorism Act, proposed expanding the government's authority to trace telephone calls to include email. It was a legacy of FBI efforts to expand surveillance powers during the Clinton administration, which had supported a variety of technology-oriented proposals opposed by civil libertarians. Now it was hauled out and approved in minutes.

One of the few voices advocating calm deliberation was Patrick Leahy. It was not clear what he would be able to do in such a highly charged atmosphere.

ACROSS THE CITY and across the country, other civil libertarians braced themselves for the fallout from the attacks. Among them was Morton Halperin, former head of the Washington office of the American Civil Liberties Union and a former national security official in three administrations. Halperin, a senior fellow at the Council on Foreign Relations, was personally familiar with government surveillance.

While working as a National Security Council staffer in the Nixon administration, Halperin was suspected of leaking information about the secret U.S. bombing of Cambodia. His house was wiretapped by the FBI, and the taps continued for months after he left the government.

Now, twenty-four hours after the attacks, he read an email from a member of an online group that had been formed to fight a Clinton administration plan to make publishing classified materials a crime. The writer warned the plan would be reprised. Halperin had been anticipating this moment for years. More than a decade ago, he wrote an essay predicting that terrorism would replace communism as the main justification for domestic surveillance. "I sat and stared at that email for a few minutes and decided that I could not do my regular job, that I had to deal with this," he would say later.

Halperin banged out a call to arms on his computer. "There can be no doubt that we will hear calls in the next few days for congress to enact sweeping legislation to deal with terrorism," he wrote in the email to more than two dozen civil libertarians on September 12. "This will include not only the secrecy provision, but also broad authority to conduct electronic and other surveillance and to investigate political groups. . . . We should not wait."

Within hours, Jim Dempsey, Marc Rotenberg from the Electronic Privacy Information Center, and others had offered their support. Their plan: To build on Halperin's call for legislative restraint while striking a sympathetic note about the victims of the attacks. They started putting together a meeting to sign off on a civil liberties manifesto: "In Defense of Freedom at a Time of Crisis."

Underlying the discussion about how to respond to the terror attacks was the mid-1970s investigation, led by Senator Frank Church (D-Idaho), into the government's sordid history of domestic spying. Through hundreds of interviews and the examination of tens of thousands of documents, the Church Committee found that the FBI, the CIA, and other government agencies had engaged in pervasive surveillance of politicians, religious organizations, women's rights advocates, anti-war groups, and civil liberties activists.

At FBI headquarters in Washington, agents had developed more than half a million domestic intelligence files during the Cold War. The CIA had secretly opened and often photographed almost a quarter-million letters in the United States from 1953 to 1973. One of the most egregious intelligence abuses was an FBI counterintelligence program known as COINTELPRO. It was, the Church Report said, "designed to 'disrupt' groups and 'neutralize' individuals deemed to be threats to domestic security." Among other things, COINTELPRO operations included undermining the jobs of political activists, sending anonymous letters to "spouses of intelligence targets for the purposes of destroying their marriages," and a systematic campaign to undermine the Reverend Martin Luther King, Jr.'s, civil rights efforts through leaked information about his personal life. "Too many people have been spied upon by too many government agencies and too much information has been collected" through secret informants, wiretaps, bugs, surreptitious mail opening, and break-ins, the Church Report had warned.

CHRISTOPHER PYLE, a professor at Mount Holyoke College, remembers those days well. In 1967 and 1968, while serving in the Army, he taught law at the Army's intelligence school at Fort Holabird, Maryland. One of his classes focused on CONUS intelligence and spot reports, the Army's shorthand for intelligence in the continental United States. No one told him exactly what to teach, so he concentrated on what he thought the Army might need to quell riots, the use of maps, layouts of city parks for bivouacs, the configuration of bridges, so that Army trucks would not get stuck under them or fall through them on the way to a crisis. One day an officer directly involved in actual CONUS intelligence operations approached him.

"Captain Pyle, you don't know much about this, do you?"

"No," Pyle said. "What can you tell me?"

Pyle and another instructor arranged for a briefing. They were taken to a huge building that once had been used to assemble railroad engines. It had a large black arch and, in one brightly lit room, an interior cage made of mesh wire. Pyle walked into the cage, where an officer showed him books containing mug shots. He looked in the first volume and saw a familiar face. It was Ralph David Abernathy, Martin Luther King's assistant. Officers called the books the "black list." As Pyle recalled it, they were actually labeled: persons active in civil disturbances. On a bench near the books was a stack of computer punch cards, the kind used in the 1960s to program the cutting-edge machines of the day. Written on the cards in pencil were the names of people whose information the cards contained. The top card was about Arlo Tatum, a man Pyle knew as the head of the Central Committee for Conscientious Objectors in Philadelphia, a group of activists who advised soldiers and others about their rights. Outside the cage, Pyle saw more than a dozen teletype machines. The head of the CONUS intelligence section told him they were spitting out reports from some fifteen hundred Army operatives about demonstrations with twenty people or more. Pyle was starting to understand how naive he'd been. He began formulating a plan. He would be getting out of the Army soon. He could tell the world about what was going on. When he joined the Army he took an oath to defend the country against all enemies, here and abroad. In his mind now, that included the Army's intelligence operation. They turned in their security badges and left the building.

"So I turned to the briefer and said, 'This is really terrific stuff. You are doing a great job. Do you have anything I can show my students?'"

The briefer gave him teletype printouts for the week of March 11–18, 1968. One of the reports on it told of undercover Army agents attending a meeting at a Unitarian church. Pyle thanked him and turned in his security badge for the building. "It was very clear to me that we had just witnessed the essential apparatus of a police state," Pyle said. "It wasn't that these people were trying to create a police state. They were very nice people. The kind that you would want as your friends and neighbors. But they were creating a reporting apparatus that was covering millions of Americans engaged in completely lawful activity."

Pyle left the Army as planned, and in January 1970 he wrote a long story about the Army's vast and growing spy operations. The article, which won a Polk Award in 1971 for *The Washington Monthly,* began: "For the past four years, the U.S. Army has been closely watching civilian political activity within the United States."

PYLE'S JOURNALISM PROVIDED one of the first major revelations about the depth and breadth of government spying. His stories prompted hearings by Senator Sam Ervin, which Pyle helped organize. As a result of the scrutiny, the Army soon shut down its domestic surveillance efforts.

Similar operations came to light in the next few years, including those run by the FBI, CIA, and other agencies, and Congress responded to them as well. The result was a series of laws aimed at curbing government abuses. The Privacy Act of 1974 gave individuals new rights to know and correct what the government was collecting and sharing about them. The Foreign Intelligence Surveillance Act (FISA) of 1978 gave broad powers for counterintelligence officials to monitor the agents of foreign countries. It also created restrictions. Under FISA, authorities had to demonstrate, to the supersecret Foreign Intelligence Surveillance Court, that the principal purpose for their surveillance was foreign intelligence. But the law also restricted the use of those powers for domestic criminal investigations and prosecutions.

Those laws provided ballast for civil liberties protections for three decades. Civil liberties activists even consider FISA a key safeguard against domestic spying. This despite all the secrecy surrounding it, and the fact that the FISA court almost never denied an application for electronic surveillance. Some conservatives have contended that the law created unnecessary, even absurd barriers between criminal and intelligence investigators.

By the time of the Patriot Act debates, the Bush administration believed those barriers were getting in the way of uncovering terrorist cells operating in the United States and abroad. Law enforcement authorities chafed at internal guidelines imposed by the Justice Department in response to the Church Committee revelations. They claimed agents weren't allowed to monitor religious services without evidence of a crime, for instance, which made it hard to investigate mosques that might be harboring terrorists. Ashcroft claimed that the rules even prohibited investigators from surfing the Web for information about suspects.

When Dinh and his team began taking stock of needed legal changes, the legacy of the Church Committee loomed large. They saw a chance to turn back the clock. Standing in their way were people like Dempsey and Halperin.

SCORES OF PEOPLE streamed into the ACLU's white stucco town house on Capitol Hill on the Friday after the attacks, responding to Halperin's email and calls from ACLU lobbyists. As with so many privacy battles, there were some strikingly strange bedfellows in attendance: liberal immigration rights groups, libertarians from the conservative Free Congress Foundation and Eagle Forum, technology-savvy activists from the Electronic Privacy Information Center and the Center for Democracy and Technology.

They filled the main conference room downstairs, overflowing through French doors into a garden, and up the stairway to the ACLU's offices. The ACLU's headquarters, later relocated downtown, had been the site of countless strategy meetings over the years on abortion rights, civil rights, freedom of speech, and religious freedom. "I had never seen that kind of turnout in twenty-five years," said Laura Murphy, director of the ACLU's national office. "People were worried. They just knew this was a recipe for government overreaching."

They also grasped the difficulty of their position. They were trying to persuade Americans to hold fast to concerns about individual freedom and privacy while the vast majority of people were terrified. Polls that fall showed that most people were more than willing to trade off civil liberties and privacy protections for more security. Even normally privacy-minded lawmakers, including Senators Dianne Feinstein (D-Calif.) and Charles Schumer (D-N.Y.), had no intention of questioning efforts to push a bill through quickly. Representative Bob Barr (R-Ga.), a staunch conservative and dedicated privacy advocate, couldn't offer much hope. Barr and Murphy had worked closely together in recent years, though they came from different ends of the political spectrum.

When she called him after the attacks, he confessed there was probably little he could do to temper the fervor gripping Washington. After debate over how to express clear sympathy for the victims of the attack, the group worked out a ten-point statement. "We must have faith in our democratic system and our Constitution, and in our ability to protect at the same time both the freedom and the security of all Americans," read point No. 10. The document was signed by representatives of more than 150 groups, including religious organizations, gun owners, police, and conservative activists. A few days later, they released it at a press conference and posted it on a Web site.

What kind of impact did it have? Apparently not much. A year later, several key officials from the White House and Justice Department said they had never heard of the appeal.

SENATOR LEAHY WOULD DESCRIBE those days as among the most challenging and emotional of his twenty-eight years in the Senate. He was saddled with the responsibility of crafting the Senate proposal for anti-terrorism legislation. He didn't want to ram a bad law through Congress, but he also didn't want to be seen as an obstructionist. He offered to negotiate a bill directly with the White House, avoiding the time-consuming committee approval process. Now he had to come up with a way of maintaining meaningful privacy protections while expanding the government's surveillance powers.

As he worked to reconcile those competing interests, he took long walks around the Capitol and down to the Mall. Everywhere he went, the mood was grim. "I saw the same faces as I did when I was a law school student [in the District] and President Kennedy had been killed," Leahy said. "I saw the same shock, and I wanted to make sure our shock didn't turn into panic." It was crucial, Leahy thought, to take enough time with the legislation to get it right.

In the weeks before September 11, Leahy and Attorney General Ashcroft had consulted frequently on a major overhaul of the FBI, which was under fire for bungling a series of high-profile cases. But the terrorist attacks quickly strained their amicable relations. Within days, Ashcroft held a press conference and called on Congress to approve the Justice Department's legislative plan in a week's time. Leahy was surprised—and irritated. The implication, Leahy says, was "we were going to have another attack if we did not agree to this immediately."

But if he balked, Leahy risked getting hammered as soft on terrorism—or so he and other Democrats feared. Leahy, backed by other Democrats, had begun working on his own anti-terrorism bill, a 165-page tome called the Uniting and Strengthening America Act. On September 19, congressional, White House, and Justice leaders gathered in an ornate room in the Capitol to exchange proposals.

Leahy, Orrin Hatch (R-Utah), Richard Shelby (R-Ala.), and others were there from the Senate. House Majority Leader Richard Armey (R-Tex.), John Conyers, Jr. (D-Mich.), and others represented the House. From the White House came counsel Alberto Gonzales. Ashcroft, Dinh, and their entourage arrived from Justice. As the meeting got started, Dinh made a beeline for a seat near the head of the conference table. Leahy and his colleagues raised their eyebrows and shook their heads. Only members of Congress were supposed to sit at the table, one of the senators told Dinh, asking him to sit with the rest of the staff.

Dinh wasn't troubled by his faux pas. He and his staff were too focused on the forty-page proposal they'd brought with them, the fruit of several all-nighters at Justice. During the crash drafting effort, Dinh had slept on a black leather couch, beneath an American flag, not far from a worn paperback copy of *The Federalist Papers*. He handed out copies of his proposal. Leahy did the same with his draft, stressing that he thought the group should move forward deliberately.

It turned out the proposals were similar in some key respects. Both bills called for updates to the pen register and trap and trace laws, clarifying how they applied to email and the Internet. Both included provisions bolstering money-laundering and wiretap laws. They also proposed making it easier for authorities to get approval for wiretaps in spying and counterintelligence cases. The administration proposal, however, went much further. It called for indefinite detention of any noncitizen the attorney general "has reason to believe may further or facilitate acts of terrorism," as well as the unrestricted sharing of grand jury and eavesdropping data throughout the government. It permitted Internet service providers or employers to voluntarily allow the FBI to tap email. And it made a small but important modification to the FISA law, changing the legal language so that foreign intelligence had to be

only "a" purpose of an investigation, rather than "the" purpose, to secure surveillance authority.

Leahy and some of the other lawmakers murmured about those last
provisions. Giving criminal investigators unchecked access to FISA
powers could break down constitutional safeguards against unreasonable searches and seizures, leading to abuses against U.S. citizens. Dick
Armey, one of the most conservative members in Congress, also expressed concern. It was Armey, in fact, who was already discussing a
"sunset" provision to the new law, placing time limits on how long
parts of it would remain in effect. A sunset provision would guarantee
that some of the most troubling new powers would be revisited by Congress, giving lawmakers an important check on executive authority.
"There were a lot of people in the room, both Republican and Democrat," Leahy said later, "who were not about to give the unfettered
power the attorney general wanted."

Armey also warned that it might take a few weeks to adopt a bill. In
effect, he was urging Ashcroft to back away from his public pressure
to approve a law in the next few days. When the group emerged from
the meeting, Ashcroft changed his tone slightly, telling reporters that
he wanted to pass a bill as quickly as possible. Leahy likewise struck a
conciliatory note. "We're trying to find a middle ground, and I think
we can," he said that day. "We probably agree on more than we dis-
agree on."

Leahy also made it clear he would not be rushed into approving a
bill. "We do not want the terrorists to win by having basic protections
taken away from us," he said. It was a boilerplate rendering of a quota-
tion from Benjamin Franklin that Leahy invoked repeatedly: "Those
who would give up essential liberty to purchase a little temporary safety
deserve neither liberty nor safety."

THE TRUCE BETWEEN LEAHY AND ASHCROFT didn't last long. Despite
Ashcroft's shift in tone, the pressure to move quickly on legislation in-
tensified. For Jim Dempsey, it was depressing. One afternoon in late
September, he was invited by Beryl Howell, Leahy's adviser, to a legislative briefing. Howell wanted Justice Department officials and civil
libertarians to describe to Senate staffers their thoughts about expand-

ing law enforcement authority. The point was to give everyone involved more ideas. Dempsey was eager to attend. "My hope was there could actually be some sort of debate," he says.

Then the Justice Department folks arrived. Howell hadn't told them they would be discussing their proposals with civil libertarians. "They were livid," Dempsey says. "They explicitly said, 'We don't think outsiders should be here, and we won't talk unless they leave the room.'"

Howell quickly brokered a deal. Dempsey and the other civil liberties advocates could stay to hear Justice's presentation, but there would be no back-and-forth discussion. As soon as the Justice delegation finished speaking about their proposals, "they got up and left," Dempsey says. "I was just in despair. I just thought we are never going to be able to work this out."

At the end of September, Leahy's staff and administration officials spent hours together thrashing out questions about civil liberties, the new police and intelligence powers, and oversight by courts and Congress. In a push to come to some agreement on the bill's wording, Howell met with White House deputy counsel Timothy Flanigan in the Senate Judiciary Committee hearing room. Flanigan was representing the president as well as the attorney general in the negotiations. Howell and he tangled over whether the law would allow American prosecutors to use evidence from abroad that was obtained through methods illegal in the United States. They also differed over whether a court should serve as a check on the sharing of grand jury, wiretap, and other criminal investigative information.

Eventually, Flanigan made some concessions. He agreed that the government would not use evidence about U.S. citizens obtained abroad in a manner illegal under U.S. law, and that a court would review information before it could be shared among intelligence and law enforcement agencies within the United States. On October 1, Leahy thought he had a final agreement in hand. He was so confident that he stopped by Senate Majority Leader Tom Daschle's office to assure him: "We have it all worked out."

Leahy left the Capitol that evening feeling satisfied. He'd done what he could to protect civil liberties by providing oversight for surveillance and domestic intelligence. But he had also moved quickly to bolster law enforcement and counterintelligence operations. No one could accuse the Democrats of coddling terrorists. The next morning, Leahy sat in his office across a polished wood conference table from Ashcroft, Hatch, Michael Chertoff, chief of the Justice Department's criminal division, and Gonzales, the White House counsel. They'd come together to sign off on the deal. But Ashcroft was having second thoughts about some of Flanigan's concessions. The agreement, he told Leahy, no longer held.

Leahy felt blindsided. He'd invested his prestige in these negotiations, and now it looked like he didn't count. "I said, 'John, when I make an agreement, I make an agreement. I can't believe you're going back on your commitment.'"

Ashcroft's support was critical to the bill's approval. The Senate and the Bush administration had agreed to deliver a proposal together, and the process could not go forward without Ashcroft's imprimatur. Flanigan downplays the dispute, saying it was only one of many disagreements in a tough series of talks that ebbed and flowed.

"There were several points in the negotiations at which they recognized that they had given up too much, and there were other times that we realized we hadn't asked for enough," Flanigan says. "It's understandable. It's the pace of the negotiations.

"You know, there'd be groans around the table and nobody was pleased to see an issue reopened. But I think it all was conducted in a spirit [of] we're all trying to get to a result here."

In any case, there was no hiding the growing animosity between Leahy and the administration. Ashcroft didn't even try. Not long after leaving Leahy's office, Ashcroft held a press conference with Orrin Hatch at his side. "I think it is time for us to be productive on behalf of the American people. Talk won't prevent terrorism," Ashcroft said, adding that he was "deeply concerned about the rather slow pace" of the legislation.

"It's a very dangerous thing," Hatch agreed. "It's time to get off our duffs and do what's right."

SENATOR LEAHY WAS DEEPLY DISTRESSED by the collapse of the deal. He felt the administration was intent on steamrolling over him. But there was frustratingly little he could do about it. He didn't even have the political leverage in the Senate to push for the same sunset provision being championed by Armey in the Republican-controlled House. Leahy knew he would have to rely on the House to fight that battle with the administration. He would have to do the same on securing court oversight of the government's new surveillance powers.

Court oversight would be especially important in light of a critical but unheralded portion of the new legislation: Section 215. For many years, FISA gave investigators access to the commercial records of people under investigation in national security cases, but only from a small range of business, including hotels, storage facilities, and car rental companies. Section 215 of the bill would greatly expand that, allowing investigators to obtain records from Internet service providers, grocery stores, libraries, bookstores—in essence, any business. More important, it would remove the requirement that the target of the records search be "an agent of a foreign power."

Those changes were significant because of the data collection revolution of the 1990s. Cheaper computing power and an ever-expanding Internet enabled businesses to more easily track customer transactions. Never before had so much information been collected about so many of us—often in the name of giving us conveniences, discounts, and other benefits. Marketers knew our names, addresses, estimated incomes, the size of a family's house, the type of car we drive, the magazines we read, the beer we drink. Libraries used computers to keep track of what we read. Hotels kept electronic records of when we came and went, as well as the movies we watched. Bookstores knew what we bought. Many toll roads could register when we had driven by.

The implications of giving the government access to so much personal information unnerved Dempsey and other civil libertarians, who were disappointed that Leahy and his allies couldn't do more to stand up to the administration. While Dempsey understood the political pressures on the senators, he worried that they didn't completely understand some of the compromises they were making.

Leahy was also rueful about the outcome. His bill, introduced in the Senate two days after his acrimonious meeting with Ashcroft, gave Justice much more power than he had originally intended. He was prepared to swallow hard and support it. To do anything else was politically impossible.

Late on October 11, the Senate assembled to vote. Leahy and Daschle knew every Republican would support the bill. They wanted Democrats to do the same. But Senator Russell Feingold was refusing to go along. A liberal who routinely bucked pressure from his own party, the Wisconsin Democrat had deep reservations about the bill hurtling through the Senate. He considered the provisions "some of the most radical changes to law enforcement in a generation" and was particularly worried that Section 215 gave the government too much power to sift through people's lives. He wanted the Senate to vote on a series of amendments that would do more to protect privacy.

Feingold's stance annoyed Daschle, who cornered him at the back of the Senate floor shortly before the vote. "The bill will only get worse if we open it up to debate," he told Feingold. Leahy also chimed in, telling Feingold that while he agreed with almost everything Feingold was proposing, the votes simply weren't there. Leahy warned that if Feingold offered amendments, their conservative colleagues would try to give investigators even more extensive powers.

Feingold wouldn't budge. "There is no doubt," he declared on the Senate floor that evening, "that if we lived in a police state, it would be easier to catch terrorists. If we lived in a country where the police were allowed to search your home at any time for any reason; if we lived in a country where the government was entitled to open your mail, eavesdrop on your phone conversations, or intercept your e-mail communications . . . the government would probably discover and arrest more terrorists, or would-be terrorists. . . . But that would not be a country in which we would want to live."

Feingold offered his amendments, and they were rejected. One month after the attacks, the USA Patriot Act, short for Uniting and Strengthening America by Providing Appropriate Tools Required to Intercept and Obstruct Terrorism Act, passed the Senate, 96–1. The law's acronym spoke volumes about what the administration expected from its citizens.

• • •

LAWMAKERS AND LEGISLATIVE AIDES were lining up for nasal swabs and Cipro. Yellow police tape encircled the Hart Senate Office Building. The House had shut down for the first time in memory. On October 17, the capital was confronting a new threat: anthrax. It was contained in a letter mailed to Daschle, and no one knew how many people might have been exposed. Were there more letters? Were anthrax spores floating through the Capitol's ventilation system? Suddenly, it became more urgent than ever to get the Patriot Act to the president's desk.

Amid the panic, Leahy, Daschle, Flanigan, Dinh, and others gathered in House Speaker Dennis Hastert's office to smooth out the differences between the Senate and House versions of the bill. The House bill, which had passed in the early morning hours of October 12, included sunset and court oversight provisions Leahy had been unable to get in the Senate. There was no longer any question that the Patriot Act would include some court oversight, though not as much as Leahy and Armey wanted. The key issue remaining for those in Hastert's office was how long the new law should be in effect. Leahy and Armey pressed for a two-year "sunset," which would force the White House to win congressional approval of the most controversial provisions of the law all over again in 2005. The administration wanted no time limit but eventually agreed on four years.

Sunset in 2005.

THE USA PATRIOT ACT POWERS went far beyond what even the most ardent law enforcement supporters had considered politically possible before the attacks. And the government moved quickly to take full advantage of both the new and existing authorities. In the first year alone, more than a thousand noncitizens were detained without being charged, and their identities were kept secret. Thousands of Muslim men—citizens and noncitizens—and others were placed under surveillance by federal investigators across the country. Their movements, telephone calls, email, Internet use, and credit card charges were scrutinized around the clock—a technology-driven campaign that has resulted in criminal charges against eighteen suspected al-Qaeda operatives in or near Seattle, Detroit, Buffalo, New York, and Portland, Oregon. "We've neutralized a suspected terrorist cell within our borders," Ashcroft announced near the first anniversary of the terror attacks at a press conference about the indictments of six people in Portland charged with conspiring to aid al-Qaeda and the Taliban regime in Afghanistan. He called the indictments "a defining day in America's war against terrorism."

In 2003, the government, for the first time, asked for more secret wiretap warrants for terrorism investigations than for criminal cases. The FBI said it got more than 1,700 Foreign Intelligence Surveillance Court warrants, while federal and state courts endorsed some 1,442 warrants for electronic surveillance in other kinds of cases. Outside law enforcement circles, no one will ever know who was targeted by those FISA warrants. Thousands of men, women, and children had been detained and searched at airports, most of them innocent people whose names sounded similar to suspects on computer watch lists or who showed some sign of threat. College students were questioned by law enforcement and intelligence officials for associating with certain campus seminars.

Many people, including some lawmakers and some judges, came to believe the Patriot Act went too far. Judge Gladys Kessler of the U.S. District Court for the District of Columbia, for instance, ruled in 2002 that the government overstepped its constitutional bounds by refusing to give the names of more than twelve hundred people detained since September 11, many of them initially on immigration charges. In response to a lawsuit by civil libertarians, Judge Kessler ordered the Justice Department to release the names, saying that without the information it was impossible to know whether the government is "operating within the bounds of the law."

Kessler's ruling was overturned by an appeals court in June 2003, after the government argued that the secrecy was necessary to avoid compromising its investigation into September 11 and future terror plots. The Justice Department also challenged a decision by the FISA court not to grant criminal investigators the authority to use FISA primarily for criminal prosecutions. The FISA court said in 2002 that, long before September 11, the government had misused the law and misled the court dozens of times in its requests for search warrants and wiretaps. Those warrants and wiretaps might not have been granted in criminal courts, which, unlike FISA, require evidence of probable cause. And if the FISA court wouldn't let criminal investigators make wide use of FISA powers, the Patriot Act would provide as much investigative muscle as the administration wants.

Near the end of 2003, Ashcroft extolled what he thought of as the Patriot Act's virtues during a public tour in support of the law. In lower Manhattan, Ashcroft appeared at Federal Hall, where George Washington took the oath as the nation's first president. The attorney general was surrounded by police and prosecutors and American flags. "At times I doubted America could make it still safe, still secure today. We have had two years of safety, a sign of blessing, a sign of God's grace upon this nation and its people that we have had 728 days of safety is second a testament to you, the men and women of our nation who guard our borders, patrol our streets and enforce our laws," he said over the hum created by thousands of protesters outside.

"Freedom is not self-sustaining. It is not automatic and the security that ensures liberty does not come without effort. For two years you have expended that effort, preserving our security, protecting our liberty. All of us owe you a debt that cannot be repaid. We learned the painful lessons of 9/11.

"We once had a culture of law enforcement that inhibited and prevented communication and coordination. We have constructed a new spirit of justice. We've built America's defense, the defense of life and liberty upon a foundation of prevention, nurtured by cooperation, built on coordination and communication and rooted in our constitutional liberties. 9/11 taught us that terrorists had outflanked law enforcement in technology, communications and information. So we have fought for the tools necessary to protect the lives and liberties of the American people. Congress provided these tools in the USA Patriot Act passed overwhelmingly by bipartisan majority: 98 to 1 in the US Senate and better than a five to one ratio in the House.

"Our job is not finished," Ashcroft added, "but we have used the tools provided in the Patriot Act to fulfill our first responsibility, that of protecting Americans. We have used these tools to prevent terrorists from unleashing more death on our soil. We have used these tools to save innocent American lives."

As with other claims by Bush administration officials, Ashcroft offered few particulars. He was, in essence, asking us to accept his assertions on faith.

• • •

LONG AFTER ITS APPROVAL, Viet Dinh said he was proud of the Patriot Act and his role in creating it. He believed the law made Americans safer, just as intended. He dismisses criticism that Justice was using a heavy hand in its investigations, and that civil liberties were being compromised. While the government can examine the lives of Americans as never before, he says, the Constitution is always there as a safeguard. "It was very clear that we did not tell the American people just simply trust us, trust law enforcement not to overstep their bounds. Rather we say, trust the law," Dinh said. "The attorney general said very clearly, 'Think outside the box, but not outside the Constitution.'"

But Dinh, who returned to life as a law professor at Georgetown University, noted that the effort to protect Americans relies substantially on private information brokers and other technology companies. He knows those companies face little of the oversight of government agencies. "The amount of information publicly available to businesses is mind-boggling. It really belies the notion that each of us has an expectation to be left alone. So many people know about what we do," said Dinh, sitting in his law school office not far from where he oversaw the drafting of the Patriot Act. "The leap in technology has not been met with a proportionate response in terms of how we think of this technology. We need to think more creatively. Not put the genie back in the bottle, but make the most use of it. Like most technology, it's mixed use. It could be put to good or bad use."

The situation seems far more dire to Jim Dempsey, who since the Patriot Act's approval was named director of the Center for Democracy and Technology. Though he maintains the government needs to use information technology to protect the country, he describes the efforts by the government to make the most of personal data and the Patriot Act since 2001 as the beginning of unprecedented intrusion into American life. In 2005, Dempsey said, he will be pressing hard to curb the Patriot Act authorities.

"It's an electronic door-to-door search," Dempsey said. "You can't physically go door to door or stop every car on the highway. But now we have the [ability] to do it unbeknownst to the people. Now it can be done electronically and constantly."

Senator Leahy is convinced the Justice Department and FBI have overreached in their efforts to identify and apprehend terrorists. And like Dinh, he began to worry about the role of the private companies, their monitoring capabilities and their expanding partnership with the government.

"The temptation will be more and more—especially in a polarized society and a society where there is a fear, whether it's the Red Scare in the fifties or terrorism in this century—to use those databanks," he said, sitting at the same table in his office where he negotiated portions of the Patriot Act with Ashcroft. "At some point it doesn't matter if they're private or public, at some point they will be used by the government to determine who is a good American and who is a bad American. Not determined through prosecution, trial, but based on what came up on someone's computer screen."

2

DATA REVOLUTION

———————

CHARLES MORGAN SLIPPED THE GEARSHIFT into first and pushed the accelerator to the floor. He quickly sped up, revving the powerful engine close to its maximum 9,000 rpms. With just days to go before one of the last big events of his race career, Morgan was putting the million-dollar Ferrari through its paces, at close to 200 miles per hour.

The bright red race car was an engineering marvel, a twelve-cylinder rocket that rode just inches above the track at Sebring, Florida. Its curves flowed back and up over the wheels like a low wave. A spoiler in the shape of a T on the tail end helped keep the car pressed to the road-way. On its side was the word ACXIOM in bold letters.

Unlike a lot of companies that sponsor race cars, Acxiom is not a household name. But as a billion-dollar player in the data industry, with details about nearly every adult in the United States, it has as much reach into American life as Pepsi or Goodyear. You may not know about Acxiom, but it knows a lot about you.

Morgan, Acxiom's chief executive, has made racing a central part of his life, and in this event he was aiming for his twentieth road race victory. It is an expensive hobby, but also the fulfillment of his teenage dream: To be the man in the driver seat instead of watching from the grandstands. Keeping the Acxiom Ferrari on the road cost up to $200,000 annually. He spent millions more on racing in general, including his son's racing operation. Morgan could afford it, though, because he has made a fortune at Acxiom by leading the collection, management, and high-tech packaging of personal information.

He was not thinking about data on this warm-up day, in March 1997. He was concentrating on the track's familiar curves, the bumpy surface jostling him from side to side, his hands on the small steering wheel, his elbows bent down. Morgan hoped the car would propel him and three teammates to victory in the grueling and prestigious twelve-hour race ahead. He thought, If only we can keep the racing machine on track. Suddenly, Morgan spun out. He nicked a wall and shattered part of the car's sleek carbon fiber shell. As the team repairs the damage, they blame the mishap on cold tires with a loose grip on the road. It's an excuse often allowed for self-funded part-time racers like Morgan, guys sometimes known in the business as "gentlemen drivers."

Things seem to go better on race day, as Morgan whips around the track. After some initial troubles, he gains on the leaders. Then he is cut off by a rival heading into the pits. Morgan slams into the car, a Porsche, and breaks his right hand.

Afterward, Morgan shrugged it off. "If I were doing something really risky, I'd be racing planes or offshore boats or Indy cars. This isn't that dangerous. Really," he told a *Success* magazine writer for a story at the time. "Of course, if I stuck you in the car and took you around for a lap, you'd probably wet your pants."

TO GET TO THE PLACE where Charles Morgan made his fortune, you must drive through the forested hills north of Little Rock, Arkansas, and then along the dense commercial strip of asphalt that cuts through the small city of Conway.

Conway is a former railroad town with three colleges. Like Acxiom, the city has grown a lot in recent years, and now parts of it are overrun by fast-food restaurants, strip malls, and congestion. Despite the changes, the Acxiom campus remains a source of community pride, and Morgan something of a local hero. The company is Conway's largest employer. Because it attracts so many bright people, Acxiom also boosts the education levels of the city's adult population far above the average of one of the nation's poorly educated states. Morgan donated millions to Hendrix College, a liberal arts school in town.

Acxiom's low-slung brick buildings spread out across a campus along Dave Ward Drive, a busy road named after a local bus manufacturer whose son founded the company in 1969. Behind the modest facade are scores of powerful computers containing one of the richest collections of personal and confidential information in the world.

You enter computer center A by passing a reception area, going through a secure door, and walking up a ramp into a large air-conditioned space with a dropped ceiling and fluorescent lights. Pallets of supplies sit on the floor. In the early days, this room was the entire company, complete with executives' desks, a printing facility, and computers exhaling hot air. Now it is simply a data powerhouse. Beneath the floors snake miles of cables that connect the computers to one another and to the rest of the world. All day long, every day of the year, those cables transmit information about Americans to and from Acxiom. It's not just names, ages, addresses, and telephone numbers. The computers in these rooms also hold billions of records about marital status and families and the ages of children. They track individuals' estimated incomes, the value of their homes, the make and price of their cars. They maintain unlisted phone numbers and details about people's occupations, religions, and ethnicities. They sometimes know what some people read, what they order over the phone and online, and where they go on vacation. These are details Acxiom gently refers to as "purchase behavior and lifestyle data." But there's more.

A short walk to another building brings you to rooms with newer computers, machines that occupy far less space and hold vastly more information. It's easy to see on the tile floor where the older equipment stood. The new computers operate in spare black boxes that look like high-end Sub-Zero refrigerators. For security reasons, Acxiom does not identify the client information in each of the computers. Instead, the machines are labeled with a series of motifs. Some sport pictures of muscle cars, such as Mustangs and Firebirds. Others display characters from *SpongeBob Squarepants* or *Sesame Street*. Shark fins sit atop one group of machines that happen to hold tens of millions of financial records.

In all, Acxiom's electronic storehouses in Conway can hold what's called a petabyte of information, or a thousand trillion bytes. Grasping the meaning of that quantity is challenging, even for mathematicians or computer scientists. You might do slightly better thinking of it roughly as a 50,000-mile-high stack of King James Bibles. Just one part of this digital ocean, a core service that Acxiom calls InfoBase, comprises the largest collection of U.S. consumer and telephone data available in one source, according to company documents.

Many companies in the United States maintain data centers now, operations that became a central if little understood part of American life during the 1990s and at the start of the twenty-first century. These companies are altering the nature of business and, in some ways, our country. Working on a network of supercomputers—something Acxiom calls "grid computing"—the company systematically matches and analyzes the information it collects to create fine-grained portraits about roughly 200 million adults. Every one of them is labeled with a 16-digit code unique to each person to make the processing of their records swifter.

The company helps retailers such as Lands' End focus their catalogues, banking customers like Citigroup profile individuals for credit offers, and insurers such as Allstate decide whom to serve and whom to exclude. It manages billions of financial and personal records for the privately owned credit bureau Trans Union. It enables drug companies to target people with certain ailments. It screens people for jobs and helps track down debtors. It outlines and predicts behavior.

And since September 11, 2001, Acxiom has offered its technical know-how and raw material—the details about you, your life, and your family—to some of the largest surveillance and screening systems ever devised by the U.S. government.

NEAR THE CENTER OF THE CONWAY CAMPUS is a cinder-block room. It has durable carpet in it now and rows of desks and PCs for the administrative staff that's housed there. In the mid-1970s, this space was the garage where Morgan tinkered with his first race cars, during breaks from long hours in the computer room. One hour he might be writing code and the next his hands would be black with grease.

Morgan and his company didn't set out to be pioneering. After getting a mechanical engineering degree from the University of Arkansas, he worked for a time at IBM in the 1960s as a systems engineer. But he wanted to take his own risks, build his own company, make money, and have time to race. So in 1972 he moved to Demographics in Conway, the company that would become Acxiom.

Morgan is a native Arkansan, tall and thin, who favors wireless glasses and custom-made clothes. He likes his Jack Daniel's neat, listens to Barbra Streisand, and speaks with a twang. While giving a deposition a few years ago, he referred to an opposing lawyer he'd just met as "buddy." When he grew frustrated with questions about Acxiom's business, he said, "I mean, I'm really in a hurt here."

When he joined Demographics, an ardent Democrat named Charles Ward—owner of the Ward School Bus Manufacturing Company—wanted to use computer technology to help the Democratic National Committee raise money. Relying on voter registration lists, staff at Demographics figured out a way to pick out individuals who seemed most likely to write checks for local and regional candidates. They employed mainframe computers—sophisticated machines for the time—that were programmed with manila-colored punch cards. Among those they helped was Dale Bumpers, the governor of Arkansas who went on to become a U.S. senator and would later serve as an Acxiom lobbyist in Washington. The Demographics approach represented a big leap for political fund-raising, because it enabled candidates to far more efficiently select targets likely to give them cash.

It was an up and down business. Fund-raising was seasonal, dependent on the election cycles. The clients were sometimes frugal and often didn't pay on time. As a consequence, Demographics occasionally couldn't meet its payroll. "There were weeks when we had to float it," Morgan would say later. "And one year we had to put our executives on half salary." But the lessons Morgan and his colleagues absorbed proved invaluable. They learned how to make money by collecting, managing, and massaging information about businesspeople, housewives, graduate students, and immigrants—indeed, potential spenders everywhere. By the mid-1970s, they had come up with a brash idea: To use computers and heaps of information about people to help marketers get to know individuals better. It was a plan that would help fuel a data and marketing revolution at the end of the twentieth century—and raise new questions about what it means to live a private life in America.

Their first customer was the American Bible Society, which was looking for ways to boost donations. The Bible Society executive who arranged the deal, a New Yorker, was amazed at the high-tech operation in Arkansas. "She was dumbfounded to find this building out in the middle of a field with cows grazing immediately behind the building. She had been there about a few minutes and said, 'I gotta call my boss. He is not going to believe this,'" Morgan would say almost two decades after the fact. "She literally starts shrieking and saying, 'Joe, you can't believe it. There are cows here right outside the door here.'"

The transformation from political fund-raiser to direct marketer would make Morgan wealthy. In 1972, Charles Ward was having financial difficulties. He offered Morgan a chance to buy a stake in the company, which brought in about $400,000 in revenue that year. For $50,000, Morgan got half. Acxiom is now a $1 billion, publicly held company. With more than 4 million shares in June 2003, worth some $60 million and rising, Morgan was the single largest individual shareholder.

GATHERING AND MERGING INFORMATION about people isn't new. Throughout the twentieth century, marketers, lenders, insurers, private investigators, and of course the government continually came up with efforts to collect or traffic in names, addresses, and individuals' activities.

For marketers, it was a matter of finding people who might be most interested in their products. Banks and others wanted to track down debtors. For some, the list building was politically motivated, as when the government tracked labor activists or people who criticized World War I. Such efforts became rampant during the fifties and sixties, when the FBI, the Army, and shadowy conservative groups such as the Church League created dossiers about tens of thousands of students, anti-war activists, social crusaders, and others deemed undesirable.

Information compilers have always found relatively little standing in the way of these efforts. The laws didn't exist or were too weak to matter or they were simply ignored. Dossier builders were limited only by what their minds and file cabinets could hold. The creation of the computer in the 1940s was a boon to these kinds of initiatives. Simple and slow as they were, the early electronic brains spurred a new way of thinking about information. In just a few years, businesses, bureaucrats, and scientists realized they had the tool of their dreams: machines that could store more information and help answer more questions than ever before.

By the early sixties, some 250 businesses began specializing in brokering almost any details they could acquire. Fueling this nascent industry were magazine publishers, hoteliers, car dealerships, and other businesspeople, who soon understood they could make extra cash just by selling the names, addresses, and preferences of their regular customers. One of the notable leaders was a firm called the Dunhill International List Company. In 1964, it sold private details about people to magazine publishers and others who wanted to target their pitches. For $14, you could acquire the names of a thousand women who had bought a "bust developer" product. If you wanted to find "men and women of large means," the list cost $15. A few dollars more would get you the names and addresses of newlyweds, 500,000 in all.

It wasn't long before government agencies also got into the business. Clerks across the country began selling lists of births, marriages, new families, and tax rolls to companies like Dunhill. For some companies, information brokering became big business. The Reuben H. Donnelley Corporation became a regular buyer of information about the cars people registered. Before long, it was selling access to lists of 400,000 car owners.

The muckraking journalist Vance Packard estimated that by 1964 businesses, charities, and political groups were spending $400 million annually to buy information about individuals. Until the laws were changed, one city clerk earned the grand sum of $60,000 selling details about couples applying for marriage licenses. "There's no question about it," Packard wrote at the time, in a book called *The Naked Society*. "In bulk, we are very attractive." Increases in computing power enabled the industry to expand throughout the decade. On the leading edges of this growth in data collection were credit bureaus, hundreds of operations across the country that conducted background checks of individuals on behalf of credit card issuers and other lenders. They first gathered information from the person seeking credit. The bureaus added in their own data collected from credit issuers, newspapers, and public records. When that wasn't enough, they sent out investigators to knock on doors. These commercial gumshoes collected innumerable anecdotes from landlords, friends, neighbors, and coworkers. Most of the time, because they faced quotas, the investigators didn't have time to verify the stories. In a way that seems quaint now, an analyst, a real person, then took stock of the applicant's report before passing judgment.

A major force at the time was the Atlanta-based Retail Credit Company, later to become Equifax. It had some seven thousand investigators who compiled information on some 45 million adults. Retail Credit's customers included insurers and employers, and its reports could be unsettlingly specific. One credit report, for instance, described a retired Army lieutenant colonel as "a rather wild-tempered, unreasonable, and uncouth person who abused his rank and wasn't considered a well-adjusted person."

The bureaus insisted they handled such reports with care, making the same promises they make now: No one gets access to the information unless they have signed contracts limiting the use of the reports to credit granting. The reality, then as now, is that anyone intent on getting those reports had no trouble at all, generally for a small fee, sometimes for nothing.

This bonanza of information spurred the creation of new conveniences that we now take for granted. Instant credit, cheaper mortgages, a panoply of shopping options, and even detailed and accurate phone books. But it also was a huge step down the slippery slope of privacy encroachment for commercial gain. In 1971, a Michigan University academic named Arthur R. Miller caught the zeitgeist when he described the computer-driven changes as a "cybernetic revolution." His book was called *The Assault on Privacy.*

"The new information technologies seem to have given birth to a new social virus—'data-mania,'" Miller wrote. "We must begin to realize what it means to live in a society that treats information as an economically desirable commodity and a source of power."

• • •

FOR ALL HIS PRESCIENCE, Miller, now a law professor at Harvard, had no idea just how fast and how much personal information the world would create. Only science fiction writers really had the gall to suggest the pending magnitude of change. "In a very few generations—computer generations—which by this time may last only a few months—there will be a mental explosion; the merely intelligent machine will swiftly give way to the ultra-intelligent machine," wrote Arthur Clarke, in a 1968 *Playboy* magazine article.

An effect known as Moore's Law was driving the revolution. The eponymous Gordon Moore was co-founder of Intel, the computer chip maker. In the mid-1960s, Moore noticed that the power of the chips doubled every year. He predicted correctly the phenomenon would continue. By the early nineties, the power of computer processors exploded and the cost of data storage was sliding fast. The Internet, the global computer network developed by the Defense Department and embraced by the academic world, was becoming commonplace. Suddenly companies like Acxiom could more easily employ systems known as data warehouses, to hold the information, and data mining, to make sense of it. Instead of creating a simple list of people who bought, say, an Oldsmobile or read the *Saturday Evening Post,* Acxiom had the data savvy and computer power to combine dozens of characteristics about people.

The resulting profiles, generated by statistical models, enabled the company to better predict what people were likely to buy or do. The Internet became both the conduit for gathering data and the instantaneous delivery system. Companies could now know who you were the instant you called. "Imagine if you could obtain an instant consumer profile of each prospect at your first contact," gushed Acxiom's promotional material about the InfoBase Profiler system.

By 2004, the company had developed its grid supercomputing system, enabling its analysts to do everything faster and with far more depth. Marty Abrams, a former executive at Experian, the giant credit bureau, and a leading thinker about data policy issues, likened the technological changes to the upheaval caused by Henry Ford's assembly-line innovations or the steam engine. "It's like the revolution that occurred when we began to understand the world was round, and not flat."

Technology forecaster Paul Saffo, director of the Institute for the Future, liked to cite a toy popular a few years ago called the Furby. Using a microchip, the Furby recorded speech and appeared to talk. But far from being just a fuzzy toy, the Furby represented a technological transformation, because it had more computing power inside it than the first Apollo lunar module. That kind of power, coupled to the Internet, made it easier than ever before for one person to find out information about another. "It used to take an army of gumshoes to do what an individual can do clicking their keyboards in a matter of minutes," Saffo said.

Researchers at the University of California at Berkeley concluded that all the information collected by humanity through 1999 would more than double in the next several years—and continue to grow at an accelerating pace. That's approximately a dozen exabytes by the Berkeley team's reckoning. Just five exabytes equals all the words ever spoken. Most of this information comes in the form of benign, even banal office documents and memos that go into someone's computer and never disappear. Much of it is duplicative. But an extraordinary amount—far beyond most people's reckoning—is the telling minutiae of individuals' lives, their families, whereabouts, habits, and shopping predilections.

For more than a decade, Acxiom and its allies and competitors were, by their own account, in a sort of feeding frenzy. Acxiom alone had almost 1 million times the capacity for information in 2004 than it had in 1983, the year it first sold shares of stock in the company. Just one of its sleek black computers holds roughly the equivalent of 5 million copies of Huckleberry Finn.

Much of the information that Acxiom manages and enhances comes from technology-savvy (and very data-hungry) retailers like Sears, Roebuck, gift shop chains like Hallmark Cards, grocery stores such as Safeway, scores of mail-order operations like Lands' End and the publisher Rodale. Nearly all the top banks and credit card companies send data to Acxiom, including Bank One Financial Services, Bank of America, MBNA America Bank, and Charles Schwab. That holds true also for GM and Toyota, AT&T and other telephone companies, Pfizer and fellow drugmakers, Microsoft and IBM. They all have collected massive amounts of information about their customers, and they all work with Acxiom to learn still more about what makes their customers tick.

During a tour of Acxiom's Conway campus several years ago, Morgan paused, turned to a visitor, and, over the loud hum of the machines, marveled about what was happening. "They have gone on an information collecting binge," Morgan said about the commercial world. "There's just this insatiable appetite for more information."

"They record everything about their customers," Morgan said. "They're saying, 'We ought to convince customers this is good for them.'"

Helping businesses make sense of all this information became one of Acxiom's main goals in the 1990s. Simple lists weren't good enough anymore. But profiling people well, getting inside their heads, meant acquiring even more information about them. Acxiom began making deals with both clients and competitors. These companies underscore the breadth of the data revolution and the wealth of information they collect.

At the beginning of the nineties, Acxiom cut a deal with one of the nation's largest direct mailers, ADVO-System Inc., a little known firm that at the time delivered weekly pitches to some 52 million households. Under the arrangement, the two shared technology and information, including the names, addresses, and other information from ADVO-System computers. ADVO-System bought half of Acxiom's InfoBase. Another partner was R. L. Polk & Co., one of the oldest information services in the country and one of the few that has grown as large or as powerful as Acxiom. The cornerstone of its business is "automotive intelligence" about car owners. It also led the way in the race to build up massive amounts of lifestyle and buying information. In promotional material not long ago, Polk declared that "Information is power." Acxiom signed a long-term agreement to manage Polk's data.

In 1996, Acxiom bought Direct Media Inc., the nation's biggest list manager and broker, a Goliath that processed more than 10 percent of all third-class junk mail—hundreds of millions of pieces a year. The list of other contributors over the years to InfoBase—the service Acxiom claims is the largest of its kind in America—reads like a who's who of data compilers: DataQuick List Service, Partners' Marketing, American Data Resources, I Rent America.

One deal involved a handshake between Acxiom and a company called Abacus Direct Corp., a consortium of retailers who share information about their customers in a cooperative database. The deal signaled a momentous change for individuals, people the industry refers to as "consumers." Not only were the two companies going to share information, they were going to apply cutting-age behavior modeling to every individual. In May 1999 the companies described their partnership: "Under terms of the agreement, Abacus will maximize the power of its Alliance database, the nation's largest database of consumer catalog buying behavior, in conjunction with Acxiom's InfoBase database, the nation's premier source for demographic information, to create new, jointly marketed data products."

Just weeks before, a partnership was announced between Abacus and HNC Software, a company that specializes in artificial intelligence software. HNC can analyze billions of transactions and learn from them to predict what an individual is likely to do. It watches, for example, every credit card transaction for some companies, learns individuals' spending patterns, and tracks any anomalies, in part to root out fraud. "Under the agreement," the companies proclaimed, "Abacus will use HNC's Content Mining technology to enhance the data mining of billions of mail order merchandise purchasing transactions maintained within the proprietary Abacus Alliance database of 88 million households. In turn, HNC Financial Solutions plans to apply the Abacus aggregate prior purchasing data to further enhance the value of HNC Financial Solutions products to its clients."

This was a new kind of marketing surveillance, an emerging power that excited marketers no end. Richard Barton, a lawyer for the Direct Marketing Association, was one of many in the industry who watched all of this unfold with pride. "We have the capability to gather, store, analyze, segment and use for commercial (and many other) purposes more data about more people than was ever dreamed of," he boasted to a trade magazine. "And technology is providing us with even more ingenious ways to reach into the lives of every American."

Most individuals had no idea this was happening.

FEW OTHER PARTNERS have been as important to Acxiom as the one created by the Union Tank Car Company, a railway car leasing firm that created a holding operation called Trans Union.

Trans Union has always been in a hurry to grow. It bought the Credit Bureau of Cook County, which had maintained 3.6 million files in hundreds of file cabinets. In 1972, the fledgling company made a bold claim for a system it called the Credit Reporting Online Network Utility System, better known in industry circles as CRONUS. By the company's own reckoning, CRONUS "revolutionized the credit reporting system" by giving lenders a look at borrowers online more than two decades before the advent of the World Wide Web.

Trans Union fought its way to the top tier of a deeply competitive industry, embracing computers, networks, and other data processing technology. It bought out competitors, and because it was a privately held company, it had to answer only to its owners. By the early 1990s, Trans Union had become a national credit bureau, with information in its files about almost every American adult—at least those who weren't living in mountain cabins without electricity or credit cards.

Trans Union wanted Acxiom to help work with banking customers to target people who, based on data profiles, might be likely to sign up for credit cards. It also wanted to improve its use of data, and figured Acxiom could be a partner in developing new technology. At Trans Union's helm was Harry Gambill, a graduate of Arkansas State University who knew Charles Morgan personally. Morgan realized that his technology and information, coupled with Trans Union's fountain of personal data, could be enormously profitable. In 1992, the two companies made a deal that would help both of them expand their businesses. This sort of arrangement, played out across the financial and data industry, would dramatically accelerate the collection of personal information in the coming years.

Trans Union is one of Acxiom's closest partners. The deal in July 1992 called for Acxiom to acquire all of Trans Union's interest in its Chicago data center. Acxiom would then manage Trans Union's information and the two would work together to develop technology and services enabling them to better profile and target individuals. They would market and assess such individuals for risk, to better discriminate between profitable customers and those who should be ignored.

Acxiom agreed also to "use its best efforts to cause two people designated by Trans Union to be elected to Acxiom's board of directors." No one will say precisely how much stock Trans Union got out of the deal. Two years later, Acxiom added tens of thousands of square feet to the Conway facility to accommodate the growing amount of information it was handling for Trans Union. Over the last decade, the ties have grown stronger. In 2002, the two companies' sales forces decided to market their products together. A short time later, Acxiom paid almost $35 million for Trans Union's background screening business. For its part, Trans Union paid Acxiom more than $71 million in 2003, up from $50.6 million the year before. When pressed about the relationship at the end of 2003, Morgan acknowledged it was a close one. "We run their computers. We are the computer operators. We do the systems programming," he said about the fabled CRONUS. "We are responsible for the computer infrastructure."

THE BIBLE OF MAILING LISTS in America is a $331 document called the *SRDS Direct Marketing List Source*. Not too long ago it was the size of a telephone book for a small city. In the early 2000s, it became a multivolume document that resembles an engorged directory for New York City and Los Angeles combined.

In 1,600 pages of fine print, volume 2 of the *List Source* offers marketers' names, ages, addresses, and other details about book buyers, magazine readers, muscle car owners in Florida, and people who buy prints online from the Metropolitan Museum of Art. It has a list called Gay America Megafile with almost 700,000 names. Other lists contain the names of millions of parents and children. Marketers buy these lists, create files of the best "prospects," and go at them with direct mail, email pitches, and telemarketing calls. Direct mail, a.k.a. junk mail, lists have been around for decades, of course, but year by year they become richer, more arcane, and potentially more intrusive. Want the names, addresses of people taking Prozac for depression? No problem. Computer users who like to gamble online? Who like sex toys? Bible believers and Hispanic political donors? It's all available to almost anyone who wants to pay. There's a good reason for these changes, apart from the fact that computers make the job much easier. Marketers dream of perfect lists, filled with names of rich, compliant, and acquisitive people. The quest is never-ending and, now, always accelerating.

For all the irritation they sometimes cause, these pitches spur mil-

lions of people to respond on a regular basis. At last count, such promotions generated $1 trillion in sales in 2003, almost double the sales a
decade before.

The Trans Union people figured they could make more effective lists
by relying on details at the core of their computer system: how much
credit an individual had, the number of cards they had, whether they
had any recent loans, and so on. The problem was, the Federal Trade
Commission (FTC) considered the Trans Union lists the effective
equivalent of a credit report. A 1970 law called the Fair Credit Reporting Act was enacted to protect individuals' credit reports from abuse.
Though shaped by industry lobbyists, the law is a landmark of consumer protection in America. The commission told Trans Union in
1992 that it was breaking the law by selling its lists.

For years, the credit bureaus had been dogged by complaints. Information in their reports was chronically incorrect. They routinely failed
to correct mistakes, and seemed arrogant when individuals called. Year
after year, they were rated by the FTC as the number one target of consumer ire. Under pressure from the commission, the two other leading
credit bureaus had stopped using credit information in their mailing
lists. But not Trans Union.

In 1994, the agency formally brought an administrative proceeding
to stop Trans Union from selling the lists. Trans Union fought hard.
There was simply too much money to be made by these more refined
lists. David Medine was in the center of the fight as the FTC's associate
director for financial practices. He was intent on making use of the relatively few privacy laws to protect individuals. "It was a misuse of confidential information," Medine said at the time. "They were trading
privacy for profits."

Medine described visits from Oscar Marquis, then Trans Union's general counsel. Medine understood clearly that, so long as Trans Union
made more money selling credit information than they paid their lawyers,
they would keep doing it, until a judge told them to stop. For his part,
Marquis later said the company felt that it was entitled to continue, in
part because it was providing a good service. He said the issue was not as
cut and dried as the FTC lawyers argued. "We thought we were right and
that the FTC was overreaching," said Marquis, now in private practice as
a lawyer. "The definition of a consumer report is complex."

The case dragged on for years, with Trans Union appealing each ruling that they were violating the law. The company argued it had a First Amendment right to use information however it wanted. Ultimately, they tried to take their case to the U.S. Supreme Court. The Court's decision not to hear it out ended the case in June 2002. Now, it had to stop.

ONE SECRET TO ACXIOM'S SUCCESS is Charles Morgan's focus on business as an endurance test and his willingness to take risks. Acxiom is routinely cited by business magazines as one of the best places in America to work, in part because Morgan gives his employees, from senior staff to clerical workers, much latitude to manage. By all accounts, though, he expects them to be relentless about the company's basic mission: To find new ways to track, monitor, and profile people with data, and to find new ways to make money off of it.

Acxiom has all sorts of ways of providing these services, and it is instructive to read how the company itself describes what it does. "InfoBase Enhancement" enables Acxiom to take a single detail about a person and append, on behalf of its customers, a massive dossier. This generally happens without the individual ever knowing about it. Say someone gives a telephone number or address to a retailer. Acxiom can instantly attach details about their life, income, and family activities from the InfoBase list, the "industry-leading consumer data including demographics, home ownership characteristics, purchase behavior and lifestyle data."

The "dictionary file" of data contained in InfoBase Enhancement runs to eight pages. The document, shared with government officials after September 11, 2001, points to the many intimate details that fuel Acxiom's business. In addition to names, birth dates, genders, and addresses, it offers a wide variety of details designed to give database marketers precise glimpses at us and our families. This includes: number of adults, the presence of children, their genders and ages and school grades. It includes the home assessment, with ranges that go up by $50,000 and $100,000 leaps, the size in square feet, the market value. And it includes your occupation, net worth, estimated income, details about the credit cards you own. Another product known as Personicx takes stock of households according to income, spending habits, car ownership, and the like. In some ways, it replicates the sizing up that a neighbor might do of another neighbor, except for the fact that it automatically rates every household in America and few of them understand they're being judged. Acxiom calls Personicx "consumer segmentation," using the dispassionate language created by marketers.

One of the most compelling of Acxiom's products is the InfoBase TeleSource. When someone makes a toll-free call to a client of Acxiom to inquire about clothing or to buy some shoes, information about who the caller is and where he or she lives pops up on a screen in front of the telemarketer, even before the customer service representatives answer the call. Using TeleSource, the agent can often find out the kind of home the caller lives in, the type of cars the people in that household drive, whether they exercise. That's because the Acxiom service has amassed 160 million consumer telephone numbers, including up to 30 million that are unlisted, to help identify and profile people who call toll-free lines to shop or make an inquiry.

In the 1990s, the number of consumer calls to toll-free numbers operated by retailers and many others nearly tripled, to an estimated 24 billion a year. By 2004, the number of calls in to telemarketing centers eclipsed the number out to prospects' homes. One consequence: telephone numbers, even many that individuals pay to keep unlisted, are fast becoming consumer tags, identifiers akin to household Social Security numbers.

Acxiom officials said most of the information about the 160 million consumer phone numbers is gleaned from telephone companies' white pages and directory service files, as well as other public sources that fuel the company's giant computer system. Acxiom gets those numbers electronically or it buys the phone books and sends them abroad, where workers key them into computers. Company officials won't detail exactly how they gather the unlisted numbers, which they said represent about half of all unlisted numbers in the nation. They acknowledged that some of the information comes from "self-reported sources." Industry specialists said that could include surveys, product registration cards, and credit card applications. The company also gathers numbers from public records such as property data.

There are no laws prohibiting the collection of unlisted telephone information, according to officials at the Federal Trade Commission and the Federal Communications Commission (FCC). But Acxiom officials claim they follow limitations recommended by the direct marketing industry and are respectful of consumer privacy. Acxiom claims it won't give out unlisted telephone numbers willy-nilly; the company doesn't give out information about those numbers unless an individual calls a telemarketer.

Like others in the industry, Acxiom believes consumers grant permission to gather and use information about them when they make toll-free calls and engage company agents, regardless of the fact that almost no one knows that he or she has made such a bargain, or what it might entail. Telemarketers use phone numbers and associated personal details to provide personalized services, to tailor promotions, and to instantly distinguish profitable prospects or loyal customers from those seeking bargains. Marketers also use the phone numbers, and the information that can be appended, to improve customer service and prevent fraudulent transactions. "It's the difference, perhaps, between hunting with a shotgun and hunting with a rifle," Rick Ferry, executive vice president for the Miami-based Precision Response Corp., said about the growing power to monitor and target certain callers for pitches.

But many callers have no idea how information about them is being gathered and used. Even if someone wanted to block the identification of his home phone number, he can't because the owner of a toll-free number has a right to know who is calling for billing purposes. It's unclear whether any other company has as extensive a collection of unlisted numbers as Acxiom. But other information companies aggressively collect and use telephone numbers and data about callers. Targus Information Corp. provided a service called PhoneData Express, with the help of Acxiom, which the company says "allows you to append current name, address and other information to virtually every [U.S.] telephone number."

In the late 1990s retailers, cataloguers, and other companies on their own became adept in their use of toll-free lines and customer telephone numbers. Drug companies, for example, use toll-free numbers to attract patients and build databases. In one campaign, Merck & Co. worked with football coach Dan Reeves to promote a booklet about heart disease. When individuals called to get the booklet, they were asked their names, addresses, and a series of questions about age, health history, insurance coverage, and smoking and exercise habits—all of which went into a database. The industry has come up with its own rules governing the exchange of data. Acxiom won't share information until a "relationship" has been initiated between a caller and a company. When Acxiom appends personal information to a telephone number, most details generally do not appear on an agent's screen. Instead, the details prompt a computer to generate tailored scripts to guide the agent. Most people still assume that a telephone call remains a simple, ephemeral transaction. Fordham University law professor Joel Reidenberg, author of several books about information privacy, believes marketers are using telephone numbers as a proxy for Social Security numbers, which a growing number of people refuse to share because of concerns about privacy. "They can't go and ask you for your Social Security number," he said. "Instead, they're secretly taking your phone number and tagging your phone number."

Industry officials reject the notion that personal information is being collected surreptitiously, or that they're acting against the interests of their customers. But they acknowledge the industry's reluctance to highlight its growing technological prowess. Faced with the choice of unnerving callers by demonstrating how much they know, or discreetly using the information to direct a conversation, telephone agents generally opt for the latter course. That's why the agents rarely greet callers by name at first. "It gets people, including me, very nervous," said Gordon McKenna, president of the American Teleservices Association, an industry group, and chairman of TeleQuest Teleservices.

Acxiom underscores the growing sophistication of its services in literature about the InfoBase Profiler, which can instantly provide call centers with a caller's name, personal details, and household data, "and is entirely transparent to the consumer."

Allen Hile, assistant director in the FTC's division of marketing practices, believed this convergence will continue to dazzle consumers. But he cautioned that it may also expose them to scrutiny they don't understand or want. "It has just gotten so hyped up because computers are so much more powerful and databases are so much more accessible," Hile said in 1999. "Nobody is disclosing 'Hey, we're collecting your info.' Nobody knows."

...

ACXIOM AND OTHERS in its industry don't hide their sources. They just have never made much of an effort to disclose them in a way that most of us can understand. In financial documents on file with the federal Securities and Exchange Commission (SEC), Acxiom cites examples in the broadest possible sense: telephone directories, voter registration forms, tax assessor offices, questionnaires, warranty cards, catalogue buyer behavior information, and product registration forms. "Advances in computer and software technology have also unlocked vast amounts of customer data which historically was inaccessible, further increasing the amount of existing data to manage and analyze," says the company's annual report for 2003.

One Acxiom executive estimated that the number of warranty cards collected each year more than doubled from the mid-1980s, to 30 million by 2004. The warranty information, collected from 150 different manufacturers, represents about a third of all the households in the United States. In the mid-1970s, Congress approved a law requiring companies to automatically provide warranties. But people still believe they must always fill out the cards. In 1998, there appeared in magazines across the country a survey for a new marketing initiative. The survey asked readers to answer scores of questions about themselves by filling in many of more than seven hundred boxes. Do you suffer from depression or infertility? Experience stress or menstrual pain? What about gastritis and nail fungus? As much as this might sound like a medical form, it was actually a data collection effort by Condé Nast Publications, publisher of *The New Yorker, Vanity Fair, Vogue,* and more than a dozen other upscale magazines. It seems Condé Nast wanted to know its subscribers better. Much better.

The effort was designed to fill a data warehouse, with technical help from Acxiom. It asked for particulars about smoking, drinking (including "brands of spirits"), hobbies (collecting art or antiques, investing, and so forth), and shopping (at Bloomingdale's and other stores). It asked subscribers for the make, model, and year of their cars, the kinds of computers they own, and details about how they cruise the Internet. And it probed subscribers' intentions with regard to marriage, having a baby, and becoming a grandparent. Those getting married were urged to say when ("Please write in month, date and year in numeric format"). On page 5, readers found questions about twenty-five health-related matters, everything from "Acne/skin problems" to "Vaginal/yeast infection," all in alphabetical order. Also included are queries about drugs. "For which conditions do you or someone else in your household take prescribed medication?"

"What do you like? What do you want? Your answers to the questions that follow will allow us to target areas which interest you most and help us be most rewarding to you," says the introduction to the Preferred Subscriber Network survey. "Just answer the questions below to start the conversation and become part of this select group of subscribers to whom marketers listen first."

The survey intentionally sidestepped disconcerting questions about one's financial matters. That's because Condé Nast, like most other companies, could easily buy such data from information services like Acxiom to add to the details it gets directly from subscribers. The success of the publisher's data-warehousing effort over the next three years highlighted one ugly truth about the roiling privacy debate at the time. Even as people fret about corporate intrusiveness, they often willingly, even eagerly, part with intimate details about their lives.

Surveys are far from perfect. Some people lie. But data services like Acxiom and other marketers still rely on the answers as a rich resource. Besides, a startling proportion of people fill out questionnaires honestly, in part because they want to tell somebody about themselves. The impulse is approximately the same as when a guy starts talking about his divorce to a stranger on a crowded plane. It's worth noting that hundreds of thousands of subscribers filled in the eight-page booklets after they went out with magazines beginning in May 1998. What few of them realize is how their responses become part of a vast and growing information market.

"It's amazing. It's impotence and incontinence and all kinds of things they don't tell anybody," said Edward Nash, a marketing consultant and author of *Database Marketing: The Ultimate Marketing Tool*. "People tell us all kinds of things they wouldn't tell their neighbors.

"It's a release. Sometimes they want to let something out," said Nash, adding that surveys sometimes also make people feel like they're a part of something interesting. In some cases, they simply want to get something in return from companies they have faith in.

The Condé Nast program encouraged a sense of intimacy. In a "Dear New Yorker Subscriber" letter, publisher Thomas A. Florio said readers who responded to the survey would be those "to whom we can turn first for a valued opinion about the products you see on our pages or for a first look when there is something sensational looming on the horizon."

The company's Preferred Subscriber Network uses the responses in a program that connects readers and advertisers, including retailers, travel firms, and cosmetic companies, as well as drug manufacturers that want to market directly to patients with particular ailments. An organizer of the initiative said readers will appreciate tailored promotions. "What we're trying to do is enhance the relationship between the subscriber and their magazine," said the organizer, Stephen Jacoby, Condé Nast's vice president for marketing and databases. "In a sense, it's a benefit to the subscriber."

OTHER EFFORTS ARE STEALTHIER about their aims. A survey from General Electric asked shareholders of GE Investments for thoughts about the company's service, the quality of its products, and ways to improve. There was no place to put a name. What the survey failed to mention to the fifteen thousand recipients—most of them employees of General Electric Company, the giant parent firm—was that officials would quickly find out who filled in the circles indicating "Unacceptable," "Average," and "Outstanding." That's because the company included a code on the return envelope that corresponded with information in the company's shareholder database, allowing the company to surreptitiously identify every respondent.

A GE Investments official raved about the technique in a letter to the printer that helped devise the method. "This was, on the surface, a simple task requiring printing and collating various pieces for each shareholder's use. However, the hard part came with our request to be able to 'secretly' identify each respondent in the most discreet way," his letter to Harty Press of New Haven, Connecticut, stated.

"I must especially compliment one of your employees. . . . Her suggestion enabled us to secrete the code in a manner least likely to attract attention from the respondents," the official went on. "She's terrific!"

Such ploys have been used for years by some market researchers, who pine for personal information about individuals but know that respondents sometimes grow shy when they must include their name on a survey. But the methods have become far smoother in recent years, as computer technology makes it easier than ever before to link coupons, surveys, or other materials to databases of information about individuals.

The mechanism might be a bar code. It might be a cluster of dots. In the case of GE Investments' survey, the identifying information was contained in a series of numbers.

GE Investments is a money management arm of General Electric that oversees about $80 billion in assets for individual and institutional investors. The survey went out to shareholders of the company's mutual funds. It was intended to help the company improve service and identify the particular concerns of individual investors. Tim Benedict, spokesman for the company, noted that it did not explicitly say the answers would be confidential. Benedict said it was the first—and last—time the company used such a code. "We basically didn't ask for the customer's name and address because we wanted to encourage a response." And Benedict added: "We wanted to know who was answering. . . . It was not to pull a fast one on our customers."

That wasn't good enough for GE chief executive Jack Welch. In an extraordinary mea culpa, he sent an email message to several hundred thousand employees condemning the coded survey, saying it was "clearly wrong and should never be repeated."

CHARLES MORGAN NEVER MUCH CARED about working with the government. The red tape was too cumbersome and the profits too low, in part because the government didn't seem technology savvy enough to make full use of Acxiom'sophisticated systems. The September 11 attacks abruptly changed the equation for him. Morgan and his colleagues reached out to many of their contacts in the government and in politics. One of them was Bill Clinton.

When the planes crashed into the World Trade Center and the Pentagon, Clinton was in Australia with his daughter Chelsea. It was a serious situation, given that no one knew whether the United States was in the first stage of a war. The Bush administration, forgetting its fierce political differences, sent a plane to pick up the former president. A few days later, he was sitting in his den in the Chappaqua, New York, house when Paul Leopoulos called. Leopoulos, one of his closest childhood friends from Arkansas, worked as a sales and training executive at Acxiom.

Leopoulos told Clinton: You've got to see what we have here. We have information on a number of the terrorists. Maybe we can stop future attacks. We can help find these guys.

Based on a few scraps of information in newspapers after the attacks, Acxiom queried its data and found names, addresses, links among the terrorists, and telltale inconsistencies. The data showed the attackers had used invalid driver's licenses and phony telephone numbers. "We were trying to figure out where these guys had lived and we were trying to figure out everything from improper use of credit cards and who they might have been associated with," Morgan said two years later.

It didn't take much to convince the former president. Acxiom was no stranger. Morgan and his crew at the company were supporters of Clinton and Hillary, donating money to their campaigns and rallying on their behalf in the state. Clinton picked up the telephone and called one of his most ardent political foes, Attorney General John Ashcroft. He urged Ashcroft to give Acxiom a hearing, and Ashcroft agreed.

Not too much later, Clinton visited Morgan's office in a new building overlooking the Arkansas River. He was guarded by a team of Secret Service agents. Morgan and Clinton sat side by side as Morgan showed what Acxiom had. "He was just sitting in my little bitty office," Morgan said. "He caught the significance of a lot of things almost before you say them." The episode was a turning point of sorts in Acxiom's history. Suddenly a new market, based on the fear of terrorism, had opened.

Morgan suggested the change grew out of a sense of civic responsibility. Acxiom, he said, was obligated to use its data and privacy smarts on behalf of the government. It knew the people, had their names, addresses, and all the rest, and could say whether they were who they claimed to be. It could monitor credit activity and track people to a large degree through their purchasing behavior. "Activities in and around 9/11 caused us to rethink that and we developed a sense among the leadership at Acxiom that for this country to be a safer place they had to be able to work with information better," Morgan said in November 2003, after refusing for nine months to discuss the company's homeland security efforts.

"And 9/11 showed us that the U.S. government and its information processing capabilities were at the level we were at in 1973. And that it—if we were going to have a safe country the government was going to have to do a lot of upgrading and investing. And we also knew that would have to be done in an environment where privacy and data use and practices have got to be carefully thought out so that we don't create the fear, doubt and concern of Big Brother. Big government, Big Brother. We thought we could help work on that balance."

In other words, the company decided to become a major player in the war on terror, to use its reservoirs of personal information in a new way.

THE FLETCHER ROOM was a space deemed by bureaucrats at the Department of Transportation to be among the ugliest in all of Washington. It had no windows, ancient chairs in frayed maroon polyester cloth, walls covered in dingy cream fabric. Into this drab scene walked retired Army General Wesley K. Clark, a West Point graduate and Rhodes Scholar who was contemplating a run for the presidency. Clark carried great prestige, having served as Supreme Allied Commander in Europe. When he retired in 2000, Clark was awarded the Presidential Medal of Freedom, the nation's highest civilian honor.

On that day in December 2001, he was an Acxiom man. An Arkansan, Clark had recently joined Acxiom's board of directors. At the same time, he worked as a hired hand, using his prestige and connections to open doors for the data giant. He appeared impressive as he described the company's audacious plan to team up with another little known company, HNC Software, to create a massive passenger profiling system. At the core of Acxiom's effort would be a program called AbiliTec, which uses a 16-digit number as a stand-in for names, an approach that dramatically accelerates the processing speed.

The system Clark described to transportation officials would combine personal data along with information about the reservations and seating records of every U.S. airline passenger. Acxiom was offering only a subset of the information it manages. Under contracts with other data providers, Acxiom cannot share some information gathered for marketing purposes. What Clark was suggesting, however, would more than do the trick to clearly identify people and, if necessary, their associates. In a matter of seconds, HNC software would take the information and, using software that can learn from massive amounts of information, examine it for subtle signs of deceit or malicious intent. It would authenticate the identity of every passenger.

Government authorities would then use artificial intelligence and other sophisticated software, along with behavior models developed by intelligence agencies, to determine whether the passenger was "rooted in the community"—whether he or she was well established in the United States—and find links to others who might be terrorists. According to a secret government document, it was to be an "automated system capable of integrating and simultaneously analyzing numerous databases from Government, industry and the private sector . . . which establishes a threat risk assessment on every air carrier passenger, airport and flight."

Clark was well paid for his presentation and for his efforts in general on behalf of Acxiom. In 2002 and 2003, he received nearly half a million dollars. Before the announcement of his presidential candidacy in September 2003, he received an annual $150,000 retainer plus commission "for new business." Acxiom got what it paid for: access. Even as he took care to keep a low public profile, Clark worked assiduously on Acxiom's behalf to open doors in Washington. He arranged meetings with FinCEN, the Treasury office that collects and data-mines suspicious activity reports from financial institutions. He took the company into the intelligence agencies. He sat in on an intimate session with Vice President Dick Cheney in the vice president's office in the Senate. Early in 2002, Clark approached a new operation at the Defense Department called the Office of Information Awareness. Run by former Vice Admiral John Poindexter, who had been Ronald Reagan's national security adviser, the office aimed to create unimaginably large data systems and surveillance networks. The system Poindexter envisioned would be larger and more powerful than even the global eavesdropping technology run by the supersecret National Security Agency

(NSA). Poindexter and his colleagues were impressed by Acxiom, according to internal email.

Joining Clark as Acxiom lobbyists were other well-connected Arkansans, including former Transportation Secretary Rodney Slater and former Arkansas senator Dale Bumpers, who had benefited from Acxiom's fund-raising prowess so many years before. Former Clinton chief of staff Thomas F. (Mack) McLarty III, who also sat as a director on Acxiom's board, received consulting fees of about $175,000 annually, through a company he runs called McLarty Management Company.

Acxiom was like other information services on the make—indeed, high-technology companies of all kinds. The company used people like Clark, Clinton, and other representatives to transform its own image. Suddenly Acxiom was also an anti-terrorism company. Not only could it better target people for marketing and weed out fraud for businesspeople. Morgan's staff told the government it could now authenticate people and truth-squad the information they shared about themselves.

MAGICIAN DAVID HARRIS stood beneath a large silver globe, barking out his pitch from the Acxiom booth on the floor of the Jacob Javits Convention Center in New York. The occasion was the Direct Marketing Conference of June 2003, a glitzy affair that gives data-driven firms a chance to sell their services to one another. "Ten seconds," he boomed. "Watch one trick!"

As people gathered around, Harris handed out three worn paperback books, including Dale Carnegie's *How to Stop Worrying and Start Living*. He told the crowd he was going to read their minds, and he focused on one woman holding John Grisham's *The Client* open in her hands. She looked back and forth from the book to Harris's face. "I see an 'e' toward the end of your word. It's not the last letter. It's the second to the last letter, and the last letter is 'r,'" Harris said. He tilted his head, leaned forward, and pointed to the woman. She mumbled her assent. He asked her a few more questions, then declared the word she was looking at was "photographer." He was right.

As the hired entertainment, his job was to convince visitors at the conference that his parlor tricks added up to real magic. He drew them in, dazzled them with his show, and then let the Acxiom sales team, including a guy named Rob, do its thing. Harris, who made his living as a "hired gun" working at conventions for a wide array of companies, salted his patter with words like "content" and "data." "Rob and I can tell you in forty-five seconds what we do," he boasted at the conference. "We help manage, grow, and keep customers."

On cue, Rob the salesman jumped in with his own patter. "We are a one-stop solution," he told the crowd, noting that the company's latest product had information on almost 200 million people living in 110 million households. "What we do is no illusion. It's straight up."

Acxiom officials convey the same message about personal privacy: We're straight up. In promotional material and on Capitol Hill, the officials portrayed themselves as working in the best interest of consumers. At the same time, the company also lobbied hard against legislation that might curtail its access to personal information. Over and over, company officials worked with lawmakers to fashion rules that preempted tougher state laws. (One of their arguments: that a variety of strict state laws might confuse people.) They claimed to support what is known as fair information practices, but they resisted following some of the basic tenets. They talked about how everything would cost more if Acxiom and its competitors lost access to information about you. The economy would suffer.

Acxiom knew that concerns about privacy, were they to become acute enough, could lead to legislative and regulatory reforms. Almost $1 billion in revenues was at stake. At the same time, the company knew perfectly well that its business would be considered massively intrusive by many people—at least for many of those who understood that business. Former spokeswoman Marice Gardner once made a joke about it: "My mom says I work for Big Brother."

The company was relatively lucky. It had managed to stay off the radar screen of regular Americans, even as it promoted itself aggressively to major financial institutions, direct marketers, insurers, retailers, and the like. Regular people seemed more worried about the impact of the World Wide Web.

JENNIFER BARRETT WALKED into a sparsely furnished office high up in Acxiom's new $50 million administrative building, a handsome facility that overlooks the muddy Arkansas River and a highway heading in the direction of Texarkana. Not far upriver was the Clinton Presidential Library, still under construction.

Barrett has a computer science background, and in the early days when Acxiom was still called Demographics, she wrote code. She has worked as a product developer and, in recent years, as the company's "privacy officer." Her job involves serving as an internal watchdog and the face and voice of Acxiom, particularly during policy discussions about laws and regulations that might curb the company's access to personal information.

Barrett has red hair and deep brown eyes that can sparkle one moment and grow wary the next. She laughs easily, giving the impression of spontaneity, but she also relies heavily on pat phrases and arguments of the sort she uses frequently in congressional testimony and policy papers. Like any good marketer, she rarely strays from the pitch she is making. To her way of thinking, Acxiom serves as a trusted third party that oversees personal information. And the company helps provide individuals with more shopping opportunities, quicker loan approvals, targeted marketing promotions, and an array of conveniences. She believes that most people don't know or care how their information is used to generate these Information Age benefits, as long as they keep coming. "They love it. They don't have any idea why they get it. There's a total disconnect," she said. "I have a personal belief that the consumer doesn't really want to know."

Barrett underscored her idea by pointing to the light switch on the wall. She compared the flow of names, financial records, spending habits—and the many other digital details that comprise our lives—to the flow of electricity that keeps the lights on. "I don't care to know how the electricity gets to that light switch over on the wall. But when I punch that light switch, I want the lights in this room to come on and I want them to come on pretty quick, okay?

"The value the information brings to the consumer is a little bit like that. We're living in a very information-, infrastructure-rich society today. It used to be, you know, technology and electricity and all the things that we went through in the industrial revolution. And now that we're in an information revolution—or whatever you want to call it—information has become the grease that gets things done faster, quicker.

You know, it makes the engine run. And without it, things slow down. We're a very time-sensitive society."

This is Barrett's buildup to her core message, the one Acxiom has used so effectively over the years in Congress. Don't regulate information services heavily—or else risk losing all the Information Age benefits we have come to expect. "Politicians in general—there are always exceptions—are beginning to recognize that writing good information management law is very tricky," she said. "And you do not want it to be driven by anecdotes or incidents. You really want to understand. I mean, we don't outlaw knives, even though people are stabbed to death."

THAT'S BARRETT'S JOB, to make that kind of argument. She does it well, both for Acxiom and the industry in general. Despite her title as privacy officer, and the claims the company makes as a leader of privacy policy in America, Barrett's role often is to fend off anything that might constrain Acxiom from gathering and using whatever it can to bolster the company's bottom line. It's a brash approach, to say the least, and very effective.

In March 2002, as the company was pressing hard to win contracts to provide data to the government for screening and surveillance initiatives, Barrett and Morgan teamed up on writing a briefing paper on privacy. In a magazine-style brochure called *Beyond Consumer Privacy to Consumer Advocacy,* they argued, somewhat paradoxically, that the more information that flows to Acxiom and its clients, the more privacy individuals will have. More important, they wrote that there would be huge economic costs if the flow of data to marketers and companies like Acxiom were slowed.

"There's no question that protecting consumer privacy is important and should be done," their paper about consumer privacy stated. "At the same time, we cannot ignore the fact that the free flow of information has a positive impact on consumers' pocketbooks. So are privacy and responsible data usage somehow mutually exclusive? Absolutely not."

Morgan and Barrett used their briefing paper to tout AbiliTec, which Acxiom claimed could dramatically improve a client's ability to draw together information about a particular customer. The executives said AbiliTec could help a company "move from being merely concerned about consumer privacy to becoming an aggressive consumer advocate."

By the spring of 2003, though, their claims for AbiliTec had evolved. Now the technology was also being packaged and sold as a risk management and screening tool for the government's war on terror. "We also believe that in the post–September 11 environment, certain governmental agencies have a need for the type of data integration solutions enabled by AbiliTec," the company wrote in its annual report. "Since September 11, 2001, we have been actively pursuing government contract work in this regard."

Barrett has spoken to Congress about privacy on a number of occasions. In a September 2002 appearance before the House Subcommittee on Commerce, Trade and Consumer Protection, she represented Acxiom; Experian Marketing Service, an arm of the giant credit bureau formerly known as TRW; and Trilegiant Corporation, one of the nation's largest direct mailers. At issue was legislation that might limit the kinds of personal information direct marketers could gather. "Our clients represent a who's who of America's leading companies, and we are always proud of the reputation for helping them sell better products, smarter, faster, and at a lower cost," Barrett began.

Her main goal that day was to ensure that legislation under consideration would not require companies to say how they are collecting and using personal information, or give individuals a chance to say no. She opposed rules or laws that would put oversight of company activity in the hands of the government. She also wanted the committee to be sure to prevent states from writing tougher consumer protection laws, saying in effect that that wouldn't be fair to consumers. "Nothing will be more confusing to consumers than to have differing privacy laws in each state or locality," she said.

Implicit was the idea that a variety of state laws would cost Acxiom and its clients a lot of money and, perhaps, cut back on its access to information about people. But she never said this outright in her testimony.

Barrett applauded the panel's plan to limit the ability of individuals to seek access to the files companies maintain about them. Providing that kind of access is a part of the fair information practices Acxiom professes to support: proper notice to individuals about what is being collected about them, the individual's choice not to participate, and the ability to access any information that's being collected to ensure it's accurate. But it also is inconvenient for the company and costs money to provide.

As she spoke to Congress, Barrett pulled off the trick of seeming to support these fair information principles while in fact opposing their spirit almost head-on when they cut too close to Acxiom's business. Or at least trying to bend them in Acxiom's direction. "Each of the four fair information practices principles—notice, choice, access and security— must be applied uniquely to strike a balance between the value gained by the consumers, business and society and the associated cost," she said. "The primary purpose of access is to assure that information a company maintains about an individual is accurate.

"However," she added, "access for the sake of curiosity is never justified." Her courting ways worked, and she continued in her unusual role as the company campaigned for government business, much of it cloaked in secrecy. In 2002, Barrett counseled a senior counterterrorism official in the Transportation Security Administration (TSA) on how to handle questions about privacy at a public forum. John Poindexter's Information Awareness Office was also smitten with her reputation on privacy. "Acxiom is the nation's largest commercial data warehouse company. . . . They have a history of treating privacy issues fairly and they don't advertise at all," one official said in an email to Poindexter. "As a result, they haven't been hurt as much as ChoicePoint, Seisint, etc by privacy concerns and press inquiries. . . . Ultimately, the U.S. may need huge databases of commercial transactions that cover the world or certain areas outside the U.S.," the official wrote. "Acxiom could build this mega-scale database."

In order to avoid panicking people, Acxiom officially suggests a different approach: Don't build one giant database. That's bad for public relations. Use networks to link those data systems together.

BARRETT HAS LONG INSISTED that regular people don't care as much about data collection and privacy as they sometimes claim. "It's not about the collection, it's all about the use," she liked to say, echoing the gist of her message to regulators over the years. "I think the consumer is saying, 'I want the information about me to be under control, not necessarily under my control.'"

But a series of privacy storms in the late 1990s and early 2000s showed that privacy had become an incendiary issue and frequently riles both liberals and conservatives.

In 1998, a company called Image Data sparked a national debate by quietly buying state driver records, including driver photos. Officials from Image Data portrayed themselves as working in the public interest. The company said it intended to build a national database of photos and personal information to help retailers prevent identity theft, an epidemic crime in which fraud artists use victims' personal information to run up bills in their names or empty their bank accounts. Company officials claimed the service could head off billions of dollars in fraud by giving clerks an instant, tamperproof way to verify the identity of customers.

Like Acxiom and others, Image Data was taking advantage of cheaper data storage and networks to devise a completely new service. It appeared promising. Image Data bought the photographs for less than a penny each. Those images were to be cross-referenced to personal information gleaned from public and private sources. In addition to a name and address, the company's databases held an individual's Social Security number, age, sex, race, and other details from a driver's file, as well as limited information about each transaction. Image Data's plans called for a national database to come into play whenever a customer at a participating retailer attempted to use a credit card or check. Identifying data was sent to Image Data computers, which would respond by sending a photo back to a small screen mounted discreetly near a cash register. The transaction would proceed only after a clerk verified the customer's identity.

The company's desire for motor vehicle files was far from novel. Acxiom, for example, depends heavily on such files to locate and describe people. These records were routinely sold by many states and had become a computerized staple for direct marketers, information services, and others. But by adding photographs into the mix, Image Data had crossed into new territory, raising on the one hand the possibility of improved security for consumers and retailers and, on the other, new questions about personal privacy.

The service was part of a growing number of surveillance and identification systems that take advantage of computers, electronic networks, personal information, video images, fingerprints, and other identifying data, generally in the quest for security. Law enforcement authorities now use computer-assisted cameras to "read" license plates of cars that have run through red lights. Casinos use such cameras to watch for the faces of con artists or card sharps in their digital picture files, and police in Britain are using them extensively in public areas to automatically scan for known criminal suspects. Some automated teller machines now require users to offer a finger for scanning rather than a bank card to get access. And growing numbers of banks, including First Union, require some people to provide a thumbprint before cashing their checks.

Privacy activists said they feared that once photos are released by authorities in digital form, they will be used for other purposes by private detectives or telemarketers who want to match a face to other personal information. "It contributes to an atmosphere where people feel they are being watched," Robert Smith, publisher of *Privacy Journal* newsletter, said at the time. "What you create is a mug file of law-abiding citizens."

Image Data downplayed the concerns. Company officials said they only wanted to stop fraud. "What we're looking for is security of the entire process," Image Data spokeswoman Lorna Christie stressed. "This is a great example of how technology can be used to protect citizens and business."

It turns out that in 1998 Image Data had quietly accepted nearly $1.5 million in federal funds and technical assistance from the U.S. Secret Service. Congressional leaders who helped make those arrangements envisioned using the photo file to combat terrorism, immigration abuses, and other identity crimes—applications that appear to go beyond company claims the database would only be used to prevent check and credit card fraud.

"The TrueID technology has widespread potential to reduce crime in the credit and checking fields, in airports to reduce the chances of terrorism, and in immigration and naturalization to verify proper identity," stated a letter about Image Data LLC from eight members of Congress in September 1997. "The Secret Service can provide technical assistance and assess the effectiveness of this new technology." Thousands of people in South Carolina, Florida, and Colorado complained they were never told their images, at least 22 million of them, could be sold. As the company lobbied to gain access to motor vehicle files, officials apparently told few people about its ties to the Secret Service or the money it received from Congress.

With help from an influential Boston public relations firm, the Rasky/Baerlein Group, Image Data hired lobbyists in Florida and South Carolina. The company spent about $25,000 on the South Carolina lobbyist—five times the cost of the database it eventually bought. It contributed $500 to state Senator John Land, the legislator who sponsored a bill enabling the sale, as well as $1,000 to former Governor David Beasley. Image Data also received help from eight legislators on Capitol Hill. They include Senator Judd Gregg (R-N.H.), who received $2,000 in campaign contributions in his last campaign from the company's officials or their families, and Representative Charles F. Bass (R-N.H.), who received $3,000 in contributions from company officials since 1995, according to Federal Election Commission data.

State legislators, motor vehicle administrators, and others who worked with the company said they had no inkling that federal officials might be involved. When the arrangement became public, people went nuts. Several officials from Florida and South Carolina said they felt misled by the company. Florida governor Jeb Bush canceled a contract to sell 14 million photographs. Colorado governor Bill Owens halted the sale of 5 million images, while the state legislature pushed through a bill that would ban the transfer. South Carolina attorney general Charles M. Condon sued the company for the return of 3.5 million digital photographs already being used in a pilot project there. State legislators, meanwhile, proposed laws blocking future sales and a South Carolina woman filed a class-action lawsuit on behalf of others seeking to stop Image Data from using the images. Officials in Florida, Colorado, and New York have said they intend to study sales of personal information by their states, with an eye toward new restrictions. Congress requires states to change the rules on the sale of such records, or risk losing transportation funds.

Robert Houvener, the founder of Image Data, portrayed himself and his colleagues, some of them veterans of the direct marketing world, as well-meaning corporate newcomers overwhelmed by attention from the media and policymakers. "We've been forthright with everyone," Houvener said. "There's nothing inconsistent here at all."

THEY GATHERED IN LITTLE ROCK, chief executives and privacy officers from Internet, marketing, medical, and banking companies, all there at the request of Charles Morgan and Jennifer Barrett. The idea was to talk about pending battles with regulators, Congress, and activists over how to properly harvest and use the many details about individuals' lives. Though the September 11 terror attacks were still a year away, the meeting offers insight into how Morgan and his colleagues think about their place in the world.

The group Morgan had assembled was intimately aware of a series of intense controversies that had made privacy a touchy national issue. In addition to Image Data, a national uproar over medical records had been caused by a small Massachusetts company called Elensys. It seems that with no public discussion, Elensys had made arrangements to collect prescription records from pharmacies and, on behalf of particular drug companies, to send out "educational materials" reminding patients to take their medicines. Problem was, they never asked the patients for permission. The ensuing outrage prompted CVS and Giant pharmacies to back away from Elensys and buy full-page newspaper advertisements to apologize to customers.

Before that, Intel withdrew plans to include a unique identifier on every processor it produced, after computer users howled with indignation. The online advertising giant DoubleClick had been hammered for its plan to combine online browsing habits with offline shopping records compiled by a data cooperative called Abacus, a company allied with Acxiom. There were plenty of other examples. The government created its own stink with Know Your Customer, a proposal to require financial institutions to monitor customers more closely for signs of money laundering. That plan was loathed and blasted by conservatives and liberals alike, leading the government to abandon the plan.

On the day of Morgan's roundtable meeting in Little Rock, financial services companies were facing a costly and cumbersome federal requirement to provide privacy notices that, for the first time, would disclose how they collect, sell, and use customer records. Americans, including Congress, were beginning to understand. They were being watched, analyzed, tracked like never before. They loved the Internet and thought it was nifty when companies seemed to know them better. But they wanted some control over their own information.

Morgan set the tone with his remarks. The transcript of the meeting shows he was intent on selling a vision in which companies like his maintain responsibility for policing themselves. He was all for privacy— as long as it didn't hurt his business.

He clearly didn't believe Congress was up to the task of striking that balance. "My observation in general is that industry is moving as quickly as possible to address a lot of these issues and even what I would call opportunities that are offered by the better use of information," Morgan said. "Also, my further observation is most of these companies are acting in a very responsible manner vis-à-vis privacy. They want to do the right thing. They really don't want to invade people's privacy.

"But my big concern right now is that legislation or regulation is potentially actually going to get in the way of all this happening. And, obviously, it's going to impact the potential success of companies, as laws are passed that restrict the flow of information.

"What is particularly alarming to me is that the guys who are framing these issues—the lawmakers who are casting votes on Capitol Hill—are not really wired into these issues."

Morgan used a colorful analogy that he believes lawmakers and others should consider before imposing restrictions on his industry—the same analogy Barrett used with me three years later.

"There's a very large inherent risk in having a 70-mile-an-hour speed limit on the Interstate," he stated, "because we know that about 40,000 or 50,000 people die in automobile accidents each year. But we've decided that 70 miles an hour and 41,000 deaths are an acceptable risk and return.

"If we legislate a five-mile-an-hour speed limit, 41,000 people would live next year. However, the lifestyle that we enjoy would be severely changed." Morgan told the group that "You can put sort of that same analogy in the flow of information. If you just totally stop it, we're going to suffer a lot."

. . .

AT THE END OF 2003, Acxiom began work on a fence around its Conway campus. The fence would keep unwanted visitors at a distance. The
company had never had to think about such things before, since very
few people had ever heard about it. That's changing as more and more
people come to know Acxiom, not all of them friendly.

One of those curious people was a young Ohio man named Daniel
Baas, a systems administrator for a data-mining company in Cincinnati
called Market Intelligence Group. The Cincinnati company was hired by
Acxiom to analyze some data. As a consequence, Baas had regular access to an important Acxiom computer server.

Baas is bright, somewhat nerdy, a hacker. He liked to explore computer systems, and got excited about finding gaps in security and exploiting them. That wasn't hard at Acxiom. During one of his electronic
forays he discovered a file containing encrypted passwords for some of
Acxiom's largest customers—banks, credit issuers, retailers, and other
businesses who maintained billions of customer records there. Baas had
hit paydirt. Using a widely available software program, he decrypted the
passwords. He found one that opened all the files. Then he began
downloading. Authorities say he took the names, credit card numbers,
Social Security numbers, addresses, and other details about an estimated 20 million people. The information was burned on about thirty
CDs.

The breach was grave, but far from uncommon. Like so many other
companies and government agencies, Acxiom had failed adequately to
secure the information it had collected. The company did not even detect the lapse. It was local sheriff's investigators who turned up Baas's
name during the probe of another hacker in the area. The investigators
found logs of online chats between that hacker and Baas. They later
searched Baas's home and found the CDs containing the Acxiom data.

The case was turned over to federal prosecutors. In the summer of
2003, they said Baas "exceeded his authorized access" to a protected
computer. In December of that year, Baas pleaded guilty to one count.
Though Baas had offered to share the information, he never did.

Acxiom officials flew up to Cincinnati to talk with the hacker, who told them how he had entered their system and taken the information. They informed their clients about the breach. But they didn't bother to tell individuals their information had been stolen. A company official said the information was simply not that sensitive and "did not meet a threshold that would require customer notification."

They told prosecutors that the information Daniel Baas obtained had a market value of $1.9 million. They estimated it cost them $1.3 million for security audits and encryption software to fix the gaps he had exposed. It turns out that wasn't the only incident. When Acxiom examined its files, it found that other hackers from Boca Raton, Florida, had gained access for months—also by taking advantage of access through a business associate of Acxiom.

Security specialists shuddered at the episodes, not only because Baas got into the Acxiom system so easily but because the company did not feel obligated to reach out to the people whose names, addresses, and other personal details ended up on Baas's CDs. "Obviously, they should have protected the data better," said Kevin Poulsen, who wrote about the incident at SecurityFocus.com, a Web site devoted to such issues. "The fundamental problem is we have no rights to have our data protected, because it doesn't belong to us."

LONG AFTER the terror attacks, Charles Morgan had high hopes about the company's new ties to the government—and business in general. Morgan predicted that Acxiom and other information services were just beginning to learn how to exploit the oceans of data they had collected.

"The information is all there, but the ability to analyze it has really not been there on the grand scale until fairly recently," he said, charming but focused as ever as he steered his way through difficult issues about privacy and security. "We have built database marketing systems that are a snapshot in time, but in general we have a today snapshot in time. And what we are saying today is we are going to keep that snapshot and tomorrow's snapshot and next year's so that we have years of those historical snapshots that can go into the analytical process."

Morgan was asked whether people should trust Acxiom to do the right thing with those snapshots—the virtual dossiers they can pull together so quickly about almost anyone in the United States—for marketing or security.

"I think that regular Joes on the street pay little attention to Acxiom. But should we come to their attention, we need to make sure they feel there are the appropriate laws in place and that they are comfortable with our published information," Morgan said.

"And the average person probably doesn't care. But for those who do, they need to be able to find the information out that gives them the level of comfort that they need."

3

WHO AM I?

MICHAEL BERRY PROWLED the streets of south-central Los Angeles in a rented silver Volvo, searching for a clue. He turned onto a residential street called 12th Avenue, peered at each home, and then slowed the car almost to a stop. Off to his left was the address that had obsessed him for months. He saw a well-tended bungalow with crisp green grass. Watering the lawn was a man covered in tattoos and wearing a sleeveless undershirt and aviator sunglasses, who watched closely as Berry drove by.

"Oh crap, I didn't do this right," Berry muttered, gripping the steering wheel a little tighter and trying not to stare back.

It was the summer of 2002. Berry had come 2,700 miles from his town house in Arlington, Virginia, to scope out the place that had appeared on credit reports as his new home. Somebody using this address had opened at least fifteen new credit card accounts in Berry's name and run up thousands of dollars in bills for clothing, flowers, gasoline, and telephone calls. Berry had always taken pride in paying his bills on time. At thirty-three, he was the chief operating officer of the Independent Women's Forum, a conservative women's group, mingling regularly with Washington lawmakers and Republican activists. The theft of his identity was changing everything: threatening not just his credit rating, which was in tatters, but his respectability, his very sense of himself as a man in control of his own life. Now, as he drove by the tidy house in L.A., he was at a loss. "I felt," he said, "totally helpless."

He had tried to report the financial problems to the L.A. police. Because he wasn't a resident, and the fraud was not considered large enough, they brushed him off over the telephone. When he called police in Arlington, a friendly officer took his report. But he got no promises. Arlington, the officer said, had no jurisdiction in California.

Berry pulled up on the street, turned the car around, and parked. Pretending to do paperwork in his lap, he kept watch for anything suspicious. He had good reason to take care. Just days before, he'd learned from a Florida homicide detective that a man who had assumed his persona—using his Social Security number and carrying a driver's license with his name—was a convicted murderer who was wanted for fresh killings in two states. That meant that Berry, the real Berry, was liable to be taken into custody as a wanted man at any time.

SITTING IN HIS OFFICE in south Arlington in January 2002, six months before his visit to Los Angeles, Berry dialed a toll-free number and waited for the computerized voice at Chase Manhattan Bank to prompt him. He punched in the number of his Chase Platinum MasterCard. He was trying to consolidate his debts onto one low-interest card. He sat back in his chair as he told the clerk his current income and how much credit he wanted. When he hung up, he was certain the bank would comply because he had never missed a payment, even when he was between jobs. A few days later, he heard the news. He was rejected. "I'm sorry," the clerk told him. "You have opened too many cards lately."

Berry was puzzled, but not particularly upset. "This is a mistake," he thought. He'd get it fixed. Berry was used to working through problems and, eventually, getting where he wanted to be. As an undergraduate at the University of Southern California, he'd found his way into the state headquarters of the 1988 Bush-Quayle campaign, landing a volunteer job recruiting and coordinating college activists. He became head of the Trojan College Republicans at USC, one of the state's largest college political groups. After transferring to Pepperdine University in his junior year, Berry parlayed his burgeoning Rolodex into prestigious internships at Ronald Reagan's post–White House office and in the Bush administration, where he worked as an advance man for Vice President Dan Quayle.

He had every intention of staying in Washington as a political operative. But he cut short his plans after his father had a heart attack. Berry moved back to his home town in central California and took a job as a teacher, following in the footsteps of his father. He worked his way through the education bureaucracy and became an elementary school principal. He never lost interest in politics, though, and had decided to move back to D.C. a few years ago. He became a special assistant to Texas senator Kay Bailey Hutchison on the Hill before moving over to the Independent Women's Forum.

Berry tried to put his savvy to work for him. After the rejection from Chase, he made a round of calls to the top three credit bureaus—Trans Union, Experian, and Equifax—companies that operate near the center of the U.S. economy. Working with banks, retailers, landlords, car dealerships, and an array of other enterprises, the credit bureaus collect and share rich financial details about nearly every adult in America: where we live, how much money we owe and to whom, and whether we pay our bills on time.

Credit bureaus sold some 1.2 billion credit reports in the United States in 2002, more than double the number a decade ago. Many of the transactions that characterize American life depend on those reports. They are factored into mortgage loans and credit offers, used to weed out risky tenants and screen people for mobile phone service. Some identifying personal information in them, including addresses and Social Security numbers, also has helped fill the reservoirs of information brokers, who resell data to lawyers, debt collectors, police, reporters, even jilted spouses searching for wayward mates. The reports are perfect fodder for identity thieves.

The credit bureaus mailed Berry his own reports, which were sullied by all kinds of purchases he hadn't made. According to the credit agencies' computers, he had sought, received, and quickly used thousands of dollars in instant credit from Gap and Old Navy. He had maxed out a $1,500 limit obtained a few weeks before from the QVC shopping channel. He had charged hundreds of dollars' worth of gas in the Los Angeles area on a new Exxon card, along with $462 on a new phone line in Riverside, California. Berry felt a rush of anxiety. He'd been paying off his car loan early and sharing a town house with two roommates to save money, but he knew all the wild spending attributed to him would damage his credit rating. If he didn't get this cleared up, he might have trouble buying a house.

Berry discovered from other businesses that his fictive counterpart had sent hundreds of dollars' worth of roses and a stuffed bear to a Los Angeles woman named Joann. "These flowers are from You Know Who," read the note that accompanied the flowers. "I love you a lot and your conversation." A few days later, You Know Who sent another pile of roses to a woman named Maisha, this time with a contrite note attached: "I am sorry for lying, cheating, being selfish."

It was as though You Know Who—and maybe others—was in a spending frenzy, trying to squeeze as much money as possible out of Berry's identity before the scam was shut down. In some cases, the fraud artist or artists got cute, using "Bebe Hooker" as his spouse's name on one credit application and "Lucy Love" as his mother's maiden name on another. But the incorrect information didn't get in the way of the applications being approved. Old Navy had decided to open a new account, in January 2002, for instance, even though the man impersonating Berry used the wrong address. At the same time, the company that issues cards for Old Navy—Monogram Credit Card Bank of Georgia, a subsidiary of General Electric Capital Corp.—also had granted the impostor credit cards for Exxon, Gap, and QVC.

Monogram knew it took a risk on those accounts. About a month after the Old Navy account was maxed out, Berry received a computer-generated letter from Monogram. The company expressed its uncertainty and asked Berry to say whether a mistake had been made.

"Dear Cardholder," it began. "We have recently opened up a credit card account, in your name, with OLD NAVY. Since, the address in the application did not match the address contained in the consumer credit bureau report, we are writing to you to confirm that the credit card account was opened at your request. If you did apply for this account, you do not need to respond."

When Berry called Monogram, a representative assured him the Old Navy account would be closed and the charges removed from his credit report within six weeks. Berry felt better after hanging up the phone, a sense of relief that wouldn't last long.

IDENTITY THEFT IS PERHAPS the most glaring symptom of the ills that have accompanied the data revolution of the 1990s. Bounced checks; loan denials; harassment from debt collectors. Victims of identity theft—and there are millions of them—are often haunted by the consequences for years. But no one was certain of the magnitude, certainly not the credit bureaus or credit issuers, who tended to downplay the problem. Until the middle of 2003, some government officials estimated that as many as 750,000 people a year were victimized. Others thought that number was way too low. In July 2003, Gartner Inc., a business research group, estimated that 7 million Americans had fallen prey to identity thieves in the previous year alone, an extraordinary figure mirrored by a new survey from Privacy & American Business, an industry-funded think tank. Then came a survey by the Federal Trade Commission which showed that more than 27 million Americans had been victims. That included almost 10 million in the previous year.

David Medine, the former FTC and White House official who became a leading information law specialist at Wilmer, Cutler & Pickering, had an unscientific test he used to judge the extent of the problem. He asked friends at Washington parties if they'd been a victim or knew a victim. Medine said almost everyone had a horror story to contribute to the conversation. "You have this seemingly low-level crime that, cumulatively, is a national crisis," Medine says.

The financial costs were staggering, though no one could put a precise dollar figure on them. The FTC estimated the losses to financial institutions had reached $48 billion, a burden shouldered largely by the nation's financial institutions as a cost of doing business. Victims estimated they had lost $5 billion of their own.

Yet identity thieves are growing not only more numerous but more menacing. Scam artists and grifters have been joined by criminal groups from abroad and street gangs that once specialized in robberies or extortion. And as September 11 and the subsequent investigation made plain, identity fraud also has become a favored technique of terrorists. It is one of the salient national security challenges facing lawmakers and counterterrorism officials alike. Often using documents generated by desktop computers, they take on fake names, Social Security numbers, birth certificates, and driver's licenses in schemes to cloak themselves and raise money for their operations. It is, law enforcement authorities agree, frighteningly easy for them to get away with it.

THE NATURE OF IDENTITY has always been the stuff of mystery stories and film noir. One of the great American novels of the twentieth century, *The Great Gatsby*, has questions about the mutability of identity at its core. Now those same issues have become the stuff of national security debates. One of the most vexing questions facing those responsible for protecting Americans from crime and terror is this: How can we prove that someone is who he or she claims to be? For most of our history, that was fairly easy to answer for the majority of Americans. We defined individuals' identities by their parents, siblings, and friends. By the town they lived in and the schools they attended. By the clubs and organizations they joined. In many cases we knew them by sight, or at least knew someone who could vouch for them. Those who wanted to remake themselves, to break free of the bonds of their own histories, had to move away.

In our lifetimes, all that has faded away, as Americans conduct more and more business electronically, move from town to town and job to job, and generally know one another less well. Now, as often as not, the practical terms of our identities are defined by "data elements" contained in thousands of computers: our Social Security numbers and addresses; our mothers' maiden names and middle initials; our birth dates and the special numbers and nicknames we use as our passwords; the things we buy, the cars we own, and the way we use our credit cards. These details, combined by computers and analysts, now authenticate us in the way that personal links used to, serving as virtual keys to financial accounts, retail outlets, communication, air travel, and government services. "What are the last four digits of your Social Security number?" we are asked. "What's your Zip code?"

The problem is, the "data elements" required to authenticate customers on the fly are often available to criminals at little or no cost, sometimes openly on the Web, other times for a price from information brokers. The brokers, who run the gamut from legitimate businesses to questionable characters operating out of their living rooms, peddle all sorts of personal information for as little as $25 a pop. Some even manage to get their hands on credit reports, which are especially prized by identity thieves: In November 2002, federal prosecutors arrested three men who had stolen some thirty thousand credit reports for resale and use in identity theft schemes. Then there are the hackers skilled at stripping computers of names, Social Security numbers, and financial records. In one recent case, hackers plundered 10 million Visa, Master-Card, and American Express numbers from a company that processes transactions for merchants. Cardholders didn't learn about the intrusion until the FBI jumped in to investigate. Bob Blakley, chief scientist for security and privacy at IBM Tivoli Systems, a software maker, says that most Americans mistakenly assume their old notions of identity still apply, that computers and clerks can accept at face value an individual's answer to the question: Who are you? "That's really a profoundly false view of the way that identity works," said Blakley, who recently served on a National Academy of Sciences panel examining these issues. "There's a great deal more opportunity for confusion. It's really complicated to sort out who's who."

SOMETIME IN THE SPRING OF 2002, a man posing as Michael Berry moved into Bay Run II apartments, a working-class complex in Orlando, Florida. He'd come from California and sublet the place from a friend of a relative. His real name was Demorris Andy Hunter, the police said, and he was a convicted killer who'd spent thirteen years in Folsom State Prison for a 1985 murder. He looked nothing like Berry, a big man with pale Irish skin who stands 6 feet tall and weighs close to 200 pounds. Hunter was smaller—only 5 feet 7 inches and 150 pounds—and African-American. A police photo of Hunter shows a tired-looking man with a shaved head and a slight scowl.

None of those differences mattered when Hunter showed up in Orlando. People assumed the California driver's license with Berry's name and Hunter's photo was legitimate. A fake Social Security card displaying Berry's number also passed muster. Those documents helped Hunter get a job at B's, a barbecue joint where he washed dishes and bused tables. Bay Run residents who met the man calling himself Michael Berry considered him a friendly if somewhat wary character. Soon after moving in, he was attending parties and getting to know some of his neighbors. One of his new friends was Theresa Green, a part-time hospital secretary who lived one floor up with her fourteen-year-old son.

On May 25, 2002, Hunter and Green attended a party in an apartment in the same building. According to witnesses who were there, the two drank copiously and danced to the loud music until the party ended at about 2:30 am. But Green didn't want to leave, and when Hunter pulled her away, the two started arguing and somehow fell down a set of stairs. Later, their yelling could be heard through the walls of her apartment. About 7 am, Hunter approached Joseph Butler, the neighbor who had held the party. Hunter gave Butler the keys to a borrowed van and, without explaining why, asked that Butler follow him to a drugstore in a suburban town more than fifteen miles away. Hunter himself drove Green's white Oldsmobile, although she wasn't around. After leaving Green's car in the drugstore parking lot, police said, Hunter dropped Butler off and disappeared in the van. Green was found early the next day. She was dead, stuffed into the trunk of her own car. It appeared she'd been strangled.

Orlando homicide detectives Roy Filippucci and Barbara Bergin received pages on Memorial Day afternoon. When they went to Green's apartment, they found drywall broken in one spot and some personal items on her bed that had been rifled through. As the two made the rounds in the neighborhood, talking to people who knew Green, they turned up a suspect in no time: a man named Michael Berry.

WITH A FELT-TIP PEN, the real Michael Berry outlined several lines of charges noted on his Trans Union Personal Credit Report and Score. "NOT ME!" he sketched in. "FRAUD." He circled the last word five or six times out of frustration, as he thought about what to do next. It was spring 2002, about the time that his impersonator had moved to Orlando, and as usual Berry was working to offset the damage.

He had lost count of the telephone calls he made to the credit bureaus, the banks, and the stores that drew him unwillingly into their business. He had filled white legal pads on his desk with contact names, reference numbers tagging his complaints, and dollar amounts. His boss and coworkers knew about his trouble and now and then asked for updates or offered to help him. To make up for all the time he was spending on the telephone and writing letters, he worked later each day. His usual sixty-hour workweek grew even longer.

"I was totally in war room mode," Berry said. "Every single day I was calling . . . The applications were pouring in every single day."

From December to May 2003, there were new requests for cards from MBNA and Household Bank, two of the nation's largest credit issuers. One came in for Macy's. Another report alerted him that someone was trying to open a Cingular cell phone account in his name. Berry noticed the thief's methods changing, growing cheekier with time. In some applications, the thief started to use Berry's parents' address and his birth date. Someone also was making up information about him, writing on one application that he was a lawyer who worked for the city of Los Angeles and earned $75,000 a year.

It was a grind, but it seemed like Berry was making headway. He had placed a "fraud alert" in all his credit report files, a service that tells companies inquiring about creditworthiness to be careful in granting additional credit or new loans. "I felt like I was getting near victory, when I was catching them before they were being issued," he said. "I absolutely thought the worst of this is over."

In fact, his troubles were just cresting.

Berry discovered that he had almost no legal standing as a victim to make a formal report to authorities. That realization dawned on him when he called Detective Dave Harned, a veteran in the Commercial Crimes Division of the Los Angeles Police Department. Harned took the calls about identity theft and directed them to the right place. He made it clear where Berry's report was going: into an inactive file. Not only was Berry not a Los Angeles resident, Harned told him, his claims didn't come close to meeting the department's informal threshold for investigation. "We wait for the retailers or credit bureaus to make a report," he told Berry.

Berry tried persuading Harned to change his mind, explaining that he knew exactly where all the fraudulent mail was going. "Even if you have an address, you have to prove he did it," Harned explained later.

"People call me every day and say, 'I've got an address. We've solved the case.'"

Harned likens identity theft to "financial rape," and blames it on the financial and data-driven businesses that traffic so freely in personal information. "The credit card companies and everybody else make it so easy," Harned said. His department had resources to investigate only a tiny fraction of the 100-plus identity theft complaints it receives every day. "You almost have to pick and choose what case you're going to work, because of the volume," he said in 2003, adding, "Last year was bad, but this year is going to be worse."

THE REASONS FOR THE SURGE in identity theft are complex, but the problem ultimately comes down to a few salient facts. For one, we are awash in information about ourselves. Twenty-four hours a day, every day of the year, the credit bureaus, information services, groceries, pharmacies, toll collectors, banks, and other institutions gather information about us. They build models about what we are likely to buy and, sometimes, learn more about us in refined mercantile terms than we know ourselves. They often resell or share information about us. At the same time, the institutions responsible for safeguarding all this data often do a poor job of it. The information industry—including brokers, database marketers like Acxiom, and the main three credit bureaus—has steadfastly and successfully opposed much government regulation, arguing that it would make life less convenient and more costly.

The data revolution did indeed spur an explosion in new credit opportunities. Those who once could not afford to borrow, or were not given access to loans, can now get credit cards in the time it takes to buy a pair of shoes or a T-shirt, thanks to electronic networks, the credit reporting system, and regulatory changes over the years. Banks such as First American claim they can provide "preapproved" credit cards, via the World Wide Web, in under three minutes. Credit issuers drum up business through junk mail solicitations, almost 5 billion of them in 2002, according to a company called Synovate, which tracks such offers. Never mind that only a fraction of the people who receive these pitches embrace them—or that they have made life easier for identity thieves, who sometimes search through mailboxes as a starting point in their scams. Many of these offers come from banks that have no tellers, no branches, no people at all of the sort who once came to know customers over a period of many years. From the standpoint of credit card issuers, the solicitations have been a roaring success. There are now more than 3 billion Visa and MasterCard cards in circulation around the world, generating huge profits for the companies that issue them. Two thirds of all American adults have credit cards now, about ten apiece on average.

Peter Tosches, a spokesman for Monogram, said that retailers, in a desire to make life easy for customers, will often approve credit cards for individuals who provide only a picture ID and an unverified Social Security number. While companies like Monogram insist they try to guard against identity fraud in such circumstances, Tosches said the thieves have become increasingly sophisticated in sidestepping security measures. The reality is, the security at checkout counters and online is often incredibly lax. It's intended to make transactions more efficient, not fraud-proof.

The credit bureaus also have a checkered history of responding to complaints about identity theft and mistakes. After years of complaints, Congress amended the Fair Credit Reporting Act in 1996 to force credit bureaus to be more responsive to individuals, particularly those worried about mistaken reports. Among other things, the bureaus were supposed to provide easy access to their clerks by maintaining toll-free telephone lines. They didn't do a good enough job, at least according to the FTC. Despite the clear message from Congress, hundreds of thousands of telephone calls to the three credit bureaus went unanswered, or met with a busy signal. In January 2000, the bureaus paid $2.5 million to settle FTC charges that they were not properly responsive. Many people complain they still aren't. In one eye-opening case, an Oregon woman named Judy Thomas sued Trans Union for allowing errors to remain on her credit report. She spent six years calling and writing to the company, trying to get Trans Union to permanently remove damning details such as unpaid bills that belonged on another woman's report. Court records showed Trans Union mistakenly assumed Thomas was the other woman. Her report would be fixed one month only to show up tainted again several months later. After hearing her story in 2002, a federal jury awarded Thomas $5.3 million for her trouble. While the judge reduced the award to $1.3 million, it was still a record. Trans Union wrote a check to Thomas early in 2003.

Evan Hendricks, a consumer advocate and editor of the *Privacy Times* newsletter, who testified on Thomas's behalf, believed her problem was related to the fact that so much of our information is processed automatically by computers, not people. "Human beings cost money that the credit bureaus and the credit granters don't want to spend," he explained. "That's why this is going to get worse before this gets better."

IDENTITY THEFT is almost laughably easy to commit, and terribly difficult to prevent, at least at present. Consider the strange case of James Rinaldo Jackson, a genial con artist from Memphis, Tennessee. He knew that major financial institutions routinely gave out confidential customer account information to callers. Standing before U.S. District Court Judge Deborah Batts in Manhattan in 2000, Jackson described how he easily took advantage of that porous security, duping information brokers, banks, credit card companies, and even a funeral home. Before he was caught in a sting operation, he netted some $730,000 in diamonds and Rolex watches by using the information he gleaned.

Jackson got the idea from a magazine ad that showed diamonds for sale online. As he looked at the slick photos, he thought, "I would sure like to get some of these diamonds to just have." He described how he gathered bits and pieces of information about his targets, including Gordon Teter, the late chairman of Wendy's International; Nackey Loeb, the former president and publisher of the *Manchester [New Hampshire] Union Leader,* who has since died; and other corporate executives. Starting with an online version of *Who's Who in America,* Jackson turned to information brokers, paying them $50 and $100 for Social Security numbers and banking details. With some of the basics in hand, he called his targets' banks and persuaded clerks to hand over account numbers. That enabled Jackson to tap the accounts directly over the phone, sidestepping the need to talk to clerks the next time around. Then it was a simple matter of calling dealers, ordering the jewels, and wiring the money. He had his booty sent to hotels, to which he dispatched a confederate to pick up the packages.

MasterCard, Visa, and American Express, along with banks in Ohio,

New York, and New Hampshire, all got taken in. In the parlance of law enforcement, Jackson's specialty was known as "pretext calling"—using scraps of personal information to trick clerks on the telephone into divulging more information. It's an old con that's become easier than ever. Jackson was so good—and security at his targets was so weak—that he convinced the Fifth Third Bank in Ohio to wire almost $300,000 from Teter's accounts to diamond and watch merchants. He also changed Teter's billing addresses to Jonesboro, Arkansas. Robert Dunn, Jackson's attorney, said Jackson would have been stopped much earlier had the companies required passwords before sharing customers' information or allowing him to act on the accounts. Regulators and law enforcement officials had warned financial institutions years earlier that identity thieves and information brokers were tricking clerks into giving them access to individuals' financial information. They urged banks to require customers to use passwords or codes instead of Social Security numbers, mothers' maiden names, and other widely available personal information to identify themselves when calling. For years, many financial institutions didn't bother.

"We don't want to make it difficult for customers to get access to their accounts," Robin Warren, then a privacy executive at Bank of America Corp., said before Jackson was sentenced. "Customers get irritated."

IN THE DAYS after Theresa Green's death, police investigator Barbara Bergin made the case a mission, and she worked all hours tracking down the killer. After coming up with Berry's name and some details about the killer, she sent off a request to California authorities for Berry's fingerprints, a copy of his driver's license, and a photo. On June 2, 2002, Bergin got a hit on some records in California. But there was a problem. The Michael Berry she was looking for was a short African-American guy. The records she received showed the real Berry.

With help from neighbors who'd heard Hunter mention his previous jail time, and from a California official who searched through records on her behalf, Bergin turned up Hunter's real name from scraps of evidence she had found. She also discovered the case was more sordid than she thought. Hunter was wanted for the slaying of an Oakland,

California, woman named Ivora Denise Huntly, who'd been shot two months before Green's death. California authorities alleged Hunter killed Huntly as she tried to prevent him from beating his girlfriend. The next day Bergin called the real Berry at his office in Arlington. "There's a serious problem here," she told him. She was putting out a national warrant for Hunter's arrest on murder charges, and would use Berry's name as his alias. "Things could be very bad for you."

Berry was scared, and he didn't know what to do. "This was the first indication I had this wasn't just a fraud problem. This was someone who was killing people, posing as me."

Bergin explained the warrant meant that he, the real Michael Berry, could be picked up for murder. The law enforcement computers would tell officers they were looking for a black man. But cops are so used to getting reports marred by mistakes, she said, they might ignore that detail if they had the right name. The two agreed he should get letters from police in Orlando and Oakland testifying to his real identity. "The last thing I wanted, after everything he had been through, was for him to be on the ground, at gunpoint, in handcuffs," Bergin explains. "That could very well happen."

MICHAEL BERRY HURTLED WEST on I-66, sitting in the passenger seat of a friend's car. On his way to dinner, Berry tried hard to loosen up, but it wasn't working. Ever since he'd received the call a few days before from Bergin, he'd worried he might be mistaken for a killer. In the mornings, he feared he could be stopped while driving his car. Even now he wondered what would happen if police asked for his ID.

He was pulled out of his reverie by the buzzing of his cell phone. When he checked his messages, he heard the voice of his friend Arthur Estopinan, chief of staff to Florida representative Ileana Ros-Lehtinen. "Hey, Mike, it's Art," the message said. "You were just the lead story on *America's Most Wanted*." Berry called him back.

America's Most Wanted features detailed crime reports and information about fugitives. It urges viewers to call in with tips about suspects, and the show's host, John Walsh, boasts that he has helped authorities capture more than 750 people wanted for crimes. On this particular night, Walsh did an episode on Demorris Hunter. "Let's get down to

business. We got to stop a real ladykiller," said Walsh in a jazzy segment to begin the show. A photo of Hunter filled the screen.

"Hunter uses the alias Michael Berry," Walsh said. "Look out,
Hunter. Now you're our prey, because the manhunt starts right now!"

"Oh my God," Berry exclaimed to Estopinan, "every policeman in
America is going to be after me."

The next morning at work, Berry clicked his way to the *America's
Most Wanted* Web site. When he saw Hunter's photograph, he laughed.
"So this is the son of a bitch who is pretending to be me," he said, in-
credulous that he could get away with the impersonation. "He's not
even my height."

Then Berry looked at Hunter's biographical material. Once again, he
couldn't believe what he was looking at. Below a line naming Berry as
Hunter's alias was Berry's Social Security number. "I'm not looking at
my Social Security number on the World Wide Web," Berry thought. "I
cannot be looking at this. Any person in the world can be looking at
this page right now."

Berry wrote an email to an address set up for crime tips and asked
that the number be removed from the site. To help out, his sister did
the same thing. "I never got a response," he says. Eventually Berry's Social Security number was removed from the Web site.

TV officials later said the police had suggested including it as a detail
that might lead to Hunter's arrest.

As HORRIFIED AS BERRY WAS about being caught up in a financial tan-
gle with a convicted killer, that was nothing compared with the dismay of law enforcement and intelligence officials after September 11,
2001. For some time, the FBI could not say exactly who the hijackers
really were. In their quest, agents resorted to low-tech investigative
techniques, knocking on doors and handing out grainy photographs of
the suspects, even as they sifted through a morass of electronic intelligence.

Suddenly, identity theft wasn't just a consumer issue anymore. It was
an aspect of global terrorism. The hijackers used phony identifications,
Social Security numbers, and birth dates to establish bank accounts and
set up their lives in the United States. Landlords, flight schools, banks,

and other institutions took them at their word. Seven of the hijackers got identification cards through the Virginia Department of Motor Vehicles even though none of the seven lived in the state. They took advantage of rules allowing individuals to meet residency requirements with a simple notarized letter. The system had long been abused by immigrants seeking to establish themselves in the region—with help from immigration lawyers and local notaries. But despite warnings from the FBI and DMV investigators, the department maintained the system as a convenience until shortly after September 11.

"We were seeking to balance legitimate needs with the potential for fraud," DMV spokeswoman Pam Goheen explained.

The link between terrorism and identity crimes goes much deeper. Specialists believe that such fraud is becoming a chief source of income for terrorists. Money raised through credit card scams, the resale of goods purchased under assumed names, and other types of identity fraud enables cells to remain free of any financial ties to their leaders or patron states. Authorities allege that al-Qaeda terrorists, for example, took on bogus identities to run a credit card scam in Spain to raise money. They also allegedly used stolen telephone cards and IDs to communicate with colleagues in the Middle East.

Dennis Lormel, the former chief of the FBI's terrorist financial review group, an organization established after the terror attacks, underscored the point when he told Congress that identity fraud posed a looming national security problem. Not much changed in the months after he testified, he said. "I don't think people have really gotten the message. We have known terrorists out there who are exploiting identity theft and identity fraud vulnerabilities."

Ahmed Ressam, a member of an Algerian group with close ties to Osama bin Laden, was caught in December 1999 at the U.S.-Canadian border with a trunkful of explosives. He had assumed the name Benni Norris, which he used to obtain a passport and open bank accounts. He also got a false birth certificate and a student ID. A member of the Armed Islamic Group, or GIA, Ressam told authorities that he relied on welfare and petty crime, including credit card fraud and trafficking in identity documents, to support himself in Montreal. He was linked to a theft ring suspected of funneling money to radical Islamic groups around the world. Authorities believe the ring stole more than five thousand items, including computers, cellular phones, passports, and credit cards, with the goal of financing Muslim extremist groups.

There was also the case of Ali Saleh Kahlah al-Marri. A native of Qatar, al-Marri was detained in Peoria, Illinois, where he was a student, and charged with participating in an identity fraud scheme. When al-Marri was detained in December 2001, federal agents searched his home and found a document containing thirty-six credit card numbers in the names of other people. A laptop computer contained 1,000 other credit card numbers. A review of the credit card activity showed that a phony company—AAA Carpet, with the address of a cheap hotel in Illinois—had been set up to process credit card transactions. Federal authorities were convinced they had an al-Qaeda sleeper, so they dropped the identity fraud charges and declared him an enemy combatant. Marri denied the claims.

"Identity theft—credit card theft, bank fraud—is hugely important to al Qaeda, as it is to many terror groups. I've been astonished that there's been so little attention paid to it," Magnus Ranstorp, director of the Center for the Study of Terrorism and Political Violence at the University of St. Andrews in Scotland, told *Newsweek* magazine at the end of 2002. "The pattern was very clear within the North African contingent of al Qaeda members operating in Europe. Every time you arrest one of them he has 20 different identities and 20 different credit cards."

BY THE TIME HE FLEW OUT to Los Angeles in June 2002, Michael Berry was out of patience. He needed to see for himself the address that mocked him from the pages of his credit reports. Maybe it wouldn't do any good, but maybe going to the house would turn up evidence that would spur an investigation of the case. If nothing else, it would help Berry feel in control of his life again. As he drove into south-central Los Angeles, he wondered how he'd been targeted. He had been treated for his testicular cancer not far away at UCLA Medical Center some years before. Had someone there shared his information? Could it have been a state motor vehicle official? Someone in a credit bureau?

He called Janie Haskill, a close friend who'd once served as Berry's vice principal at an elementary school in central California. On this day, she served as a security blanket for a determined but frightened man.

Speaking on his cell phone from his car, he described for her the house and the man in the sunglasses. He was still describing the scene when a sharp-looking young man in a Lexus sedan pulled up to the house. The fellow on the lawn disappeared inside for a moment, reappeared, and walked into the street. He handed the visitor a six-inch stack of mail. Berry watched in amazement. "I wonder how many of those letters have credit cards with my name on them," he thought. Then the two men looked directly at Berry, and he almost lost his cool. "I'm scared," he admitted to Haskill. "I want you to know if anything happens."

"This is wrong," she said back. "Michael, get the hell out of there." Berry left and never discovered who lived in that house.

WHILE LEGISLATORS, law enforcement authorities, and entrepreneurs recognize the problem of identity theft, they can't agree on what to do about it. After September 11, many people called for a national ID card, among them the technology guru Larry Ellison and the Harvard law professor Alan M. Dershowitz. The American Association of Motor Vehicle Administrators also started working on a plan to create a de facto national ID system that would link state databases to uniform, high-tech drivers' licenses containing computer chips, bar codes, and biometric identifiers, such as fingerprints or iris scans.

Government agencies, including the new Transportation Security Administration (TSA), have begun requiring workers to use such hardened IDs. The Pentagon has millions of plastic "smart cards" containing name, rank, photograph, and fingerprint. But despite widespread support at first for some sort of national ID system—some surveys found that in the fall of 2001, almost seven of ten people welcomed one—the idea foundered. Technical problems and, more important, a long-standing aversion to the concept undermined enthusiasm. Some critics invoked the specter of Nazi tyranny, bristling at the notion of authorities demanding, "Your papers, please."

But the idea of improved identification received a substantial boost from the 9/11 Commission, which described identity issues as central to national security. Among their recommendations: to combine passports with biometric identifiers, improve terror watchlists and travel checkpoints to find known terrorists, and ease travel for those people who don't appear to pose a risk. There are already technological solutions in the works, some that have begun stirring other kinds of privacy concerns. Data companies like Acxiom are aiming to use vast caches of personal information to help airports, retailers, police, and other authorities determine, instantly, whether someone is who they claim to be. They're betting their initiatives to resolve identity will make their data surveillance systems very profitable—and helpful—for many years to come. Businesses, schools, and other facilities are relying more on fingerprints and face recognition to ID people.

Banks and other financial institutions, meanwhile, must now verify the identities of new customers and make records of customer transactions available to law enforcement and counterterrorism officials upon request. Some banks are turning to the same commercial services to authenticate the identities of their customers; others are banding together to create their own verification systems.

STEVEN BRILL'S CORNER OFFICE on the eighth floor of a Rockefeller Center building overlooked the complex's famed ice rink. It was the hub of his latest effort to build a new empire. Hanging on his walls were signs of his earlier ventures: *Court T.V.*, Brill's *Content* magazine, *The American Lawyer*. Now he was teaming up with one of the nation's giant data services, ChoicePoint, to create an ID system.

It was a system that would do what the government for political reasons won't: Use data mining, fingerprints, high-technology cards, and an ever-expanding network of checkpoints to verify that someone was who they claimed to be.

Americans have always chafed at identity systems, of course, but Brill and his partners reckoned that times have changed, and that people would be more willing to accept an identity card managed by a private company. Brill said the idea came to him during his most recent project, an extensive well-received book called *After* that spelled out how the government was reforming itself in reaction to the terror attacks. Over and over during his research, Brill discovered that identity was at the core of many security conundrums. He reasoned that since a national ID card system would never be accepted, he and ChoicePoint and their other partners would be doing a public service by creating one themselves. They would do it more cheaply than traditional government contractors, and in so doing make life more convenient for people who don't want to wait in security lines.

Brill spoke to dozens of other people, in the industry and government, about the identity issue. Among them were Attorney General John Ashcroft and Homeland Security czar Tom Ridge. "So by the time I finished the book I sort of knew a lot about this stuff and was really sure that I wanted to do this business idea," Brill said. "There was a need for some kind of reliable credential that would be recognized in more than one place." The card, initially dubbed V-ID, was later renamed Verified Identity Pass. The company describes it in promotional material as a "nationally recognized, voluntary biometrically secure identification system. . . . The V-ID will combine convenience with security—without putting the government in the business of identifying and tracking American citizens."

"It's not a government national ID," Brill said. "It does use some data mining at the outset to do what you want to do, which is have someone prove they are who they say they are."

Starting with just a few clients in early 2004, the company planned to gradually expand its use to office buildings, sports facilities, concert halls, and even airports across the nation. It marketed the card as the answer to "securing the homeland" at the vast majority of vulnerable facilities that are privately owned. According to plans, the card would cost up to $50 upfront and require monthly payments to maintain membership. Those applying must take an "ID quiz" that ChoicePoint will score. The applicant's name will be run through ChoicePoint's background screening system and checked against government watch lists. Under the USA Patriot Act, the government can share that sensitive information with private companies. Based on the outcome of that process, ChoicePoint decides if an applicant "qualifies"—or is too risky, based on criteria from the government. When individuals are approved, they will provide a fingerprint that will be maintained in the company's computers.

Those who have the cards will be allowed to use a fast lane outfitted with a fingerprint-scanning system. That system will be operated by another Brill partner called TransCore, a company that runs the electronic toll booths in New York and across the country. TransCore computers will instantly assess whether your fingerprint belongs to a person who has paid the necessary fees and been declared a low risk. Everyone else will have to use a slow line.

To encourage adoption of the card, Brill and his partners intend to allow companies who adopt the card to put their own logo on it. Brill says he is counting on the marketplace pressures to ensure the card "keeps its promises of quality and integrity." As for privacy concerns, Brill said, no record will ever be kept of any transactions. That's a promise that will be difficult to verify.

For his latest venture to succeed, it seems Brill needs government cooperation. He has developed many relationships over the years and through the work for his recent book. He also has another set of partners from Civitas Group, a company formed after the attacks to help develop homeland security products. Among the senior executives at Civitas is Samuel (Sandy) Berger, a former national security adviser to Bill Clinton, and Charles Black, a former adviser to Presidents Ronald Reagan and George H. W. Bush.

"Every day I worked on the book," Brill said, "I'd confront another example of how in the September 12 era we needed a new solution to the old problem of balancing security with liberty and privacy, not to mention balancing our new need for added security with the problem of not having bottlenecks every time one of us wants to go into a building or a theater, or get on a train or airplane. Sure, a lot of those bottlenecks faded away in the year after the attacks," he added, "but many haven't, and, more important, there are now all kinds of new efforts underway, many encouraged or even mandated by Congress or the Department of Homeland Security, to secure venues like ports, ferries, sports arenas, industrial facilities, and office buildings. Those efforts will be accelerated overnight and could become chaotic after there is any kind of new attack."

Brill said he's not at all worried about criticism that the ID card will be turned into an identity system of the sort that Americans have abhorred over the years. His comfort level is due in large part to his partnership with ChoicePoint, a company that in his view works hard to improve security without undermining privacy and autonomy. "They seemed committed to the kinds of things I wanted this thing to be committed to, including a really strict, careful, accountable privacy policy," Brill said.

ON DECEMBER 4, 2003, Michael Berry was back in the White House as a guest of President Bush. Berry was serving as the stand-in for everyone who had been the victim of identity theft. The occasion was the president's endorsement of the Fair and Accurate Credit Transactions Act of 2003. By now, Berry's story had become public. He was excited that something productive might come of it, that his story was being used by the White House to promote change. The law gave every adult the right to one free credit report each year. It required merchants to blank out most digits on credit card receipts. The law also required the creation of a "national system of fraud detection to make identity thieves more likely to be caught."

"Michael Berry is with us today. Thank you for coming, Michael," the president said. "In January of 2002, Michael was applying for a credit line increase. He'd always paid his bills in a timely manner. He's a good citizen. But his application was rejected. They told him that he had taken out too many credit cards recently. It came as quite a surprise to Michael, since it wasn't true. He discovered that someone had stolen his financial identity. He made countless calls to credit bureaus and tracked down credit card purchases he had not made. He even found the address of the person who had taken out the cards.

"Nearly two years later, Michael is still fighting the effects of the fraud. The system was broken. Michael is living testimony to what I'm saying when I said the system was broken," Bush went on. "See, in an age when information about individuals can be found easily, sold easily, abused easily, government must act to protect individual privacy. And with this new law, we're taking action."

Berry's excitement soon dimmed. It dawned on him that he was simply a prop, helping to promote a law that did not address some of the fundamental problems, including the lack of follow-through by law enforcement authorities and the lack of adequate security by the companies that use personal information so profitably. Several months later, the president approved more identity theft legislation, adding two years to prison sentences of criminals convicted of misusing using personal information and five years to the sentences of terrorists who misuse such data. It remains to be seen whether identity thieves or terrorists even know about the penalties.

The kind of system mentioned by Bush for reporting identity theft, meanwhile, had been announced earlier that fall by a group called the Financial Services Roundtable, one of the industry's most influential lobby groups. According to Kate Ennis, the group's spokeswoman, the announcement was timed to coincide with debate about identity theft in Congress. "It was to demonstrate our commitment to this issue," she said in an unguarded moment. "Obviously, Congress was hearing about this."

When the effort was unveiled by lobbyists in the Capitol, it wasn't clear whether it had broad support among the group's own members. There was no system in place. Even Ennis expressed skepticism at the time. "I said, 'Wait a minute, there's no there there.'" By March 2004, the program had secured just $1.5 million in sponsorship from fifty-one of the group's member companies. But it was already behind the scheduled May start-up date. The group also said it would only be a "pilot" program. Ennis said the program's future depends on how people respond to it.

Despite his disappointment with the White House, Michael Berry at least had the satisfaction of knowing that the suspect in his case was behind bars. An acquaintance had sent him an email, including a copy of a newswire service account of how police and the FBI captured Hunter in Houston earlier in 2003. Police found the van Hunter had been driving in Orlando, burned and abandoned, not far from the house where he was captured. Hunter was moved to Alameda County, California, where, early in 2004, he was awaiting trial in the Oakland murder case. The Orlando charges were still pending.

Apart from confirming that Hunter impersonated Berry, authorities still knew little about the identity theft or who the mastermind was. By the summer of 2004, they had not conducted an investigation or filed any charges. Berry may never find out how Hunter latched onto his Social Security number and driver's license. Or who was living in that bungalow on 12th Avenue. Or how many people were filling out credit card applications in his name.

Early in 2004, Berry was still wrestling with the mess made of his finances. One charge—$462 to Pacific Bell—was particularly troublesome. Before Berry could get the debt erased, it was sent to a collection agency, a red flag on any credit report. One immediate casualty was Berry's Chase MasterCard Platinum credit card. Even though it was Chase that had tipped Berry off to the identity theft in the first place, the bank decided that he was somehow responsible for his troubles. Viewed now as a credit risk, Berry was given a choice: Pay a much higher interest rate or close out the card. He closed it out.

While most of the fraudulent charges were eventually removed from two of his credit reports, the third remained marred by purchases he didn't make. For many months, Berry continued to fill out form after form to take care of the problem. Each says essentially the same thing: that it was a thief and not Berry who made the charges. "It is a total and complete nightmare," Berry said in an email, "and completing the paperwork alone could easily be my full-time job."

He carried around the letters he obtained from police in Oakland and Orlando for a long time, neatly folded in a black leather wallet. "Michael D. Berry is not the felon fugitive that is being sought by several agencies," said the well-worn missive from the Orlando police. "It is our intention to clear any confusion as to Mr. Berry's identity."

The police assured him that he didn't need the letters after Hunter's arrest. Somehow, he couldn't bring himself to throw them away.

4
THE MATRIX

———

TWO DAYS AFTER the September 2001 terror attacks, Hank Asher
leaned against the tile counter in his kitchen, a room the size of
many New York City apartments. In his hand was a mug-sized martini.
Sitting nearby was Bill Shrewsbury, a special agent from the Florida Department of Law Enforcement and one of the many cops Asher had cul-
tivated over the years. They were brainstorming about what they could
do to fight back. Shrewsbury pondered the kinds of clues the terrorists
might have left behind. Asher, owner of an information service called
Seisint Inc., talked about the profiling power of his massive data reser-
voir.

Asher made a fortune in the data broker industry with a service that
delivered billions of dossiers about Americans to police, private investigators, lawyers, reporters, and insurance companies. For much of the
year before the attacks, he had worked at most a day or two each week.
He spent much of his time at home in a gated community mansion, or
on his sport fishing boat, a gleaming white 65-footer with four cabins.

Now he felt his life of leisure was over. Asher was certain that
Seisint's 20 billion records could help the government, if used the right

way. His way. After gulping some of his icy drink, he put the glass down and looked at Shrewsbury. "You know," he said to his friend, "I think I can find these fuckers."

ASHER HEADED INTO HIS BEDROOM, with Shrewsbury close behind. It is a cavernous space with vaulted ceilings, a king-size bed, and desks topped by two computers with large screens. Glass doors opened out onto an expansive lawn and pool. He sat at his desk, hunched over his keyboard, and began typing in commands. Now and then Shrewsbury looked over his shoulder without a clue of what he was doing. "Look," Shrewsbury said after about two hours, "I got to go, man." Asher continued to bang away. He was on a digital safari.

Using artificial intelligence software and insights from profiling programs he'd created for marketers over the years, he told Seisint's computers to look for people in America who had certain characteristics that he thought might suggest ties to terrorists. Key elements included ethnicity and religion. In other words, he was using the data to look for certain Muslims. "Boom," he said, "32,000 people came up that looked pretty interesting."

Over the next several hours, he managed to narrow the list sharply. One of those he identified as a potential threat was Marwan al-Shehhi. Asher didn't know it at the time, but al-Shehhi was the hijacker who flew the second American Airlines plane into the World Trade Center. What he did know was this: The data held the truth. You just had to know how to look for it. And he knew how.

Though he'd dropped out of high school, Asher was a computer savant who'd created a company called Database Technologies and a groundbreaking product called AutoTrack. Starting in the early 1990s with a single database of automobile records in Florida, Database Technologies added in driver's licenses. Corporate records came next. Over the next few years, it absorbed property ownership details, marriage and divorce records, professional licenses, even information about handicap parking stickers. By 1998, Database Technologies, later known as DBT Online, had more than 8 billion files about Americans. Through his programming innovations Asher figured out how to deliver those electronic records—long, rich dossiers—in seconds.

Seisint, Asher's latest company, had even more information. And its supercomputers worked even faster.

In his darkened bedroom that night, he put the system through its paces over a swift connection to Seisint. "I got down to a list of 419 through an artificial intelligence algorithm that I had written," he recalled later. The list contained names of Muslims with odd ties or living in suspicious-seeming circumstances, at least according to Asher's analysis.

At midnight he called Tim Moore, commissioner of the Florida Department of Law Enforcement and a friend, to tell him what he had done. Asher and Moore had known one another for years, in part because Asher was a police booster who provided services for hundreds of law enforcement agencies and routinely donated money to police organizations. "I think if you can put together the right team of government officials and directors of departments, that we can catch these guys," Asher said.

Moore was impressed. He told Asher state investigators would be at Seisint headquarters in the morning. It was the beginning of a public-private collaboration that would lead to the creation of Matrix—a surveillance engine that would soon capture the attention of the most powerful law enforcement and intelligence officials in the country.

There was an irony here. The technology Asher was preparing to use in the name of justice might once have targeted him, a man with a questionable past of his own.

A FEDERAL PROSECUTOR named Michael Mullaney and an FBI agent named Sal Hernandez walked into Seisint's high bright foyer in Boca Raton, Florida, on Sunday morning, September 16. Asher had called federal authorities repeatedly, trying to get their attention. It was Mullaney who agreed to pay him a visit.

Mullaney and Hernandez seemed skeptical. Here they were, meeting with a guy who seemed to know—before almost anyone else—details about some of the terrorists who had caused the greatest number deaths on U.S. soil since the Civil War. "What do you have?" one of them asked brusquely.

Asher showed them to a long desk that held his computer. As he typed at a keyboard, they focused on an oversize monitor. Asher demonstrated what he had managed to do the days before. He typed in some queries and instantly pulled up detailed biographies of some of the same characters. He showed links among them, based on where they had lived, the telephone numbers they used, and other details in the system. The feds inched their way closer to the screen. Their reserve melted away. "As they would ask me questions, I would actually run what they were asking in front of them," Asher said later. "And the FBI guy would come out of his seat about six inches and say, 'Can you print that?'"

"We went back to the FBI and said, 'This is amazing,'" said Mullaney, who later became principal deputy chief for counterterrorism at the Justice Department. "I sat down and said, 'These guys have the computer that every American is afraid of.'"

They weren't the only ones to get a personal demonstration. In the days after the attacks, the Secret Service showed up, asking some of the same questions. So did a host of officials from the Florida Department of Law Enforcement, other agencies across the country, and even competitors. During the data revolution of the 1990s, a growing number of data services had filled their own computers with billions of personal records about Americans to enable private investigators, police, insurers, and others to track people, weed out the frauds, hunt down the debtors. The credit bureaus and a variety of specialized information services constantly recharged the reservoirs of DBT and its competitors, without drawing attention to such relationships.

In the anxious months after the attacks, many of them gave away their knowledge and expertise for free. But Seisint seemed to deliver the data more quickly, at least according to some of those who saw the company's operation. As a Florida intelligence official said later, it was unnerving how much information came rushing at analysts using the system. "It's scary," said Phil Ramer, director of state intelligence at the Florida Department of Law Enforcement. "I can call up everything about you, your pictures and pictures of your neighbors."

Asher was adamant about making this power available to police for a long time to come. On the morning of September 11, people had crowded into his part-time office on Seisint's Boca Raton campus to watch the image of smoke billowing from the World Trade Center. After the second plane disappeared into the second tower, Asher told all those watching to call the FBI and Secret Service and other police agencies across the country. Give them free accounts, he ordered, give them whatever they need.

By the end of that week, Asher decided to build a secure room at Seisint for law enforcement authorities to use, twenty-four hours a day for the foreseeable future. It would be safe from hackers, while giving investigators access to all the public records and classified information they could use. "Shredders, computers on desks, white boards, pictures on the walls, plants in the corners," Shrewsbury said, describing the room that Asher built one weekend with his own money.

Before long, the company created a "terrorism quotient" that tagged certain individuals as having a "High Terrorist Factor" score. Asher and his colleagues gave federal and state authorities 120,000 names of people with the highest scores, along with a "1 percent list" containing the names of the 1,200 people deemed the biggest threats. That refined list provided leads in scores of investigations and led to some arrests. Unknown to Asher at the time, five of the names he generated were hijackers on the planes crashed on September 11. Agents from the Secret Service, FBI, the Immigration and Naturalization Service, the U.S. Customs Service, and state police joined Mullaney in making Seisint's headquarters an outpost in the war on terror.

ASHER BECAME A DATA PIONEER in the early 1990s partly out of necessity. He had lost his job as a computer programmer. He had child support to pay to a former wife. The economy was in a recession, and Asher had to find work. An insurance industry official in Tallahassee wanted to collect all the state driver information as part of a new service. The man explained how the information would be collected, cleaned up, and then transmitted electronically to customers over telephone lines. "I can do that," Asher told the man.

"Well, son, there's twenty-six million records in Florida," Asher remembers the man saying with a deep southern accent.

"That's no problem." Asher said. "I can handle that."

"Well then, son," the man said, "we're going to make a lot of money."

That is the exchange that Asher said preceded the creation of DBT and AutoTrack. Few people had ever used such a system, or even imagined something like it could be created. This was before most people had personal computers. The Internet was a creature still known chiefly to academics and scientists. The World Wide Web as we know it now didn't exist. But suddenly customers could dial in to Asher's computers and swiftly and legally obtain a wealth of information about customers, targets of investigation, fraud suspects, and the like.

Local police soon heard about Asher's trove of information. Authorities in Boca Raton called him about working as a programmer. Asher declined, but mentioned his new service. He showed them his system— some thirty computers linked together—and the many millions of records. They went crazy for it. Before long, his customers included the insurance industry, private investigators, lawyers, and newspapers. Among his favorite accounts were the hundreds of police agencies that tapped in to the system on a daily basis. He liked to tell cops: "I find 'em, you fuck 'em."

His timing was ideal. When he sold shares in DBT in 1999, Asher took away between $117 million and $147 million; reports vary. In less than a decade, he and his company had collected more than 8 billion records. By now, the lookup service industry was relatively crowded. There was LexisNexis, a newcomer called ChoicePoint, divisions of all three credit bureaus, and scores of smaller operations that, like DBT, focused on finding people and their assets, not on selling them something. But the demand for personal information was exploding. They could all make money.

"I've been very fortunate, I've never chased money," Asher said. "I built products with passion and the money followed. I was trying to feed two children when I built DBT, not make $150 million."

He wasn't through after he sold his shares of DBT. Anxious to build on his success, Asher decided to cash in on the fervor about the potential of online commerce. The Internet was exploding. It was the height of dotcom mania. There seemed to be endless amounts of money for digital entrepreneurs promising new ways to exploit the global computer network. Asher resolved to create a direct marketing firm that could profile consumers better than ever before. He poured money into the new venture, hiring a team of computer scientists and drawing in investors from the direct marketing and data worlds.

The result was eventually named Seisint, a company that Asher hoped would turn the data industry upside down and make him even richer.

ASHER SUMMONED HIS TEAM of software developers to his Seisint office a few days after the attacks. Make something extraordinary for the terror investigators, he told the group. Use every resource at the company. Money was not an issue.

While lawmakers struggled over the response to the attacks that became known as the Patriot Act, Asher and his team worked at a feverish pace to enable investigators to ask questions of the data that could never be answered before. They had neither the time nor the inclination to think about congressional debates, political trade-offs, and privacy concerns.

After four weeks or so, they had built the system later to be dubbed the Multi-state Anti-Terrorism Information Exchange, better known as Matrix. Its very name suggested the same computer dominance portrayed in the science fiction movies starring Keanu Reeves. A police intelligence official in Florida who helped develop the system said he thought the allusion would be amusing.

At the core of Matrix was a lightning-fast computer system called HOLe, short for the first names of it inventors, Hank Asher and Ole Poulsen. The HOLe system was a series of linked central processing units that added up to a supercomputer. HOLe, pronounced "Holy," was created during the dotcom boom for eData.com, the name of the company before it was called Seisint. The company's focus initially was direct marketing, both online and off. That meant using massive amounts of information to target and profile the people most likely to spend money on a particular product. The industry's buzz phrase for such efforts was "customer relationship management," something that became a mantra in the marketing world.

The marketers' idea was to use computers, the fast-dropping price of data storage and networks to collect enough information to anticipate the needs and wants of customers. To track them and their desires. In promotional material, marketers across the country held out the promise of recreating the experience of small-town America a century ago, when butchers knew your favorite cut of meat and tailors remembered your measurements. Some data marketers seemed to believe the hype.

In *The One to One Future: Building Relationships One Customer at a Time,* a cheerful how-to book popular with many marketers, Don Peppers and Martha Rogers described the pending change in breathless terms as "a paradigm shift of epic proportions." "Technology has brought us back to an old-fashioned way of doing business by making it possible to re-member relationships with individual customers—sometimes millions of them—one at a time, just as shop owners and craftspeople did with their few hundred customers 150 years ago," Peppers and Rogers wrote in 1993. "It would not be an evolutionary change, but a revolutionary one."

LIKE ITS MORE ESTABLISHED COMPETITORS, Seisint wanted to go be-yond simple conclusions about people. It aimed to plumb the data to discern details about people they might not know themselves. Key to this vision was personal information that was now widely and system-atically available from the public records, credit bureaus, and marketing services companies: details about homes, cars, and incomes, families, travel, and buying behavior. It was HOLe's power that would be the driving force.

"I have a computer that can run thousands of times faster than any-body else's computer," Asher boasted. "My computers are so much faster than any computers that exist, I have redefined what computers can do."

Some of this work was geared toward traditional direct mail. In June 2001, Seisint and Equifax, an investor in the private company, an-nounced an alliance to do target marketing for the credit industry. "The company's parallel processing technologies will enable Equifax to ac-cess, analyze, manipulate and store massive amounts of information across disparate databases in fractions of seconds," the companies said in a press release.

Seisint made similar expansive claims for a marketing service it was offering with Accenture, another partner and investor. "In their global alliance, Accenture and Seisint are uniting their considerable strengths to help organizations fully capitalize on massive amounts of data to reinvent their customer relationships," the companies said. The company then also had a subsidiary called eDirect, which focused on sending email, mostly to people who had signed up for sweepstakes online, filled out warranty cards, and otherwise shared their email address. Company officials claimed eDirect only targeted people who gave their permission. Some critics accused the company of being one of the nation's most notorious spammers.

The eDirect subsidiary was sold off and eventually became Naviant, an email marketer that in turn was bought by Equifax for $135 million. Seisint maintains close ties to both Naviant and Equifax. Seisint managed Naviant's data and that company's former president sat for a time on Seisint's board. Equifax is an investor in Seisint, and was a regular source of its data.

Seisint's ties to the marketing world would be supremely important after September 11, 2001. Without regular infusions of fresh information about Americans, Seisint's extraordinarily swift computers would be of little use to police and intelligence officials.

WITH AUTHORITIES DEMANDING MORE of the company than ever before following the attacks, Seisint had one distinct advantage: computing speed. Not only did it have a sea of data and a supercomputer, it had a digital identity system that somehow managed to tag every adult American citizen with a unique code.

Americans have long opposed the idea of a national identity number or card, on the grounds that such a system would enable authorities to track them too easily. That's partly why the pervasive use of Social Security numbers has come under attack so frequently by civil liberties activists. In 1996, LexisNexis created a national storm with a service called P-Trak that made Social Security numbers available on the Internet; the company was forced to back down. A few years later, Intel became the subject of national scorn after it became public knowledge that the company wanted to put a unique identifier on every computer chip—part of a plan to make life easier for marketers. Those concerns didn't hinder Seisint. Asher, Poulsen, and the rest of the design team implemented their own universal identity system. The innovation (similar in concept to those used by Acxiom and other data companies) enabled HOLe to automatically link records to particular individuals. These electronic tags verged on the mysterious. Seisint considered the process of applying them a corporate secret. However it's done, the links dramatically eased the process of digitally conjuring dossiers on demand.

The identifiers would be a milestone on the road to preemptive law enforcement surveillance—the ability to predict when someone might commit a crime. But few people outside the company know about them. Even Asher refers to the process as "mystifying."

"We have created a unique identifier on everybody in the United States," said Poulsen, the company's chief technology officer. "Data that belongs together is already linked together."

FEDERAL PROSECUTORS joined the team of investigators at Seisint headquarters. They didn't have a clue about the technology, but they improved its performance through the power of the law. They issued subpoenas that gave Matrix access to data that otherwise would have been out of bounds: financial records, credit card activity, who knows what else? The company won't say. "They had to get a subpoena first," Poulsen said. "But they did."

Seisint's identity product, called Accurint, became the backbone for Matrix. Many of those who have seen the system, including counterterrorism and law enforcement officials, were impressed with its power to answer complex questions instantly. What are the interesting ties among these millions of people? How many of them are Muslim, immigrants, transients? Where did they travel and with whom? Analysts could now ask deeply layered questions that, in essence, became profiles. One might search for all the brown-haired, Caucasian people driving red pickup trucks in a particular Zip code, with a license plate that has an "S" and a "7" in it. Want to add in people who bought something in a particular store or who use post office boxes? Rent apartments with other men?

Asher and his colleagues downplay the implications of their process, because they know they face a potential backlash from people concerned about profiling. They stress that Matrix contains only records that law enforcement authorities could always obtain. At the same time, they insist those records can be gathered and analyzed faster than ever before. In effect, they created a new kind of information from the old. Matrix gave investigators new power to discern patterns and apply models that select people based on precise characteristics—all those details contained in the billions of commercial and criminal records.

"When enough seemingly insignificant data is analyzed against billions of data elements," says a Seisint brochure about Matrix, "the invisible become visible."

It had the appearance of being a perfect tool for law enforcement authorities who before the terror attacks, for civil liberties reasons, would never have been allowed to create anything similar themselves. In *The Naked Crowd*, Jeffrey Rosen, a writer and legal scholar, refers to this kind of process as "personal dataveillance—designed to collect information about individuals who have been identified in advance as suspicious."

Poulsen, one of HOLe's creators, was openly ambivalent about what he helped to create. He'd been recruited to build a marketing machine and now it was being transformed into a profiling powerhouse for the government. "I'm uneasy. I don't like the idea of an overseeing body with all the information about individuals," Poulsen said. "We're dealing with massive amounts of data. . . . It's full of errors and noise and wrong information. On the other hand, I think there's a need for it because there's a threat out there."

Asher doesn't share those doubts. In fact, he said, it is so much better than anything he had invented before. He estimated he spent as much as $20 million of his own money on its development; Florida officials put the figure at well over $10 million. "Matrix is an order of magnitude more mystifying than AutoTrack was in its brightest day," Asher said. "Blows me away to sit there and run it. To realize the core technology underneath it and the interface is mostly my design makes me shiver. Just to run, to know that we built it, just blows me away."

He promotes Matrix as the product of selfless patriotism, but it also held out the promise of making him even richer if Seisint were to win a government contract for a national criminal intelligence sharing program or if Seisint were sold.

HANK ASHER GREW UP in Valparaiso, Indiana. Asher never made it through college. He dropped out of school in the tenth grade. "It wasn't a forum that I learned in well," he once said.

Not that he wasn't smart. To be sure, he was brilliant. He had to master trigonometry in less than a week to secure a job as a draftsman, for which he drew electrical switches and circuits. When he turned eighteen, he took a job as a painter at Bethlehem Steel, which paid much more. "We were up 450 feet hand-brushing 40 gallons a day of paint, walking on 3-inch beams," Asher said. "We were making $6.50 an hour which was the highest wage at the steel mill . . . I was rolling in dough. Bought a little MG sports car and had things my friends didn't have."

It was grueling work, so he started his own painting company. The problem was that most of his business was outside and he couldn't work enough during the winters. He moved to Fort Lauderdale, as he tells it, with $7 in his pocket and great expectations. He went to work for another painting firm and was soon earning $34 a day, enough for a cheap hotel and all the beer he could drink. After he learned how things worked, he figured he could do a better job and make more money by doing things his way.

Four years later, he had some 100 employees who helped him scrape, clean, and paint building exteriors. By the time he sold the business in the early 1980s, he had invented a machine that blasted away old paint, speeding the process of his jobs, and he had almost 250 employees. It was through the painting business that Asher first taught himself how to use computers. He found a way to target his prospects in South Florida—those buildings that needed painting or roofwork—much more effectively. "I tracked every high-rise in Broward, Dade, and Palm Beach County, and kept really good records with them," he said. "For a painting company it was pretty sophisticated."

About this time Asher first got his airplane license. A self-described adrenaline junkie, he began traveling, living large on the apparent income from his painting business. He once claimed it was worth $3 million. In 1982, he sold the business to some South Africans and New Yorkers, though he did not recall their names, according to a deposition he gave several years ago for a lawsuit. He claims he got $600,000 down payment for the business but no more before the company "went into liquidation." He built a small house in the Bahamas, rented a place in Belize, and began flying, quite often, throughout the region.

Asher liked to describe himself as retired then, but in fact he led a very active life. Not only did he fish and dive, he flew an air ambulance. He also got involved in a number of business dealings that he claims took him throughout the Caribbean and Latin America. In a deposition during a business dispute several years ago, he said his destinations included Haiti, the Dominican Republic, Puerto Rico, the Virgin Islands, Mexico, Belize, Chicago, New York, and San Diego. Asher claimed his trips involved small grocery stores and a liquor company. "I did business with some Bahamian people and would fly through the Caribbean with them to further business causes," he stated under oath.

Asher loved the flying. "You know, when somebody would have a heart attack on an island, with no lights on the runway, no way to get in there, nobody would go in there," he said. "I'd go in a heartbeat . . . I'd go in the worst weather, you know. I did it for two reasons. One, it made me feel good to help somebody. But two, I loved the adrenaline."

The group he ran with those days lived fast lives. Asher said he was impressed by their charm and apparent sophistication. "I got hung up on the fact that these were more important people than I had ever been around before," he said, "and they were classy and everything else."

As it happened, some of them were drug smugglers. And before long, so was Hank Asher.

BASICALLY, ACCORDING TO ASHER, there were two kinds of people in the drug trade back then: the hard-core criminals, some of them ruthless members of Colombian cartels, and the more laid-back, Jimmy Buffett–loving adventurers. He insists he fell into the second group. "I could tell a rascal from a criminal in a heartbeat and I'd like to say that my friends were really of the rascal nature."

Asher's new group of friends recruited him into their black market business as a pilot. At the time, Asher said, it seemed like fun. His trips involved flying to Colombia, Belize, and elsewhere, picking up tightly wrapped packages, and flying back to remote farms in central Florida. (Confidential police memos quote Asher associates as saying some of the contraband was cocaine.) When interdiction efforts grew in Florida, they flew to even more remote airports in Oklahoma. One trip involved picking up 1,100 pounds of marijuana in Orangewalk, Belize, a sugar cane–growing region. Asher flew into the area on a foggy night. He and a companion met their contact in the morning. They had planned to fly out from a dirt runway, but at the last second, they decided to use a small highway as their runway instead. Asher said he got $5,000 a trip. A former smuggling colleague said the pay was at least double that.

"I was a pilot. I had no employees. I didn't know anybody. I didn't know anybody at one end, I didn't know anybody at the other end," Asher said. "I was an airplane driver.

"I didn't feel like I had done a crime until it occurred to me I had just done a crime. All of a sudden I realized, I had just done a crime. I was a criminal."

ASHER CLAIMED HIS ROLE was limited to seven trips or fewer. He said he feels a deep and abiding sense of remorse. And he claims he has never broken the law since then. Records maintained by police, and interviews with a colleague who served time for running drugs, suggest the story is not so clean cut. One housemate who was with Asher during the Belize pot deal later served six years in federal prisons for his drug activities. In an interview, he said Asher was "a partner in our smuggling gang."

Other drug smugglers told Florida investigators that Asher flew more than 600 pounds of cocaine to Florida on one trip alone. It's a story that investigators deemed reliable. By the late 1980s, none of this was much of a secret to the Florida Department of Law Enforcement. Documents show that state investigators had evidence Asher was a smuggler as early as 1986. When the state began using his own AutoTrack service in 1993, they conducted a standard background check on Asher that underscored the questions about his drug smuggling. An internal state police document from October 1993 shows that senior officials at the Department of Law Enforcement knew exactly who they were dealing with. One of the officers mentioned in the document as an investigator was Bill Shrewsbury, Asher's friend and now a Seisint employee. Another state police memo, written a decade later, said that "Asher was by his own admission a drug smuggler in the early 1980s." In 1999, the Drug Enforcement Agency and the FBI also caught on to his past. Hearing that Asher might be using his data system to monitor their drug investigations, a fear that Asher later dismissed as ludicrous, officials at the federal agencies suspended their contracts for AutoTrack. When asked about the internal 1993 memo, Commissioner James T. (Tim) Moore, perhaps Asher's greatest advocate in the state police, said he had read it, but he continued to claim the allegations about Asher's past were overblown, even as he promoted Matrix to state and federal officials.

AFTER ASHER BEGAN FLYING contraband drugs to the United States, an acquaintance approached him with a different kind of scheme. Some American mercenaries were stuck in Nicaragua, the man told him, and needed help escaping. Would he be willing to help? Asher was worried about the legal implications, but he couldn't resist. "If we get caught down there we're screwed," Asher recalled the man telling him. "But there was nothing illegal about this in the United States."

Asher put out the word that he was looking for people to join his team, and soon he had some recruits. "We kind of knew each other— these weren't guys I'd smuggled with or anything else," he said. "This was a different group of people."

More than two decades later, Asher claimed he bailed out of the incursion when his associate said they might have to fight their way in and out of the country. "If I could have flown into a little runway or something and a bunch of American guys that were stuck jumped in the airplane and we got the hell out of there, I would have felt good about it," Asher said. "Going down with a bunch of guys that were going to have a shoot-out at the OK Corral, I didn't feel good about it."

Several alleged co-conspirators, interviewed by Florida investigators in August 2003 as part of a background check on Asher, told tales of mercenaries, million-dollar payoffs, and drug-running plots that also involved planned assassinations. According to confidential police documents, one man asked his state interviewer if they "wanted to know about 'the Contra thing.'" "Speaking on the condition that his name not be revealed [he] stated that Asher was protected from testifying in [a] drug trial because of his knowledge to assassinate a major political figure from the Contra affair," the confidential police report said.

Another man stated that "Asher attempted to recruit him and several others, to assassinate then Nicaraguan president Daniel Ortega.

********* stated that he and Asher had two separate discussions on the planned assassination. ********* stated that Asher offered to pay him $1,000,000 for his involvement and he (*********) thought the United States Government sanctioned the assassination plan," according to the police document.

Asher dismissed such talk as nonsense. "I may have been in meetings with those guys when it was about picking up guys who were not incarcerated down there, that I was all for doing. I was at the meetings when they said, We're going to have to bring some boys down, they got them in custody. And it might have been the next day that I called the guy back and said, I'm out. And I know that they continued to meet afterwards." Asher said that he had no idea the operation might have been part of a secret government operation until years later, when he read about the Iran-Contra scandal.

The brief state police investigation of the allegations, in the summer of 2003, proved inconclusive. "Investigation revealed information that Asher may have been involved in 'planning' a scheme to support covert paramilitary activities in Nicaragua that was reportedly sanctioned by the U.S. Government. There was no indication that any plan was actually implemented."

HANK ASHER HAS the large forearms of a laborer and the gut of a man who likes his cocktails. His hair is turning gray and his eyes are watery. He favors T-shirts, wash-and-wear pants, and boat shoes. Despite his apparent lack of polish, though, he often captivates those around him. "He has the look of a pirate. He talks like a sailor and he has the mind of a scientist," said Ira Siegel, a member of Seisint's board of directors and the former president and chief executive of LexisNexis.

His persona helped to explain why Asher made so many friends over the years—and why some of them have decided to ignore the many signs of his checkered past. That includes Martha Barnett, former president of the American Bar Association. She is a Seisint director and Tallahassee lawyer whose firm once pressed the state years ago to hand over entire databases of records to Asher. She defended Asher, saying he had never been convicted of any wrongdoing.

"This is America. This is the land of opportunity. This is the land of rags to riches. . . . Hank is the American dream," she said. "The story to me is about what he has created."

Many people are drawn to him, in short, because he seems larger than life. He has also won praise, attention, and access by sharing his personal wealth far and wide. He has given untold amounts of cash and services, for instance, to the National Center for Missing and Exploited Children, the quasi-government agency that uses massive amounts of data to help law enforcement authorities track down abducted children. The group won't say exactly how much Asher has donated, but a spokeswoman said "it's huge."

John Walsh, the star of *America's Most Wanted* and another big supporter of the center, said Asher is an unsung hero. Walsh said he has known Asher for fifteen years and spoke of him as a next-door-neighbor kind of guy who might invite people over for a barbecue. "He doesn't look like the developer of some ass-kicking program . . . like a hunter of criminals and pedophiles and terrorists," Walsh said.

When asked about Asher's drug-smuggling past, Walsh said: "I think it's mean-spirited bullshit. You know that old thing, 'Don't let the facts get in the way of a good story.' He was never charged or indicted."

Asher is proud of his support of the center—and of the recovery of missing children in general. "What I've given the National Center is access to my system since 1993, and what the National Center has given me back is a paycheck for the soul that couldn't be measured in money," he said. "I've looked into the eyes of over a hundred parents who've lost their children because of stranger abductions, where they're either still missing. . . . or found dead. And I see the same thing in every set of eyes I look in. I see hollow eyes and a hollow soul." Asher also has given tens of thousands of dollars of cash and services to police groups, though exact numbers remain hard to come by. He spent money freely to hire former cops, including Shrewsbury and agents from the DEA and the FBI. Hal Robbins, the executive director of a group called the Florida Police Chiefs Association, said Asher personally gave $80,000 or more in recent years. In turn, the group gave him an award that Asher displays on Seisint's World Wide Web site. "We don't have that many contributors, certainly not like him," Robbins said. "I don't want to upset him. It was done very quietly."

One of Asher's law enforcement friends is North Miami Beach chief of police Bill Berger, who tested early versions of AutoTrack. Berger used to be head of the International Association of Chiefs of Police. After September 11, Berger said, Asher called to complain that some law enforcement officials weren't returning his phone calls. So Berger reached out to his own network, including Secret Service director Brian Stafford, who returned the call promptly. "He actually called me from *Air Force One*," Berger recalled. A day later, the Secret Service had people at Seisint.

Stafford went to work for Asher in early 2003. He became chairman of the board in March 2004.

NO ONE COULD ACCUSE ASHER of being a tightwad. In recent years, he has donated more than $750,000 to Democrats and Republicans. Recipients include Democratic senators Bob Graham, Barbara Boxer, and Hillary Clinton, and Republican representative Katherine Harris. In 1999 and 2000 alone, he gave $150,000 to the Democratic National Committee. In 2001 and 2002, he gave $100,000 to the Democratic Senatorial Campaign Committee and $50,000 to the National Republican Campaign Committee. Harris, the freshman representative from Florida, received $2,500.

Asher said he donates freely to people and causes he believes in, regardless of political affiliation. It is not, he insisted, a bid to gain access, win favors, or seek political help.

In 2002, he apparently took a shine to one of Senator Bob Graham's pet causes. Graham, a Democrat who was then chairman of the Senate Intelligence Committee, was one of the leaders of an initiative in Florida to create a more centralized structure to the state's university system. The effort required a change to the state constitution. To generate support, a political action committee was formed. Asher donated $10,000 in May of that year. He chipped in another $5,000 in September. But his biggest donation came in the fall, just days after Graham paid a visit to Seisint.

As described by an aide, Graham was touring the state on behalf of the education initiative. At the same time, he knew about Matrix and sought out a demonstration. Days later Asher donated $50,000 to the political action committee, becoming one of its single largest individual contributors. In the next few months, Graham promoted the Seisint technology to the Senate Intelligence Committee and to the Justice Department. At the time, Graham's staff was inundated by pitches from technology and data companies, but they singled out Matrix for special attention.

"He was impressed enough with the technology—and what he had heard about it from state law enforcement officials, especially Tim Moore at the Florida Department of Law Enforcement—to ask the staff director of the Intelligence Committee at the time to follow up and see if the technology would have value to any federal agencies," Paul Anderson, Graham's communications director, said. Those meetings led to a $4 million grant from the Justice Department that allowed the state to pursue expansion of the Matrix system to other states. A dozen states committed to using the system, which would rely on a Justice-funded computer network to share information.

Richard Ward III, the former deputy director of the Bureau of Justice Assistance, who helped arrange that grant, said he did not recall hearing details about Asher's drug-smuggling exploits. Even if he had, Ward said, it probably would not have mattered. Calling the system "mind-boggling," Ward said the technology is too good to ignore. "I'm too much of a pragmatist to worry about that," he said. "If a bad guy develops a tool that's useful to law enforcement, and he has no way to use that tool, I don't care. What's important here is the product."

Graham also persuaded members of the powerful Senate Appropriations Committee to offer their continuing backing. In a written statement submitted to the *Congressional Record* in July 2003, Graham made his support for Matrix clear:

"I can attest to the success the MATRIX program has had in our home State of Florida. Time is critical in preventing acts of terrorism. Our law enforcement officials in Florida tell me that, with the advantages of the MATRIX system, they have seen significant improvements in cases involving kidnapping, identity theft, drug trafficking and terrorism, just to name a few. MATRIX has been a resounding success, with the program set to expand to 12 additional States in the near future, including Kentucky, Pennsylvania and Texas.

"Yes, for the first time, States will be able to share information through this integrated database system, providing law enforcement officers with the information they need to investigate threatened acts of terrorism or domestic crimes. The same results would have required many hours to accomplish. Those hours can now be compressed, freeing up limited law enforcement resources to focus on critical priorities, such as responding to terrorist threats."

PREMKUMAR WALEKAR DROVE his cab into a Mobil station just outside Washington, D.C. At 8 am on October 3, 2002, Walekar opened the gas tank lid and inserted the pump. Then came the crack of a rifle shot. He staggered, collapsed against a van filled with children, and slid to the ground. The killing spree by the Beltway Sniper had just begun.

Less than a half hour later, Sarah Ramos was leafing through a book on a bench near Leisure World, a home for the elderly. One of the men who lived in the community strolled by, heard the clap of a rifle shot, and saw that Ramos was covered in blood. A short time after that, Lori-Ann Lewis Rivera pulled into a Shell gas station to clean her van. She was shot dead with the same rifle that killed Ramos and Walekar. So was Paschal Charlot, who had the misfortune to set out for a walk that day in the neighborhood where he had spent his whole life.

The sniper seemed invisible. For the next three weeks he would stay that way, terrorizing the Washington region, moving from place to place, gunning people down, young and old, black and white, men and women. It didn't seem to matter who the victims were. "For you, Mr. Police, call me God," said a note left behind at one of the killing scenes. "Do not release to the press. PS, your children are not safe."

As the hysteria built, Hank Asher thought about the rifle of his childhood, a .223 with a scope on it. He had used it to track down squirrels, shooting them from a distance. He and his friends never trespassed when they were hunting. They always stayed on familiar ground, calculating that landowners might be inclined to shoot them if they trespassed. Asher had a saying: "You don't go where you don't know."

In thinking about the Beltway Sniper, Asher reasoned the same strictures must hold true for killers. It didn't make sense to him that the sniper would travel at random, hunting people on ground he didn't know. Asher also rejected the prevailing theory among investigators that the shooter was a former military man. In his mind, the killer had to have geographic ties to areas where the shootings occurred. This was the kernel of his newest profile, which he ran through the Matrix. It wasn't long before he had a suspect and passed along the man's name and number to police.

His work was a testament to the power of Matrix. It was also wrong. "So I ran a profile of the distance of every one of the murders, and I came up with a guy that lived like a hundred feet from one of them, five hundred feet from another, two thousand feet from another. I mean, the glove fit," he said. "And I sent that up to them and I can't imagine what that poor fellow . . ." Asher laughed in an embarrassed way about his mistake.

"Hopefully he was cleared easily with alibis and excuses," he said. "But I thought I had caught him."

In the end, Matrix still played an important but unheralded role in the case, joining other information services that responded to requests as fast as police issued them. At the same time Asher was pursuing his gut feeling, an FBI agent named Thaddeus Knight and a state police investigator named Jeff Portz were camped out at Seisint's headquarters, testing other ideas on Matrix. Portz was becoming an expert on the system. He knew the kinds of questions to ask and, increasingly, the power of Matrix.

Asher had been frustrated by the unwillingness of investigators in the D.C. area to send data to Matrix. His sources in law enforcement and Congress called the FBI repeatedly, urging the bureau to send down forensic details that might help solve the case. Finally, after a woman named Linda Franklin was shot down outside a Home Depot in Fairfax County, Virginia, they agreed. Three hours later, Asher said, federal authorities shared data about the case. Police were almost frenzied in their determination to capture the suspects.

Asher looked at the data that came in and predicted it would take just over a week to identify the killer. "Next Tuesday he's mine," Asher announced to his colleagues, who took up the call: "Next Tuesday he's ours."

On the evening of October 23, Portz and Knight got a call from the sniper task force. They had left the Seisint office for the day, but the task force wanted their help. We need it now, they were told, we're that close. The investigators went back and fired up Matrix. They also established a Web link to suburban Maryland, enabling the investigators there to watch their work in real time. The task force had the name of a suspect, John Williams, and an address in western Florida. Portz and Knight said that person's profile didn't add up. He didn't have any Army postal addresses in his dossier, for example, or any ties to the Northwest.

Investigators believed the real shooter should have both. Portz and Knight said the Florida guy was probably not the right suspect. They tailored their search to pinpoint their man from a universe of some 21,000 John Williamses in the United States. Based on what the task force was telling them, they concluded the likely one came from Tacoma, Washington. The address and other demographic information appeared instantly on the computer screen of the sniper task force in Maryland.

The next day, authorities cut down a tree at the residence in Tacoma. It had been used for target practice. Authorities quickly discovered .223-caliber slugs from the same rifle that had dropped sixteen people. It was the confirmation they needed. They released the license plate number of a Chevrolet Caprice, a dirty former police car that, as it happened, had been seen several times near the shootings. A trucker spotted the car at a rest stop in rural Maryland, and at three-thirty in the morning on October 24, a police team rushed the car and arrested the man identified by Matrix and his young accomplice, John Lee Malvo.

Shrewsbury, who was with Portz and Knight, said investigators would have found the killer before long, but he insisted Matrix helped speed the process. "We feel very strongly we could have saved some lives," Shrewsbury would say long after the killers were apprehended.

A reward that had been promised for tips leading to the killers went to the trucker who spotted the Caprice, not to Seisint. "I'm not saying I'm any kind of Kreskin or anything, but I set a goal and it was met," Asher said. "Certainly we could have said, 'Part of this reward money should be ours.'"

THE ROOSEVELT ROOM in the West Wing of the White House is named after Theodore Roosevelt and Franklin Delano Roosevelt, who served as the twenty-sixth and thirty-second presidents. Once nicknamed "the morgue" because so many people had to cool their heels there while waiting to see the president, it is an ornate working space a few steps from the Oval Office and across the hall from the cabinet room. Above a carved wooden mantel at one end of the room hangs an equestrian portrait of Teddy Roosevelt. Dominating the center of the space is a long wooden conference table, flanked by leather-covered chairs.

Hank Asher walked into this room in January 2003. Despite his criminal past, he had been invited to share his Matrix technology with Vice President Dick Cheney, FBI director Robert Mueller, and Tom Ridge, who was going to be sworn in as director of the Homeland Security Department. Joining Asher was his friend Tim Moore, commissioner of the Florida Department of Law Enforcement, and Paul Cameron, president of Seisint.

Their escort was Florida governor Jeb Bush, the president's brother, who had seen his own demonstration of the system two months before. Bush was so impressed that he asked the Seisint people whether they had demonstrated it for Washington officials. They hadn't. "Well, then, we need to get this up there," Bush told the Seisint people.

Asher's visit to the White House showed the lengths to which the White House and the government were willing to go to secure new surveillance and profiling technology. Even the nation's top cops were willing to trust Asher.

The room was set up for a live demonstration. Since they couldn't use the secure White House data lines, Seisint officials had worked with technicians from the White House to run 1,500 feet of high-speed cable from a remote location into the room. Cameron's laptop computer sat on the conference table. A pull-down screen stood nearby to show the results of the Matrix queries to the crowd of officials.

Governor Bush opened the meeting with a background description of what state officials were doing with Seisint. Asher made some brief remarks. Then Moore introduced Cameron, who described the genesis of the program—the partnership with the state police, FBI, Secret Service, and other federal agencies—before turning to his computer. As usual, it was a startling demonstration. Cameron put in certain variables and instantly pulled up long dossiers. He showed how to call up driver's license photographs of suspects—and photographs of their neighbors. The system charted unseen links among suspects, telephone numbers, driver record information in the blink of an eye.

At one point, Cameron recalled, Ridge twisted in his chair, turned toward Cheney, and nudged him with his elbow. Afterwards, Cheney praised the group and applauded the fact that it was a state-driven initiative.

"It's not a federal project," Cheney said with approval, "it's a national project."

When told about the visit, good government advocates seemed aghast. Charles Lewis, director of the Center for Public Integrity, questioned the motives of Cheney, Governor Bush, and the others. He said Asher's presence, at the center of government, was inappropriate. "How did this man get so close to those people in the White House?" he asked. "It strains credulity there wasn't some awareness at a very high level, that they didn't know about this past."

Moore said Asher had nothing to do with organizing the meeting. "Governor Bush saw the product, understood it," said Moore. "We weren't there selling something."

But that apparently was the effect. Those at the White House were sold. After the Roosevelt Room meeting, Ridge ordered the Department of Homeland Security to grant $8 million to speed the Matrix program.

Sitting in his office in the Justice Department more than a year after the visit to the White House, Attorney General John Ashcroft was untroubled by Asher's past or by his White House visit. It was, Ashcroft said, a matter of national security. "We are not in the business of disqualifying technology by the author. We are in the business of qualifying technology, using technology based on its ability to help the American people."

LATE MORNING ON A HOT AUGUST DAY in 2003, almost a dozen police intelligence analysts assembled in a classroom on the first floor of the Georgia Bureau of Investigation headquarters. Each of them had signed on to a personal computer with a lightning-fast link to Seisint's machine in Boca Raton. At the front of the class were officials from Seisint and the Florida Department of Law Enforcement. The director of the Georgia agency, Vernon Keenan, looked on, his excitement showing on his face.

As soon as the Matrix demonstration began, the Georgia analysts began shaking their heads. These were veterans who used databases every day. LexisNexis, ChoicePoint, the national criminal database known as NCIC, you name it. They couldn't believe what they were seeing here. They ran names and addresses and instantly had pages of records. They sought and found links among people. Photographs materialized the moment they were requested.

"They were in awe," Keenan said. "It's one thing to have the capabilities of Matrix explained. It's another thing to see it in real time."

That training session was the culmination of more than a year of work by Vernon Keenan. He had been taken with this project from the very first. After seeing a demonstration by Asher more than a year earlier, at a session organized by Tim Moore, Keenan had volunteered to use his own Social Security number. "God damn!" he said when his dossier began appearing on the screen in front of a group of police. "After just a moment there was display after display after display."

Keenan grasped what Matrix could mean for his analysts. Projects that might take months could be done in hours. Searches for suspects in drug cases, abductions, and other crimes could happen instantly. Instead of having to tap in to dozens of record systems, they would have to turn to just one. "It's one-stop shopping," Keenan liked to say.

Keenan's Georgia bureau soon turned over criminal records to Seisint, and began negotiating with the state motor vehicle administrator to deliver driver's license records and photos as well. Keenan had great hopes that Georgia would be at the forefront of a technological shift in law enforcement. But the training session on August 14, 2003, was probably as far as the agency would get with Matrix.

Even before Matrix became public, state motor vehicle officials had already complained about the cost. It would set the state back hundreds of thousands of dollars to deliver the records, and almost $2 million a year to participate in Matrix. They seemed ambivalent about the legality of turning over the records to a private company in another state. There were also simmering questions about Asher's past.

WHEN DETAILS ABOUT MATRIX emerged as a news story that summer, civil liberties and privacy activists jumped in. They were alarmed that officials had so suddenly mixed criminal and commercial records into one blinding-fast system. Citing privacy concerns, California's attorney general refused to share state records with Matrix. Other states put off joining the system for the same reasons. In October, Georgia governor Sonny Perdue pulled the plug, saying he couldn't abide the cost or the impact on privacy.

Among those attacking the very idea of Matrix was former Georgia Republican congressman Bob Barr, a former U.S. attorney and a prominent conservative privacy advocate. "This is a battle for what kind of society we want to live in," he said. "Do we want to live in 1984, or do we want to live in the kind of society that America has always been?"

Those sorts of questions spooked a lot of people who otherwise couldn't wait to get their hands on Matrix. Suddenly, their prized project was caught up in the politics of privacy. Almost everyone who cared about privacy had been focusing on federal surveillance initiatives. John Poindexter's Total Information Awareness program was target number one. But even Poindexter, who had seen a demonstration of the Matrix, condemned the project, in part because of Asher's involvement. "I question his character," Poindexter said. For many critics, Matrix provided the clearest evidence that much of the work of knitting commercial and criminal data together in this new war on terror was happening at the state level, orchestrated by the information services. "The government no longer has to build that database. That database has already been built by private entities," said Jim Dempsey, now the director of the Center for Democracy and Technology, who closely followed the debate about Matrix. "If you're trying to locate somebody, if you're trying to profile, this is where you go."

Dempsey and Barr weren't the only ones with questions. The American Civil Liberties Union now vowed to go after Matrix, declaring it a state-level version of Total Information Awareness. Though Georgia and several other states had bailed out, others were pining for a chance to sign up to the system. The ACLU didn't want that to happen. "In essence, the government is replacing an unpopular Big Brother initiative with a lot of Little Brothers," said the group's opening salvo, a press release announcing its intention to shut the system down. "What does it take for the message to get through that government spying on the activities of innocent Americans will not be tolerated?"

New York, Texas, and Wisconsin, among other states expressing interest, soon dropped out. Utah put its participation on hold. Connecticut, Florida, Michigan, Ohio, and Pennsylvania continued to work with the system. Because of the controversy about his past, Asher earlier had distanced himself from Matrix and put his Seisint holdings into a trust. Anyone interested in learning more about the project was urged to contact a private, nonprofit group called the Institute for Intergovernmental Research, which managed the federal funding for Matrix. But don't expect to get any detailed answers on this—or much else to do with Matrix. As a private operation, one of the group's officials once said, it's not obligated to share any information about participants, their contracts, meetings, and the like.

The institute began working on a request for proposals from other companies, such as ChoicePoint, or LexisNexis, which maintained its own data warehouses of public records, legal documents, and newspaper and other media reports. The idea was to find the cheapest way possible to run the system and fulfill state obligations not to offer single-source contracts. Seisint still had a very real chance of continuing to win the contract. ChoicePoint was already quietly connecting law enforcement agencies around the country to its own supercomputer-driven system, which it claimed provided the same lightning-fast service. Call it Matrix Redux.

Asher didn't have to wait long for another payoff. Just months after he was forced out of Seisint for public relations reasons, the company and its Matrix system were acquired by information giant LexisNexis Group for $775 million in cash. Asher's take? Something in excess of $250 million.

LexisNexis, a subsidiary of the UK-based Reed Elsevier Group, maintains billions of records, including media reports, legal documents, and public records collected from thousands of sources around the world. Officials there gushed about the impact of Seisint's supercomputer technology on all that data. They claimed the deal would boost the company's already extensive role in homeland security initiatives, while expanding services it already provides under contract to police departments across the country and federal agencies such as the Justice Department and the CIA. At the same time, they played down the role Matrix would play in LexisNexis strategy, suggesting the system might disappear. Make no mistake, though: Asher's technology will be there, working behind the scenes, no matter what it is called, and now quite possibly on a global scale.

On the day the sale was announced, in July 2004, Asher said he was proud of the company he had built and expected it was only going to blossom in the coming years. "To me, my inventions are like children. I want them to grow up and be great adults. Lexis will see that that happens."

5

LOOK ME UP SOMETIME

O N NOVEMBER 7, 2000, Matthew Frost stepped out of a sporty green Mercedes and walked toward his polling place in Tampa, Florida. Frost was excited about making a small mark in history by voting. At thirty-three years old, he had never cast a ballot for the White House. He had never bothered in his college years. Then he lived abroad for six years, studying Chinese in Taiwan. Now he was married, the father of two, and, he thought, properly registered. He was supporting Democrat Al Gore.

Frost stepped up to a table at the entrance and gave his name to an electoral worker. The elderly woman riffled through some computer printouts. "Sorry, sir, you have a felony," the woman told him. "You can't vote." Frost blushed, embarrassed that people around him had heard her. He had received a letter from state officials months before, telling him he was ineligible. But he had never been convicted of a felony and dismissed it as a mistake. Then he got a second letter telling him where to vote, so he assumed all was well. Frost was a hotel franchise salesman and prided himself on his powers of persuasion. He urged the election volunteer to check the list again. "I can talk myself out of anything," Frost said later. But not on that night.

Along with hundreds of other legitimate voters across the state, he was victim of a botched attempt to use a private data contractor to help purge the electoral rolls of felons and other ineligible people. State officials said they had the best of intentions: to rely on new information technology to ensure a clean election. But the outcome, overshadowed at the time by other problems, provided a glaring demonstration of what can happen when the government and private data services team up to target individuals. The use of computerized personal information can—and often does—spin out of control.

Frost was more than disappointed. Not only was he prevented from voting in one of the closest elections in American history, he had no idea how he could clear up the mistake. If the computers considered him a felon, he might not be able to get certain jobs. He might not be able to coach his kids' sports teams or volunteer in their schools.

Frost dreaded having to tell his wife and children about the question that had been raised about his past. On his way out into the warm Tampa night, he put an I VOTED sticker on his lapel to hide his sense of shame.

THE COMPANY BEHIND Frost's exclusion was DBT, the pioneering operation founded by Hank Asher in the early 1990s. DBT had been bought in a $444 million stock deal in early 2000 by a fast-growing data giant called ChoicePoint.

DBT's primary mission was helping police, and one of its customers was the Florida Department of Law Enforcement. Company executives had promised they could use immense storehouses of information to help state police and election officials purge the electoral rolls of illegal voters. A new law, approved after voter fraud ruined the 1997 mayoral elections in Miami, mandated such arrangements. It seems that great numbers of ineligible convicts and an untoward number of deceased persons cast ballots that year, undermining faith in the outcome. The apparent winner was quickly told to pack up and go home. In 1998, DBT said that for about $4 million it would prevent a similar outcome in 2000 for the presidential contest and other races, by comparing names of registered voters against lists of known felons, deceased people, and duplicate registrations. Company officials called this cleansing

process "list maintenance" and claimed they could help the state identify precisely those voters who should be excluded. To electoral officials
it seemed like an ideal solution. Government agencies across the country had come to rely on private data companies for an array of services.
By outsourcing this role, the government aimed to save money.

Very little about the effort went as planned. Information obtained
from other states about felons who had moved to Florida turned out to
be flawed. Thousands of electronic documents from Texas, for instance,
mistakenly included misdemeanor convictions. As late as May 2000,
DBT discovered that 8,000 of the 66,000 people identified as felons
were in fact Texans convicted only of misdemeanors and therefore entitled to vote. Another 2,000 people on that long list also should not have
been there: though convicted of felonies, they came from other states
that automatically restored voting rights to felons.

The methodology was questionable from the beginning. State officials demanded a comprehensive list of anyone whose name and other
personal information contained even a slight indication they might be
ineligible. Election officials insisted their workers would verify all the
names beforehand. DBT officials, however, had warned the state about
the likelihood of "false positives," that is, the identification of someone
who had every right to vote. They cautioned that local election supervisors would not understand that the list was only a starting point in the
weeding-out process, not a definitive accounting.

Their complaints had little effect. When state officials dismissed the
concerns, so did DBT and ChoicePoint executives. The contractor continued to do the work despite the mistakes and its own persistent
qualms. "Oh well," one of the firm's executives wrote in an email to a
colleague a few months before the election. "Their [sic] the customer."
Thousands of people in Florida got form letters saying it was up to
them to clear up any mistakes. "According to information received from
the Florida Department of Law Enforcement, *you have a felony conviction*
and have not had your civil rights restored," said one version sent out
by officials in Miami-Dade. "Therefore, your name will be removed
from the voter registration rolls thirty (30) days from the date of this
letter unless information is received that you have not been convicted
of a felony or have had your civil rights restored."

Lawyers, a judge, and even an election official were told erroneously they had felony convictions. Former convicts who had worked hard to win pardons or obtain clemency, some specifically so that they could vote, were unable to clear their names in time. Things became so chaotic and uncertain that many county election supervisors decided to ignore the lists. One of them was Linda Howell, the supervisor of elections in Madison County. She knew there was trouble when she herself got an erroneous letter from the state police. "It said they had verified the information sent to them, and I was a convicted felon," Howell said. "I said, how can this be?"

Howell saw a few friends on the lists she was given. One was a lawyer who told her his record, for a youthful indiscretion, was supposed to have been expunged. Another was a minister who had been granted a pardon. She thought about what that taint could mean to their careers. "The thing that upset me the most was how careless it seemed to be. They were dealing with people's lives," Howell said. "It could destroy a life."

So much about the election remains clouded by confusion that it may never be possible to learn the true extent of the fallout from the exclusion effort. It's quite possible, though, that it gave George W. Bush the edge he needed. Bush of course defeated Gore by a scant 537 votes in Florida, an infinitesimally small proportion of the 5.9 million ballots counted. (The victory in Florida, upheld by the U.S. Supreme Court, gave Bush the necessary electoral college votes to win the White House, even though he lacked a majority of votes in the nation overall.) An analysis by the *Palm Beach Post* found that at least 108 people on the exclusion list were prevented from voting even though, like Matthew Frost, they had never been convicted of a felony. At least another 996 Florida residents with felony convictions in other states, who had automatically had their rights restored, also were prohibited inappropriately from voting that day.

The U.S. Commission for Civil Rights, in a damning report issued in August 2002, concluded that the cleansing effort had a disproportionate impact on African-American voters. The commission estimated that as many as one in seven people identified by DBT were on the list inappropriately. Others put the figure much higher.

Among those disenfranchised was Sandylynn Williams, who was blocked from voting because election officials mistook her for her sister, a convicted felon. Her incredulity, long after the election, was common. "They sent me a letter of apology, and I just laughed," Williams said. "I was cheated out of voting."

As for Matthew Frost, the salesman, it appears he got on the list because he had been the victim of identity theft while living in Taiwan. A credit card fraudster, convicted of a felony in 1995, had used his name. That fraud apparently provided a tenuous link in the data between Frost and a felony—a link that DBT found and noted in its exclusion list. After the election, Frost complained to officials, and he eventually got a letter declaring him free from taint. Frost voted for the first time in 2002, in state and local elections. By his reckoning, though, that was two years too late.

NEITHER DBT NOR ITS PARENT COMPANY, ChoicePoint, suffered in any obvious way from the role they played. In January 2001, the NAACP and other civil rights groups sued. They accused the company and a variety of state officials of violating the federal Voting Rights Act. Rather than fight the allegations, ChoicePoint settled the case, paying $75,000 to the NAACP. Company officials contend they bear no responsibility for the trouble. They blamed the state and moved on.

At the same time DBT was becoming an important building block of ChoicePoint's expanding data empire. Its cache of public and criminal records gave ChoicePoint sweeping reach into the lives of regular Americans. It also gave the company a vast customer base. Before long, every major federal law enforcement agency, some 2,100 state and local police, and almost half of the nation's top corporations used DBT's AutoTrackXP public and criminal records. Starting with fewer than 1,000 clients in 1997, ChoicePoint had more than 50,000 by 2004.

Based near Atlanta, ChoicePoint started in 1997 as a spin-off from Equifax, the credit bureau and information service. It was considered an underperforming division—its main source of revenue at the time was the insurance industry. ChoicePoint examined credit records and other personal information to help all the top insurers to assess customers and vet their claims for signs of fraud. But ChoicePoint officials wanted much more. Intent on becoming a national data and analysis clearinghouse, they went on a buying spree. In the first seven years of ChoicePoint's existence, the company acquired more than fifty other information broker, background screening, and identification companies. There was nothing inherently new about ChoicePoint's underlying aim: to enable frightened or uneasy clients to systematically look into the lives of others to lower the risks for themselves or their businesses. That was the point of credit bureaus, after all, and of private investigators. It's also why ChoicePoint and similar companies are called "lookup" services. For decades, businesses with enough money conducted surveillance and background checks on sensitive employees. A half century ago, even entertainment and advertising companies turned to specialists to check out employees or contractors for indications they might be considered un-American, something that could spark a boycott or federal investigation, which they feared would cut into profits.

In *The Naked Society*, Vance Packard describes the operation of one busy investigator he named Mr. Diggs. Mr. Diggs made his career checking out the political "desirability" of performers. He often worked closely with authorities sympathetic to his mission. Mr. Diggs routinely got access to the Senate's confidential records, indexes of witnesses who testified about subversive activities, and lists of targets compiled by Senator Joseph McCarthy and others. He also checked the private records maintained by the American Legion and a shadowy organization called Aware, Inc., a "vigilante group dedicated to fighting 'the Communist conspiracy in entertainment communications.'" For an additional fee, Mr. Diggs's checks included questions about morals and criminal activity. Some reports included details about mental health, tax problems, and the use of "stimulants" by one performer's wife. In all, the security consultant examined tens of thousands of records for two thousand reports.

ChoicePoint's marketing plan is based on the fact that the company wants to make the country a safer place, not simply check on workers' political affiliations. The manual approach used decades ago was far too narrow and haphazard for ChoicePoint. Its executives hoped to examine billions of records at a time, deploying blazing fast computers, networks, and analytical tools to help track and profile people like never before. Even the industrious Mr. Diggs could not have foreseen the scale of ChoicePoint's ambition.

• • •

CHOICEPOINT'S STRATEGY was to become, in effect, a National Nanny that for a fee could watch or assess the background of virtually anybody. ChoicePoint also wanted to be an enforcer that would determine whether someone was entitled to the "rights and privileges" they claimed. That might mean a job, access to public facilities, the right to vote, or a whole array of other activities. To accomplish this aim, ChoicePoint had to create a broad digital web that brought together a great deal of data.

One of its earliest acquisitions was called DATEQ, which enabled ChoicePoint to buy and sell credit reports more efficiently. ChoicePoint makes extensive use of credit reports to "score" or profile people seeking to renew their insurance. Another acquisition, Customer Development Corporation, helped the company to "address its customers' increasing need for targeted customer acquisition and retention programs." It soon had demographic and lifestyle records about 220 million American adults.

ChoicePoint's employee screening business expanded in February 2000 when it bought the National Safety Alliance, a large drug testing company that screened new employees for signs of illicit drug use. A year later, it acquired BTi Employee Screening Services, a high-volume operation in Dallas that had three thousand clients. It also took on employee screening businesses from Pinkerton Services Group and other companies. The purchase of Applicant Screening and Processing improved its ability to examine the background of would-be tenants.

ChoicePoint took on the operation of yet another employee screening system, called Esteem. Started under the direction of Target, Home Depot, and other national retailers in the mid-1990s, it is intended to offset the problem of shoplifting. The industry estimates the value of shoplifted goods at almost 2 percent of all sales—40 percent of which is linked to employees. Those costs are often passed on in the form of higher prices. Since only about a third of apprehensions by stores lead to prosecutions, the retailers, along with ChoicePoint, felt they had to take matters into their own hands.

"Most employees who steal do not end up in public criminal records. Dishonest employees have learned to experience little or no consequences for their actions, especially in light of the current tight labor market," ChoicePoint tells interested retailers. "A low-cost program is needed so companies can afford to screen all new employees against a national theft incident database and to make employees aware of the consequences of counterproductive activities at work."

The database works as a sort of blacklist of people who have been accused or convicted of shoplifting. Dozens of retailers now contribute reports to the system, in turn using it to block the hiring of people included there. ChoicePoint calls Esteem a "private database" and describes the information it contains as "legally-shareable." The database includes accusations of thefts backed up by "signed confessions"—documents that are sometimes extracted from individuals by security officials threatening to press charges. Individuals can be included in Esteem's database if they have been referred to authorities for prosecution but not yet convicted. To encourage participation, ChoicePoint notes in promotional documents that retailers are unlikely to face defamation lawsuits for furnishing information to Esteem. Besides, the document says, "consumers CANNOT sue a furnisher for making a mistake, only for repeating it or failing to adequately re-investigate it."

By 2003, ChoicePoint could claim to have the leading background screening and testing business in the nation: that included job applicants, soccer coaches, day care workers, and Boy Scout volunteers. There's no question these checks snare former convicts, sometimes in very sensitive jobs. About 5 million criminal records searches by clients in 2003 turned up almost 400,000 applicants who had a criminal record in the previous seven years. People who'd been convicted of drug crimes or theft or robbery accounted for the highest proportion of those hits. A review of almost 200,000 Big Brother and Big Sister volunteers turned up 38 murderers and 67 sex offenders.

ChoicePoint executives saw the need to know the very essence of individuals. On May 1, 2001, they announced the purchase of Bode Technology Group in suburban Washington, D.C., the largest private forensic DNA lab in the nation. Bode specialized in the use of DNA to identify people. It was a prescient purchase. Bode was later given the grim task of identifying the bone fragments of victims of the attacks on the World Trade Center, the largest disaster DNA identification effort ever.

ChoicePoint officials envision a day when their databases of DNA—something they consider "IDNA" or "the ultimate identifier"—or fingerprints or other biometrics banks will be employed routinely to identify everyone, dead and alive, innocent and criminal alike.

They also wanted to control the documents that proved who we are. In December 2002, the company snapped up VitalChek Network, a Nashville, Tennessee, company that provides the technology and networks to process and sell birth, death, marriage, and divorce records in every state. After paying $120 million for the company, ChoicePoint officials said it would more than earn its way in the homeland security market. This also meant that ChoicePoint was integrating itself more deeply into the structure of state and local government. It would soon control the records that defined who we are. And it would be ChoicePoint that would certify that those aptly named "vital records" were accurate.

"ChoicePoint's core competency is verifying and authenticating individuals and their credentials," said ChoicePoint chief executive Derek V. Smith. "We also believe the increased emphasis on homeland security means vital records are becoming even more valuable in proving you are who you say you are."

ON THE WAY TO DEREK SMITH'S OFFICE, you go through ChoicePoint's lobby, a bright and airy space with architectural reminders that the building was a manufacturing plant before it became the center of a high-technology empire.

Directly in front of padded benches where visitors wait, several presentations try to put the company in the best light. As at Seisint and other competitors, there's an award ChoicePoint has received from the National Center for Missing and Exploited Children, to which it has donated many millions of dollars worth of services and data. One display describes the criminals the company has helped police to catch. A second display illustrates something the company calls "ChoicePoint Gorillas," offering a glimpse of the fierce dedication and drive the company expects from its employees. "Gorillas in the wild are intelligent, fearless and bold animals with many admirable traits. They stand their ground and protect their family. They are courageous and make their presence known. Like gorillas, ChoicePoint associates strive to show these same positive behaviors. Our gorillas believe in our vision, mission and principles."

In essense, Derek Smith is the company's alpha gorilla. He is tall and lean and altogether too boyish-looking to be taken at first glance as the chief executive of a three-billion-dollar corporation. But he's fierce, almost evangelical, about what he does. His background as an athlete provides some foundation for this. Smith lettered in three high school sports and played wide receiver at Penn State under the famed Joe Paterno. Leaning against a wall is an antique putter with a wooden shaft, a reminder that at forty-eight he was a scratch golfer obsessed by the sport. "To me athletics is about coming together to win against a common enemy," said Smith, who sometimes wears a golf shirt, slacks, and loafers but no socks to the office. "And I love that."

He accumulated shelves full of trophies for his athletic accomplishments. Around the office are a different sort of glass trophies. Called "tombstones" by the investment bankers who give them, they document the many mergers and acquisitions he has overseen at Choice-Point. After working at Equifax for sixteen years, Smith guided the spin-off of the insurance services division that became ChoicePoint. Since then, he and his company have been on a tear. When the company first sold stock in August 1997, it raised some $500 million. By the beginning of 2004, the stock was worth about $3.2 billion. Much of the company's revenue still comes from the insurance industry, which pays hundreds of millions of dollars a year to have ChoicePoint profile individuals and track their claims. But a large and growing proportion of the company's profits come from "risk mitigation": background checks, employee screening, and the sale of dossiers to police, government officials, and intelligence agencies.

Smith expresses great pride in the way that ChoicePoint came to straddle the public and private worlds. He said that life has become so constantly risky that authorities need help to keep up. Laws and fences aren't enough. We must use personal information "responsibly," he said, to prevent crimes and terrorism. Otherwise "we will be threatened by enemies"—against us, our businesses, and our nation. When Smith talks about risks, he's thinking not only about looming terrorist threats but about officeworkers, nannies, soccer coaches, even the people who deliver pizzas and Chinese food. A few years ago, a ChoicePoint-commissioned study purported to show that one in four pizza delivery men had recently been in jail. ChoicePoint said it knew how to help prevent one of those drivers from robbing or hurting your family: a simple online criminal check. "Are you willing to take the risk associated with dealing with a company that doesn't screen their drivers?" he asked.

Smith and his colleagues decided ChoicePoint should extend its services beyond the usual customers: government agencies, police, and corporations. They wanted to sell peace of mind to regular Americans. In 2002, the company began allowing individuals to buy dossiers, including criminal checks, education records, and other personal details. Basic reports started at just $25. A notable move into this new market came in November 2003, when ChoicePoint offered "Employee Background Check" in a box at Sam's Club, a division of Wal-Mart, the world's largest retailer. The $39.77 package included a *How to Hire Quality Empoyees* handbook, a CD containing an online background screening package, and one complimentary drug test. "Conduct Background Checks Quickly & Easily!" printing on the box declared.

It was a milestone of sorts for ChoicePoint—and for the country. For the first time, the nation's largest background screener was offering its services directly to the mass market on the aisles of a giant retailer. Gone were the days of Mr. Diggs, Aware Inc., and expensive corporate sleuths. Now everyone would soon be able to dig into the past of suspect acquaintances or employees, for the price of a modest night out. A senior ChoicePoint executive said the service would "empower" an increasingly mobile society to feel as secure as it once did decades ago, a notion that echoed the promises of database marketers. September 11 changed everything. "The fact the world has changed in the last three years has made it a ripe time," said ChoicePoint vice president Deslie Quinby. "We're kind of reconnecting people via technology."

To minimize the potential for abuse, ChoicePoint requires buyers of the kit to get written consent from the subject of their check. They must keep that document on hand in case ChoicePoint ever comes calling for an audit. No one at the company specified when that would be.

The background-in-a-box was the embodiment of Smith's most salient message: You can never be too sure. When asked whether the company was stoking the public's anxiety for profit, Smith explained that his motivation goes far beyond simply making money. "I truly believe this stuff," Smith said. "And it drives me every day."

Smith once said he has "this incredible passion to make a safer world" because he's on a spiritual mission, something that became clear to him after the terror attacks. Smith said he had come to believe that all his adult life—his education and professional experience—has been preparation for this time.

"I believe that all of us are here for a purpose, a purpose that's greater than ourselves. And so I've always sought in my life to find places where I could make a quantum difference," said Smith, a Presbyterian. "It's grounded in the fact I believe there's a higher power that guides all of us in what we do.

"I don't think there's a lot of difference between my personal mission in life and the mission of ChoicePoint," he added. "And I think that's why it has come together so well."

The business of security has come together well at ChoicePoint. In the anxious times following the terror attacks, when businesses and the government clamored for more information and intelligence about people, ChoicePoint profits soared to new heights. And so did Smith's compensation. He was paid about $20 million in 2002, just over 50 percent more than the year before.

As a public company, ChoicePoint routinely discloses new acquisitions and its financial condition in filings with the government. But it has no obligation to discuss the details of its contracts and dealings with the government. When asked for such details, company officials often decline. The government also is not very obliging. The nation's Freedom of Information system is intended to guarantee openness in government. But it can take years, luck, or expensive lawsuits, to secure requested documents.

Chris Hoofnagle, a young lawyer who works at the Electronic Privacy Information Center (EPIC), a nonprofit advocacy group in Washington, D.C., has spent several years of his career trying to chart ChoicePoint's rapid ascent and its growing ties to law enforcement and intelligence agencies. Along with a variety of conservative and liberal activists,

Hoofnagle believes that ChoicePoint and other information services routinely skirt the principles of federal privacy regulations enacted in the 1970s to curb the tendency of authorities then to spy on American citizens.

Hoofnagle was born in 1974, the same year that the Privacy Act provided "certain safeguards for an individual against an invasion of personal privacy" by government officials. The law followed the revelations about covert domestic spying campaigns by the FBI, the Army, and other agencies. In spelling out the need for the new law, Congress stated that the increasing use of computers "has greatly magnified the harm to individual privacy that can occur from any collection, maintenance, use, or dissemination of personal information; the opportunities for an individual to secure employment, insurance, and credit, and his right to due process, and other legal protections are endangered by the misuse of certain information systems."

Among other things, the law restricted the government from building databases of dossiers unless the information about individuals was directly relevant to an agency's mission. Of course, that's precisely what ChoicePoint, LexisNexis, and other services do for the government. By outsourcing the collection of records, the government doesn't have to ensure the data is accurate, or have any provisions to correct it in the same way it would under the Privacy Act. There are no limits on how the information can be interpreted, all this at a time when law enforcement, domestic intelligence, and foreign intelligence are becoming more interlinked. "This limitation to the Privacy Act is critical—it allows [data brokers like ChoicePoint] to amass huge databases that the government is legally prohibited from creating," Hoofnagle wrote in a paper about ChoicePoint in 2004.

Hoofnagle grew up in suburban Washington, attended law school at the University of Georgia, and joined the Electronic Privacy Information Center in 2000. Though he's too young to remember the country's anger about COINTELPRO and other domestic surveillance transgressions, he knows his history. And he has long bridled at the idea of authorities taking advantage of individuals. Hoofnagle said he recognizes that ChoicePoint's services can help law enforcement authorities and those charged with protecting homeland security. But he said that information—the extraordinary reservoirs, coupled with analytical software—is becoming the infrastructure of a surveillance society. By outsourcing data surveillance assignments to ChoicePoint and other information services, the government is sidestepping the laws intended to protect individuals from government intrusion. "ChoicePoint creates efficiency in law enforcement that could never have been envisioned by the framers of the constitution," he said. "It alters the balance of power."

Hoofnagle works hard to bring the government's use of data to light. Along with his colleagues at EPIC, the American Civil Liberties Union, and other groups, he regularly files Freedom of Information requests. By 2004, EPIC had collected some 1,500 pages of documents about ChoicePoint and other information companies. When the Justice Department or other agencies balked, his group sued in federal court. That's how the country ultimately learned that the Justice Department had a $67 million contract with ChoicePoint.

Hoofnagle and his colleagues at EPIC worry that ChoicePoint's massive computer systems will alter the dynamic of a society that has always treasured its "Don't Tread on Me" autonomy. That's because, accurate or not, data is forever. He envisions a day when everybody will be held to account through background screening for even relatively minor or old infractions or crimes. He calls that a "scarlet letter society."

ChoicePoint counters such criticism by saying that anyone can request their files and correct mistakes. That's a central tenet of the self-regulatory principles that ChoicePoint and its industry endorse. When Hoofnagle requested his information, ChoicePoint released his file, which contained information about where he had lived, the names and addresses of his roommates, the kinds of cars they drive. However, company officials would not allow him to opt out of their databases, saying they were not obliged to do so. As ChoicePoint states in its privacy policy:

"ChoicePoint limits access to its information products to government and businesses with legitimate business purposes for the data, such as detecting and preventing fraud, performing legal due diligence, locating criminal suspects, finding missing children, and managing business risks in a variety of ways. We feel that removing information from these products would render them less useful for important business purposes, many of which ultimately benefit consumers."

Those principles were carefully crafted by industry lawyers to give ChoicePoint and other brokers a great deal of flexibility. Hoofnagle contends that that leaves individuals seeking some degree of control over their information out in the cold. "The question is what rules will be applied. What due process will be present. What accuracy standards will be required. Right now, ChoicePoint is performing government functions without any of the legal restraints normally applied to government.

"It is," Hoofnagle said, "an equal opportunity dossier builder."

ONE BIG PROBLEM with the data industry are the inevitable mistakes. The authors of the 1974 Privacy Act knew this. More and more, as the country turns to ChoicePoint and its competitors to screen and assess individuals, the consequences of those mistakes are going to loom ever larger. Forget the old adage, "If you've done nothing wrong, you have nothing to hide." If recent history serves as a guide, the innocent, such as Matthew Frost, are going to be routinely caught up in these digital dragnets, right alongside those who have been accurately targeted. ChoicePoint acknowledges as much. The company gets up to fifty complaints a month from individuals about credit and background reports. But it often blames county clerks, data contractors, and others for providing bad information that leads to bad decisions.

A struggling Kentucky woman named Mary Boris found that out in 2002 when she sought to renew her homeowner's insurance. Boris was a single mother with three children, who worked as an administrator at a heavy equipment company. Her major financial asset was a brick A-frame house in the middle-class Hikes Point section of Louisville.

Boris had no reason to suspect she had any problem with her insurance. Apart from a few minor claims for water damage, her record was clean. She discovered by accident that she was no longer covered when an insurance representative said that her record was sullied by four claims for fire damage and one theft. Boris was aghast. She checked with other insurers and their story was the same. "They started telling me, one by one, you've had four fires," Boris said. "I said, no, this can't be happening."

It turns out that like most major insurers, these companies relied on reports from ChoicePoint's Comprehensive Loss Underwriting Exchange. Boris's report portrayed her as a substantial risk. Not many people know about the exchange, known as the CLUE system, but it has become a major force in the insurance industry, in large part by taking advantage of the same information technology that transformed the direct marketing world: computers, profiling software, and lots and lots of information about people. Using almost 200 million records, contributed by all major insurance companies, CLUE creates a "score" on virtually every policy holder in the country. That score determines how much an individual should pay in premiums—or whether someone like Boris even qualifies for homeowner's or auto insurance. In 2003, it was used in more than 100 million transactions. "We help ensure it's a *fair* transaction," ChoicePoint said in its promotional material.

Boris had never heard of CLUE until she tried to fix her record. When she contacted ChoicePoint officials, she was bounced around from one official to another. They blamed her insurance company for providing bad information and did little to help. Boris contacted the Kentucky Department of Insurance, which then called ChoicePoint on her behalf and convinced the company to work with her insurer to clear up the mistakes. Finally, she thought, I can breathe easy. "My fear was that something would happen," she said. "The house would burn down. We'd have another flood. I'd lose everything."

She let her guard down too soon. While looking for lower insurance rates several months later, she discovered the inaccurate claims were back on her report. They would remain linked to her report, on and off, for more than two years. Now, on top of everything else, she worried that ChoicePoint was suggesting, in effect, that she was a high risk and could not be trusted.

She turned to her brother for help. Bernard Leachman, Jr., was a veteran lawyer in Louisville. After reviewing her papers, he was outraged at the recurring mistakes and the implications for her family. "This is defamation at the very least," he told her, adding that it put her at risk of being wiped out financially.

Leachman eventually filed a lawsuit against ChoicePoint in federal court under the Fair Credit Reporting Act. Among other things, the law requires companies like ChoicePoint to maintain accurate records and to be responsive to consumers. Leachman argued to a jury that Choice-Point was doing neither. "Essentially, information gathering organizations reduce human beings to bits of data and don't give a lot of consideration to the disastrous effects that these reports can have on people," Leachman said, summarizing his argument to the jury. "It's not unusual for those things to get into people's records. It's just sometimes problematic, difficult, even nightmarish, to get them out."

ChoicePoint claimed it wasn't responsible for the troubles, blaming Boris's insurance company for failing to provide it with good information. The company says that it gets complaints on only six of every ten thousand items put into the data system, which may have something to do with the fact few people know enough about CLUE to complain. In court, ChoicePoint lawyers said that Boris had to prove not only that ChoicePoint had made a mistake but that it had been negligent. The lawyers also attacked Mary Boris directly, questioning why she didn't go to church and suggesting she might be in the case only for the money. The jury agreed with Boris, awarding her $447,000 in compensatory and punitive damages. A judge reduced the compensatory damages somewhat after ChoicePoint appealed, but not before sharply chiding the company for "a complete lack of sympathy" for Boris and the problems with its data.

"Not one of ChoicePoint's employees ever accepted responsibility for the accuracy of the claims data and, in fact, everyone blamed others," Circuit Court Judge John G. Heyburn II noted in his March 2003 opinion.

Mary Boris said the case still makes her uneasy. She understands she never could have fixed her report without the help of her brother.

AFTER THE TERROR ATTACKS, drugmaker Eli Lilly decided like so many other companies to take stock of its workforce, including contractors. It hired ChoicePoint to do the work. Among those being screened was Sandy D. Snodgrass, an airflow technician who had worked as a Lilly contractor for eighteen years. Not long after the checks began, he got a letter from his boss. "Due to concerns raised by the background check," the letter said, "Lilly requests that you no longer assign this employee to perform services for Lilly effective immediately." The fifty-six-year-old Snodgrass had never had any troubles with police. But the problem became clear when he got his report from ChoicePoint. The company's computers had mixed up his Social Security number with that of a younger relative with the same name. The younger Snodgrass had been convicted on misdemeanor charges relating to the theft of a can of Skoal, as well as a battery conviction for an altercation he had with the woman who became his wife.

Even when the company gets it right—that is to say, in the great majority of cases—the outcome can sometimes seem harsh to those who have been targeted. The same sweep that snared Snodgrass identified a host of other employees for run-ins with the law, infractions that cost them their jobs. Kimberly Kelly, a forty-six-year-old single mother who worked as a pipe insulator, lost her job after the background check turned up the fact that she had bounced a $60 check two years before. Cris Lochard, a twenty-eight-year-old asbestos removal contract worker, lost the job he had had for five years. It seems he had broken into a school as a teenager and, with a group of friends, stolen a guitar, a VCR, and a Camcorder. Donald Ade lost his $70,000 annual income as a skilled sheet metal worker when his company learned from ChoicePoint that he had been convicted a decade earlier of possessing a pound of pot. For his transgression then, he spent one night in jail and paid $1,115 to the court. Now he was paying again.

"Are we sorry? Of course we are," one contractor told the *Wall Street Journal* for a story about the layoffs. "As a subcontractor, we're bound by our contractual provisions."

That's cold comfort for Kelly, the pipe insulator, and the others, who feel as though they're paying a big price for earlier mistakes. "I never would have thought a sixty-dollar bounced check would cost me my job," Kelly said. "And I loved my job. I wish I had it back."

CHOICEPOINT KNOWS what its critics say. Its response is simple and to many ears compelling: There is growing demand for the company's services because they work. In some cases, that means helping to solve horrible crimes. One of those cases involved a series of rapes, four in the Philadelphia area and seven others in Fort Collins, Colorado. One of the victims was a Wharton student who was raped and killed.

Based on DNA evidence, police concluded one man was responsible, but all they had was a general description from the victims: A man in his twenties, between 5 feet 8 and 6 feet tall, who lived in either Philadelphia or Fort Collins. Philadelphia police put out a bulletin. Detective Glenn Kerns, who is assigned to the Joint Terrorism Task Force in Seattle, took particular interest in the case.

In the summer of 2001, Kerns saw the teletype. A data specialist who instructs other officers how to use information systems, he had worked closely with ChoicePoint in the past. He called his contact at Choice-Point, an executive responsible for government contracts. They agreed that ChoicePoint would do a special program at no cost. It would be a profile that incorporated all the details Kerns knew about the suspect: the height, hair color, approximate age, and the ties to Philadelphia and Fort Collins.

"We've been using the database and we all knew how incredible it was," Kerns said. "This is just a hobby of mine. This is a passion for tracking people."

The profile came back with six names. When Kerns turned the information over to a Philadelphia investigator, he said: "Dang it. Two of those names are already suspects!" The Philadelphia investigator looked deeper into the ChoicePoint records and found one of the men at an Air Force base in Fort Collins. His name was Troy Graves. His fingerprint had been captured at the scene of one of the rapes, so a DNA test was ordered. Graves pleaded guilty in the spring of 2002.

Kerns was very enthusiastic about ChoicePoint, praising its easy access to credit reports, insurance records, and all the rest. "In my eighteen years, it's probably been the biggest boost to law enforcement I've seen.

"They call me a lot on this stuff. 'How can we improve?'" he said. "They'll do anything. The biggest thing is tracking people who try to hide. But you can't hide from this stuff."

THE QUEST TO EXPAND AND REFRESH the information maintained by ChoicePoint is a mammoth task that never ends. Like some competitors, the company relies on thousands of researchers, employees, and other firms to gather public records. Carolyn Lucas is one of these gleaners, a veteran whose roots in the business go deep. In the 1970s she started out with the Atlanta-based Retail Credit Company, the firm that would later become Equifax. Now she works for National Data Retrieval, which ChoicePoint acquired in January 2003.

Lucas is what the business calls an "independent collection contractor." She specializes in culling personal details from bankruptcies, civil judgments, and liens. She is a determined woman, sixty-one years old, who lives in a brick ranch house in rural Sims, North Carolina, next door to the home where she was born. She works a circuit of about eight county courthouses, driving by tobacco and cotton fields on her way to the careworn facilities she has come to think of as almost second homes over the years.

One morning in November 2003, she went to work at the Wilson County Courthouse, a handsome building with a portico, great wide columns, and a memorial out front dedicated to Robert E. Lee. She carried a steno pad, a black Bic Round Stic pen, and photocopied forms. On the way in, she said hello to the clerks and made her way to oversize volumes containing the latest court judgments. Then she began her familiar routine. She pulled one book off the shelf, put it on a rib-high table, and copied the names, addresses, and other information. She doesn't trust computers, so she does everything by hand. In one case, she jotted down the name, date, and judgment details about a man who the court ruled owed the local Terminix extermination company $3,500. On some days, she made as many as 120 of these reports. When she had a stack about two inches high, collected over several trips, she mailed them off to her contacts at National Data Retrieval.

Think of this work as a small creek that flows into a stream of data that eventually makes its way into oceans of information. Day after day, massive numbers of other records join this progression in the form of tapes and feeds online from state officials, affiliated companies, and other data services. In all, it collects personal data from some several thousand sources. That includes almost a billion records from Trans Union about twice a year. The telephone companies add in phone numbers, listed and unlisted, from about 130 million people. Nearly every time someone makes a claim on their automobile insurance, details about the transaction are wired to ChoicePoint's Comprehensive Loss

Underwriting Exchange, or CLUE, which includes almost 200 million records about individuals. Many of these records flow into Choice-Point's National Criminal File. With almost 100 million records, then, it is one of the world's largest private storehouses of criminal activity.

ChoicePoint has a total of about 17 billion online public records, a figure that grows by more than 40,000 every day, in part because of the deliberate efforts of Lucas. All told, the company has more than 250 terabytes of data regarding the lives of about 220 million adults. That's enough information to extend some 21 million miles, if printed out on copy paper carefully laid end to end. As one ChoicePoint official proudly put it: "That's roughly 77 round trips to the moon."

None of this much interests Lucas. She doesn't care where her reports end up. She has no idea really how the information is packaged, sold, and used. People have criticized her now and then over the years, blaming her for getting them into trouble by passing on details from their court records. She has also heard people express concerns about civil liberties and privacy. "I did not invent the records. I am not a judge or the keeper of the records," she said. "I collect records. Someone's going to do it. That's just how I look at it."

MUCH OF THE RAW INFORMATION that ChoicePoint holds is in itself not unique. Personal data has become a commodity that is bought and traded essentially like sow bellies, or soybeans, or newsprint. Acxiom, LexisNexis, Seisint, and the credit bureaus Equifax, Experian, and Trans Union all gather essentially the same names, telephone numbers, and addresses. What they don't have in the way of extras—say the magazines you read or the car you drive or the vacation you went on last year—they buy from one another.

Competition in the industry often comes from their differing ways of processing and delivering the data. Seisint's calling card is its super-computers, those long strings of PCs that provide rocket fuel for data processing, deliver personal dossiers so quickly. Acxiom prides itself on its relatively new AbiliTec software, which the company claims provides better clarity than competitors for the identity of individuals.

One way ChoicePoint is trying to distinguish itself is through the strange talents of a man named Jeff Jonas. Jonas is a high school dropout, and founder and chief scientist of Systems Research & Development, a Las Vegas company full of engineers and computer scientists.

At the company's core is analytical software that can examine billions of records, tag each file, and identify people and the ties among them in a uniquely powerful way. It's called NORA, for Non-Obvious Relationship Awareness, and it discerns things no human ever could. As one writer put it, adding NORA to ChoicePoint data is like putting "a supercharger on a V-12 Ferrari." Jonas serves as one of ChoicePoint's most interesting bridges into the world of homeland security and the war on terror. His company is partly owned by Reed Elsevier, the parent company of LexisNexis, which acquired a 16 percent chunk in 2003. LexisNexis worked closely with intelligence and Homeland Security officials to build the aviation screening program known as CAPPS II. Another investor in Systems Research is SAIC, a giant government contractor that often works with our nation's spy organizations. One former SAIC executive is Tony Tether, who headed the Defense Advance Research Projects Agency, or DARPA; another SAIC executive helped create the Total Information Awareness project while working at the agency.

Jonas is an adviser at the Homeland Security Department, the Department of Defense, and the three-letter intelligence agencies. And he was a frequent visitor to former Admiral John Poindexter, who consulted with Jonas about the Total Information Awareness project at the Defense Department. He has received millions of dollars in funding from In-Q-Tel, the private investment arm of the Central Intelligence Agency. In February 2003, his company signed a contract with the supersecret National Security Agency—a contract that was doubled in size eight months later. In other words, he not only spends a lot of time making ChoicePoint's data more incisive, he gives Derek Smith and his colleagues valuable contact in Washington.

Jonas is 5 feet 9 inches, has a thick goatee, long sideburns, and a suntan. He is as fit as can be, crackles with energy, and is always ready to laugh. A triathlete, he rides and runs dozens of miles at a time in the mountains near his home outside Las Vegas. The best way to see him in action is in the casinos, where he honed NORA while helping casinos thwart the clever, determined sharpsters and insiders who have become adept over the years at cloaking their identities and intentions.

Jonas calls this an "asymmetric threat," a phrase that defense and intelligence agencies have used for years to describe terrorists. During a tour of Las Vegas in the fall of 2003, he bounced his way through one upscale casino, pointing out the scores of cameras: above the gaming tables, along every walkway, high in every corner. He kept moving because he knew the surveillance systems—or the people running them—would detect something suspicious in his movements. Since this was a client, he didn't want to spook them. Jonas said casinos have become among the most sophisticated and aggressive users of surveillance gear in America. Some of the cameras are linked to face recognition programs, systems originally developed with funding from the Defense Department. But cameras are not enough. That's where NORA comes in. The system can examine large amounts of information—billions and billions of records about people, their identities, addresses, telephone numbers, and the like—and instantly know which record belongs to whom and the sometimes obscure ties among them.

Forget trying to transpose the numbers of your Social Security number or altering your address or even changing your name. Such obfuscation melts under NORA's ceaseless gaze. Jonas calls this process "entity resolution." NORA works in some forty languages, knows scores of ways to spell Mohammed, and can find the links between you and the president of the United States, if need be. That's called "relationship awareness." And the more information it has to work with, the better NORA gets at identifying people and their relationships to one another.

There's no end to the scams it has unearthed. Gamblers at roulette tables will sometimes try to bet after the ball has dropped. Success typically depends on an accomplice, who can distract the dealer with a yelp, spilled drink, and the like. In one instance casino security saw the bet and apprehended the fraudster, but they did not see any form of distraction. "I'm so embarrassed," the dealer complained, according to a story about Jonas in *Men's Journal*. "Arrest him."

When security officials entered the cheater's name and address into the computer system, NORA discovered the problem. The cheater had the same phone number as the dealer. That was the link. The dealer, the cheater's roommate, was in on the scam.

The story of Jonas's ties to the casino industry involves fish. Jonas licensed some software to a large accounting firm in 1987. The company asked him to help a client—the MGM Mirage company. The brilliantly colored inhabitants of the casino's giant aquarium kept disappearing. Managers wanted Jonas to find out why. The database he created tracked all the fish and soon determined which ones were having lunch at the others' expense. In 1994, the casino began using NORA, another system, to identify gamblers listed on the official blacklist. Casinos use the system to authenticate the identities of the high rollers and check whether they have any links to employees, who might be tempted to help illegal schemes.

Since then, a number of casinos have adopted NORA. One examined all twenty thousand employees, the company's vendors, and its VIP players. It found scores of potential problems, including obscure or hidden ties between employees and vendors. Two dozen VIP players had obscured their real identities. They were actually alleged crooks who had been previously arrested for fraud and were on the gaming blacklist in Nevada known as the Griffin Book. Said Alan Feldman, an MGM Mirage spokesman, "We've been able to keep people out who otherwise would have gotten in."

That is exactly what ChoicePoint officials want from NORA: to be able to better monitor people, on behalf of the government and other clients, at lightning speed. "Our work is about perpetual analytics, instant intelligence, as fast as something is introduced, instantaneously being able to tell if that means something important to you," Jonas said.

"You're sitting under an ocean of data, and every day millions of gallons are being added, and every day you have to go through zillions of drops to find out whether there's something important in there," Jonas went on. "You're slicing time down to the nanosecond, so you can see every drop hit. So when each drop hits you can see where it lands, what it's next to. You can measure the ripples, and there is an instant where you can make interesting decisions about what has changed."

ON THE LAST DAY of her life in October 1999, Amy Boyer's stalker knew exactly where she would be. As the twenty-year-old dental assistant slipped into her Honda Accord, on a quiet road just off Main Street in Nashua, New Hampshire, the obsessed young man pulled up, shot her repeatedly, then turned the gun on himself. The murder-suicide drew nationwide attention because the gunman, a former classmate named Liam Youens, had bought her Social Security number and other personal information from a broker in the gray market online. That broker in turn had bought it from I.R.S.C. Inc., an information service in California that ChoicePoint acquired. The killing outraged privacy advocates, who had been railing about the ubiquitous use of Social Security numbers. At first police said Youens parlayed Boyer's number to find details about her workplace. The situation was uglier than that. Youens's broker, Docusearch Inc. of Boca Raton, Florida, went beyond simple database searches. It also employed "pretexting" to sate his desire for more information about Boyer. For a $75 fee, Docusearch hired a Brooklyn, New York, woman who called associates of Boyer's and obtained the work address: 5 Main Street. By the time of the shooting, Youens had a rich dossier about his victim.

The case was a public relations nightmare for the information industry. The circumstances suggested that information brokers—from giants like ChoicePoint on down to the many shoestring operations like Docusearch—cannot maintain real oversight over the data they sell. As with background-in-a-box, ChoicePoint and the others required the brokers to sign agreements to adhere to privacy laws and to sell only for permissible purposes. But they often did not have the time or resources to vet their clients. One major service acknowledged that it routinely sold personal information to online clients using fraudulent credit cards, something the company considered a cost of doing business.

Amy Boyer's death spurred calls for a crackdown on the sale of Social Security numbers. After hearing appeals from her parents, Senator Judd Gregg led the way. Suddenly the industry was under fire. So important was easy access to Social Security numbers that ChoicePoint warned investors, in documents on file with the SEC, it could face serious financial losses if their use was ever sharply circumscribed. The identifier was crucial to the easy collection and sale of information. Credit bureaus cautioned that such limits might drive up the price of loans.

Privacy advocates warned that the burgeoning reliance on Social Security numbers would lead to an explosion in identity theft. They also complained that the numbers opened the way to systematic data surveillance, in a way that was not possible a generation ago. With Gregg's initiative, critics assumed they had a chance for a rollback. What they weren't counting on was the influence of an industry association called the Individual Reference Services Group.

The group was formed in 1997, following the privacy firestorm over a LexisNexis service called P-Trak. The LexisNexis service marketed Social Security numbers and other personal information online. LexiNexis figured that people would clamor for the service. But their timing of the service could not have been worse. Most computer users were just then being exposed to—and often spooked by—the extraordinary reach of the Internet. Suddenly they had to confront the fact that their private details were part of a giant and growing market. Congress asked the Federal Trade Commission to examine the implications. That was a sign that some regulations might be forthcoming, threatening a very lucrative if somewhat stealthy business.

At the end of 1997, Acxiom, ChoicePoint, LexisNexis, and others made the case to the FTC that they would police themselves. Far from being a threat to privacy, they claimed they were consumer advocates acting in the best interests of society. It worked, but their efforts didn't end there. The association soon evolved into something more: a strong lobby opposed to heavy data regulation. And unknown to the privacy advocates, the group's members helped Senator Gregg shape the Amy Boyer bill. "Your bill strikes the right balance by providing strong privacy protections without undermining the range of important and socially beneficial activities by business and government that have developed based upon the use of SSNs," the group wrote in a letter to Gregg about the proposal they helped to craft.

There was nothing new about an industry shaping legislation for a lawmaker—it happens all the time in Washington—but critics were outraged, calling the Gregg bill a Trojan Horse. The law included provisions allowing giant data brokers, banks, marketers, and even private detectives to exchange or sell Social Security numbers among themselves. That meant such companies would be free to use Social Security numbers to track down debtors or deadbeat parents, collect personal data, conduct fraud investigations, and build profiles about what people buy and do. In short, it gave the industry a nearly free hand. It wasn't just privacy advocates who complained. Boyer's stepfather, who originally asked Gregg to introduce the bill, backed away. President Clinton promised not to sign the bill if it came to his desk unchanged. Because of the controversy, the law lost steam. The process underscored the great pains companies like ChoicePoint and others in the industry would take to remain unfettered.

In the years since, the company has expanded its influence in Washington, D.C., by other means. Among other things, it strengthened ties to a group called Privacy & American Business, which had an almost singular role in the public discussion about privacy. Founder Alan Westin was a pioneer in the study of privacy, a law professor at Columbia University who wrote a landmark book in 1967 called *Privacy and Freedom*. By the late 1990s, though, his tone had become much more skeptical, more like that of the companies he represented. His partner in the group was Robert Belair, a Washington lawyer and lobbyist who represented ChoicePoint, Equifax, and other data services on Capitol Hill. Both men and their group have accepted fees and contributions from information industry companies.

ChoicePoint was one of the group's supporters and sometimes sponsored its studies or conferences. The firm described these efforts as public-spirited, but they sometimes carried the aura of well-crafted public relations. In 2002, ChoicePoint sponsored a workplace privacy survey. "When ChoicePoint learned that a decade had passed since anyone conducted a major national survey on employee privacy issues, we realized the importance of this project and felt obligated to lead on this issue," Derek Smith stated in a newsletter to customers. Smith said the workplace had changed in recent decades, with people moving in and out of jobs more frequently. It has become harder to know colleagues, especially those who serve as temporary or contract workers.

"The implication of this ever-increasing anonymity in our workplaces creates greater risks and more severe consequences. Without access to quality, objective information—such as public records, psychological profiles and the results of drug tests—employers are left to make high-risk decisions without appropriate tools," Smith added.

The survey came as ChoicePoint was pressing to expand its background screening and identification businesses. Designed by Alan Westin, the survey seemed to show strong support for the kinds of services that ChoicePoint sold. Employees had great faith in their bosses' use of information. The vast majority welcomed more background screening. They also supported the use of IDs containing a biometric, such as a fingerprint or retinal scan. "There is an unmistakable post–September 11 tone in these findings," Westin said in a ChoicePoint press release. "Clearly, workers want to know that employers are doing everything they can to keep inappropriate people out of workplaces."

Those findings were the centerpiece of a Privacy & American Business conference that year. It was entitled "Privacy and Security in the New America Workplace," and ChoicePoint was a sponsor.

DEREK SMITH AND HIS COLLEAGUES wasted no time seeking new business after the terror attacks. On September 12, 2001, while much of the world was bracing for more destruction, the company was preparing a pitch for the U.S. government. "Today ChoicePoint is the nation's largest provider of online and on-demand public records," the company wrote in its memo to the government that day. "ChoicePoint expanded its data collection efforts in 2000 to include international data to complement its U.S. public record products. Since then, ChoicePoint has added significant international data assets through acquisitions, direct relationships with various foreign governments, and by expanding its international network of trusted data vendors."

ChoicePoint said it would give the INS unlimited access to all the information for $1 million a year. ("Pricing in future years subject to change based on the availability of new data sets," the company added at the end.) Among the details it was offering to sell: A nationwide listing of Mexican voters, including names, addresses, ID numbers, birth dates. A national registry of Colombians, including their physical descriptions and "parentage." The passport and national identification of Costa Rican citizens. The national ID number of Argentinians and all of their phone numbers.

The memo was a model of the ChoicePoint approach. It promoted the company's data prowess, while attempting to disarm skepticism about how it came to amass the trove of information, details about some 300 million people in ten countries. ChoicePoint "goes to great lengths to verify that the data offered in ChoicePoint products is being acquired legally from official sources." And just in case, the company said it required its foreign data brokers to promise they had not broken any laws.

The new service was embraced by an array of other federal authorities, who raved about its potential for tracking suspects, both in the United States and abroad. In the fall of 2001, the online database helped border patrol agents identify the bodies of fourteen Mexican immigrants who perished in the Arizona desert. It also helped authorities track down the smugglers who left them in the blazing heat to die. Drug enforcement authorities relished the new discretion they had to create dossiers of Latin American citizens, without having to alert local police, who might be corrupt and inclined to tip off their suspects.

U.S. authorities felt comfortable using ChoicePoint's services. Shortly after the terror attacks, the FBI Office of the General Counsel ruled in a classified document that it was perfectly fine to rely on the data for "foreign intelligence collection or foreign counterintelligence investigations." The document concluded that "individuals do not have a reasonable expectation of privacy in personal information that has been made publicly available." There was one big problem. No one bothered to tell authorities or the citizens in Latin America that the U.S. government was outsourcing intelligence work to ChoicePoint, which in turn was hiring contractors to collect the information. When the ChoicePoint service was revealed in May 2003—the Electronic Privacy Information Center turned up details—a scandal ensued.

"It's espionage," said Alejandro Bendana, director of the Institute of International Studies in Managua. "The U.S. is going to know more about the Nicaraguan people than the Nicaraguan government." Authorities in Mexico, Nicaragua, and Costa Rica opened investigations, determined to learn how ChoicePoint got the information. Mexican authorities quickly issued an arrest warrant for one data broker. They also invited Choice-Point executives to Mexico City. The company declined. In June that year, a Mexican official visited the Atlanta consulate instead to formally receive computer files of the Mexican voters' information. The company said it had erased the information from its databases. In November that year, Mexican authorities arrested three officials from Soluciones Mercadologicas en Bases de Datos, a company that allegedly sold information to ChoicePoint. The government was considering charging them with treason. ChoicePoint asked for a statement from Mexican officials, declaring that its employees had done nothing wrong. They were rebuffed. Said Mexico's special prosecutor for electoral crimes: "There is a presumption that a crime has been committed."

ChoicePoint officials said they did nothing wrong. They claimed they had been misled by unscrupulous data brokers, who had signed documents pledging to uphold the law. "ChoicePoint acted in good faith," said J. Michael de Janes, ChoicePoint's general counsel. "Unfortunately, our Mexican data supplier abused its position of trust and took advantage of the people of Mexico and ChoicePoint."

DESPITE THAT MISSTEP, the terror attacks appear to have had a lasting beneficial impact on ChoicePoint's business prospects. Suddenly everyone was uneasy, and not just about terrorists. The number of criminal background checks alone increased nearly tenfold in the months after the attacks. At a Web site devoted to homeland security clients, Choice-Point had a link that bore the headline: *Tighter Security Focus Boosts Prospects Here.* The story behind the link, a piece by *Investor's Business Daily,* said the company's bottom line was only going to grow.

At the end of 2003, the company reported revenue of more than $800 million, 30 percent more than it earned the year before the attacks. Part of that revenue came from a contract with the Justice Department that was signed after the attacks. The department agreed to pay ChoicePoint $67 million, in a four-year deal that gave access to investigators, transportation authorities, and anti-terrorism units across the country.

ChoicePoint also scored a $19 million contract to conduct criminal and credit checks on almost forty thousand baggage screeners. But that project hit some bumps when Department of Homeland officials questioned whether ChoicePoint was thorough enough. The department's inspector general investigated allegations that dozens of screeners with criminal backgrounds were hired inappropriately.

IN EARLY 2004, the company made two more acquisitions, neither of which drew much attention. One was a company called Templar Corporation. It specializes in sharing information between government agencies and delivering it to any computing device: desktop, laptop, or hand-held. The other, iMapData, does something called geospatial visualization, turning massive amounts of data into detailed maps.

For insight about the importance of these firms to ChoicePoint's new aims, consider *Homeland Security White Paper: The Right Information at the Right Time in the Right Place.* At first glance, it looks like any other marketing material. But with each page, it becomes more interesting. ChoicePoint had teamed up with Templar, iMapData, and another little known company called Orion Scientific, a private intelligence-gathering specialist with close ties to the Defense Department, to produce the document. The paper described how the team was preparing networks that would serve as a public-private clearinghouse for all kinds of data. This wasn't limited to the 17 billion commercial records maintained by ChoicePoint. The system would also help police combine such information with details from their own database and then use software tools to automatically look for suspicious patterns or links among people. All this would be done with the help of a supercomputer akin to the ones used by Acxiom and Seisint. Added into this mix was Jeff Jonas's NORA system. When police had a suspect or a name to check out, it would be run through NORA to determine who the person really was. ChoicePoint has used NORA since September 11, 2001, to tag every person with a single identity code. The speed of the company's services has increased dramatically.

It was in many respects another Matrix, only this service relied on many computer systems instead of just one. And it spits out the information to law enforcement authorities anywhere in the field, not only those in an office. By March 2004, company officials said, there were already eighteen installations. To guide ChoicePoint officials in this new direction—as well as open doors in Washington—the company retained some key people at the end of 2003 to serve on an advisory board. One of them was Dale Watson, a former FBI executive assistant director of counterterrorism and counterintelligence. Another was William Crowell, the former deputy director of the NSA. Still another was Viet Dinh, a law professor and Patriot Act author.

"The partnership between ChoicePoint, Orion, Templar, and iMapData brings together unique industry-leading technologies that focus directly on the issue of information, thus providing end users with the ability to obtain the right information at the right time, analyze and derive intelligence from the information, and organize and disseminate the information to the right sources," the white paper stated, adding that it offers investigators "the ability to access all relevant information with a single query."

ChoicePoint is no longer merely a background screener. Or a drug tester. Or an insurance fraud specialist. It doesn't just provide dossiers to police across the country or tease out the links among people for intelligence and counterterrorism officials. It does all of that and more. By 2004, it had become perhaps the world's largest private intelligence operation. Its services mirrored what good intelligence analysts do, only ChoicePoint identifies the patterns and links and potential tendencies much faster, and with a sweep that would make James Bond's colleagues envious. Besides, as a data contractor, it often can work with aggregated details about American citizens in ways that police and intelligence officials sometimes by law cannot. The company's aims are apparent in its marketing documents. The phrase the company used in an annual report to describe the essence of what it sells was "Actionable Intelligence."

Company officials make no effort to advertise to the general public what the company is becoming. They worry the reality would scare people. They also don't think that most people would believe them.

6

THE IMMUTABLE ME

T HE EMAIL ARRIVED in Joseph Atick's laptop on the last day of 2002. It was from a senior official at the Justice Department Atick had met while pitching his prized invention, a computerized face recognition system. Call us, the note said, we need your help. Atick dialed the number. The voice on the other end of the line seemed strained. We've got a problem, the man told him. Intelligence agencies had received an unsettling tip from a Pakistani forger. Five men had entered the United States under assumed names and phony IDs. It appeared they planned an attack in New York during New Year's Eve celebrations. But no one knew where or precisely when. Atick was both awed and thrilled by the call.

The government wanted him to match images of known suspects against some 35,000 digital photographs of people who had recently entered the country. It needed to know who was preparing to strike, where they were last seen, the names they were operating under.

For years Atick had worked on automated face recognition. First as a path-breaking scientist, then as an entrepreneur. He had promoted his software as the world's response to identity fraud and security questions, and some states and intelligence officials had embraced his innovations. But Atick also had been deeply stung by civil liberties activists, who accused him of profiting from an intrusive, Orwellian business.

Now the government was counting on his invention in a crunch. It was about 9 am. Atick had only a few hours to gather a team together at his company's office in Minneapolis. "No problem," Atick said.

FACE RECOGNITION IS A KIND of biometric, a word that encompasses "biology" and "measurement." It is one of several kinds of technology that rely on the body's immutable characteristics to identify people. In addition to face recognition systems, there are fingerprint readers, iris scanners, voice analyzers, even computer-linked cameras that recognize the way people walk. For many years this was the stuff of science fiction. Now these identity systems routinely give millions of people access to their offices, ease ATM transactions, or authenticate that people are who they claim to be over the telephone or on computer networks.

In 2004 the biometric industry was still in its infancy, though, roughly like TV in the 1940s or computers in the fifties. The technology is far from fully realized. Face recognition doesn't work well unless lighting conditions are just right, and electronic fingerprint readers can be fooled. But it's going to be a very big business in our lifetimes.

In 1994, at a time when few people knew the fledgling biometric industry even existed, Joseph Atick founded a firm called Visionics to develop and sell face recognition technology. In part because of his tireless advocacy and innovation since then, biometric technology is fast becoming an integral part of the world's information and security infrastructure. Government officials and many others see it as a powerful weapon to combat identity thieves, computer hackers, terrorists, and crime. After the terror attacks, Atick worked hard to put face recognition at the vanguard of how to respond. He lobbied government officials ceaselessly to use his surveillance systems as a screen for terrorists and criminals. Calling his plan Operation Noble Shield, Atick called for a nationwide network of cameras at airports, all of them linked to a database of suspects' faces. His system, known as FaceIt, would automatically scan the faces of travelers for people whom authorities be-

lieved posed a threat. For three months, he practically lived out of hotels in Washington, D.C. He was an indefatigable salesman. Atick said
in the busy time after the terror attacks, "I'll be taking this as a personal
crusade."

Atick had some notable successes. Several airports installed FaceIt
on a trial basis and he was quoted a lot in newspapers as an authority.
But it was the 2002 New Year's Eve call from the Justice Department
that gave him the greatest hope that financial success and his reputation as an inventor would be secure. "It was," he said later, "vindica-
tion."

Immediately after that call, Atick rallied a small team to implement
the operation. They worked out of Visionic's facility in suburban Min-
netonka, Minnesota, a nondescript single-story glass office building just
off I-494. By noon, his four technical guys had managed to hook up
with their peers in the government. Working on secure links over the
Internet, they transferred all the photographs. Then they went through
the process of mapping some eighty coordinates from each picture, the
bumps, curves, and angles that make each face unique. Those maps
were turned into digital codes, and those codes were matched against
one another in a search for pairs. After several hours, it appeared they
had a match. The photos were transmitted to Atick, who could not tell
the difference. He sent them along to his Justice contact. And then he
waited. About 11 pm, intelligence officials ruled out any connections
between the photos. It was a false alarm. Based on information gleaned
from other sources—along with the face recognition analysis—they decided the tip was probably a hoax. Atick was told that he and his ex-
hausted team could go home. He was disappointed that his software
had not saved the hour, but he got a call from Justice the next day.
Would he come to D.C. and talk more to senior officials about his products?

JOSEPH ATICK IS A SHORT, dapper man, who speaks softly with a vague
Middle Eastern accent. Like his neighbors in Manhattan, he tends to
wear expensive black clothes. From a certain angle, he resembles the
British actor Peter Sellers.

He was born in the Christian quarter of Jerusalem in 1964, the son of a businessman who sold T-shirts emblazoned with the images of pop icons. As a child, Atick showed unusual aptitude for abstract thinking. He became so adept intellectually that he dropped out of high school and began writing a book about modern physics for college students. Week after week, he scrawled out a 600-page draft on the back of sheets of paper showing pictures of Bruce Lee and John Travolta.

Atick was not a political kid, but he'll never forget the ominous political currents in his childhood homeland, the sense of insecurity and uncertainty, and the inability to do anything about it. It was terror experienced firsthand, and Atick loathed it. "We stood on the sidelines watching wars that we could not affect," he said. "This was a time of armed resistance. Security measures were everywhere. Buses were searched. You had to stand on line for hours waiting to prove your identity."

At fifteen years old, Atick moved with his family to Miami. Unsure what to do, he contacted a nuclear physics professor he admired at Stanford. The professor recognized the name. The physicist had just come back from a conference in the Middle East, where someone had brought Atick's book to his attention. Why don't you come to Stanford as a graduate student? the professor suggested. Atick agreed, took an exam, and was in the next year. His subject of study: String Theory, also known as the Theory of Everything. It was a wildly ambitious examination of the first few moments of existence. After Atick got his doctorate in mathematical physics in 1987, he received a call from the Institute for Advanced Studies in Princeton. The institute had been founded in the 1930s as a base for Albert Einstein. It was later home to some of the greatest minds of the twentieth century, including J. Robert Oppenheimer, who directed the development of the first atomic bomb. Atick went to the institute to continue his String Theory studies. Wanting a better connection to the world, he moved into the arcane field of computational neuroscience, a new field that examined whether mathematics is involved in the operations of the brain.

"When we look around us, our sensory systems and brain are processing information at a phenomenal rate. It became clear that there are problems that a conventional computer cannot solve," he said. "There had to be a discovery that would explain, how do we convert massive amounts of data to knowledge and actionable items."

Atick's first Eureka moment came during a walk across the Princeton campus from his apartment on Einstein Drive to his office at the institute. He was kicking around the idea of perception, trying to imagine how the brain actually "sees" people. It seemed like a data-crunching problem, how to process millions of subtle pieces of information. But he realized on his walk the solution lay in the opposite direction. It was all about using as *little* information as possible. All he wanted to do was grab a pen and paper to write down his insight. He ran the rest of the way to his office.

At the end of 1991, Atick was asked by Rockefeller University in New York to form a Computational Neuroscience Laboratory there. Three years later, he saw that his earlier insight at the Princeton campus was right. Atick had programmed a computer in his office to accept data from a black and white camera. It looked at a few dozen points on a face and used those points to create a face print. One morning, he walked into the office with several other people. Without expecting it just then, Atick heard the machine speak. With the metallic inflections of an artificial voice, it said: "I recognize Joseph Atick."

Atick experienced a glee that most scientists can only fantasize about. After years of study and tinkering, after pondering the nature of human perception, his theories had spurred a technological leap. Machines could now recognize people. "I felt so elated," Atick said. "I felt like the birth of a child."

He wasn't the only one excited. The Department of Defense offered him grants to continue. Hundreds of thousands of dollars that, over the next decade, would become millions. Atick gratefully accepted the help. He had great hopes for improving security and helping people clarify their identities. His federal sponsors, though, had their own ideas about how to use this nascent surveillance power. And they would be there every step of the way to help make the technology better.

THE PROBLEM BIOMETRICS tries to solve goes far back in human history. In *Database Nation: The Death of Privacy in the 21st Century,* Simson

Garfinkel retells the story of King Solomon to spell out the core issue. As readers of the Old Testament know, two women had recently had children. One of the babies died, but both of the mothers claimed to be the parent of the survivor. Called on to resolve the dispute, Solomon asked for his sword. He would, he said, split the baby in half. Solomon knew of course that the real mother would rather give up the baby than see it harmed. When one woman disavowed the child, he knew he had resolved the question of identity. She was the real mother.

Ever since then, people have struggled to find better ways to verify identities. The most venerable biometric is a fingerprint, those unique patterns of ridges and whorls that everyone is born with. In ancient Babylon, merchants used fingerprints on clay tablets documenting deals. Chinese authorities in the second century B.C. impressed thumbprints on clay seals to secure important documents. In 1563, the Portuguese explorer João de Barros noted how Chinese merchants took ink prints of children's palms and feet to distinguish them from one another.

A century later, a professor of anatomy at the universities of Bologna and Messina examined skin under a microscope and noticed that fingers all seemed to have characteristics. Marcello Malpighi did not suggest using his insight to improve identification at the time, but the discovery was a turning point. Two centuries after that, a British anthropologist named Sir Francis Galton published a book called *Fingerprints*. Galton, a cousin of Charles Darwin, reckoned that the odds of two people having the same fingerprints were 1 in 64 billion. Given the number of people on earth, that meant there was roughly no chance at all.

It was only a matter of time before law enforcement authorities understood the utility of this unique stamp. Credit for solving the first murder with this new science goes to Eduardo Alvarez, an inspector for the Argentine police. In 1892, he worked with Juan Vucetich, who had opened the first fingerprint files the year before. Using those files, and evidence collected at the scene, they were able to identify a woman who had killed her two sons.

The size and sophistication of fingerprint files improved steadily through the twentieth century. Scotland Yard in the United Kingdom, the

FBI in the United States, and law enforcement authorities across the world turned to fingerprints as a key to making investigations. By the 1980s, most of them had adopted the Automated Fingerprint Identification System. Instead of examining the loops and ridges, the system employed computing power to find anomalies. In the late eighties, the system could match up to six hundred prints per second. That rate increased by ten times over the next decade and continued to quicken.

California police solved the notorious "Night Stalker" case using the system, better known as AFIS. Authorities in Baltimore soon found they could handily identify hundreds of suspects who had given false names to police. Police agencies across the country have solved many thousands of cases with fingerprints. In 2004, the FBI was maintaining some 250 million sets of prints on files from some 40 million people. They get about 37,000 new fingerprint cards a week. "If all the fingerprint cards on file were stacked on top of one another, they would equal one hundred and thirty three stacks, each the size of the Empire State Building!" says a bureau Web page. "Finding space to keep all of these fingerprint cards is difficult!" But the FBI's fingerprint system was not up to the demands placed on it and some of its computer equipment was way out of date. By 2004, however, that was changing fast. One in three files came in as a digital image, making it easier than ever to store this oldest of biometrics. And the bureau was using its storehouse to digitally review some 100,000 prints a day.

IN THE LATE NINETEENTH CENTURY, a Parisian criminologist came up with another way to identify people. Alphonse Bertillon had been pondering how to pinpoint the names of petty thieves who deceived police about their identities. At the time, Paris and many other cities were being inundated by newcomers. Businesspeople and authorities confronted the same dilemma we now face: How can we know and trust the many strangers we come into contact with every day?

Bertillon reasoned a crook might change his name, but he could not change his face or his features. Over several years, he took thousands of measurements of people who had been arrested. He arranged these files—including the suspect's name—by his measurements. Large heads in one stack, small heads in another, and so on. He called this "anthropometrical signalment" and over the next several years authorities used the approach to index some 120,000 Parisians.

Other authorities, including those in the United States, took a keen interest in his work, and at least twenty prisons and seven police departments adopted signalment with a zealousness that would be familiar today. "The process of signalment would take the place of passports at every national frontier, and signalments would appear on all life insurance policies, permits and other papers whose value depends on the establishment of personal identity," Major R. W. McClaughry, the warden of Illinois State Penitentiary, wrote in an American edition of a ninety-five-page pamphlet in which Bertillon spelled out his ideas. "It would then be possible to find any person at once whenever desired, whether for his own good or that of society at large."

It wasn't until the rise of computers and networks a century later that Bertillon's vision for these systems—and the social control they enable—became broadly feasible. Computers can now recognize voices. They can distinguish the geometry of hands, read handwriting, sense the unique way that an individual taps on a keyboard. Cameras can pinpoint a person in a crowd based on how he or she walks. They can even look into someone's eyes and know—better than a lover or a spy— whether that person is who he claims to be.

IN 1993, JOSEPH ATICK faced a tough choice. He could stay at Rockefeller University, continue studying the technology, and cross his fingers that it would some day catch on. Or he could take a risk, like many other scientists of his time, and build a company around his work.

Atick decided to leave the university and create Visionics Corporation. But it would not be a clean break into the private sector. For years, Atick and other face recognition innovators had been receiving funding from the Defense Department and other federal agencies determined to nurture the new technology. Once Visionics opened for business, the government continued to fund Atick's research. Atick estimates that over the years he and his company received some $4 million in government grants, including from a program at the Defense Advanced Research Projects Agency called Human Identification at a Distance, or

HumanID. The National Security Agency paid another $4 million for FaceIt gear and services.

"Government grants helped expedite the research," Atick acknowledged. "There were people in Washington that understood the potential impact, but also that it would be ten years away."

That support for biometric technology was critical. Without it, Atick and the rest of the biometric industry would be years behind. But it also meant that prime sponsors—including the Office of Naval Research, the Immigration and Naturalization Service, and the Defense Department—would be expecting to use the surveillance gear as soon as they could.

Few people outside the government had any idea it existed until 1997, when Atick unveiled FaceIt PC, a security program that regular folks could use to log on to their personal computers, using their faces as the keys. Visionics took FaceIt PC to Comdex 97 in Las Vegas, the largest information technology conference in the country. Participants went wild when they saw what Atick had done. Of almost seven hundred new technology products—including from giants of the technology world—FaceIt won the best of show. "The judges saw the potential for a paradigm shift," Atick said. "They understood it would change the world in the next twenty years." After that, Atick could barely keep up with the calls. In July that year, the company secured four federal contracts. The NSA, the INS, the Army Research Laboratory, and the National Institute of Justice at the Justice Department all wanted to tap the nascent surveillance prowess of FaceIt for investigations and security.

"FaceIt is the only face recognition technology capable of performing continuous monitoring," Visionics boasted at the time. "It can locate, extract, identify and track human heads in real-time, totally hands-off and without user or operator action required."

That's exactly what officials in London were about to ask him to do as part of the first computerized surveillance camera system put on a major city's street.

THE TELEVISION MONITORS flashed with ceaseless activity. Shoppers crossed streets. Lovers embraced. Cars pulled up to intersections. Now and then someone looked up directly at a camera, their face enlarged by a close-up. Some of the TVs showed multiple scenes at once, like net-work coverage of a football game. Each of the images came from a cam-era that could rotate almost 360 degrees. The cameras were linked to Joseph Atick's FaceIt software.

This was the control room of the London borough of Newham, the first neighborhood in the world to install automated face surveillance. Newham had once been home to a thriving shipping industry, but the East London docks had fallen on hard times. Increased unemployment had fueled the crime rate. Borough authorities decided in the mid-1990s it was time to expand their use of technology to fight back.

At first they put closed-circuit cameras on the street, accompanied by signs warning people they were under surveillance. It was a bit of law enforcement theater that seemed to frighten the criminals away, at least for a while. "We reduced crime by sixty percent in the area where we posted the signs," Bob Lack, who ran the borough's system, told Jeff Rosen, author of *The Naked Crowd*. "Then word on the street went out that we had dummy cameras."

That's when Lack reached out to Joseph Atick. Hoping to reinforce the credibility of their surveillance threats, borough officials began adding FaceIt software to the computers in 1999. It had an undeniable gee-whiz appeal to it. When the machines sighted a wanted person, an alarm was sounded for analysts in the control room. The analysts then compared the captured image to one called up by the computer. If they believed there was a match, they called in a police officer for advice. But there were some problems that tarnished the theory's glossy veneer. For one, there were few faces in the computer. In the summer of 2001, the system still contained only about sixty faces. And the system was linked to only about thirteen cameras at a time. There was no clear pol-icy as to whose image should be in the system. Lack said he wanted only local criminals who had recently been identified by intelligence as active. They never caught any violent criminals or terrorists or anybody at all in the first three years of operation. None of that mattered to Lack and his colleagues. They considered it a great success because overall crime—mostly petty crime—had dropped. Lack said that most people in the borough seemed to welcome the cameras. Far from worrying about Big Brother, "they're demanding that something be done" about the crime. Lack insisted face recognition wasn't just about catching criminals, it was about dissuading them from committing crimes in the borough. If that meant mixing technology with the smoke and mirrors of public relations, so be it. "We went live in a blaze of publicity," Lack boasted one day to a visitor.

Atick was proud of the system as well. "Newham had high crime, petty crime, people felt fearful. They were building a state of the art system helping law enforcement deployment. Instead of cops on the beat, they decided to put in cameras. That was the first application of facial surveillance in a challenging environment. Crime dropped dramatically," he said. "That's not all due to face recognition, the publicity helped too. The end result was that the old ladies came out again."

Rosen, in *The Naked Crowd*, calls this a "Wizard of Oz" effect. Bombast coupled with the Defense Department–funded technology. It demonstrates a fundamental problem with many data surveillance systems. The technology doesn't work as well as advertised, even as it gives individuals the sense of being watched as never before.

THE RISE OF this technology could be a balm for Information Age problems. A universal biometric system could help protect people like Michael Berry, the identity theft victim who struggled so hard to clear his name. Not many people would try to take on Berry's persona if they had to come up with his fingerprint or the contours of his face. It also could be a godsend to people who have been overwhelmed by passwords. As we learned in the 1990s, passwords are deeply flawed. Think about those times you were standing at the ATM, with people in line behind you fidgeting because you couldn't think of the correct sequence of numbers. Was it the date of your daughter's birthday, the combination to an old high school locker, a favorite lottery number? Good luck remembering.

Since the late eighties, people have been forced to collect passwords like janitors collect keys. There now are passwords for office equipment, passwords for cellular telephones, and, of course, passwords for computer networks. Some people have passwords to electronic organizers where they keep track of all their passwords. It had become a frustrating situation indeed. People began experiencing overload, so they used easy-to-recall combinations but that made security-conscious network administrators cringe. Hackers can crack passwords such as 1111 or those based on the names of children, pets, and favorite words or phrases, like "Kung fu" or "Trekkie," almost as easily as they crack their knuckles. They use computer programs that can test millions of number or word permutations to unlock accounts. The security of both computers and vast networks has been undermined repeatedly because of such laxity. Specialists estimated that up to three quarters of all people use passwords that were easily guessed by others. To be effective, people needed to come up with nonsense jumbles of letters, numbers, and symbols, passwords that resemble nothing so much as a cartoon cuss. The problem is that people generally aren't cut out to remember random strings of numbers and the like. "It is a major problem," said Kent Norman, a psychology professor and director of the Laboratory for Automation Psychology at the University of Maryland. "Machines are very good at coding numbers and text. We're very bad at it." No one using their own characteristics would have to remember a code. They just had to be themselves. That's partly why the demand for biometric systems soared in the nineties, as the price of equipment plummeted. In 1990, the industry sold just under 1,300 units for about $5,100 each; by the end of the decade, about 145 companies had sold some 115,000 biometric devices for about $547 each.

After the terror attacks, interest in biometrics surged even more. Entrepreneurs saw a tremendous new market. William Rogers, publisher of *Biometric Digest*, estimated that by the end of 2004 the number of manufacturers and re-sellers of the identity gear and related services had more than tripled in just five years, to some five hundred. Businesses wanted to control access more efficiently. The government rushed to make use of the devices at border checkpoints, in office buildings, and, surreptitiously, around sensitive or vulnerable facilities. Some analysts predicted that worldwide sales would grow from about $601 million in 2002 to more than $4 billion in 2007. "We're just starting now," Rogers said. "This is ground zero."

IN THE SCIENCE FICTION MOVIE *Minority Report*, Tom Cruise walks through a long corridor. The billboards along the way scan his eyes,

sense that it's him, and offer personalized greetings and marketing promotions. It's the ultimate in customer relationship management. It's also
a reminder that everywhere Cruise goes he's being tracked by the very
sensors designed to make life more convenient and secure. Though it is
set five decades in the future, the scene is startling with its plausibility.

More than any other technology, biometrics serves as the emblem
of what civil libertarians fear most these days: that identity systems
will accelerate the erosion of our most essential freedoms. Face recognition, iris scans, and related technology hold out the very real possibility that one day, everyone will be identifiable, everywhere, whether
or not they want to be. And companies like ChoicePoint and Identix
already are refining systems to link individuals' dossiers to face and
fingerprints.

Authorities routinely photograph protests, saying they want to
record illegal activity. Through the use of face recognition, they may
soon be able to instantly identify people, innocent and suspect alike.
It won't be long before police turn to video data mining to document
all the faces that appear at different protests. And even if no names
are attached to those images, they can already turn to systems that
match those photos with lightning speed, against driver's license or
passport images.

It's a safe bet that law enforcement methods also will become expansive. Suppose the face of an African-American or Hispanic businessman
is captured in a largely white neighborhood about the same time as a
rape or robbery. If the visit seems unusual, say, because computers
show he does not often travel that way, police may be inclined to pay
the man a visit, even though there's nothing else to indicate his involvement. The same phenomenon could hold true for a white professional who shows up in the wrong place at the wrong time, or who
appears to show unusual or suspect travel patterns, as documented
electronically by face or iris prints and computers.

The use of biometric identifiers shifts an enormous amount of power
into the hands of those who control the equipment—power to track
people in minute ways, or to give or withhold access to buildings, airplanes, and innumerable other facilities. Think of our fingerprints,
irises, and faces as akin to the online "cookies" put on personal computers to ease browsing and track computer users. Only these identi-

fiers will never go away. As in *Minority Report,* marketers will relish the chance to know their customers' habits better, something we might be inclined to embrace or to dismiss as merely annoying. But what about when the government turns to those records to satisfy its obsession for security? We're only a few years into the twenty-first century, but suddenly the idea that we can be tracked in these ways is not so far-fetched as we might want to believe.

TWO CENTURIES AGO, the British jurist and philosopher Jeremy Bentham envisioned a form of surveillance that would enable authorities to watch individuals without being seen themselves. As spelled out in his *Panopticon Writings,* authorities would create circular buildings where control was most needed: prisons, schools, "work houses," and such. Cells would be situated on an outer ring. Each cell would have an opening facing toward the center, where a guard tower was situated. Shielded by a screen, authorities would see every cell's occupant but not be seen themselves. Bentham's idea was to maximize the exercise of authority with the least effort and expense. "Panopticon" systems achieved this efficiency though the "apparent omnipresence" of the observers. Prisoners would come to sense they were under close scrutiny, at all hours, even if there were no guards present.

This is what civil libertarians worry about, that with biometric technology and computer networks authorities will soon convey the sense of omnipresent surveillance, that the United States will soon become a Panopticon society. Anyone who walks by a camera linked to Atick's FaceIt or similar technology might suddenly be subject to a high-tech search. "What it tells us is that we are really on the cusp of a surveillance society where you're not going to be able to go anywhere without being subject to both surveillance and identification," Barry Steinhardt, director of the ACLU's Technology and Liberty Program, told a newscaster. "I find it chilling."

Supporters of face recognition and video surveillance get frustrated by such remarks. They want people to focus on the utility of their machines. They also correctly note that individuals don't have any right to privacy in public places. Courts have ruled that the Fourth Amendment of the Constitution, which bars warrantless search and seizures, does not protect an individual from having his face print taken surreptitiously. But Steinhardt and others argue that video surveillance has a powerful effect on psychology. People aren't just paranoid, in other words, they really are being watched. "When people fear surveillance, whether it exists or not, when they grow afraid to speak their minds and hearts freely to their government or to anyone else, then we shall cease to live in a free society," Senator Sam Ervin said in the 1970s, after examining domestic surveillance in America.

There are other troubling questions. We know now that once data systems are created, their use almost invariably evolves. It happened with the Social Security numbers. Public records about real estate, voter registration, drivers' and professional licenses are now used intensively for marketing. In 1989, cameras made in America and installed to help control traffic in China were used instead to track down subversives after the protests in Tiananmen Square. The government counterterrorism initiatives now rely heavily on mountains of data collected by private companies.

What would happen if computers containing face prints and other biometrics were breached and the biometrics sold? What about masks or makeup that tricked FaceIt or other biometric systems? Atick and others said that's not possible, but there are no guarantees. In a world where we all have to share our thumb- or face prints to buy, travel, and work, that would be the ultimate theft of identity. ChoicePoint has made clear its plans to create a central clearinghouse of biometric information for commercial uses.

There is some evidence that the devices can be tricked. Tsutomu Matsumoto is a Japanese cryptographer who wondered about the security claims made for fingerprint readers. As a university teacher, he made his inquiry part of a student exercise. Using readily available supplies—including Gummi Bears gelatin and a type of molding plastic—they fashioned model fingers from live subjects that fooled every major fingerprint reader eight of ten times. "If he could do this, then any semi-professional can almost certainly do much much more," wrote security specialist Bruce Schneier in his *Beyond Fear*. "Be very careful before believing claims from security companies."

• • •

WE OFTEN ASSUME that pictures don't lie, and that sophisticated technology won't fail us. But the mix of those two assumptions, coupled with human error, can be misleading and dangerous for the people under surveillance.

On June 29, 2002, a woman named Denise Mansfield was found strangled in her Prince George's County, Maryland, home, where she ran an accounting and computer business. Mansfield had been dead for a week. In a search for clues, detectives turned to her bank. They scored almost immediately, securing evidence that seemed almost too good to be true. Not only did the bank have records of activity for Mansfield's ATM card, it also had videotape that showed $200 being withdrawn from her account.

The video, grainy and halting, showed three women gathered around a cash machine at SunTrust Bank, not far from Mansfield's home. The time records on the video showed that two of the three women withdrew money just when Mansfield's card was being used. Thanks to the mix of technologies, investigators had their suspects. Now, they just needed to know their identities. For that they turned to *America's Most Wanted*, the television show that features unsolved crimes, such as the murders involving Michael Berry's identity theft case. The show displayed a snapshot of the video and, as the *Washington Post* reported in an examination of the case, a viewer called in to finger the three women.

Virginia Shelton, her teenage daughter Shirley, and her friend Jennifer Starkey had traveled from their homes in Arizona to Silver Spring, Maryland, to help Virginia's mother sort out some legal papers. They also planned to visit the Air and Space Museum and other landmarks, including Six Flags in Largo, Maryland. Before going to the amusement park, though, they needed cash. The video machine captured the short few moments they were at the SunTrust Bank.

For ten months, police weren't sure who was responsible. The trio had headed home to Arizona the next day. After the television program, though, police had the names they needed. Determined Prince George's County investigators traveled out to Sierra Vista, Arizona, and, on April 22, 2003, questioned the women at a local police station on and off for seven hours. Virginia Shelton and the two others acknowledged they had been in the bank, but they denied having murdered Mansfield. That didn't matter to police. To them, the grainy video told the real story. It was the only physical evidence listed in an affidavit submitted to the court by police. The women were charged with murder. Shelton and Starkey were sent to jail, Shirley to a juvenile detention facility. There they languished until authorities in Prince George's realized they had placed too much faith in the technology.

As it happened, the video had correctly recorded their images, and the ATM electronically noted the time when the murder victim's account was being pilfered. The problem? The two systems were not in synch. On their way to the amusement park that day, the women had used SunTrust's ATM a few minutes before the real suspect had tapped in the stolen passcode. Detectives had records showing the discrepancy, but Starkey's father, who had the same documents, had to fly from Arizona to point it out. More than three weeks after they were thrown in jail, a prosecutor arranged for the court to set them free.

The same kind of misidentification—in the same case and based on the very same video—had occurred a few months before. Police charged two sisters from Washington, D.C., with Mansfield's murder. A third sister had identified the two from still images that ran on local TV news programs and in the newspapers. One woman was freed at long last after showing she had been traveling on business the day the video was taken. The other had to share DNA to prove she was not responsible for the murder.

For Shirley Shelton, the teenager, it was as though police were weighing her word against the technology's, and they chose to believe the latter. "I felt like one detective wanted to take his gun out and shoot me for not telling the truth," she said.

SHELTON'S EXPERIENCE was relatively mild compared to what Brandon Mayfield faced in the spring of 2004. A lawyer and a convert to Islam, Mayfield was accused of participating in the March 11, 2004, terror bombing attacks in Madrid that killed 191 people and injured 2,000 others. The FBI claimed his fingerprints matched those found on a plastic bag in Madrid containing bomb detonators. His house was turned upside down, many of his papers were taken, and on May 6 he was detained as a "material witness."

Spanish authorities had raised doubts about the fingerprints, and the thirty-seven-year-old Mayfield protested that he had nothing to do with terrorism. Mayfield said he abhorred violence. But the FBI, relying on its Automated Fingerprint Identification System and three outside analysts, said the evidence was "absolutely incontrovertible." Even an expert hired by Mayfield's attorney seemed convinced. But that confidence, based on a biometric system used by law enforcement authorities around the globe, melted away. Soon after Mayfield was put in jail, Spanish authorities said the print actually belonged to an Algerian man. A federal judge ordered Mayfield released and all copies of documents taken from him destroyed. The FBI blamed the confusion on a print "image of substandard quality" provided by the Spaniards. They also did something extraordinary: They said they were sorry. "The FBI apologizes to Mr. Mayfield and his family for the hardships this matter has caused," the bureau said in a statement on May 24. The FBI also promised to review what went wrong.

The FBI claimed that Mayfield's religious affiliation, and the fact that he had once represented a convicted Taliban sympathizer in a child custody case, had nothing to do with their decision to jail him.

As for Mayfield, he was overwhelmed by the implications of his brush with the global war on terror. "I am two or three days out of the detention center, and I'm just now starting not to shake," he told the *Washington Post.*

NO ONE EVER CONSIDERED the La Playa Market in Inglewood, California, a technology hot spot. At the end of 2002, it had just one lane for checking out. Its shelves overflowed with canned goods, juices, baby food, and the other staples of mom and pop shops everywhere. But the dusty Inglewood bodega distinguished itself as a twenty-first-century operation in one remarkable way: It used an electronic fingerprint reader to identify customers. Grocery stores all over the country, many of them much larger than La Playa, have begun embracing these devices. Thriftway stores in the Seattle area allow thousands of customers to use thumbprints instead of debit or credit cards. Kroger stores in Texas require customers to share finger scans in order to cash paychecks. At the end of 2003, some 176 Bi-Lo markets in Georgia, North

Carolina, South Carolina, and Tennessee had agreed to deploy a similar system. Groceries might seem unlikely turf for such exotic technology, but they consider fingerprint systems, which dropped sharply in price in the first few years of the new century, an efficient way to cut down on fraud and track customers better.

Operating the systems are little-known companies that collect and store customers' fingerprints and personal information on behalf of the groceries. Leaders of this burgeoning industry include Biometric Access Corp. in Texas and BioPay LLC of Herndon, Virginia. Their approach is similar to ChoicePoint's, in that they want to enforce rules. They're betting that Americans will be more than willing to trade off personal privacy for convenience.

Consider the approach used by BioPay, whose name suggests something out of a cyberpunk novel. Customers who want to participate must hand over their driver's license to be scanned. Then they put their index fingers on an electronic device about the size of a computer mouse to electronically capture their prints, which are converted to a digital code. The information is all stored on databases.

When customers want to cash a check, they put their finger on the scanner. The system then instantly reports earlier transactions—at any store in the network. All this service for about $75 a month from each store. Every machine costs about $10,000. "If the person has any negative transactions with any other BioPay merchant in the country, advanced alert mechanisms warn the clerk, enabling the transaction to be declined before it is processed saving Bi-Lo money it may have otherwise lost. A customer with a history of positive transactions allows Bi-Lo to cash the check with confidence," stated a BioPay announcement.

When asked by a *Los Angeles Times* reporter about the impact that privacy concerns might have on BioPay's prospects, the company's president, Tim Robinson said: "You have already given away all your privacy."

Such networks could run across grocery chains and even include other kinds of businesses and government services, such as the Food Stamp program. It might be possible to link terrorists or criminal watch lists or even scofflaws to the fingerprint networks one day.

The use of this gear by groceries shows how far along the biometrics industry has come. Many other businesses and organizations also use biometrics. Hundreds of casinos rely on face recognition to identify both unwanted customers and VIPs. An Atick competitor called Viisage acquired a company in 2002 called Biometrica, which operated the Surveillance Information Network, or SIN—a service that enables casinos to trade the images of undesirables. Biometrica had sold its systems to 150 casinos. Among the SIN customers were the Trump, MGM, and Foxwoods casinos. After the terror attacks, the government asked Biometrica for advice about how to create its own biometric-sharing network.

The National Security Agency has used Atick's face recognition systems to control computer access and track people through its own facilities. State motor vehicle offices and electoral officials in Mexico used his software to target identity frauds. Atick also offered "video data mining products" that could review existing photographs or video recordings long after when they were taken. The company stated in financial documents on file with the government that its data-mining service is "a state-of-the-art automated full-time facial surveillance and identification engine that allows each camera of a surveillance system, whether new or old, to serve as a diligent observation point, even when the video is not being actively observed."

Banks use iris scans and fingerprints to verify the identities of customers. Dozens of credit unions have started deploying electronic fingerprint systems at kiosks to allow members to do business remotely. And businesses everywhere use machines to read the geometry of employees' hands as they check in and out of work.

In November 2003, ChoicePoint teamed up with a company called BIO-key International to deploy fingerprint readers at check cashing and retail outlets. Once again, ChoicePoint was promoting the service as a way to "create a safer and more secure society." Tom Colatosti, BIO-key's chairman—who had served earlier as chairman of Viisage— described it in promotional material as a way to "deter the multi-billion identity theft crisis in America," particularly in the "high volume and rugged retail environments where identity theft breeds."

YBOR CITY IN DOWNTOWN TAMPA, Florida, has the paradoxical feel of being both gritty and glamorous. It has blocks and blocks of former warehouse buildings, large brick affairs built for shipping and manufacturing a century ago now filled with bistros and pubs, ice cream shops and boutiques. On any given weekend, tens of thousands of young, hip, and affluent people converge on Ybor City to party.

For city and business leaders, the health of the entertainment district was a blessing, a sign that their town was a place to be. For police, it was a giant headache. Fights often broke out. The crowd was a target for pickpockets and con artists. There also was more pressure than ever from city bosses to prevent any crime that might taint Ybor's good fortune. Much as Bertillon struggled to identify criminals in Paris during his day, Tampa police wanted a better way of knowing who they were dealing with, or at least who they ought to watch out for. They turned to surveillance.

Police are a suspicious breed. They sense danger almost everywhere, and almost all the time. Given a chance, they'll snoop. The Tampa police were as aggressive as any. With support from city leaders, they had bought all kinds of electronic gear to watch people and listen to what they say. During the 1990s, that included high-powered cameras, some with night vision, for a fleet of helicopters and boats. They had miniature cameras mounted on the ends of fiber-optic wands that could slip under doors, around corners, and even through holes in walls. The Tampa police also had listening devices that enabled them to eavesdrop.

Behind some of these efforts was a detective named Bill Todd, a weekend sailor in love with technology. To his mind, police could never have too much surveillance gear on their side. It was all about efficiency. "We've been aggressive at looking to technology," Todd said in 2003. "In our time there's nothing that replaces the witness of the video camera."

Todd and his colleagues figured they could improve their efficiency simply by installing cameras on the streets of Ybor City, which is what they did in 1998. But they didn't stop there. They had heard about face recognition and wanted to try it out. Their first deployment came at the Super Bowl in 2001. Working with Viisage, Atick's most aggressive competitor, a company that also received government grants, Tampa police surreptitiously recorded the faces of the 72,000 spectators. Viisage used a different approach to the technology, but the broad aim was the same: To identify people by the unique irregularities in their faces. Like Atick's company, Viisage also worked closely with state motor vehicle agencies, which used face recognition to search databases of driver's license photos for people who have more than one license.

At the Super Bowl, Viisage's FaceTrac software matched the images of fans against a hodgepodge of criminal photographs they had downloaded from area authorities. The software had been developed in the labs at the Massachusetts Institute of Technology. It was an Information Age experiment, with Tampa's massive sun-splashed stadium as the petri dish.

The result? The computers and cameras found nineteen people whose photographs had been entered into the system beforehand. These were people police had identified as known troublemakers. No arrests were made, but Tampa police were thrilled. Tom Colatosti exulted about the fact the software worked. He also secured massive amounts of publicity for the publicly traded company. "It was a phenomenal success," he said. "If you had told me the day before that we'd get one, that would be great. The fact that we caught nineteen, that's astounding!"

Civil libertarians said it was unfair to "search" people without permission. They had heard about the borough of Newham's experiment, and suddenly the use of face surveillance in the United States was no longer theoretical. But Colatosti said people always reject new technology. "They said this about penicillin. They said it about TVs. They said it about television and the Internet," he said. "We're on the other side of it. We believe this offers a level of security and convenience that is far beyond what we experience today.

"This technology gives greater freedom and greater privacy to individuals," he went on, turning the criticism on its head. "We wouldn't be doing it for any other reason."

JOSEPH ATICK WOULD NOT be outdone. Not long after the Super Bowl, he offered hundreds of thousands of dollars worth of equipment to the Tampa police. They wanted to use it to mind their weekend visitors and search for sex offenders and other violent criminals. At the beginning of the 2001 summer season, signs appeared along the streets: AREA UNDER VIDEO MONITORING.

Police had connected three dozen cameras to a database with one thousand images of known felons and runaways, a figure that would nearly triple over the next few years. The system operated out of a donated, makeshift backroom just off one of the main streets of Ybor City. It was cramped and a bit grimy, but it gave police officers a clear view of nearly everyone passing by.

Bill Todd, the technology-minded detective, strolled through the room one afternoon in 2003 when the streets were nearly empty. He showed the computer servers that held Atick's technology, and demonstrated the way police use joysticks attached to computers to move the cameras. There were nine monitors to look at. The images were somewhat fuzzy. But they included a date and time, down to the second. One monitor showed some police in bulletproof vests and baseball caps having a drink. Another aimed at a woman using an ATM. Todd typed a password into one of the computers and accessed the face recognition system. He targeted a woman outside, who was rubbing one eye, oblivious that she was being watched. A green question mark appeared on Todd's screen, as the software sought a match of her face in its database. Then it disappeared. No match.

Todd said he didn't mind the paucity of hits. Like the officials in Newham, he insisted that even when it fails to match faces, FaceIt deters criminal activity. (Crime statistics for the area don't appear to back up this assertion. When pressed on the matter in early 2004, a police department spokesman said that "it didn't have any impact.")

There was something acutely voyeuristic about the process. It was possible to follow the woman at the ATM by remotely moving the cameras, and then by switching from camera to camera as she walked down the street. Researchers in England found that attendants often spent their time using the cameras to follow women on the street. Todd said the same thing happened in Ybor City, but downplayed its significance. "Police officers are human beings. When there is a pretty girl walking by, I am not going to tell you that the officers don't look at her through the cameras," he said, fiddling with the equipment. "But there is nothing that they can see through these cameras that you can't see on the street. They are not looking into bedroom windows, they are looking in public places."

ATICK SAID HE HAD donated the equipment, software, and services with the idea of showing the world how useful FaceIt could be. He clearly also had a profit motive. But even as police and other authorities around the world clamored for access to FaceIt, Atick wondered whether the civil libertarians were right. Suppose an oppressive regime in North Korea or Iran got a hold of FaceIt? Would it help them to crush or even liquidate dissidents? Israel already uses the software to register and check Palestinian workers, and that is a relatively benign form of control. Other countries were calling.

He was expressing an inventor's regrets, acknowledging that his invention and others like it could be used for both good and bad. "Fifty years down the line, when I look at my life achievements, I don't want to be the person that people say: 'Well, he's like the guy who invented the atomic bomb,'" Atick said. "Mass surveillance. That should never be allowed to happen."

"I will try, with all the energy I have," he pledged in a taped interview on August 16, 2001, "to prevent Big Brother.

"I cannot allow this technology to go out without me ensuring I have full control over this until the law takes that burden from me," he added, without detailing how he would shape public policy in other countries.

For all the apparent passion, Atick's qualms didn't last long. A few weeks later, within days of the terror attacks, he was meeting with any government official who would see him. He laid out his ideas for Operation Noble Shield, a sweeping multi-billion-dollar plan. Then he entered one of the fiercest competitive rivalries the young biometric industry had seen.

Atick's Visionics and Viisage both promoted their products as technological leaps beyond passwords and personal identification numbers for security and authentication to fight terrorism, identity theft, and other kinds of crimes. With their stock prices soaring, the companies' officials crisscrossed the country to meet with aviation, defense, and immigration officials. When testers of a new system at Fresno Yosemite

International Airport in California were dissatisfied with their Viisage software, Atick quickly offered his services. Soon after, Viisage representatives met with executives of T. F. Green Airport in Rhode Island. They thought they had a deal, but Visionics got a foot in the door and a commitment it would be allowed to make its own pitch. Both companies got a chance to compete for a possible contract at Boston's Logan International Airport. This was war, a business contest Atick was determined to win. "They think that we are the enemy, we're the one to beat," taunted Colatosti, then the chief executive of Viisage, who accused Visionics of being too aggressive. "They get into this PR stuff, this 'Spy vs. Spy.'"

Atick played down any rivalry. "The opportunity here is bigger than both of us combined. May the best technology win," he said. "I'm confident we have a technology that's a quantum leap ahead of our competitors."

It was becoming clear, though, that Atick and his rivals were getting ahead of themselves. Government tests of face recognition in 2002 mandated by the USA Patriot Act showed that FaceIt and other systems had improved in the previous two years but remained far from perfect. They did not work outdoors very well, because of variable lighting and other factors. The systems identified men better than women, and older people better than the young.

Even the best of systems, including FaceIt, could only detect and identify people about 80 percent of the time. And then it had a relatively high rate of false identifications, a trade-off that become obviously significant when considering the many millions of passengers who fly in the United States each year. False alarms could completely undermine the point of the system. The system in Ybor City set off false alarms a couple hundred times, leaving it up to officers to decide whether there was reason to approach a suspect. To get the most out of face recognition, authorities had to carefully control lighting conditions. They also had to persuade people it was in their interest to go along, that face recognition was not intrusive. For these reasons, by early 2004, few airports had adopted the systems to screen passengers. Tampa dropped face recognition in 2003. In two years, it enabled police to watch and record a lot of people. They saw some drug deals go down. But FaceIt never once found anyone it was looking for.

• • •

EVEN IF JOSEPH ATICK had pressed to limit the spread of face recognition and other biometrics, he would have faced almost insurmountable odds. Other companies were being as aggressive as his, and the government was backing them with cash.

Early in 2003, the New Egypt Elementary School in Plumsted, New Jersey, turned on a security system that relied on iris scans, one of the most effective biometrics. It was the first time that an American school had ever deployed such equipment. Later that year, authorities installed a face recognition system at the Royal Palm Middle School in Phoenix, Arizona. Neither school could cite a pattern of crime or abuse it was trying to prevent. Both had contacts with businesses intent on experimenting with their equipment—and getting good publicity.

Plumsted is a bucolic town, with no discernible crime trouble. The school's usual security procedure—asking parents to check in—had always worked. In a grant application, though, organizers cited an incident in 2000 in which a "deranged National Guardsman from neighboring Fort Dix shot his sergeant and drove a stolen Army Humvee on a rampage through our area." "It was a frightening day," the application concluded, never making clear how the iris-scanning system would have made the children safer.

That was good enough for the Justice Department's National Institute of Justice. It awarded the project some $293,000 as part of a study to see how biometric systems might be deployed more widely. Behind the project was an enthusiastic and ambitious local security consultant named Raymond L. Bolling III. After September 11, Bolling calculated that interest in biometrics security would soar. He figured that a project involving children was a sure thing, since everyone worries about the safety of children, even though there was no obvious threat. "It kind of symbolizes a small town that could be any place in America," Bolling said. "We felt we needed to push the envelope as far as we could."

The software driving the system—produced by a private New Jersey company called Iridian Technologies—had been used with cameras installed in hospitals, airports, and office buildings, even the Pentagon

Officer's Athletic Club. Employees at JFK International Airport in New York could sign up to use the scan to pass through security checkpoints. United Nations officials used the technology in Pakistan to prevent refugees from getting more assistance than they were entitled to.

At New Egypt Elementary, it was teachers and parents like Lauren Lindsay who registered. On a morning in June 2003, Lindsay arrived at the school with her two sons, Connor, eight, and Austin, six. Normally, she would have stopped by the front desk to check in. Instead, she bent toward a metal box mounted just outside the main entrance, looked into a small camera, and waited for a signal. After snapping several images of her iris, a personal computer matched it against the images she had shared during a voluntary registration. The lock on the door released automatically, allowing Lindsay and her sons to walk in.

Like many other parents at New Egypt, Lindsay praised the feeling of security the technology gives her. She talked about how she hoped it would prevent another incident like the one at Columbine High School in Colorado. Never mind the fact that the killers in that terrible rampage were high school students who by definition have open access to the school campus.

"I'm hoping this thing proves itself," Lindsay said. "I'm thinking ten years down the road, when the price comes down, I'll get one for my home."

The project came at a good time for Iridian. Business had improved markedly after the terror attacks. The company had just had its best quarter of revenues ever. Lina Page, director of global marketing, was pleased with how things were going at the school. In her mind, parents like Lindsay understood what Iridian was all about. "There's always going to be a big trade-off between privacy, security, and convenience," Page said. "You have to volunteer to say, 'I want to give this up to preserve my security.'"

At Royal Palm in Arizona, the situation was similar. There was no obvious problem with crime, but a new government contractor called Hummingbird Defense System donated $350,000 worth of face recognition gear. Sheriff Joe Arpaio, who was beginning a local reelection campaign, endorsed it strongly. Arpaio liked to call himself America's toughest sheriff. He dressed prisoners in striped uniforms, worked them on chain gangs, and made them wear pink underwear. On his campaign Web site, he urged voters to support his "Get Tough" tactics. "Under my watch, prisoners are treated like criminals and not like guests at the country club," the sheriff pledged.

Arpaio brought that get-tough approach to the project. Just two cameras were linked to a database of abducted children supplied by the National Center for Missing and Exploited Children. It also had some images of their abductors, who often are parents involved in custody disputes. And the database contained pictures of Arizona sex offenders. Arpaio acknowledged the likelihood of snaring someone with two cameras was remote, but said the surveillance was still worth the effort. "If it works one time, locates one missing child or saves a child from a sexual attack," he said, "I feel it's worth it."

Both he and Hummingbird officials hope the project will be a model for a national network for schools—something that sounds a lot like Atick's vision for a Noble Shield.

ATICK WAS GETTING USED TO people thinking of him as an authority, someone whose thoughts on security and biometrics mattered. As a founding member of the International Biometrics Industry Association—and a NATO adviser and biometric expert who had testified several times before Congress—he was becoming a familiar figure of the industry. But demand for face recognition wasn't growing enough to suit his business goals, so he decided to branch out. In June 2002, he merged Visionics with a fingerprint specialty firm called Identix. The deal created one of the world's largest biometric firms.

Atick had gotten some fingerprint business through a far smaller merger a year before. Identix gave them a global reach. Now Atick's firm provided the wherewithal not only to scan faces but also to help record many millions of fingerprints. Customers included police in every state, federal immigration officials, and authorities in at least four other countries. Social services agents in some states used his machines to manage assistance payments and fight against identity fraud. More than a hundred airports employed them for background screening. By 2003, as many as 60,000 of the 100,000 fingerprints sent to the FBI each day were captured by Identix machines or analyzed by the company's BioEngine software. The company was also increasingly linking the fingerprints to demographic data.

In 2003, more hospitals, banks, and other organizations embraced fingerprints as a way to authenticate computer users and secure their networks. The company really did well when it secured a five-year "Blanket Purchase Agreement" from the Department of Homeland Security. Worth an estimated $27 million, it was one of the largest contracts of its kind ever issued. Atick was effusive. "We believe that this win has the potential to be a defining point for the biometrics industry and that it reaffirms Identix' leadership position," he stated in a press release.

The company still had not turned a profit. But there was more good news. Starting in January 2004, Identix would be providing the United Kingdom's passport service with both fingerprint and face scanning equipment. Just months before, a group called the International Civil Aviation Organization had issued a set of technical standards to guide how face recognition should be used around the world. The group is responsible for creating uniformity in the world aviation system so, for example, a ticket from one country can be read in another. By setting a standard, the aviation organization was giving its imprimatur to the technology. The UK program, a test pilot program that would run through much of 2004, conformed to the new standard. "What matters is that facial recognition has arrived," Atick said. "It's no longer a rogue technology."

In the first few days of January 2004, the U.S. government began one of the largest biometric deployments ever to screen foreign visitors at airports and seaports. Called U.S. Visit, the system relies on digital fingerprint and photograph devices to ensure that millions of passengers coming to the United States each year with visas are the same people who obtained travel documents at U.S. consulates overseas. In a trial run, authorities employed the system to catch several people with criminal records or using a phony ID.

Citizens of European countries didn't have to participate initially, since they don't have to use visas to enter the United States, but every traveler to the United States will eventually need to carry passports that contain a fingerprint, face print, or other biometric identifier—documents that can be read by a machine.

On June 1, the government granted the contract for a massive expansion of U.S. Visit to Accenture. The deal, worth up to $10 billion, will bring together an array of information and surveillance industry subcontractors.

Among the possible partners is Acxiom, which struck a deal in December 2003 to be Accenture's "customer analytic factory . . . to accelerate and enhance the core customer information processing." Seisint may also play a role. Accenture was an original investor in Seisint, and former Accenture executives work at Seisint or serve on its board.

In the coming years, Accenture will be helping to build sprawling computer networks and identity systems to enable the government to track foreign visitors to the United States. The company aims to create digital folders containing visitors' fingerprints, photographs, and details about their travels. The new systems will also rely on radio frequency identification and face recognition software. It is another ambitious surveillance initiative, and another sign of what is to come.

In promoting the program on television, Homeland Security Secretary Tom Ridge said there's no doubt where all this is headed: Before long, every country in the world will likely require similar digital documentation, leading to new efficiencies in the verification of identity. Ridge said the United States has no intention of tracking people once they enter the country. But when biometric systems become more widespread, that could always change. U.S. officials are already bracing themselves for new requirements in other countries that demand U.S. citizens do the same abroad.

In March 2004, Identix acquired another biometric, one that few people in the world had ever heard of: skin print. It's based on the insight that every patch of epidermis contains unique patterns established, as Atick puts it, in the womb. The technology can look at a digital photograph of, say, a square of skin under someone's eyes and enable computers to know, forever, it's theirs.

Atick claimed that tests showed the combination of face recognition and skin print identified people as clearly as a single fingerprint. His homeland security and intelligence contacts were equally enthusiastic. "This is, in my opinion, the missing piece," he said. "It can even tell twins apart." It was also a sign of things to come. Not only would more people have to share a biometric; they would have to share more than one with authorities who want to be doubly sure who they are.

ATICK STROLLED through the Hyatt Regency in Crystal City, Virginia, past booth after booth of high-technology surveillance gear. One small competitor displayed a three-dimensional face recognition system. Another demonstrated iris-scanning machines. A hand geometry company touted the efficiency of a system that clocked employees in and out of work. Everywhere Atick went, he was treated as a star.

When the Biometric Consortium Conference began in 1996, it had perhaps three tables in a seminar room. Less than a decade later, it was a full-blown trade show, with hall after hall filled with business executives, intelligence officials, police, and biometric products. Atick gets some portion of the credit for that growth. That's due in part to his salesmanship, and because he helped found an industry group called the International Biometrics Industry Association. The association's aim was to make biometrics acceptable enough to be profitable for all concerned.

It's not just the gear that makes the conference interesting. It's also the organizers, a little known government group called the Biometric Consortium. Behind the consortium is the secretive National Security Agency (NSA). Starting in 1992, the consortium began talking about ways to improve identification technology. Three years later, the group was officially sanctioned by the Clinton administration. Now the consortium is the government's main source of technical information about biometrics. That is to say, the nation's most powerful spy organization was working hard to nurture the biometrics industry, in part to develop identity technology and applications that may never become public.

Atick made his way to his own booth. It featured a cheery display with director's chairs, some fingerprint readers, and a small machine with a rubber handle that looked like a dustbuster vacuum cleaner. The device was dubbed IBIS, short for identification based information system. Atick, with obvious pride, called it "gangbuster." He held it against his torso, like an oversized handgun, and showed off its features. At the front was an opening for a finger. The opening was embedded with a small scanner that electronically captured "forensic quality" prints.

Above that was a lens about the size of a dime. It took digital photos. On the back, facing the machine's operator, was a screen about the size of a PalmPilot. Police can use IBIS to instantly transmit the information back to headquarters on a wireless network. The small screen displayed any information sent back with details about the person.

Now it wasn't just one biometric that would identify people. It was two. And the machine was as mobile as the police using it. An electronic checkpoint could be established wherever they wanted.

As Identix put it in financial documents submitted to regulators, "security and identity should never be limited to the requirements of a particular established location, situation or environment. Police officers in the field, agents securing borders and ports, and roaming security officers all have a critical need to be able to identify people in real-time at any location. Identix offers a patented mobile identification system, called Identification Based Information System."

"It's allowing law enforcement to improve efficiency," Atick said. "We have a solution to a problem that used to take three hours to solve and used to involve a traditional desktop."

Atick wanted to create vast wireless networks to enable authorities to use IBIS anywhere. Not surprisingly, the Justice Department is helping to pay for his vision. In June 2003, the National Institute of Justice granted Identix $3.2 million to help authorities adopt the machine. By the end of the year, police in Minnesota, California, and Oregon were using IBIS. The results? A few thousand searches, a few hundred detentions, and the identification of four suicide or murder victims.

Atick said any sense of intrusiveness at having to give a fingerprint and photo is offset by the improved ability to quickly authenticate people. As for the images and prints captured by the machines, he said they were routinely destroyed after a short time, at least according to police policy at the time.

Besides, Atick said, he would never do anything that would undermine the rights of individuals. Not with the portable IBIS machine. Not with FaceIt. Not with the many thousands of fingerprint readers popping up in unlikely places around the country. He said that's because he values autonomy and privacy as much as the next person. "For me, I believe one of the most precious liberties that attracted me to the United States was the idea that I could live a private life, be anonymous, be living without someone intercepting me at every checkpoint," he said.

But that principle runs hard up against Atick's fear of terrorism, his desire to help, and his responsibility to make profits.

"I think trying to make the world a little safer is something I value because I grew up in an unsafe world," he said. "I do believe as a human and a member of a civilization I think it is important to protect society, but to do it in a way that does not rob us of the most fundamental and most precious things we have, our freedom and our civil liberties. Those are important factors."

In other words, Atick said, he does not want to live in an Orwellian world.

7

TOTAL INFORMATION AWARENESS

———

THE INTELLIGENCE ANALYSTS would work in secret, staring at computer screens, watching the world. With a few keystrokes, their machines would summon the mundane stuff of life from around the globe. Travel records. Chemical purchases. Telephone calls and email. Medical reports and financial transfers. Voice prints and face prints and faint bits of intelligence. All this and much more would be swept up by a vast web of electronic sensors, sifted in colossal digital reservoirs.

Classified electronic tools would help them make music from the noise. One program would instantly interpret foreign languages. Others would endlessly examine the same data, searching for patterns and links that no unaided human ever could see. To debate the meaning of their insights, analysts anywhere might one day even be able to meet face-to-face in virtual rooms, using holographic stand-ins.

At the end of the day, this intricate and supremely sensitive network would differentiate groups of good people from those with ill intent. It would be the ultimate security tripwire, an ever vigilant system that would give those charged with keeping America safe a better chance at heading off terror attacks.

This was the vision known as Total Information Awareness.

When the project idea was first unveiled, in June 1999, by a Defense Department official at a technology conference, the audience listened politely. But few of them treated it as anything more than a curiosity. It was still two years before the September 11 attacks, and despite the many signs the threat was looming, no one at the time seemed much to care.

ON SEPTEMBER 11, 2001, traffic in the Washington, D.C., region was bad as usual. Former Vice Admiral John Poindexter was stopped in his car on Chain Bridge, crossing the Potomac River from Maryland to Virginia, when his mobile phone rang. It was his wife, Linda, calling from home. Do you have the radio on? she asked. Poindexter turned on the car radio, listened to the news, and sunk into himself a little. The World Trade Center was burning far above Manhattan and an airliner had just slammed into one side of the Pentagon.

Poindexter always knew something like this was going to happen. Since his days as national security adviser to President Ronald Reagan, the world had become a much less stable place. With the demise of the former Soviet Union, a power vacuum had been created, opening the way for the rise of lethal, ad hoc terror organizations. Unlike the cold war, when he and other national security officials knew their enemies well, the new era presented shadowy groups, whose members roamed undetected around the world.

He continued driving to his office in Arlington, Virginia, where he worked as a contractor for the Defense Advanced Research Projects Agency, or DARPA. As a trained scientist and former naval commander, Poindexter didn't dwell on his emotions that day. He thought about what he could do. One project stood out in his mind, a computer-assisted intelligence apparatus he had named "Genoa." He wondered whether it might have helped prevent the attacks. For five years he had plugged quietly away on Genoa, a mix of machines and procedures he believed would dramatically boost the ability of analysts to identify, assess, and resolve crises. The government had devoted some $40 million to the project. The work went to the heart of questions Poindexter had asked himself while serving in the Reagan White House. How can intelligence analysts better understand fast-moving events and prevent disabling attacks? And how can they collaborate, often over great distances, to come up with accurate and effective responses?

He was certain the answers lay with better data, faster communication networks, and computer programs that could help people think more clearly. The world's problems had become far too complex, the flow of intelligence too torrential, for human beings to handle without help from computers. His was a very American faith that technology can solve almost any problem, even the inherent fallibility of the human mind. Few people in the intelligence community seemed to share this faith. They were slow to adopt his suggestions from the Genoa project, and Poindexter was frustrated.

As he mulled it over on that awful day, he thought, "Maybe they'll be more receptive now."

THE NEXT MORNING, Poindexter called his old friend J. Brian Sharkey, the former deputy director of the Information Systems Office at DARPA. Sharkey had worked closely with Poindexter in recent years. He was the man who introduced Total Information Awareness in 1999 at a technology conference in Denver called DARPATech. Now he was vice president at the giant government contractor SAIC.

Parked on the side of a road off a suburban parkway in Maryland, Poindexter talked with Sharkey about technology, intelligence, and the national security lapses that preceded the attacks. They agreed that their research, particularly the Genoa technology, which enhanced collaboration among intelligence analysts, might have helped. But one new tool like Genoa wasn't enough. The terrorism threat was too big and too amorphous. The government needed a new technology framework, a revolutionary system like Total Information Awareness. It needed to collect information both from open sources, like the World Wide Web, and from government and private databases; to scan the data constantly for faint signs of terrorist activity; and to narrow the boundaries between people and machines. Automate surveillance, in other words, to the greatest degree possible.

The thought that their research might gain traction now was exciting to them. They really believed that it could work. At the same time, neither man appeared willing to return to government service. Sharkey didn't want to give up his SAIC salary or his stock holdings in the company. Poindexter had been forced out of the government a decade before because of his involvement in the Iran-Contra scandal and for misleading Congress about it. He knew he would be a lightning rod for political attacks if he took another government post. But they felt compelled to at least try to do something.

Several days later Sharkey called Dr. Anthony Tether, the DARPA director, and set up a meeting at a restaurant in Arlington called Gaffneys. Over dinner in a private room, Sharkey told Tether about the earlier plans for Total Information Awareness, how the program had not gotten traction since Sharkey left DARPA, not long after launching it. Sharkey said he thought the program had a place now. Tether agreed wholeheartedly.

More than two years after the fact, Sharkey said, "Tony tried to hire me that night. He said, 'This is great, we've got to do this, we've got to start an office. And I want you to lead it, and we've got to resurrect this thing.'"

"Tony, I've got a couple kids going into school and a lot of financial stuff started here and until the kids are through school I can't do this," Sharkey told him. "And he said, 'Don't worry about it, I can make it worth your while.'"

Tether's best offer still wasn't good enough for Sharkey. So they decided to go in another direction. Tether asked for recommendations. The one that stuck out was Poindexter. Sharkey and Poindexter talked about the possibility while sailing on Poindexter's sailboat. Before long, Tether met with Poindexter and liked the idea of hiring him, despite his notorious role in the Reagan White House. After a meeting with E. C. (Pete) Aldridge, Jr., undersecretary of defense for acquisition, technology, and logistics, Poindexter got the offer.

Everybody knew John Poindexter's involvement was incendiary. But Poindexter himself believed that an unorthodox global war was underway and, he said, he wanted to prevent another catastrophic attack. "I'm convinced," he said of September 11, 2001, "that that was just the opening round."

"I understood the technology, the intelligence problem, the decision-making process," he said. "I had a lot to offer to tie it all together."

It was the beginning of an ill-fated program that would become one of the most sweeping, controversial initiatives in the war on terror. It would also prove to be a sort of blueprint of where the country's security infrastructure was headed, with or without Poindexter.

AS HE BEGAN OUTLINING how he would run the new DARPA office, in the fall of 2001, Poindexter envisioned a crash development program as ambitious and urgent as anything the government had done before. Initially it was to be called the Manhattan Project II or MP2, after the secret effort during World War II to build the atomic bomb. Scores of leading scientists and intelligence specialists would work behind fences, sequestered in an old warehouse, for a common cause. It wouldn't be only a government project, or even a permanent part of the Defense Department. Joining in would be experts from the information industries and university campuses. Poindexter was swept away by the possibilities. Even two years later, he spoke more quickly and appeared more determined as he described his plan.

National security wasn't the only reason they wanted to move so quickly. They were already counting on a public battle because of Poindexter's involvement.

"That was in my calculation and I think it was in John's as well. We all kind of knew that it was a matter of time of John getting hit based on being put in that position," Sharkey said. "And we had a desire to move fast and I recall at one of the meetings he was describing what he wanted to do.

"And he made a comment which I will always remember. We were trying to sensitize him to some political issues that might be raised and I remember John saying, 'Damn it, I want to break some eggs.' And so I think at times John is kind of unaware or kind of not savvy that even when you are moving very fast you've got to consider all of the facts and you have to handle some of them at a slower more political pace. I think John has sometimes a blind spot to knowing that he can't break eggs as a way of building relationships and moving fast."

When Poindexter's Information Awareness Office opened for business in January 2002, the ambition of his research plans trumped them all. For months he had been busy talking to old friends in the military and government, mixing salesmanship with technical descriptions. His office wasn't going to work off in a corner. It would be a tactical research shop, sharing breakthroughs as soon as possible with military, intelligence, and law enforcement authorities. Its mission statement: "to integrate advanced technologies and accelerate their transition to operational users." Poindexter entered into negotiations with the FBI, to help improve their counterterrorism computers. Before long, working in secret, his staff was advising transportation officials on the merits of technology companies seeking to help build the passenger screening system program. Among its biggest partners was the U.S. Army Intelligence and Security Command, which had begun a program called the Information Dominance Center. (The Army has since changed the name to the blander Information Operations Center.)

The Information Awareness Office was actually a combination of a variety of different programs, some of them, like Genoa, already underway. It had a planned budget of some $200 million annually. Authorities already had access to a wealth of information about individual terrorists, but they typically had to obtain court approval in the United States or make laborious diplomatic and intelligence efforts overseas. Poindexter's tools would dramatically ease the way for sorting through "ultra-large" data warehouses and networked computers in search of threatening patterns among everyday transactions.

Poindexter envisioned his automated tools serving as digital cops in the virtual world. They would help analysts search randomly for indications of travel to risky areas, suspicious emails, odd fund transfers, and improbable medical activity, such as the treatment of anthrax sores. Poindexter once predicted his system eventually would provide a more detailed look at data than the supersecret National Security Agency. "The problem is much more complex, I believe, than we've faced before," he said several months after the Information Awareness Office opened. "It's how do we harness with technology the street smarts of people on the ground, on a global scale."

Much of the data would be collected through computer "appliances"—some mixture of hardware and software—that would, with permission of governments and businesses, enable intelligence agencies to routinely extract information. Those same theoretical appliances would somehow also protect innocent individuals, particularly American citizens, against unwarranted intrusions. (Advising Poindexter on the appliances, without charge, was Jeff Jonas, the computer entrepreneur who works closely with ChoicePoint and the intelligence community.)

At the outset, though, Poindexter's project and international counterterrorism effort didn't have the appliances to get going. It already had a lot of information to work with—"hundreds of millions of events every day," according to a Defense Department document. That included information about Americans collected domestically, something that's allowed as long as it falls within rules limiting the scope of counterintelligence activities. "Executive Order 12333, signed 4 December 1981 by President Ronald Reagan, gives the Intelligence Community its authority to collect foreign and domestic intelligence and counterintelligence information," a Defense Department document stated.

Few people know these rules. To those uninitiated in the ways and ambitions of the intelligence world—that is to say, most Americans—this was very spooky stuff. Poindexter was proposing tools that would give the U.S. government an unprecented look into the lives of individuals. Even those unfamiliar with J. Edgar Hoover's misdeeds and the nasty sweep of domestic surveillance three decades before would soon understand that Total Information Awareness might hold out new perils.

AS STRANGE AS THE PROJECT sounded, the reach of its research was routine at DARPA. Created in 1958 as the Advanced Research Projects Agency, DARPA had the mandate to ensure that U.S. military forces maintain technological superiority over the Soviets and other foes. To accomplish their mission, agency leaders focused on high-risk, high-payoff research, much of it costly and secret. The combined budget in its first four decades totaled some $50 billion. Probably the most prominent fruit of DARPA research is packet-switching technology. First developed for a nuclear bomb–proof data network for defense, it made the Internet possible. Agency-funded discoveries also led to the creation of the F-117 Stealth fighter, the B-2 Stealth bomber, wearable computers, and space-based surveillance. Some of DARPA's projects are very far out indeed, such as "speed-of-light weapons" research, based on lasers and particle beams. It also helped fuel development of face recognition. Giant technology companies such as Sun Microsystems and Cisco Systems have thrived on DARPA-funded discoveries.

By definition, Poindexter's office was almost entirely focused on information technology, a vast and expanding horizon that gave his plans extraordinary reach. Its stated aim was for nothing less than a "counterterrorism information architecture" that would be dependable and easy to use and ready to deploy by 2007. Poindexter had a metaphor he liked to use in describing his vision for Total Information Awareness. The ideal system would replicate the experience of walking into a room, where you saw a television, a bookshelf, chairs, and carpet. "You immediately recognize all that and it gives you context for the room you are in. But there also is a lot of other information in the room. If you get down on your hands and knees and look at the carpet, you can see fibers and the dust and you might see mites," Poindexter said, once using his own living room as an example. "There is a tremendous amount of information available in this room. And the level of detail that you might absorb depends on what you come into the room for. If you come in the room for a meeting, you aren't particularly interested in the fibers in the carpet. If you are trying to find a lost earring, then you get down to that greater level of detail." His technology, in other words, would approximate the experience of walking into the world in the search for terrorists.

As with other work at DARPA, the Total Information Awareness research was farmed out to private companies and universities. Among them were familiar names in the military and intelligence contracting world: Hicks & Associates Inc., a national security consultant; Booz Allen Hamilton Inc., a management and technology consultant; and Raytheon Corp., a technology company that would provide search and data-mining tools. Joining in were Lockheed Martin Corp. and CACI Dynamic Systems, as well as more than two dozen universities, including Cornell, Columbia, and the University of California at Berkeley. In November 2002, Poindexter estimated the program would receive up to $200 million a year.

In addition to Genoa, the earlier research that focused on collaborative technology, the information awareness efforts included a project called Genisys. It would develop what Poindexter called appliances that would let analysts and investigators get information without having to know where it's stored. (Genisys would also include technology, eventually, to *"provide security with privacy"* by prohibiting access to unauthorized information and enforcing laws and regulations.)

Another line of research was "Evidence Extraction and Link Discovery." It focused on computer programs that could find relationships "among people, organizations, places, and things." Researchers here weren't just trying to connect dots. They were trying to decide which dots were worth examining. The emphasis was on individuals, places, or groups that seemed to behave like terrorists, at least according to profiles the office planned to create. Poindexter's machines would learn "patterns to discriminate as accurately as possible between real concerns and apparently similar but actually legitimate activities."

A related effort was dubbed "Scalable Social Network Analysis." It sought to distinguish terrorist cells from legitimate groups of people, through a look at patterns of telephone calls, meetings, and financial transfers. Other programs aimed at combing real-world surveillance with pattern recognition machines. "Human Identification at a Distance (HumanID)," for instance, was based on the notion that cameras and other sensors, coupled with biometric identifiers, could "provide early warning support against terrorist, criminal, and other human-based threats." This would require more than just face prints. Poindexter wanted the computers to be able to know someone's identity, in the dark and all kinds of weather, by the way he or she walked. In that spirit, "Activity, Recognition and Monitoring" was a research program built around the idea that machines could watch, record, and learn how people behave. The ultimate result would be "human activity" models that would help computers linked to cameras, low-power radar, and radio frequency tags, like those used for electronic tolls, discern whether an individual or groups were acting suspiciously.

"The counterterrorism problem is characterized by new challenges for intelligence analysts, operators, and policy makers," Poindexter wrote in a report to Congress in May 2003. "More than ever before, attempts to 'connect the dots' quickly overwhelm unassisted human abilities.

"By augmenting human performance using these computer tools," Poindexter wrote, "the TIA Program expects to diminish the amount of time humans must spend in discovering information and allow humans more time to focus their powerful intellects on things humans do best—thinking and analysis."

Poindexter clearly saw men and machines along the same continuum for the problem he was trying to solve, an engineering approach that undoubtedly gave him the best chance of success in creating Total Information Awareness. But it also doomed the project. Though he acknowledged squishier human concerns like the impact on privacy and civil liberties from the very beginning, in his intense engineering focus he never realized just how incendiary they would be.

JOHN MARLAN POINDEXTER comes across as a reserved man, a mix of engineering professor and battleship commander, a technocrat who has strong feelings but isn't always comfortable talking about them, or even acknowledging they exist. He is about 6 feet tall and slightly stooped, balding, with close-cropped gray hair on the sides and a bristly white mustache. His eyes seemed small for his face and a little sad at the corners, softer than when he last served the government more than a decade ago. Like much of official Washington, he often wears dark blue or gray suits. His dress shirts are habitually secured around his wrists by cufflinks bearing the White House emblem, a none-too-subtle reminder of the peak moments of his career. He often has a pipe in his hand.

Poindexter was born in August 1936, the son of a small-town banker in Indiana who had never graduated from college. From the beginning he was an impressive, focused, and driven kid. Though he was not an athletic sort—his nickname as a teenager was "Brain"—he won the affections of his classmates. In high school, they once elected him King of the Fall Festival. As a Boy Scout, he didn't just go on camping trips and accumulate achievement badges, like most other boys. He also secured a place in the exclusive Order of the Arrow, an elite group that focused on self-reliance and integrity. His mother marveled at her oldest child. "John was never a little boy," she once remarked. "He was born an old man."

Poindexter left the Hoosier State for the Naval Academy in 1954. He graduated, four years later, with an engineering degree, first in his class. In *The Nightingale's Song*, an illuminating study of the academy and five prominent graduates, Robert Timberg described Poindexter as a student who never seemed to have to work as hard as his classmates. Even as a plebe, Poindexter seemed to take less heat from upperclassmen than his peers.

In the résumé Poindexter posted on the DARPA Web site, he listed "goal oriented" as a defining personal characteristic. Under the heading "Experience Summary," he says: "Noted for creative solutions to difficult issues and ability to quickly grasp the essence of new tasks."

Poindexter suggested he liked to think of himself as an individualist, someone who will go his own way when need be and thumb his nose at authority. When he converted to Catholicism in August 2001 (his wife, a former Episcopal minister, converted three years before), he chose Sir Thomas More as his patron saint. That was in large part because More defied the religious edicts of Henry VIII, costing him his life. "The easier thing to do would have been to do what King Henry wanted," Poindexter said.

The reality is that Poindexter readily followed orders throughout his career and rarely had to go his own way. He was almost always successful, if not first in line, at whatever he did. "Bucking the system was not his style," as Timberg put it in The Nightingale's Song, adding: "Poindexter was comfortable with the system from the start."

Toward the end of his days at the academy, the Navy had begun a new scholarship program to encourage the deep study of science. Called the Burke Scholar program, it was started after the Soviets launched the Sputnik satellite. American officials feared they had fallen behind the technology of their enemies. Poindexter applied and, to no one's surprise, secured one of the slots.

He decided to attend the California Institute of Technology. Though he would have to take additional math courses to qualify for the Ph.D. program, he would be accepted. He got his master's in physics in 1961 and his Ph.D. three years later. Among the people he studied under was Rudolph Mössbauer, who won the 1961 Nobel Prize in Physics. On the panel that reviewed his doctoral thesis was Richard Feynman, the great physicist who would win the Nobel in 1965. Mössbauer later recalled that Poindexter—who had done an enormous amount of detailed calculation for him—"was the most orderly person I had in my Caltech experience."

• • •

ON MARCH 30, 1981, President Reagan was shot at close range while leaving the Washington Hilton Hotel. The president, who had just given a speech to union officials, was rushed to George Washington University hospital with wounds to his chest. He quickly recovered and returned to the White House, the gunman sent to an asylum.

But the episode had rattled his staff. Though there was no interruption in the chain of command or government operations, behind the scenes they questioned whether the White House Situation Room operated as well as it should have in the crisis. Later that spring, Poindexter received a call from the office of Richard V. Allen, then the president's national security adviser. Would Poindexter be interested in serving as a military aide in the White House and reviewing the Situation Room?

For years, Poindexter had been preparing for a question like that. His career since the Caltech days had been every bit as stellar as before. He had served on numerous ships at various times as executive officer, chief engineer, and commander of a destroyer squadron. Along the way, he had pioneered the use of computers to manage ship overhauls. On land, between oceangoing assignments, he had served as executive assistant to the chief of Naval Operations and administrative assistant in the office of the secretary of the Navy. In short, it was an extraordinary run.

In June 1981, having accepted the offer from Allen, he was off and running in the White House. In his study of the Situation Room, Poindexter concluded that the White House technology was way out of date. Even then, he fretted that policymakers needed "technology to help manage the complex world we live in today." "The most sophisticated piece of information technology hardware at the time was a typewriter," he would say later.

His solution took full advantage of cutting-edge technology. By 1984, he had harnessed computers, networks, and a video teleconferencing system for a $14 million crisis management center. He also introduced something to the White House that in two decades' time would become ubiquitous in America: email. He had seen how much time national security staffers wasted on telephone tag with one another. So he turned to IBM, which installed a prototype network linked to a mainframe computer called Professional Office System, also known as PROFS. "The advantage was you can handle the communications on your schedule. You don't have to be there when they want to talk to you. This meant that the whole process of interoffice and intraoffice communications was greatly enhanced," he said later. "We later moved to personal computers and we were then some of the first to use laptops."

The irony is that PROFS also kept track of everything, even notes they thought they had deleted. That was something Poindexter and a young lieutenant colonel named Oliver North would discover to their dismay a few years later, when a special commission began investigating the scandal known as the Iran-Contra affair.

ON NOVEMBER 25, 1986, Attorney General Edwin Meese spoke at an ad hoc press conference to announce that as much as $30 million raised through covert arms sales to Iran was being diverted, by National Security Council staff, to Nicaraguan Contra rebels.

A cargo plane had been shot down in Nicaragua the month before. The rebels had paraded a survivor, Eugene Hasenfus, before television cameras, where he described his links to the White House. Unpublicized at the time was a note from a CIA operative in the region. "Situation requires we do necessary damage control," said the note. A few weeks later, a Lebanese newspaper described how national security adviser Robert McFarlane and Oliver North secretly traveled to Iran to arrange arms sales. Both deals ran counter to promises President Reagan had made. In particular, he had pledged an arms embargo for Iran because of its support of terrorists. They also appeared to violate the Boland Amendment, in which Congress specifically said it did not want intelligence agencies sending money to anti-Communist rebels in Nicaragua known as the Contras.

It was a scandal that embroiled some of the highest figures in the government and ended Poindexter's career in the White House. Poindexter had been named national security adviser by Reagan the year before, replacing a worn-out Robert McFarlane, who had recommended him for the post. Since then, he had been directly involved in the concurrent efforts: One was to bolster the rebels against a well-funded Sandinista army, which received support from the Soviet Union. The other was to free hostages in Lebanon, whom authorities assumed were being held by terrorists managed or controlled by Iran. Both efforts were managed by North, a brash former field commander who served on the NSC staff. Poindexter was directly involved in both initiatives, and communicated routinely with North, who frequently traveled to Central America to meet with rebel leaders.

Shortly after Meese's speech, Poindexter resigned. During congressional hearings about the scandal, Poindexter told questioners 184 times he didn't remember details about his participation in the events. In their book about the scandal—*Men of Zeal: A Candid Inside Story of the Iran-Contra Hearings* (1988)—Senators William S. Cohen and George J. Mitchell employed a surprising phrase to describe what they heard. "There was an Orwellian quality to Poindexter's testimony."

On March 16, 1988, Poindexter was indicted on criminal charges alleging conspiracy, obstruction of justice, and lying to Congress. A jury in the District of Columbia found him guilty and sentenced him to six months in prison. He appealed, saying that Congress had granted him "use immunity" for testifying during its earlier hearings. In November 1991, a federal appeals court overturned the conviction. He dodged another effort to put him away the following year, when the Supreme Court declined a request by the special prosecutor to reconsider the conviction.

Years later, Poindexter remained bitter about the long episode. The jury that convicted him did not understand the laws, he said. Fueling his anger was the fact that civil libertarians still treated him like a felon. "That's what ticks me off. The civil libertarians—of all segments of our society—need to understand the legal system has many phases and the end result is what's important."

ON NOVEMBER 14, 2002, Poindexter's past caught up with him. *New York Times* columnist William Safire excoriated Poindexter, all but calling him a liar and saying he could not be trusted with Total Information Awareness. Just days before, stories had appeared in the *Times* and the *Washington Post*, spelling out the program. Safire's piece, which ran in

more than six hundred papers in the United States and around the
world, was a clarion call, a warning that American's privacy was threatened. It was headlined: YOU ARE A SUSPECT.

"This is not some far-out Orwellian scenario. It is what will happen
to your personal freedom in the next few weeks if John Poindexter gets
the unprecedented power he seeks," Safire declared. He added: "This
ring-knocking master of deceit is back again with a plan even more
scandalous than Iran-Contra."

Safire's column was like a blowtorch on dry tinder. The questions
about Poindexter's program seemed terrifying to many people. Even
under the most controlled of circumstances, its very possibility seemed
to threaten what Supreme Court Justice Louis Brandeis once famously
referred to as "the right to be let alone." Given the secrecy of the national security community, how were we ever going to make sure Total
Information Awareness wasn't being misused? Senator Frank Church
had made a prophetic warning about this years before when, after
studying the domestic surveillance abuses in the late 1960s and early
1970s, he said: "In the need to develop a capacity to know what potential enemies are doing, the United States government has perfected a
technological capability that enables us to monitor the messages that go
through the air."

Poindexter became the political target of the season, his program
serving as a stand-in for all the fears associated with the USA Patriot
Act and government surveillance in general. Paul Werbos, a computing
and artificial intelligence specialist at the National Science Foundation,
doubted whether the information awareness "appliances" could be calibrated to adequately filter out details about innocent people that
should not be in the hands of the government. "By definition, they're
going to send highly sensitive, private personal data," Werbos said at
the time. "How many innocent people are going to get falsely pinged?
How many terrorists are going to slip through?"

Former Senator Gary Hart of Colorado, then a member of the U.S.
Commission on National Security/21st Century, was blunter. While
there was no question about the need to use data more effectively, he
described Poindexter's program as an overkill of intelligence that would
waste huge sums of money. "There's an Orwellian concept if I've ever
heard one," Hart said.

To be sure, some of the criticism was opportunistic. Many people believed that John Poindexter needed a good political thrashing for daring to go back into government. Among those jostling to be first in line were lawmakers on Capitol Hill.

A FEW DAYS AFTER the Safire column, civil liberties activists from across the political spectrum went on the offensive. In a brief and tart letter to Senator Tom Daschle, the senior Democrat, and Senator Trent Lott of the GOP, they called on Congress to halt Poindexter's project. "There are no systems of oversight or accountability contemplated in the TIA project. DARPA itself has resisted lawful requests for information about the program pursuant to the Freedom of Information Act," they wrote. "We urge you to act immediately to stop the development of this unconstitutional system of public surveillance." Signing the letter were activists from watchdog groups such as the Electronic Privacy Information Center, the Free Congress Foundation, the Federation of American Scientists, the Eagle Forum, and others.

Then came the lawmakers, who voiced their own concerns. Senator Chuck Grassley of Iowa, a Republican who was assuming chairmanship of the Finance Committee, wrote to the Pentagon's inspector general, asking for a complete review of Total Information Awareness. Grassley said he was worried about the impact on privacy, but he appeared confused about what was actually going on. He questioned, for example, why the FBI and the Justice Department were not involved. "I am at a loss to understand why DoD resources are being spent on research for domestic law enforcement," he wrote. "In addition, to develop such a program in a vacuum from federal law enforcement seems to be asking for taxpayer dollars to be sent down the drain."

The momentum against Poindexter's program seemed almost inexorable from then on. Senator Ron Wyden of Oregon was especially aggressive. Like Safire before him, Wyden seized on the seal that Poindexter and his colleagues chose to represent their program. It was a pyramid, topped by an all-seeing eye, scanning the world. A vivid, spooky image. (It was also an inside pun that echoed the Information Awareness Office name: The eye represented the I of Information, the pyramid the A of Awareness, and the round earth was an analog for the

O in Office.) Beneath that emblem was the office's Latin motto: *Scientia Est Potentia* or "Knowledge Is Power." It was about as foolish a combination of images and words as could be devised, given the sensitivity of the endeavor, an emblem so over the top it practically begged for questions, or even caricature.

Standing on the floor of the Senate on January 15, 2003, Wyden warned that Total Information Awareness could create "virtual blood hounds" that could easily undermine the privacy of all Americans. "It is time for the Senate to put some reins on this," he intoned. "Clearly, to fight terrorism, we have to have the confidence of the American people that in doing so we are protecting their rights. My concern is the office of Total Information Awareness, as it is constituted today, tips that balances, tips that balance against the procedural safeguards that are needed to protect the rights of millions of Americans."

The next day, Wyden and Wisconsin senator Russ Feingold, the only senator to vote against the Patriot Act, announced legislation to stop funding Poindexter—at least until Congress could investigate. The Senate passed the law one week later. In February, Wyden and his colleagues approved another law that limited funding for the DARPA project, some $54 million in the president's budget for 2004, until Poindexter and his colleagues issued a detailed report about the program. Poindexter had just ninety days to get it together.

POINDEXTER DELIVERED the report, a detailed summation of the program's aims and efforts. It was consistent with what he had been saying all along. But it didn't help. His critics, Wyden included, wanted to kill it outright. They delivered a fatal blow on July 28. In a hastily arranged press conference, Wyden and Senator Byron Dorgan of North Dakota took aim at one of the smaller programs in the Information Awareness Office called the Futures Markets Applied to Prediction, or FutureMAP.

It was a strange program, but it was rooted in some core economic theory. It sought to use stock market–style techniques to help anticipate what was in store in the future. It hinged on the idea that markets often predicted the future price of livestock, oil, elections, and a range of commodities.

One example cited by Wyden and Dorgan as the sort of question the system might examine was: "Will terrorists attack Israel with bioweapons in the next year?" They described it as a bizarre scheme to allow "traders" to bet on terrorism. And they complained the program was an appalling waste of money. At the time of the press conference, DARPA had spent $600,000 on the program. The agency was seeking $8 million more in funding for the following two years. "I mean, the idea of a federal betting parlor on atrocities and terrorism is ridiculous and it's grotesque," Wyden said. "It's a bizarre plan that we are describing today, and it is one that fritters away hard-earned dollars of our taxpayers, and it needs to be stopped immediately."

It was another public relations blunder. The next day, the Defense Department announced it was shutting down what Wyden called the "terror market." "Today's cancellation of the terror market should be another step toward shutting down the entire TIA program," Wyden said. "With data-mining, gait-mapping and now with terror betting, TIA has consistently crossed the line on Americans' privacy, civil liberties, and good sense, and it's time to end it once and for all."

POINDEXTER TOLD DARPA director Tony Tether he was resigning, effective August 29. On September 24, 2003, House and Senate leaders agreed to eliminate Total Information Awareness, now called Terrorism Information Awareness. "In the highly-charged political environment of Washington, positions on highly complex issues are taken and debated using glib phrases, 'sound bites' and symbols," Poindexter wrote to Tether in his resignation letter.

In that letter, which he uncharacteristically made available to the press, Poindexter reminded people that he remained adamant that the threats were real, and his solutions sensible. "The United States and free-world continue to face an enormous threat to our freedom and way of life by those who choose to use terrorism to destroy what we cherish," he wrote.

"It is my sincerest hope that our country's children and grandchildren can understand that, in my opinion, the complex issues facing this nation today may not be solved using historical solutions and rhetoric that has been applied in the past, and that it may be useful to explore complex solutions that sometimes involve controversial technical concepts in order to rediscover the privacy foundations of this nation's strength and the basis for its freedoms."

POINDEXTER'S PROGRAM, which had quickly become a touchstone for worries about the impact of the war on terror, was suddenly ended. But even as Poindexter was stepping back into private life, other branches of the government were already engaged in projects that closely echoed the spirit, if not the particulars, of his initiatives.

Everywhere you looked, government officials were scrambling for ways to know more about people, identify the patterns of their behavior, even predict what they were likely to do through the use of computer profiles. The efforts frequently had a science fiction feel to them. And almost invariably they involved private contractors, some of them seeking to cash in on this new security-industrial partnership.

After winning the battle over the Patriot Act, for instance, the Justice Department increased its spending on state and local initiatives that embraced new technology. That included millions of dollars for Seisint's Matrix system and millions more for biometric programs, like the one in Plumsted, New Jersey, involving Iridian, the iris-scanning specialist.

Officials in the FBI at first swept up data from across the country, and not only from ChoicePoint, Seisint, LexisNexis, Acxiom, and the other information services. Sometimes with subpoenas, sometimes without, they also received records from airlines, Internet service providers, credit reporting agencies, libraries, banks, apartment complexes, even grocery stores. More far-reaching, though, was the FBI's own crash program to build a centralized information system, initially called the Data Intel Mart. It was a data-mining operation that would combine criminal, intelligence, and commercial records. It also would give agents and analysts a wide array of commercial software programs for automatically linking people and events together.

The CIA began a data-mining program called Quantum Leap. One official, in an unguarded moment, told a writer at *Fortune* magazine it was "so powerful it's scary." There also was the development of the CAPPS II program to screen air travelers, the largest domestic surveillance program ever seriously contemplated.

At the new Department of Homeland Security, the idea was to spin out new technology and surveillance networks as fast as possible. One division started work on a computer network that would rely on data to assess identities at border crossings. "The resulting system will identify individuals who have already entered our country, either legally or not, and who engage in hostile behavior after crossing the border. The system will particularly focus on individuals who attempt to change their identity or borrow someone else's identity," according to an information sheet provided by the Department of Homeland Security. "Plans are already underway to share information among Mexican and U.S. border states in order to catch persons with hostile intentions attempting to cross the border."

Another division, fashioned on the DARPA model, was called Homeland Security Advanced Research Projects Agency. It began making plans in the spring of 2004 for automated surveillance and intelligence initiatives that would help authorities identify suicide bombers before they attack. The new agency, which began operation in the fall of 2003, was preparing what it called a "scene awareness" project. The aim was to use computers and cameras to assess risks in crowds.

There was a program funded initially by the Defense Intelligence Agency—then absorbed by Homeland Security—called Joint Regional Information Exchange System. It relied on technology originally studied by the Information Awareness Office to link police intelligence units across the county.

Much of the technology and information these other operations turn up will inevitably move toward the new terrorist screening center, known as the Terrorist Threat Integration Center. Started on September 16, 2003, at the direction of President Bush, the screening center is operated jointly by Homeland Security, the Justice Department, and the CIA. Among other things, it is obligated to "maintain a consolidated terrorist screening database that is continuously updated." The database includes "all information the U.S. government possesses to [sic] the identities of individuals known or appropriately suspected to be or have been involved in activities constituting, in preparation for, in aid of, or related to terrorism."

In addition, the Information Awareness Office linked systems with the officials involved in counterintelligence field activity and the Joint

Intelligence Task Force at the Department of Justice. They also worked closely with the Joint Forces Command at the Defense Department.

When it killed Total Information Awareness, Congress allowed some of the programs to continue, but only under the auspices of the intelligence community. The details are now classified.

None of these programs rivals the scope of Total Information Awareness. But they are continuing to strive in that general direction, using the same technologies and concepts. J. Bryan Sharkey, the man who introduced Total Information Awareness in 1999, said government interest in the program's research actually broadened after it was apparently killed by Congress.

"We've briefed all of the intelligence organizations about what we call the major technical threads for approaching these big problems," said Sharkey. "All of these organizations and agencies that have similar problems have not conceptualized approaching it that way. But they all want to now. And so we are finding ourselves being thought of as a good model. Not just TIA, the model of collecting information and trying to root out early warning good guys. But the higher level conceptual stuff, the technical approach being used to define the methodology and apply algorithms in a systemic approach. It is now being looked at seriously as a model for how to solve the problems that every law enforcement agency has.

"I brief all of these organizations about what we are doing," he continued. "And even more so now because the big problem in the last year has been that most of these intelligence organizations, although they were connected, were reluctant to participate because of the Poindexter factor. And because it was getting such media attention. They didn't want to touch this thing. They all liked it and thought it was great but they didn't want to touch it.

"Now there is a keen interest in what was done and what was the value, so now I am briefing folks who are interested in absorbing some of these thoughts and technical processes into their programs."

SOME FAR-REACHING RESEARCH also came from the National Security Agency, which had discreetly expressed great interest in many of Poindexter's programs. Many people have heard about the agency, but few understand its size or power. It began operation in May 1949, when the Defense Department established the Armed Forces Security Agency to pursue electronic, or signals, intelligence. Three years later, it took on its current name and much more authority. More than a half century later, "Crypto City," as some people call it, has become the largest and most secretive intelligence operation in U.S. history.

In *Body of Secrets*, one of the few books to offer an inside look at the agency's operation, James Bamford describes it as "an odd and mysterious place, where even the priests and ministers have security clearances far above Top Secret, and religious services are held in unbuggable rooms." It sucks up electronic communication—signals intelligence—from around the world and then works to make sense of it all. "Crypto City is home to the largest collection of hyperpowerful computers, advanced mathematicians, and language experts on the planet," Bamford wrote. "Within the fence, time is measured by the femtosecond—one million billionth of a second—and scientists work in secret to develop computers capable of performing more than one septillion (1,000,000,000,000,000,000,000,000) operations every second."

All that was not enough after the terror attacks. The agency put out word, through its office of Advanced Research Development Activity (ARDA), that it was embarking on a new line of research. No one outside the National Security Agency and perhaps some members of Congress knows for sure how many projects the agency has underway. The several that have become public seem to focus on finding microscopic electronic needles in mountains of digital hay. One of them is known as the Information Exploitation initiative. If successful, the research will yield even faster networks and computers that can extract, synthesize, and display intelligence "from vast repositories of raw and structured data" in "all the human languages." That data might include telephone calls, email, credit card purchases, television video, photographs, even the images transmitted by mobile phones. The list could go on for pages. "ARDA's Information Exploitation programs are attempting to significantly advance the state of the art in some of these areas with the expectation that advanced analytic tools will emerge," an ARDA document said.

More ambitious yet was the program descriptively named "Novel Intelligence from Massive Data" (NIMD). Here the intelligence commu-

nity was looking for ways to squeeze more meaningful information—
"actionable information"—out of the same sea of details. It proposed
that analysts would have to routinely sift through *petabytes* of information—the equivalent of Acxiom's entire data system. That's because
some "intelligence data sources grow at the rate of four petabytes per
month," a rate that continues to accelerate. "Thus, NIMD is about
human interaction with information in a way that permits intelligence analysts to spot the telltale signs of strategic surprise in massive data
sources—building tools that capitalize on human strengths and com-
pensate for human weaknesses to enhance and extend analytic capabilities," an ARDA document said.

The NSA declines to provide more detail about its projects.

ON MARCH 1, 2004, a group convened by Defense Secretary Donald
Rumsfeld to examine Poindexter's information awareness project delivered its assessment. "TIA was a flawed effort to achieve worthwhile
ends," concluded the group, known as the Technology and Privacy Advisory Committee. "It was flawed by its perceived insensitivity to critical privacy issues, the manner in which it was presented to the public,
and the lack of clarity and consistency with which it was described.
DARPA stumbled badly in its handling of TIA, for which the agency has
paid a significant price in terms of credibility in Congress and with the
public."

The report did not confine its analysis to the newly named Terrorism
Information Awareness program. It offered a sweeping, sometimes
chilling look at data mining by the government in general, citing CAPPS
II, FinCEN, Matrix, and efforts by the Department of Homeland Security. It called for "clear rules and policy guidance, adopted through an
open and credible political process."

"The stakes could not be higher," the report stated. "Those laws and
standards are also necessary to protect informational privacy, which is
both important in its own right and is often critical to a range of fundamental civil liberties, including our rights to speak, protest, associate,
worship, and participate in the political process free from government
intrusion or intimidation."

• • •

JOHN POINDEXTER KNEW all about the other initiatives. After his resignation, he hinted with some satisfaction there were others deeply buried in the Defense appropriations bills. Poindexter professed to be over the contretemps about his effort. He had started another company, JMP Consulting, and he maintained close ties to the intelligence and technology worlds.

"One of the remarkable things about ideas is that once you surface an idea and it is a good idea, in the long term there is very little that can be done to stop it," Poindexter said confidently. "So I am convinced that research and development will continue, one way or another."

It seems that history is already proving him right.

8

THE GOVERNMENT'S
EYES AND EARS

DEPUTY TRANSPORTATION SECRETARY MICHAEL JACKSON walked into the Delta Airlines headquarters in Atlanta, prepared for a meeting he figured would be part business, part courtesy call. In December 2001 the aviation industry was still reeling from the terrorist attacks. Business was abysmal. Many people still feared flying.

Jackson figured they'd be talking about vital but unglamorous matters such as security and aviation economics. Instead, Delta chief executive Leo Mullin and his senior staff were about to make him a data believer.

They gathered in the Harvard Room, a plush space not far from Mullin's office. Framed flight schedules from the middle of the last century adorned the walls, and large windows looked out on the Delta campus. The group settled onto leather chairs, around a large cherry-wood conference table. They began working their way through a checklist of industry issues.

Jackson didn't have much time for this meeting. He was in the process of creating a huge new agency, the Transportation Security Administration (TSA), and he couldn't get it up and running fast enough.

Part of that responsibility was the creation of an electronic screening system that would somehow detect terrorists before they attacked. Congress had made it a mandate that fall. Nothing like it had ever been tried on the scale he was contemplating. "I'm looking at my watch," he said, "and thinking, 'I've got to catch a plane.'"

That's when one of Mullin's staff offered to show Jackson something the airline thought might prove important. Seisint, the Florida data service, had approached Delta with an extraordinary offer. Seisint could run names through data systems containing some 20 billion records, a virtual landscape of information about Americans. Using supercomputers, electronic profiles, and classified data provided by the law enforcement officials in Florida, the Boca Raton–based company promised it could pinpoint terrorists and identify their stealthy allies in America.

A Delta aide dialed up the company on the telephone and then established a computer link. A voice from a speaker at the center of the group asked somebody for a name and Social Security number. Others in the room, who had been through the demonstration before, kept mum. It was Jackson who piped up with personal details.

A moment later, much of his life flashed before him. On the projection screen, in the terse summation of data brokers, unscrolled details about everywhere he had lived as an adult, the dates he had moved, the cars he owned. The list showed his marital status, the name of his wife and information about her family. There was even a link to his credit history. What's more, they showed how the computer system could examine huge numbers of passenger records for signs the people were rooted in their communities, a telltale signal of whether they posed a threat. In the demonstration that day anyway, the known terrorists ended up near the top of the list of questionable passengers. To industry insiders, it was a swift and familiar display of data prowess. To Jackson, it was a revelation. He later recalled that the presentation was as good a sales job as he had ever witnessed. On the plane back to Washington, he went through the demonstration over and over in his head. He compared notes with a colleague who also had witnessed it. Together they marveled at the lightning speed of the computers, their amazing ability to create instant profiles and then find individuals who fit them. Both men recoiled at the potential intrusiveness of the system. They even looked at each other at one point and used a well-worn but still spooky phrase, "Big Brother." But they agreed, something like it was destined to become the anchor to aviation security in America.

"Wow," Jackson told his colleague. "We just saw the future."

JACKSON, A FORMER philosophy professor and Lockheed Martin executive, won a reputation in Washington as part entrepreneur, part management whiz. He turned tasks into missions and found people to work for him who made his causes their own. He was a sharp-looking bureaucrat, favoring crisp shirts and tailored suits. He had longish graying hair, a neatly trimmed mustache, and rimless eyeglasses.

The day after his trip to Delta's Atlanta headquarters, Jackson resolved to tap the power of computer technology to find terrorists who might be planning a repeat attack. "It was a turning point, where we made the connection," Jackson said. "Literally the next day I started trying to task people."

He knew it would not be an easy job, and not just because of the technological hurdles. Judging from his own reaction to the demonstration at Delta, there'd be resistance to any surveillance proposal. Privacy was going to be a big deal. Jackson would have to draw on his experience both in Washington and at Lockheed. In the late 1980s and early 1990s, he had served at the White House and as chief of staff to the transportation secretary. Then, during the Clinton years, he worked as chief operating officer for a Lockheed Martin subsidiary called IMS, running an operation that focused on improving transportation efficiencies.

Both experiences altered his view of the world. The earlier government posts gave Jackson an appreciation for the art and challenges of getting the vast Washington bureaucracies to move. At Lockheed, he was immersed in the details and practical policy of using tracking technology to improve transportation. One project was the installation of electronic toll booths in New York, now known as E-ZPass. Another, more complicated effort involved the use of monitoring transponders in trucks, equipment that could be read from roadside monitors. The idea was to automate the process of weighing trucks, to ensure they complied with state and local laws and to increase operating efficiency.

Unlike many bureaucrats, Jackson felt easy around computers and with technology in general. In the early 1970s, he had worked his way through the University of Houston as an undergrad by operating old

IBM mainframes. The trucking project had posed a new, almost psychological challenge. From the moment truckers heard about it, they assumed the worst, fearing the states would use the systems to track their every move. Some worried the system would be used to catch them for speeding or check their routes. "The truckers were extraordinarily skeptical about the government owning that data," Jackson said. "I thought it was a valid concern."

The project brought into focus just how incendiary the issue could be. The question he faced in trying to get support from truckers had been simple: How could he win their trust that the information would not be misused? After much thought—and many talks with union leaders and others—the answer seemed equally simple. He had to make clear-cut promises that data collected for one purpose would not be used for another. "'What all men believe to be true is true,'" Jackson paraphrased one of the philosophers he had taught over the years. "At some point, you have to deal with that," he said. "What you have to do is build a system to address that worry and prove to them you can and won't abuse the information."

The solution had been to create a nonprofit organization that would collect and manage the trucker data. To operate the system in real time, information would be shared with state officials; then it would be destroyed, and in short order. Before long, the process of weighing trucks across much of the nation improved markedly. "The cops loved it and the truckers loved it," he said, adding, "People couldn't go dipping in the data."

That set an important precedent for Jackson. After September 11, he embraced the idea of using computers and massive amounts of data to screen people for threats. He also knew the resulting system had to be used narrowly, otherwise the country could explode in a fury of resentment and mistrust. Jackson wanted to be the man remembered for protecting Americans' privacy even while fulfilling his mission to make the country safer. "We're not looking for deadbeat dads and people with parking tickets. We're looking for terrorists who want to get on airplanes.

"We're telling our law enforcement colleagues, 'This is not a universal law enforcement tool.'"

• • •

THE AVIATION SECURITY SYSTEM Jackson and his colleagues set out to fix was profoundly troubled. The U.S. aviation network is by far the most complex, the busiest, and the most difficult to secure in the world. Every day, aircraft take off and land some 200,000 times in the United States. Every year, they carry almost 700 million passengers. The airlines knew only in the most general terms who they were carrying.

Government security experts had long pushed for more intensive screening of passengers. The airlines, worried about costs, pushed back. They argued, through industry lobbyists, that they could take care of the problem themselves, that it was in their interest to avoid a catastrophic attack. It may not be a coincidence that Congress went along with that line of reasoning. In the decade between 1987 and 1996, at a time of growing anxiety about security, the airline industry gave some $7.5 million and free tickets to members of Congress, according to the Center for Public Integrity.

Government watchdogs concluded during this time that the U.S. aviation system had one of the least stringent screening programs in the developed world. For years airline screeners allowed people carrying phony credentials through checkpoints, sometimes without even looking closely at the documents. One group of undercover investigators, using simple ruses and bogus identity cards, managed to gain access to planes at eight airports two out of three times during probes in 1998 and 1999. They boarded aircraft more than a hundred times.

The screeners also were not very adept at finding the objects they were hired to snare, and they seemed to be getting worse at it over time. In the late 1970s, guns, knives, and other weapons inside luggage slipped through in about one out of eight tests. By the late eighties, that figure rose to about one in five times. Authorities refused to provide the precise failure rates through the nineties, saying they now consider it security-sensitive. But reports from the General Accounting Office and inspectors general assert the rate continued to worsen sharply until shortly before the attacks. At some airports it would be impossible to find, at the busy Christmas travel season, the same people who were there screening passengers the previous New Year's. A 100 percent turnover rate was commonplace. At one airport, fewer than 150 of nearly 1,000 screeners remained after one year. A big part of the problem was the pay. On average, they received about $6 per hour, less than many workers receive at Starbucks coffeeshops. They rarely had decent benefits, and the job was exceptionally boring, about like flipping burgers or sweeping floors at a fast-food restaurant, an industry that also suffers from high turnover. The fast-food workers at airports actually earned more on the whole than the screeners who bought their burgers and fries for lunch.

At one time, the Federal Aviation Administration (FAA) claimed it had a zero tolerance policy regarding terrorists, guns, and other weapons on airplanes. But after the industry complained about spotchecks from inspectors—tests that exposed vulnerabilities, leading to fines for the airlines—the agency decided in 1993 to be less strict.

After the explosion of TWA Flight 800 in 1996, a commission led by Vice President Al Gore recommended that airlines be responsible for matching every piece of luggage to a passenger. The idea was to cut down on the chances of bombs making it onto planes. They were concentrating on hijackers, though, not suicide bombers, who had not yet targeted airplanes. The proposal created an angry stir in the industry. The Clinton administration decided to abandon the recommendation, prompting praise from the aviation industry. "A week later, American Airlines delivered $250,000 in 'soft money' to the Democratic National Committee," stated the Center for Public Integrity in *The Buying of Congress,* suggesting the timing was not coincidental.

Mohamed Atta and his terrorist gang knew about gaps in the system. Even if they never read the government reports that documented the chronic lax security in a pointed series of reports, they learned what they needed by hanging around airports.

In the months leading up to the attacks, operating out of spare apartments in Fort Lauderdale, Florida, and Laurel, Maryland, Atta's Muslim extremists cased the system. Several of the nineteen highjackers flew to a rendezvous in Las Vegas. Now and then, they would visit one another at flight schools across the country. Security cameras recorded them moving through checkpoints. One photo shows Atta and a colleague as they went through security in Portland, Maine, on the morning of the attacks.

"The September 11 terrorists spent a great deal of time and effort figuring out how America works," FBI director Robert Mueller said a few months later. "They knew the ins and outs of our systems."

The terrorists made mistakes. Nine of them were selected for closer scrutiny because of those lapses. One man was targeted because he was traveling with a companion who had shaky identification. At least four of them bought tickets using the same address. Three bought tickets together. These details could have triggered a computer screening system that mandated a close electronic check of their checked baggage. That rudimentary screening system, first developed more than a decade ago, was supposed to be employed by each airline to examine passenger records for signs of threat. It was supposed to be the Information Age answer to hijackers. But it was only applied to passengers who checked in luggage—another concession to cost-conscious airlines. In this case, it created no more than an insignificant blip of attention. All the terrorists boarded their three doomed flights.

The email arrived at the fledgling Transportation Security Administration in early 2002. Former national security adviser John M. Poindexter was offering to share any promising research from the Information Awareness Office at the Defense Department. Poindexter wasn't the only government agency pining to get involved. The National Aeronautics and Space Administration (NASA) floated a notable proposal to find a way to assess risk by examining passenger brain waves with "non-invasive neuro-electric sensors." This may have been outrageous, but it was no joke. In a proposal to Northwest Airlines, NASA suggested a collaboration to develop and deploy such gear at airports. It wasn't one of the space agency's sparkling moments, though. After Northwest shared passenger records with NASA and that fact leaked out, the agency quickly disavowed the project.

Dozens of companies also said they would help Michael Jackson solve this mammoth problem—for a price. It can be frustrating to work with the government as a contractor, but companies everywhere recognized the huge potential payoff in the post-9/11 world. Billions of dollars seemed to be at hand. Biometric companies rushed to the nation's capital to propose systems that would record and analyze faces, fingerprints, iris patterns, and other immutable characteristics to authenticate the identity of passengers. Seisint and a slew of other information services insisted the solution lay in massive reservoirs of personal data maintained by information services, credit bureaus, and other private companies. Accenture, the consulting firm, came forward with a plan. So did ChoicePoint, IBM, the travel reservation company Sabre, and other high-tech firms.

Almost all of this activity was cloaked in secrecy. From the beginning, Jackson and other government officials declared it a matter of national security. They threatened to cut off vendors who discussed their efforts. But enough government documents leaked out to suggest what was happening: the creation of a mammoth risk assessment and surveillance system. (Jackson and others winced at the word "surveillance," but they acknowledged that it is the essence of what they were contemplating.)

The proposed system was to be called CAPPS II, shorthand for the second-generation computer-assisted passenger screening program. Plans called for entirely overhauling the existing profiling system, which officials became convinced was antiquated and undermined by leaks about how it worked. The new system would piggyback on the data revolution of the 1990s, using mountains of demographic, public record, and consumer files to pluck out terrorists from the mass of people who posed no threat at all. It was to be a perpetually watchful network that would electronically absorb every passenger reservation, authenticate the identity of the travelers, and then create a profile of who they are. Then it would examine that profile, instantly and relentlessly, looking for anomalies in behavior or lifestyle that might indicate ties to terrorist groups.

Jackson knew there was more at work than simple altruism from these offers of help. Though every pitch was couched in the language of patriotism—and some companies initially gave away information and services for free—vendors clearly hoped to cash in. "They were scheming about it for the profit motive," Jackson said. "And they were scheming about it for the patriotic impulse as well."

AMONG THE MOST IMPRESSIVE of these companies was Acxiom. Almost immediately after the attacks, Acxiom had run some tests for the Immigration and Naturalization Service. At no charge, the company took lists of names, ran them through its systems in Conway, Arkansas, and identified a host of characters known to the government as suspected terrorists. The company had some good friends in Washington, including former Transportation Secretary Rodney Slater, who reached out to

Jackson and others at Transportation. Former President Clinton also called Attorney General John Ashcroft for the Little Rock outfit.

In early January 2002, it was General Wesley Clark, recently retired as Supreme Allied Commander in Europe, who made the case for Acxiom's participation in the screening project. Clark's visit to Michael Jackson in January 2002 helped put Acxiom in the mix that would result in CAPPS II. Clark was accompanied by officials from HNC Software, Acxiom's partner and one of the country's most formidable data sifters. HNC Software is what is known as a risk detection specialist. Using software that can learn from massive amounts of transactions, it works for credit card issuers, telephone companies, insurers, and others in a ceaseless search for fraud. It creates profiles of individuals and then tracks how they behave.

In confidential documents provided to the government, HNC described its awesome reach. It monitors 90 percent of all the credit cards in the United States and half of those in the rest of the world—some 400 million in all—using artificial intelligence to seek out indications of fraud and deceit. (HNC Software developed its capabilities with financial help from the Defense Advanced Research Projects Agency, the outfit that brought Poindexter on board.)

Clark said that Acxiom's partner would couple Acxiom data with information about the seating records of virtually every U.S. airline passenger to discern subtle patterns and relationships. It could churn through millions, or billions, of records at a time. It would be, he suggested, a sort of truth machine to discern who was who.

Passengers would be required to provide identifying information, such as names, addresses, birth dates, Social Security, and frequent flier numbers. That information would be coupled with Acxiom data to create a composite picture of the passenger. Company officials would ask themselves: Is this person rooted in their community? Government computers would then match the person against fast-growing lists of suspects. One secret government document, generated not long after that meeting, said the aim was to create an "automated system capable of integrating and simultaneously analyzing numerous databases from Government, industry and the private sector . . . which establishes a threat risk assessment on every air carrier passenger, airport and flight."

Given that he was working for Acxiom, General Clark took time to

mention privacy. The company was excited to win government contracts, but its executives knew it would be a target for critics. They had
to make the appearance of caring, even as they proposed to make themselves a digital anchor of the monitoring system. "Information is
power," stated a paper that Clark shared with government officials during this time. "The broader the scope of integration, the greater the
power and how that power is used or could be used is already a debate
that could seriously dampen the success of our security initiatives if the
government is not sensitive to the issue.

"Success lies in building in the proper checks and balances to assure
that we don't end up with 'Big Brother,'" the paper went on, "or even a
perceived Big Brother."

BY THEN other companies had positioned themselves to take part in
this secret new world. As the remains of the World Trade Center continued to burn, for instance, the phone calls came like a torrent into
James H. Vaules's suburban Philadelphia office. They all had the same
aim. "Can you run some database checks for us," said the callers from
the Secret Service, FBI, and state police. "I need help."

Vaules worked at the National Fraud Center, a subsidiary of Lexis-
Nexis, the giant information service. As a former FBI agent, he recognized some of the names and voices. He understood their sense of
urgency. Minutes after the second plane disappeared into the second
tower, Vaules and his colleagues began probing the LexisNexis systems
on their own for details about the people on board the crashed planes.
They weren't just trying to confirm the names of the dead; they wanted
the terrorists' identities and the names of any others who might be
preparing more attacks.

Almost immediately, Vaules and his colleagues began handing out
dozens of passwords. Investigators who never thought much about the
service suddenly had free access to a vast trove of records from some
16,000 databases in the LexisNexis universe. Within days, the company
created a Downtown Disaster Task Force in Washington, D.C. It dedicated an office and two terminals in the District that remained open day
and night for law enforcement authorities that fall.

Many people think of LexisNexis as a legal resource or newspaper clip service. In the 1970s, the company built a giant law library for the Internal Revenue Service. Then it created its own telecommunications network to provide good service to top customers. A few years later, it opened up its applications for intelligence agencies. About a decade ago, it began building up a cache of public records, billions of files with names, addresses, Social Security Numbers, birth dates, and much more. The wealth of information seemed the height of technological sophistication, particularly because it was now accessible to police, reporters, lawyers, and anyone else via the World Wide Web.

Then LexisNexis trumped itself. It bought a company called RiskWise, which automatically looks at the reports about people for signs of inconsistency or potential risk. The credit industry long ago adopted the same technique when it created "credit scores" to assess the risk that a borrower might default. LexisNexis customers now could "score" individuals for a wide array of reasons. Would they be good employees? Did they seem to be lying about their past? Instead of having to search through hundreds of records, a customer could ask LexisNexis to generate a score for them.

Today, LexisNexis is a $2 billion plus subsidiary of Reed Elsevier, the giant London-based publishing company. It caters to more than 3 million subscribers, including newspapers, libraries, intelligence services, and police everywhere. It taps some 36,000 sources of information from news, business, public records, and law sources, and it adds 7 million searchable documents every week. This is not the LexisNexis most people think of. Not only did it team up with I2, the company that specializes in finding links among individuals, its parent had bought a large chunk of SRD, the company founded by Jeff Jonas and used so intensively by LexisNexis's competitor, ChoicePoint.

The work Vaules and others did after the attacks put the company on a path that led quickly to Jackson and the passenger screening initiative. LexisNexis officials realized that a tectonic shift had taken place in the government. Information was a more valuable commodity now and a vast new market had opened up. They weren't going to miss an opportunity. For several months they worked for free. The expectation was they would be paid—perhaps a lot—before long. "A lot of this was done before we had formal agreements or the contracts," Vaules said. "A lot of it was done on the come."

One of their projects involved work with the new Joint Terrorism Task Force at the Justice Department. Using their risk-scoring technology, they created a customized system to analyze the veracity of names, addresses, birth dates, and other identity information of foreigners applying to flight schools. The system coupled LexisNexis data with government intelligence computers. Authorities knew the September 11 hijackers had trained at schools in the United States to fly the planes. Another project involved the constant monitoring of suspected terrorists, more than twenty thousand in all, named in classified government lists. (LexisNexis set up its computer to flag any changes in the suspects' profiles, such as a new address.) On its own, LexisNexis analysts found a house in Florida that several of the hijackers had shared. The discovery demonstrated the conspiracy that authorities had suspected from the start.

One of the people the company worked with at Justice was named Ben Bell III, a blustery intelligence specialist who would soon be recruited by Jackson to head a new agency at the Transportation Security Administration called the Office of National Risk Assessment. Vaules had known Bell from before. They ran in some of the same intelligence circles. Now Vaules and his colleagues realized that Bell might be the doorway into the government and its lucrative business. "We had a relationship with Bell," Vaules said. "He trusted us."

Because LexisNexis was foreign-owned, there was only so far it could go in working with classified materials. Its government contacts began urging it to create a new, U.S.-based subsidiary. The result, formally begun in February 2003, was LexisNexis Special Service Inc., a company that could handle some of the nation's precious secrets. Creating the company was a laborious process, but Vaules said his parent company and colleagues all agreed it was worth it. More police and intelligence authorities than ever were tapping into their data. "Law enforcement, in the last two years, has just exploded its use and knowledge of public records," Vaules said.

By the summer of 2003, the company would become the "information gatekeeper" for the massive aviation security project. It would play a central role in the aviation screening. The relationship between Ben Bell and another LexisNexis official named Norm Willox would soon deepen—to the point that Willox, chief officer for privacy, industry, and regulatory affairs, even reached out to the media on Bell's behalf. "The relationship would continue," Vaules said about the ties to Bell, "just really on a larger scale." And now, nothing they did was for free.

WHEN DAVID SOBEL FIRST HEARD about plans for CAPPS II, he was sitting as usual in his Connecticut Avenue office, not far from the White House. Sobel is general counsel at the Electronic Privacy Information Center (EPIC), a feisty group of legal activists whose sole purpose is to track and shape privacy issues. He is a classic post-Watergate figure in activist Washington. Buttoned-down, bearded, and slow-speaking, he's careful about his facts and cautious to ground his arguments.

At first glance, EPIC's offices seem like countless other modern warrens, with PCs, copiers, and other office equipment scattered about, and files everywhere. The movie posters on the walls tell another story: *Enemy of the State, Gattaca, Metropolis,* films that feature characters caught up in a high-tech net of surveillance and oppression. Enlarged legal briefs also adorn the walls, souvenirs of the group's battles with government agencies to learn more about the official, often secret use of surveillance and personal information. In one corner is a Big Brother Award, a garish trophy featuring a boot resting on a tarnished gold head. The group gives the award to the company or person they believe violates privacy most egregiously in a given year. One year they focused on the data-mining company called Elensys, which collected prescription records and sent out "educational material" on behalf of drug companies. John Poindexter recently won the award for Total Information Awareness. The aviation screening proposal brushed up against the core of Sobel's civil liberties values. Here the government was proposing one of its largest domestic surveillance systems ever without disclosing any details to the public. He and his EPIC colleagues saw the system as an ominous legacy of the terror attacks. The very idea struck them as something out of a bad movie.

As Sobel read an account of the system in the press at the end of January 2002, he recalled the fallout from the TWA 800 explosion and the panic about air security six years earlier. At the time, Sobel questioned whether a system would really work. In a letter to Vice President Gore, who headed the White House Commission on Aviation Safety and Security, Sobel and other civil liberties activists sought to head off the mandated use of government IDs for travelers, the deployment of X-ray cameras and profiling. "All of our experience with the creation and updating of such ever-changing data bases teaches us that the likelihood of inaccuracy at any given moment is high," Sobel and the others stated in the February 1997 letter. "The FBI, for instance, recognizes that data in its computer system of criminal records has an inaccuracy rate of 33 percent.

"Such inaccuracy would lead to both a breach of safety and to violations of the rights of innocent people. This proposal is a quick fix that won't fix anything."

Sobel figured that nothing had changed since then. As it happened, he was right.

DAVID AND LEAH NELSON arrived at Portland International Airport almost two hours early. They wanted to be sure they caught their flight to Atlanta, where they were to attend a meeting of golf course superintendents.

Nelson is the owner of a public relations company in Salem, Oregon, that helps associations reach out to newspapers and television stations across the state. One of his biggest clients is the Oregon Seed Council, which represents growers of fine fescue, the grass favored by certain golf courses. His wife, Leah, works with him as the office manager.

As usual they pulled their bags up to the curbside check-in. Nelson set his briefcase down and handed the Redcap the voucher for his electronic ticket. "For some reason you're not in the system," the bag handler told him a few minutes later, after searching for Nelson's reservations. "You'll have to go inside." Nelson thought: "That's kind of strange," but he complied and walked inside. They stepped up to a self-serve kiosk recently opened by Delta Airlines, their carrier. With another attendant helping, Nelson repeatedly typed their information into the machine. No success. "Something is wrong," the man told him.

This time, the couple was directed to a long line leading up to the ticket counter. Leah got her boarding pass with no problem, but not so her husband. After clicking at a computer for more than ten minutes, occasionally glancing up to look nervously at Nelson, the clerk said he had to see his supervisor. "My computer," the clerk said, "has had a hiccup."

For ten more minutes they stood there as the rest of the line disappeared. Nelson finally lost his patience. "Can you find out where our agent went?" Nelson asked another clerk. That's when he heard the loudspeaker overhead blare his name, a disembodied voice urging him to return to the ticket counter. When his original clerk returned, Nelson, still waiting at the counter, was angry. "What the heck is going on?" he demanded.

"You'll have to talk to that security guy behind you," the nervous clerk said. Nelson turned around and saw a man wearing a shirt with a TSA emblem, a helmet, and a microphone on his shoulder.

"'You don't look like a terrorist to me,'" Nelson recalled the man saying. "'Give me your driver's license.'"

DAVID NELSON WAS STOPPED because his name was on the government's No Fly or Selectee lists, a collection of names gathered through myriad intelligence sources and distributed to airlines and security officials around the country. The lists were around long before the terror attacks, but since then they have grown tremendously, with thousands of new names culled from an array of undisclosed sources.

David Nelsons all over the country have experienced the same routine: The "who are you really" stare from clerks, the extra pat-downs, boarding delays, and missed flights. There's a state senator in Oregon—an acquaintance of the grass seed representative—who keeps getting stopped. There's a professor, David L. Nelson, from the Medill School of Journalism in Chicago. One David Nelson, a graduate student in Kansas, appealed to Representative Dennis Moore, who then asked TSA chief Admiral James Loy how to distinguish him from the wanted David Nelson. It seems the problem was getting worse. After repeatedly being detained and missing flights, the graduate student was now having trouble even booking flights. Details about the actual characters targeted by authorities remained elusive, the government refusing to discuss its activities or its mistakes.

Authorities said everything was considered national security sensitive. But a TSA memo, from October 2002, said that since November 2001, "the FAA/TSA 'watchlist' has expanded almost daily as Intelligence Community (IC) agencies and the Office of Homeland Security continue to request the addition of individuals to the No Fly and Selectee lists." That included a physician named Enrique Hernandez in Philadelphia who complained he was being stopped and searched because of his Spanish surname. Jim Thompson, city manager in Bothell, Washington, expressed his anxiety about getting tickets stamped with an "S." "I am asking your help because all other attempts to clear my name have been futile," he wrote to Representative Jay Inslee.

Many of those listed have names of Middle Eastern origin, but some of them, like Aquil Abdullah, have no ties to that region of the world. Abdullah is a Catholic African-American man who lives near Princeton. He also is a U.S. rowing champion, who joined the team in 1997, received a medal at the Pan American Games in 1999, and won the single-sculls division at the U.S. national championship in 2002. In 2004 he became the first African-American man to make the U.S. Olympic rowing team. Those achievements meant nothing to officials at Newark International Airport, where Abdullah was trying to catch a flight to Seattle for a meet. "We need you to step aside," a clerk told him. "I have to call a police officer." The same thing happened to Abdullah in Philadelphia, only that time three officers came over and asked him a long series of questions. It took almost two hours to clear his name.

Abdullah described the feeling he had during his ordeals as "shame," even though he had done nothing wrong. He said the experiences reminded him of his brushes with bigotry as a teenager. "I remembered when I would be followed around the department stores," he said, "people crossing the street when they see you."

"You feel guilty," he said.

For his part, David Nelson, the public relations specialist from Oregon, remained perplexed as to why the government uses information without giving him and others like him a chance to fix the mistakes. He joked about it with state senator David Nelson. They teasingly call each other "Muhammed" or "terrorist" now. But to the communication specialist, the heart of the problem is no laughing matter. "It's the freedom to come and go, to do your business without this feeling, in the back of your mind, you're going to encounter this inquisition: Who are you really? Give us some means of clearing it up. As far as we know, there's no way of getting off the list, of proving that we're legitimate citizens, that we're not suspects or not people who pose a threat.

"In the back of your mind you think—when you walk up to the

counter, and you know you're on the list—they may be thinking: 'Who is this creep?'"

JOHNNIE LOCKETT THOMAS WAS PULLED ASIDE the first time in March 2002, just about when Jackson and his colleagues were stepping up efforts to create CAPPS II. She was preparing for a flight from New York's LaGuardia Airport to Boston. A female guard approached with a hand on her gun. The ticket clerk urged caution, saying Thomas had not done anything wrong. They detained her for forty minutes.

The same thing happened on her return flight. Airline clerks balked at issuing her ticket and guards repeatedly questioned her identity. It happened again and again over the next year, as Thomas traveled to visit family and friends. Thomas was the seventy-one-year-old African-American widow of a senior Postal Service executive who lives in Miles City, Montana. No one had ever thought of her as a threat. As a young woman she had studied dramatic voice. Eventually she became an amateur historian.

When a U.S. Airways clerk in Boston explained for the first time why she was being singled out, Thomas was stunned into silence. As with Abdullah and the David Nelsons, Thomas had the bad luck of sharing a name with a man on the No Fly List. In her case, authorities worried she might be John Thomas Christopher, the alias of a white man wanted for murder who was already in custody. "There's nothing you can do to make this better," she recalled the U.S. Airways clerk telling her that day, six months after the terrorist attacks. "And it's going to happen every time you fly."

As a southern child—her father was the son of a slave—Thomas knows about being singled out. One night when she was ten, she lay on the floor of her family's business in Tuskegee as white protesters shot bullets into the building. The gunmen objected to the fact the government was allowing black aviators, the Tuskegee Airmen, to fly fighter planes in World War II. She said her own son gets stopped by police for "driving while black." Thomas discounted the idea that she personally was being targeted for her race, but she believes the use of lists follows a long pattern of discrimination against designated "enemies of the state."

"The pattern is always the same," she wrote in a letter from Montana, citing the horrible experience of Japanese Americans during World War II as an example.

Thomas has tried repeatedly to extricate herself from the situation, but her letters to the TSA and other agencies did not stop her detentions. Even a document from the FBI attesting to the authenticity of her identity was ignored by airport security officials. On one occasion, she was detained at Logan Airport, taken to a secure room, and told to stand, while agents searched her bags. She was released just moments before her flight, forcing her to run for the gate. "Hurry," an agent told her, "the plane is being held."

"While the FBI defines my experience as 'frustrating' I find it frightening. I am afraid because I am old. I am afraid because I am a woman. I am afraid because I have no money, no power, no position," she said in a letter. "I am afraid of being taken off into a back room. I am afraid of overly aggressive security guards.

"I am afraid," she wrote, "of hostile patriots among airline employees who labor under the misconception that if the government targeted me I must be guilty of something."

JERRY BERLIN, AN AVIATION CONSULTANT, worked closely with companies helping to shape the CAPPS II system. But by the summer of 2003, he was worried that he might be helping to develop a tool of oppression. "We're playing with dynamite," he said. He was holding details about a proposal for the CAPPS II system. One paper outlined the billions of records that would be available for the system from Acxiom. Another discussed technical details about the computer architecture. Still another document spelled out the role that artificial intelligence might play.

At seventy-four, Berlin seemed more intent than most people on listening closely, perhaps because he is also a psychologist who does that for a living. He is passionate about human development. Since he got his Ph.D. at the University of Chicago in 1961, he has focused most of his career on aviation. For years, he served as director of the Aviation Research Center at Embry-Riddle University. He studied the behavior of pilots. For several years in the 1970s, he lived in Israel with his family and served in the Air Force there as a lieutenant colonel. He was eventually named chief of training research and development.

Berlin counts among his greatest achievements the early, almost unknown role he played in the development of the nation's first profiling
system, which was secretly expanded by Northwest Airlines and embraced by the commercial aviation industry in the mid-1990s. Berlin remembered the day in the mid-1980s when he sat at the head of an
office at the Federal Aviation Administration. He was demonstrating
the first computerized terrorist profiling system, typing details about
theoretical passenger reservations into a small computer as quickly as
officials in the room could give them. One woman passenger, for example, might have bought a theoretical round-trip ticket from a travel
service near her home, used a credit card, and asked for a window seat.
A fictive elderly man was traveling with a companion. A graduate student, in the United States on a six-month visa, paid cash for his ticket.

Every fictitious detail in the scenario was meant to test a new system
that Berlin had developed, in response to the hijacking of TWA Flight
847 in 1985. (That plane, flying from Athens to Rome, was forced to
land in Beirut, where it sat on the tarmac for more than two weeks. The
hijackers called for the release of Kuwaiti and some seven hundred Shi-
ite Muslims held in Israeli and South Lebanon prisons. When negotia-
tors refused the demands, hostage Robert Dean Stethem, a U.S. Navy
diver, was shot and his body thrown out of the plane.) Officials representing the FAA and other government agencies immediately began
contemplating new ways to protect against hijacking attacks. For
months, Berlin and others gathered details about known hijackers in
the United States and several other countries. On Berlin's recommendation, they decided to use that data and other personal information
about passengers to create a profiling system that could target the
riskiest 10 percent of passengers on a particular flight. The details from
several dozen tickets became the core of the system.

Personal data included the passenger's name, age, place of birth, gender, citizenship, residence, and passport. From the ticket they collected
details about any companions, method of payment, and whether the passenger was flying round trip or one way. They examined where the trip
began and ended and any intermediate stops, the place where the
ticket was bought, and the travel agency's ethnicity. They factored in
ticket changes and baggage details, including types of meals ordered.

Berlin's model was able to identify nearly every theoretical passenger who was supposed to be a terrorist threat in the exercise. "Soon afterwards, in cooperation with the Security Department of Northwest Airlines and [with] the assistance of other federal agencies, the FAA commenced the development," Berlin wrote in a letter.

A push to expand the system strengthened after the February 1993 bombing of the World Trade Center, when a van loaded with explosives blew up in the basement garage of the towers. Shaken investigators turned up evidence of other looming threats, including plans to blow up airliners. Ramzi Ahmed Yousef, one of the trade center bombers, and others had developed an audacious plan to bomb a dozen American planes over the Pacific Ocean. Yousef and his colleagues knew they could operate freely in the United States and fly more or less when and where they wanted.

It wasn't until July 1996 that fears about such attacks crystallized with the catastrophic explosion of TWA Flight 800 off the coast of Long Island. The plane, en route to Paris from JFK International Airport in Queens, disintegrated in a flash that was seen miles away. The pieces fell on beaches near million-dollar homes and sunk hundreds of feet into the cold Atlantic—thousands of airplane parts, computers, purses, family pictures, and the luggage of people traveling to one of the world's great cities.

Some investigators mistakenly assumed the explosion was the result of terrorism and immediately called for new security measures. Though the Transportation Safety Board eventually concluded the crash was a horrible accident—a spark from a faulty wire detonated a fuel tank—the Clinton administration decided it was time to change. It created the Commission on Aviation Safety and Security.

The commission raised many questions about lax security and made many recommendations about fixes. Chief among the proposed solutions was the creation of an automated profiling system that would help identify potential terrorists. The system that was embraced, however, was used only for people checking in baggage. After September 11, 2001, Berlin was thrilled to be recruited to help develop the security plan contemplated by Acxiom and its partners. For months, he met with government officials and an array of companies selling data and technology, often commuting from his home in Daytona Beach, Florida. He collaborated with a team of mathematicians at HNC Software. He was convinced the nation had to have some sort of improved screening system to help eliminate vulnerabilities to another attack. "There are groups and individuals who would like to destroy us. You have enemies who live with us, live within our culture," Berlin said. "We must look at the person and his or her history."

Long after the attacks, he still believes that. But he was growing more worried about "the price that we pay as a people and a nation in terms of the sacred constitutional protections we have."

After watching the partnership of the government and technology companies from the inside, Berlin came to believe the system under development poses an unprecedented threat to American values. It's not just the mistakes the system will invariably make, although Berlin said he loses sleep thinking about that. It's the pressure to conform. Berlin believes that CAPPS II and other data surveillance systems will shape people by making them unwilling to stand out.

"People are losing the right to have their own private life," he said. "The final result, if carried through to its logical end, to its predicted end, would be a profound change in American culture."

THE CLOCK WAS TICKING. Michael Jackson and other transportation authorities had a clearer idea of what they wanted but still had no system in place in August 2002. Almost a year after the attacks, they were still grappling with the complexities. They could not determine the right technology to use. Jackson remained consumed by the idea of a vast network of supercomputers that would instantly probe every passenger's background for clues about violent designs. They had spent millions of dollars and innumerable hours studying how the secret profiling system might enable them to "deter, prevent or capture terrorists," as one of their planning documents put it.

In the spring of 2002, they hired four teams of technology companies that had honed their expertise in profiling for casinos, marketing companies, and financial institutions. Their stated mission was to demonstrate how artificial intelligence and other powerful software could analyze passengers' travel reservations, housing information, family ties, identifying details in credit reports, and other personal data to determine if they have an unusual history that indicates a potential threat.

A March 8, 2002, request for "white papers" had required companies to demonstrate they had experience with the financial industry, fraud detection, risk assessment, and the authentication of individuals. It also required the companies to describe how they would handle "Privacy Rights and Interests/Civil Rights/Confidentiality." Two months later, four teams received grants. Officials from the companies declined to discuss their roles in CAPPS II publicly, saying they were warned by the TSA that such disclosures might undermine national security. Documents showed the companies represented a cross section of commercial technology and data integration industries.

The Austin-based Infoglide Software Corp., for example, said in promotional materials that its software "makes it easy for the user to find relevant connections between people, places, and/or events, thereby uncovering possible incidences of fraud and threat." Another firm, Language Analysis Systems, was once so closely related to intelligence work that it could not publicly acknowledge its own existence. The company, which specializes in name recognition software, helped track some of the September 11 hijackers to Florida. A classified subsidiary of the giant military vendor Lockheed Martin Corp. was brought in to pull the different software services together. The little known division, called Intelligence, Surveillance and Reconnaissance, had a long history working with the government on secret projects.

Along with Lockheed came Systems Research & Development, the Las Vegas company founded by Jeff Jonas. Using the system called Non-Obvious Relationship Awareness (NORA), the company can sort through oceans of data in real time, seeking links among people. It also can determine when an individual has transposed names or intentionally tried to obscure details about him- or herself. "We're talking about instant, perpetual, real-time analysis." Jonas said at the time, the beginning of a campaign to lay down roots in the counterterrorism and intelligence communities. HNC Software, now a part of Fair, Isaac & Co., won the largest grant, more than a half million dollars. Acxiom, of course, was its fountain of data for the effort.

Finding the right companies and technology was only one of several tasks facing Jackson and Coast Guard Admiral James Loy, who had been hired to lead the new Transportation Security Administration. Another was selling the program to Congress and to passengers. Jackson and

Loy met quietly with individual lawmakers. They didn't know what to say publicly. The system was far from complete. Jackson also promised first to tell the American people about what he and his colleagues were building. Then the TSA would treat the system as a secret national security matter. It was a tough balance he was trying to strike. "This is going to be classified," he said. "What's inside that box contains some very sensitive intelligence."

For all the expectations inside the government, the screening program was an unfulfilled idea. "We're still between the conceptual and the reality," Loy admitted. The delay showed the extraordinary challenges facing the nation's security overall—and the lengths to which government officials believe they must go in examining the lives of ordinary Americans to avoid a repeat of the security and intelligence failures of September 11. The government's documents at the time showed that the project was nearly overwhelmed by complexity. They also remained uncertain about what level of scrutiny the public would accept. In the summer of 2002, they privately argued that given the immense importance of screening to the new air security framework, the extra few months are worth taking. For good measure, Jackson said CAPPS II not only would protect passengers, it would make life easier for travelers at the airport because screening will be more efficient.

"It's probably the most important security tool we have in our arsenal—if we develop it intelligently, which we will do," Jackson said, at the time under a cloak of anonymity. "What we now have is a chance to build a significantly more powerful tool."

SOME LAWMAKERS WERE uneasy that the TSA had not begun a pilot program, saying they worried about the nation's vulnerability to another attack. "I'm totally frustrated by it. It should never have taken this long," said Representative John L. Mica (R-Fla.), chairman of the House Transportation Committee's aviation subcommittee. "It's very serious. It leaves us exposed. We don't have a thinking system." David Sobel of EPIC and other civil liberties activists warned that privacy issues would embroil the system in controversy and undermine its effectiveness if these issues are not publicly resolved before the system begins operation. Others questioned whether it could even work, and they worried that innocent but offbeat or politically radical travelers will be swept up in the system, much as the David Nelsons and Johnnie Thomases of the world have been snared by the No Fly and Selectee lists. "This system challenges core values, such as privacy, the right to travel, and the right to engage in certain activities," said Katie Corrigan, then a leading voice on the issue at the ACLU.

Sobel pushed his campaign to learn more, even though the government's obsession with secrecy hindered EPIC's legal effort. He had filed a request for details in early 2002, as soon as he learned of the screening programs. Under the federal Freedom of Information law, the government has twenty working days to respond to requests. "And we asked for expedited processing, which means even faster than that," Sobel said.

The new Transportation Security Administration didn't bother to answer, or couldn't comply. It was experiencing acute growing pains. Though the agency was formed by Congress in November 2001, it still had only a few employees. Never before had the government created an agency so large so quickly. In March 2002, Sobel sued the fledgling agency in federal court. Three months later, the group received a pile of email and other documents. It was intriguing but limited stuff. One of the documents he received was the NASA brain-scanning proposal.

Sobel asked for more. Once again that summer, the new security agency failed to meet the deadline, and once again Sobel sued. Officials defended their handling of those requests and others by newspapers, saying they too are working in the public interest. Transportation Secretary Norman Y. Mineta described their secret initiative as "the foundation" on which all other far more public security measures really depend. "What is the government's responsibility to the citizens?" Mineta said at the time. "It's really to protect them. That's what we're trying to do here."

"If I don't have the ability to know what the government is collecting about me and the ability to see it and correct it—and that the government may be using against me—that's a fundamental violation of my privacy under federal law," Sobel said after being rebuffed by the agency more than once. "Secret determination based on a secret analysis based on a secret category of information: that's really what we're talking about," he added. "It's an extreme departure from the most fundamental principles of our society. Citizens should not be subject to secret action by the government."

• • •

WHEN VISITORS WALKED into Ben Bell's office, the first thing they saw was a doll on his desk. It was Eric Cartman, the profane and intermittently likable character from *South Park,* the cartoon series for adults. Cartman sat behind the computer, facing the door with a silly grin on its face. It's a typical joke, an implicit challenge from the unlikely choreographer of the aviation screening system, a former intelligence official who lives on a boat, wears a gold pinky ring, and once investigated the global trafficking of women and children.

Until April 2004, Bell was the director of the Office of National Risk Assessment, a division of the TSA that few people know about. He was recruited by Michael Jackson in the fall of 2002 to take charge of the aviation screening system. Jackson recognized his push had fallen short. He was not satisfied with any of the four main proposals he had commissioned earlier in the year. They didn't work, and they didn't demonstrate how to solve the privacy question. That's what Ben Bell was tasked to do.

At Bell's insistence his office was unmarked, near the NSA, which would provide technical support. It houses the computers and other hardware that run the screening program. At fifty-four, Bell has thick gray hair, a gray beard, and a substantial paunch. He wears bow ties and a massive Rolex watch. His pinky ring displays a gold coin. It's a reminder of his father, Bell said, who rued the passing use of gold coins. Bell is known in Washington's national security community as a "character." He speaks gruffly and leaps at the chance to tease or taunt the people he likes. Until the attacks, he was a deputy assistant commissioner at the INS. He ran the agency's intelligence branch, working on issues relating to human trafficking and mass migration.

Bell was the leader of operations planning and intelligence for the government's rescue of Elián González, the Cuban boy who fled with his mother to the United States. Because his mother died during their journey, Elián became the focus of an intense struggle between his father, who wanted to take him home to Cuba, and relatives in the United States, who refused to let him go. Bell's assignment, Operation Reunion, lasted almost three months. It culminated with a call from Attorney General Janet Reno, who told him to order armed authorities to seize the boy from a house in Miami. "I'm saying a prayer," he recalled her telling him. "Do it." ("That was a child custody case," he says, "not all the bullshit around it.")

On September 12, 2001, Bell was called on to sit down with John Ashcroft, who recruited him to serve as deputy director of the new foreign terrorist tracking task force. His mission was to pull together law enforcement, commercial, and intelligence data. Bell had long been interested in commercial data as a resource for his intelligence work. Though he wasn't a technical guy, he had made the use of public source data a pet specialty. It wasn't long before he was working with Acxiom, LexisNexis, ChoicePoint, and others in his new assignments. One of Jackson's colleagues had heard about Bell's work over at Justice and wanted a demonstration. Bell and his staff showed them the system that LexisNexis had set up to screen foreigners applying to flight schools in the United States. The transportation officials were amazed. A few months later, Bell was invited to the Coast Guard dining room at the Transportation Department for lunch with Jackson.

"I hear they briefed you on our new CAPPS program," Jackson said. "What do you think?"

"Mr. Deputy Secretary," Bell responded, "I think you should finish your lunch before I answer that."

In typical gruff fashion, Bell explained to Jackson that his plan was half-baked. The proposed systems seemed overly complicated, Bell said, and way too expensive. More important, they likely would outrage many of the passengers they were supposed to be protecting. "No one had considered the privacy," Bell would say later. "No one had considered the policy."

Bell moved over to the TSA on November 27, 2002. His first pronouncement to the staff was that the approaches they had been contemplating wouldn't work. (When he spoke about privacy, he used the English pronunciation, which comes across as strikingly delicate from a man who prides himself on being plainspoken.) Bell insisted on a different way. Instead of bringing massive amounts of information into the government, they would rely on subcontractors, companies that would verify individuals' identities by sifting through storehouses of commercial and public record information. His screening system would be applicable to just about any aspect of American life. "It's almost the Wal-Mart of risk assessment in the U.S.," he said one day.

But it wouldn't be Big Brother shouldering that task. It would be the private companies, the marketers and data warehousers like Acxiom and LexisNexis, who already had information about almost everybody in the United States.

ADMIRAL JAMES LOY and Ben Bell moved from group to group, chatting with a striking cross section of policy wonks and activists. Loy shook hands with Jim Dempsey, from the Center for Democracy and Technology. Bell engaged Dennis McBride of the Potomac Institute for Policy Studies, a conservative think tank that provides technology advice to Congress. Barry Steinhardt from the ACLU was across the room, along with Steve Thayer from the American Conservative Union and Lori Waters from the Eagle Forum.

Loy and Bell had asked all of these people to join them at the Wye River Conference Center on Maryland's eastern shore in March 2003, for an overnight discussion about how to improve aviation security. Jackson had just given up control of the agency, which now was in the hands of the new Department of Homeland Security, but the meeting was the fulfillment of his pledge to seek advice from critics. Loy, Bell, and their colleagues had made it clear they agreed with Jackson's approach: Use the technology well but narrowly.

"My hope is that this Workshop is just a beginning in a continuing dialogue among us, which will be enlarged to include your colleagues and the general public," Bell wrote in a note given to each guest. "Security and privacy are too fundamental to the rights and privileges of U.S. citizens to be developed in secrecy or through an adversarial process."

The conference center sprawls across 1,100 acres on the eastern shore. The land once was owned by William Paca, who signed the Declaration of Independence and served as third governor of Maryland. Wye River gave its name to peace accords between Israel and the Palestinian National Authority in 1998, after an intense series of talks there. The so-called Wye River Memorandum spelled out Israel's pledge to withdraw from disputed territory and the National Authority's promise to suppress terror groups. Unfortunately, that accord failed.

Loy was betting his reputation he and Bell could make their promises stick. Tall, bespectacled, and easygoing, Loy was widely respected as commandant of the Coast Guard. He had commanded four cutters on tours around the world. He was the recipient of numerous awards, including the Bronze Star for search and rescue operations in Vietnam. Now, as the first head of the Transportation Security Administration, he was taking control of one of the most controversial initiatives in the post–September 11 world. It was far from clear whether he had the authority to make good on his pledge to respect individuals' privacy, but he was determined to try.

Loy wanted to win the group over with descriptions of his "layered vision" for aviation security. That included improvements such as hardened doors in airplane cockpits, better metal detectors, and so on. At its core, though, would be the passenger screening system and an improved watch list. He described the current screening system as broken and ineffective. His message that night was direct and, to the people in the room, compelling: We do not have to trade off civil liberties for security. We can have both. The system would be used to defend against terrorism, not fight crime.

Ever present in his mind was the tattered copy of the Constitution with the blue cover that he has carried in his briefcase for more than three decades. "I was absolutely convinced that in the hands of the wrong folks," Loy said later, "the power of what we were doing had the potential to be troubling to all the things I hold dear."

Loy's remarks that night echoed what was said repeatedly all the rest of that spring, as Bell and others pressed hard to get the system up and running. "Security and privacy are complementary, not conflicting goals," Loy stated during congressional testimony.

"CAPPS II will not build databases on U.S. persons permitted to fly," Loy said. "We'll never see the commercial data being used to authenticate identification. We'll not search medical records or criminal records, nor seek credit ratings, overdue bills or any such data to assess risk. We'll not generate new intelligence, and we'll not keep even the risk scores after travel is complete."

Using just four pieces of personal information, the system they were building would authenticate individuals' identities. Then the system would run the identities through a black box. They had no intention of using the screening for anyone other than foreign terrorists—at least not in the initial stages. Loy understood that his position had to leave the door quietly open to expand the use of CAPPS II if need be. But most people heard him stress the former.

"This is a very focused tool designed not without potential to do other things if authorized and challenged by the Congress to do so. But at the moment we are charged with finding in the aviation sector foreign terrorists or those associated with foreign terrorists and keeping them off airplanes. That is our very limited goal at the moment."

Loy was asked: Couldn't it be used more probably to detect anyone on railways, ships, and so on if need be? "The potential there is very real, sir. And frankly at the other end of the day, even as heinous as it sounds, the ax murderer that gets on the airplane with a clean record in New Orleans and goes to Los Angeles and commits his or her crime, that is not the person we are trying to keep off that airplane at the moment."

Michael Jackson, the privacy and security pragmatist, could not have said it better.

THE NEWS CAME TO JACKSON first as rumors. People in the White House, Justice Department, and the new Department of Homeland Security wanted to use the passenger screening system more broadly to identify illegal aliens and catch criminals. Jackson had given up control of the system's development on March 1, 2003, when the TSA moved under the Homeland Security Department's vast and growing umbrella. It was not in Bell's hands, and even Bell was under pressure from more senior officials to expand the system's reach. But Jackson couldn't quite let go. For eighteen months he had pursued a vision of what he thought was a balanced approach to aviation security. He had made a lot of promises. Now it looked as though others might undo them.

In February, lawyers at the Department of Transportation had issued a plan for public review that made it seem as though the system could hold personal information about passengers for fifty years. Jackson dismissed the document at the time as a bureaucratic mistake. It certainly wasn't his idea. David Sobel, officials at ACLU, and others accused him and his colleagues of operating in bad faith.

Then in late March, an official at the White House Office of Management and Budget appeared before Congress and raised questions about the system's cost and potential effectiveness. Jackson was furious and wrote a letter to OMB director Mitch Daniels, even though he no longer had control of the system. Then came the suggestions behind the scenes that the screening system might be used by a wide range of police and counterterrorism investigators. Jackson was already contemplating resigning from the government to pursue a private business. He loathed the idea that the project he had spent so much time and energy cultivating might suddenly veer in the wrong direction.

Jackson had no qualms about the Bush administration's push overall on security. He was convinced the president, Ridge, and Ashcroft had the best intentions as they tried to secure the country. "I look at the Patriot Act and I see a bunch of people struggling to do the right thing," he said.

Jackson also understood the impulse to use it to fight crime. Or even to track down deadbeat parents. His own father had failed on occasion to make support payments after divorcing his mother. What worried him, though, was the apparent lack of understanding about what the broad use of aviation screening for other purposes might mean to regular Americans.

By early July 2003 it became clear to Jackson that the promises he had made to limit the system probably would not be kept. Senior officials in the Department of Homeland Security, in consultation with the White House, had decided it was potentially too valuable to use only to screen terrorists. This is precisely what Sobel and others had warned about: If you create a data surveillance system, someone will find other uses for it. It almost always happens.

Just days before Jackson was set to leave the government, he decided to try lobbying one last time.

JACKSON RODE IN THE BACK of a government limousine through the White House gates. He entered the West Wing and made his way downstairs to an office across from the Mess, not far from the Situation Room. Sitting in the office was Richard Falkenrath, a senior homeland security adviser at the White House. Some of his staff were also in the room.

The two men had worked together for a year and hit it off. Both had been professors earlier in their careers. Jackson said he got a laugh by describing himself as a lapsed academic. Falkenrath seemed intent on hearing what Jackson had to say about a wide range of transportation issues, a conversation that lasted almost two hours. At the end Jackson took care to emphasize his concern about the screening system and what he called its "mission creep." He worried that a backlash could wipe out the program's chances in Congress.

"Don't stretch it to the breaking point," Jackson implored Falkenrath and the others gathered in the subterranean office. "Don't make it the system to find deadbeat dads."

In spelling out his concerns, Jackson made an analogy to racial profiling. It is easy for law enforcement authorities to make a facile case that one ethnic group or another deserves more scrutiny. We know that many inner-city minorities, for example, are caught using or selling drugs. But that does not mean we should assume that black or Hispanic drivers are drug dealers, Jackson said, because such assumptions often crush the rights of innocent people. He said the president himself had come out strongly against profiling for a good reason. "It means we're committed to protecting a zone of privacy and dignity for people driving down the road," Jackson said.

Jackson made the case that that kind of "self-restraint" is important to the CAPPS deployment. Otherwise CAPPS will become—or seem to become—an all-purpose checkpoint system. Jackson said he left the meeting feeling good that he had made the effort.

Apparently, his appeals had little effect. Just a few weeks later, the Department of Homeland Security announced its plans to use the screening system to search for people charged or suspected of violent crimes. Department officials tried to focus attention on a related decision to abandon plans to keep records for fifty years. They called their decision "privacy friendly." But there was no doubt about the import: The system had not even been turned on, and already law enforcement authorities were making plans to use it more broadly. Jackson's promises to limit the scope of the system had been undone.

Jackson and Bell were disappointed. Loy privately objected, while publicly defending the move. They didn't control the system; other more senior officials at the White House and Department of Homeland Security did. And they had different ideas, and different commitments. When Loy took a job as Secretary Tom Ridge's deputy, he went along with the change.

"The problem that we set out to solve was stopping terrorism. Now it has migrated," Jackson said. "Where do you draw the line?"

IN APRIL 2004, Ben Bell resigned his post as director of the new Office of National Risk Assessment. Publicly Bell said he was ready to retire after a long government career, but privately he was angry about the direction the aviation screening initiative was taking.

Though the government had spent close to $100 million on CAPPS II, the system was more than a year overdue with no clear deadline in sight. Bell and other officials had hoped to begin testing in the spring of 2004. But that timetable had been thrown into doubt by a sharply critical report from the General Accounting Office, which said among other things the system did not properly protect individual privacy or safeguard against the misidentification of travelers as suspects.

Some senior officials wanted to blame the delays on Bell, whose brash style had annoyed them. One Homeland Security official called him the "bull in the china shop" for refusing to go along with their plans to use CAPPS II to screen for criminals. It wasn't that Bell had any problem with the idea of passenger screening. He thought CAPPS II was critical to national security, and he was largely responsible for helping to create a computer infrastructure, at government facilities in suburban Washington and in Colorado Springs, that could take stock of individuals like never before. But its mission had creeped into uncomfortable territory.

When he left his job, the system was designed to send passengers' names, addresses, and driver's license numbers to private data services like Acxiom to verify their identities. Acxion and the other services would send back a code that rates each passenger on a variety of risks. Then the government would match the identity against terrorist watch lists, and there were also plans to send it into a "neutral environment" run by private companies but under strict government controls, where the personal information of the passenger would be examined for irregularities or odd patterns that might suggest signs of terrorist ties.

Under his watch, none of the information would be maintained by the government after the screening. It was still one of the most sweeping surveillance systems ever created by the government. But Bell seemed convinced that if the system were used only as originally intended, to identify and catch foreign terrorists, it would be perfectly fine. In fact, a version of the system had been used to screen cockpit crews from abroad during a terror alert in the Christmas holiday, 2003. Among those helping on that classified project were Jeff Jonas and his company, SRD.

Because of pressure from others in the government, it took a sharp turn toward domestic criminals and terrorists. Bell said he believed CAPPS II, as planned the day he walked out of the government, ran the risk of eroding constitutional values.

"We have a right of passage and travel. To put an electronic tollbooth at the airport is a slippery slope," Bell said. "When you start going down that road, you infringe on those liberties.

"This is America," he said. "It is not a police state."

BELL HAD PREDICTED CAPPS II might be put off for the 2004 presidential election. He was right. Behind closed doors, senior officials, including homeland security chief Ridge, warned that the system was becoming too politically hot for President Bush, Dick Cheney, and their advisers.

That summer, after a long day and a meal, Ridge offhandedly suggested to some reporters that CAPPS II was dead. Never mind that his own people were poised to begin testing the system, with live data, or that the government had invested tens of millions of dollars in it.

In fact, it was far from dead. It would be scaled back. Officials intended to drop provisions to screen for criminals. Some public relations officials in the government even pressed to change its name, sort of rebrand it to garner more public support. It would now be called "Secure Flight" and be promoted as the new, improved version of passenger prescreening.

The public relations push aside, transportation security officials acknowledged they still intended to press ahead on testing of commercial information services, such as Acxiom and ChoicePoint. They also announced their intention to use passenger name records for automated analysis. And they made clear they would keep any system under wraps until the election was over.

Despite what authorities described as one of the most urgent security problems in America, the country would have to wait still longer to find out how the government would use computers, networks, and information services to screen them as never before.

9

GOOD GUYS, BAD GUYS

THE ORDER TO SCRAMBLE came on a Sunday afternoon, December 21, 2003. Most of the counterterrorism agents and analysts from the FBI had already begun their holiday break. Now they were being paged, one by one, to come back to offices on the fourth and fifth floors of the drab J. Edgar Hoover Building in Washington, D.C. The situation they faced was ominous.

For weeks, the electronic chatter among al-Qaeda operatives and their allies had been mounting. Just two days before, the voice of Osama bin Laden's chief aide, Ayman al-Zawahiri, had been broadcast by an Arabic television network. Zawahiri promised the terrorists would chase Americans everywhere, including in their own backyards. Unlike most intelligence, these intercepts seemed to include actual targets and rough timelines.

To senior Homeland Security officials, who announced the country was on Orange Alert, it appeared it was only a matter of days before there was an attack on Los Angeles, Las Vegas, New York, Washington, D.C., or Virginia's Tidewater area. Whether the weapon would be a commandeered plane or some sort of bomb wasn't clear. Their job was to find the killers before they could attack.

One of the men called back in from Christmas vacation was a young intelligence agent, a technology guy who keeps his name confidential for security reasons. He is a stocky, confident agent, who headed up the FBI's Proactive Exploitation Group, a tiny, technology-savvy operation in the bureau's new financial intelligence unit. Almost nobody had heard of Proactive Exploitation, but it was about to make a name for itself. For months, the agent and his team had been using automated computer tools to examine millions of bank reports about suspicious people for signs of terror financing. Now he would do something the FBI had never been able to do before: Using some high-tech wizardry, the agent told his superiors, he was going to create an instant data-mining operation.

IN THE DAYS BEFORE CHRISTMAS, data collection teams fanned out across the threatened cities. The FBI had been on information sweeps before, but never like this. Officials were taking full use of both the new technology at their disposal and the legal authority that obligated even the most grudging business to hand over customer records. In Las Vegas, federal agents and police swept up names, addresses, credit card numbers of holiday tourists from casino companies. They secured passenger manifests from Southwest Airlines, America West, United, and other carriers. Rental car agencies, truck-leasing companies, storage facilities, and many other firms handed over names and driver's license details of their customers. It was the digital version of an old-fashioned dragnet. But instead of rounding up the usual suspects, as in hard-boiled film noir, these G-men recorded something about everybody within their reach. It would be up to the bureau's computers to sort out the matter later.

The FBI's new approach relied on a profound change in our society: Like virtual comets in cyberspace, we all leave huge trails of electronic information behind. Our shopping habits, Web browsing, bank deposits and withdrawals, the random video images captured by cameras on the street. This trail has become so commonplace most of us no longer even notice. The Proactive Exploitation investigators didn't have to worry about what form the electronic records took. With an array of new software tools, the data mines would be able to pull out the who, what, where, almost without regard to the length of the text. When electronic documents weren't available, a special team took boxes of paper records and scanned them into computers, at some five thousands pages an hour. The blitz wasn't just a technological feat, it was also a demonstration of the agency's growing legal prowess. Even when companies objected, they had to cooperate or face the consequences. Agents and police used simple persuasion and grand jury subpoenas. Where that wasn't sufficient, as in the case of anxious casino companies, they issued secret national security letters, documents that require only a signature from a local FBI supervisor. They also had at their disposal authorities that had been much enhanced by the USA Patriot Act. These included the vastly expanded right to collect any business records deemed appropriate, as well as the easier-to-obtain warrants from the Foreign Intelligence Surveillance Court.

By Christmas Eve, the bureau had collected hundreds of thousands of business records. The intelligence agent and his colleagues in Proactive Exploitation also compiled mountains of government records: immigration files, criminal reports, and investigative records, including details gleaned from telephone wiretaps and collected from Internet service providers. Especially important were storehouses of suspicious activity reports filed by banks and other financial institutions. Few people know it, but the FBI maintains millions of these reports in its own computers, and the files are updated monthly by the Financial Crimes Enforcement Network (FinCEN) at the Treasury Department.

All of this information was poured into a fledgling investigative data warehouse, a project begun in the months after the September 11 attacks, when the bureau took enormous criticism for its poor use of computers and networks to share information, even from agent to agent. Since then, the FBI had recruited dozens of industry experts. By the time of this alert, it had spent $10 million since the terror attacks to buy news servers, software, and the like. That system and the automated intelligence tools it held were to be the magic that made sense of it all.

As an FBI newsletter put it: "Data mining serves as an automated tool that uses multiple advanced computational techniques, including artificial intelligence (the use of computers to perform logical functions), to fully explore and characterize large data sets involving one or more data sources, identifying significant, recognizable patterns, trends, and relationships not easily detected through traditional analytical techniques alone. This information then may help with various purposes, such as the prediction of future events or behaviors."

Less than a week after Homeland Security Secretary Ridge announced the Orange Alert, after a succession of eighteen-hour days, the new data-mining system was ready. Now the FBI and other government officials could compare all the records they had collected against existing criminal cases. The operation was soon generating thousands of potential leads from apparently suspicious patterns among the people whose records were in the system.

Those leads were farmed out to federal and local law enforcement officials on call around the country, who then turned to the billions of records maintained by ChoicePoint, LexisNexis, and other commercial services. In a secret opinion dated September 17, 2001, the agency's National Security Law Unit gave a clear thumbs-up to mix both government and commercial records. "You may use ChoicePoint to your heart's content," one legal adviser wrote by hand on the document.

In the end, most of the leads went nowhere. The system discovered several people with questionable identities and dubious legal status, prompting investigations by law enforcement and counterterrorism authorities. No terrorists were apprehended.

The holiday sweep was a milestone for another reason. It demonstrated a new kind of power at the FBI, a burgeoning computer system that could enable agents to peek more closely into the corners of American society than ever before. Though businesses might object, they had no choice but to comply. Willingly or not, they became collaborators in the war on terror. As for the individuals whose records were swept up, they were never told. To the agent who ran the operation, it was an unqualified success. "We created on the fly a process that had never been used before at the FBI," the agent said a few weeks later. "We were able to harvest that stuff electronically, bang it in en masse against what the FBI had, and spit out potential results."

Whether the FBI would use this new power properly, accurately, and fairly going forward was a question that would be answered at another time.

THE DATA MINE was an example of the sweeping overhaul of the FBI promised by Attorney General John Ashcroft and FBI director Robert Mueller. Their aim was a complete turnabout. At a press conference in May 2002, they said that investigating crimes was no longer sufficient. The leading law enforcement agency in the country would become an intelligence-driven, proactive force. And it would do so through the greatest possible use of computers, networks, and automated surveillance. They said that meant data mining, eavesdropping, and using other high-tech tools to find and target certain people—just as the marketers and private business had done so successfully in the 1990s.

"We have to have that capability. And beyond that, we ought to have the artificial intelligence that doesn't require us to query it—doesn't require us to query it, but automatically looks at those patterns," Mueller said at the press conference. "And that's the type of technology we need to enhance our analytical capability. We've expanded the use of data mining, financial record analysis and communications analysis since September 11. We've set up particular groups that address each of those areas."

This was a brash goal. The FBI had a history of chronic ineptitude in the handling of records and technology. Lawmakers had repeatedly accused FBI leaders of misspending many millions of dollars that had been allocated for similar overhauls in the past. Much of their work was still stored on paper, in tens of millions of old-fashioned files. Agents had a sorry past of mishandling those files with alarming frequency. The execution of Oklahoma City bomber Timothy J. McVeigh, for example, was delayed for almost a month because the FBI misplaced some four thousand documents. Many of the personal computers at the FBI field offices were so ancient that agents couldn't browse the Web. The agency's more powerful servers were poorly linked together and inefficiently operated. Robert Philip Hanssen, the FBI counterintelligence agent who spied on the United States for more than two decades, was able to get away with his perfidy in part because the central computers lacked simple safeguards that would have flagged his misuse of the agency system to check whether he was being watched. In the days after September 11, field agents in Tampa had to send photos of the hijackers by overnight mail to colleagues across the country because their PCs could not handle the job. FBI leaders later discovered with great embarrassment that the bureau overlooked a host of clues about the hijackers in their files, largely as a consequence of their poor information habits.

As the *New York Times* put it in one story, the attacks "exposed the FBI's computers as a national laughingstock, a system so antiquated and inefficient that U.S. senators quip that their kids get more bang for their byte than the nation's vaunted G-men."

Ashcroft and Mueller pledged that was all going to change. The intelligence system they envisioned would draw on any information legally available. It would link the forces of local, state, and federal authorities, soon almost tripling the number of joint terrorism task forces across the country, to eighty-eight. Investigating crimes or terror attacks was no longer good enough. The FBI would become, in essence, the Federal Bureau of Prevention. "Since September 11th, our first effort has been to overhaul our counterterrorism program from the top to the bottom. It's been an ambitious and all-consuming effort," Mueller would say later. "And for the FBI to identify and understand the threats against our nation and do so in compressed time frames, it is essential that we have the personnel and the infrastructure to crystallize the actionable intelligence out of that ocean of information. And to this end, we are in the process of building a comprehensive intelligence program."

They knew their initiatives raised the same sorts of questions that had worried Congress about the FBI three decades before, but they were sure there were plenty of checks and balances in place now—or so they said.

They weren't the only the agency moving in this direction. Unless they moved quickly, they would be left behind in the government's rush to fight the war on terror. That would be an untenable embarrassment at a time when some policymakers question whether the FBI is up to the task of protecting the country, or whether to form an entirely new agency to handle domestic intelligence.

• • •

ED MANAVIAN LOOKED OVER the shoulder of an analyst in California's Criminal Intelligence Bureau in early January 2004, as she scrolled through a series of pithy messages. It was New Year's Eve chatter from her counterparts in police departments across the country. One message had an alert about a small airplane heading toward the Rose Bowl Parade. Did the pilot pose a threat? Another was about a locked bathroom at a football game. Should they call in the bomb squad? There were inquiries about revelers on the Las Vegas strip; travelers at Los Angeles International Airport; visitors to New York City.

Manavian, chief of the state's new intelligence bureau, was thrilled. For more than a year, he had been working with the Defense Intelligence Agency to set up the system, and the Department of Homeland Security had recently taken over management of it. (The Defense Intelligence Agency and state law enforcement officials were collaborating in part because the FBI had always been perceived as overly chary with information.) Now he was looking at the fruit of his efforts. During the holiday alert, scores of state and city intelligence units used his system to ask questions or exchange information. It was exactly the kind of sharing Manavian had hoped for.

The network is formally called the Joint Regional Information Exchange System (JRIES). Manavian and his peers called it the Situation Awareness Space. It was designed to boost information sharing and analysis among the growing number of intelligence units in the law enforcement world. Though the system relied on the Internet as a medium, it was no mere chat room. Developed by Poindexter's Total Information Awareness program, it was tested initially by the defense intelligence community. Poindexter had envisioned it as a place where analysts from anywhere could meet, securely and secretly, to piece together vexing intelligence puzzles. ("JRIES has borrowed/appropriated a lot of ideas we had," Poindexter said in early 2004. "They're trying to put into practice some of the things we were working on.") Using technology from a company called Groove Networks, the Situation Awareness Space enabled more than one hundred units from states and major cities to chat, share intelligence, videos, investigative records, and more, twenty-four hours a day. "What we're doing with our concept,"

Manavian said, "is harnessing the power of all the analytical units and their databases into one virtual environment and using whatever database they have access to."

Manavian's project is part of the vision that Ashcroft, Mueller, and Ridge share—a part that appears destined to grow much larger. Manavian predicted that more than two hundred units will be linked to the system by early 2005. That's supposed to include the FBI, which was contemplating joining in 2004.

A document called the *National Criminal Intelligence Sharing Plan* provides a blueprint for that vision. Sponsored by the Justice Department, the plan was produced by the International Association of Chiefs of Police, the same group that sponsored the technology conference in Philadelphia at the end of 2003. The plan calls for computer networks that would stitch together the 700,000 local, state, and federal authorities and intelligence officials across the country. Think of it as Mayberry R.F.D. meets the CIA. While many state and federal agencies have been able to create intelligence units since the attacks, the police chiefs group argued that most local departments can't afford them. The plan says that must change: "Providing local agencies with the tools and resources necessary for developing, gathering, accessing, receiving, and sharing intelligence information is critically important to improving public safety and homeland security."

Among their recommendations is the broad adoption of Manavian's network. They also advocate using the Multistate Anti-Terrorism Information Exchange, better known as Matrix. That may not be only because of Matrix's power, though. One of the drafters of the plan was William Berger, chief of North Miami Beach and the former head of the International Association of Chiefs of Police. He's a friend of Hank Asher, the Matrix inventor and founder of Seisint. (Berger was one of the early testers of AutoTrack, the information system that made Asher wealthy.) "Data warehouse examples include, but are not limited to: The Multistate Anti-Terrorism Information Exchange (MATRIX) Program is a pilot effort that will initially connect participating states' criminal indices and investigative file databases, driver's license and motor vehicle registration databases, and other public records information for combined data query and sharing among law enforcement participants," the criminal intelligence sharing plan said.

Authors of the plan showed they were aware of the civil liberties implications, saying they recognized their recommendations might seem like an echo of the bad old days of domestic spying. They suggested that good training would eliminate this eventuality. "First, both constitutional values and an individual's right to privacy are deeply embedded in our nation's laws, culture, and expectations. Our nation's preference for government restraint has a long and conspicuous history in America," the plan states. "Second, the public perception of current intelligence work is strongly shaped by its recent history. Since the 1960s, overzealousness by some criminal intelligence units has periodically led to infringements on civil liberties. For example, some individuals have been targeted for surveillance and other investigative activities apparently based solely on their constitutionally protected exercise of free speech, expression of political beliefs, and other lawful activities."

In February 2003, President Bush endorsed the thrust of the ideas at the core of the plan. "All across our country we'll be able to tie our terrorist information to local information banks so that the front line of defeating terror become activated and real, and those are the local law enforcement officials," he said.

Later that year, at the law enforcement conference in Philadelphia, Tom Ridge gave an even stronger endorsement of the plan's central thrust. "We must create new layers of security around our cities, airports, coastlines and borders," he said. "At the same time, we must create new ways to share information and intelligence both vertically, between governments, and horizontally, across agencies and jurisdictions."

The widespread collection and sharing of intelligence was now policy, not just wishful thinking. It was the future of policing in the country. "Law enforcement officers know that the 'good guys' usually follow the rules, and the 'bad guys' try to get around them," Ridge told the cops in Philadelphia. "These measures will make it much harder for them to get away with it."

THERE'S A RUB to all of this. These new intelligence efforts will rely heavily on customer records that many companies do not want to give away, at least not openly. That notably includes Internet service providers such as EarthLink, which several years ago took the FBI to court to prevent the installation of government eavesdropping gear.

The Internet has become one of the most fruitful places investigators look for information when the FBI is trying to make a case. It's where people shop, gossip, and make plans. They express their political preferences, dissent, and ideas there. It's also where miscreants plot crimes or terrorist attacks. People often take it for granted now, but the Internet is a miracle of communications. It's also one of the most potentially intrusive systems devised, a system that has focused a vast range of once disparate activity onto one medium. Virtually everything you do online is recorded there, somewhere.

EarthLink, based in Atlanta, is one of the largest Internet service providers in the world. Starting with 7,000 users in 1994, it now has more than 5.2 million. Its data center handles about 3 billion incoming email messages a month. At the same time, EarthLink customers send out 240 million more. There's no counting the Web pages they browse—much less the pages millions of other people from around the globe view on EarthLink servers. All of this is profoundly alluring to law enforcement and intelligence authorities. To be able to tap in to such a rich communications lode is a dream come true for cops who have long had to rely on shoe leather, snitches, and good luck to break their cases. Les Seagraves, an assistant general counsel and chief privacy officer at EarthLink, knows this firsthand. Over the years, authorities have become rather brazen about the demands they make for information, forcing EarthLink to do things it would rather not do.

Seagraves is a family man, earnest but quiet, who keeps two poster-size photographs of his children on a shelf above his desk. A former prosecutor, he practiced law privately for a few years before joining EarthLink in the dotcom boom as an executive. He found his way into the company's legal office almost by accident, when someone realized he was an attorney. Seagraves recalled the time a federal prosecutor called on him to hand over information about one customer's email. It was early 2002. The authorities had already sent over a fax announcing their intentions. Then an FBI agent arrived at EarthLink's downtown Atlanta facilities. The prosecutor warned him to deliver the information immediately, or else. "They were going to throw me in jail," Seagraves recalled. "It's the tactic that they use to get us to act quickly."

The Justice Department had been eavesdropping on telephone and Internet communications for years. In 2000, the FBI acknowledged it was using a data collection device, with the suggestive name Carnivore, to sweep up online information. It approached Internet service providers, asked them to install Carnivore, and, with court approval, conducted investigations. Among the first wave of companies asked to install Carnivore was EarthLink. EarthLink objected, saying the machine, since renamed DCS1000, slowed the company's computers and took more information about customers than it was legally entitled to. The company took the government to court, a challenge that was hailed as heroic by civil libertarians and the computer digerati.

At the center of the fight was Robert Corn-Revere, a Washington, D.C., lawyer who represented EarthLink. He made the case that basic constitutional protections were at stake. Corn-Revere would later tell Congress: "We believed it would enable the government to acquire more information than the law permits, not just about the person who was the target of the investigation, but potentially about a large number of other subscribers who had nothing at all to do with the investigation." Corn-Revere made a stark case for the principles at stake. He warned that advanced eavesdropping gear like Carnivore could gut the Constitution's free speech protections, as well as blocks to unreasonable searches and seizures. It could overwhelm the ability of outsiders to keep track of the government's activity. "Over time, the cumulative effect of widespread surveillance for law enforcement, intelligence, and other investigatory purposes could change the climate and fabric of society in fundamental ways."

EarthLink lost the case. But instead of installing Carnivore, the company negotiated a settlement: It would do the surveillance itself for the government. The government agreed with that arrangement, in part because it was easier and apparently as effective. It's not only the federal authorities who understood the value of that service. More and more local police have been calling on EarthLink to deliver names, email addresses, and rich streams of information about the electronic highways and byways people have cruised online. And in every instance, EarthLink has conducted the surveillance on the government's behalf.

EARTHLINK'S DATA CENTER is a disorienting place. Hundreds of stereo-sized machines sit on rack after rack, connected by bright orange and green wires that snake overhead like candy-colored vines. The floor has the familiar white tiles of similar facilities at Acxiom and ChoicePoint. A constant loud hum accompanies the cooling air that blows up through holes in the raised floor.

As Seagraves walked through the vast rooms one day in the fall of 2003, he talked about the odd role the company plays in brokering how online surveillance is done. "So the Internet has become a part of everyone's lives, something that people use every day, that includes schoolkids, businesses. It also includes criminals and terrorists. So what the government is looking for normally happens to be now on the Internet. So whether it's communication or storing information, it's likely that those type of things are happening on the Internet.

"As one of the largest Internet service providers in the country, it's something that we have to deal with because it's likely that some of those things happen on our network, and that some of our customers are using the Internet for good things, and for bad things."

Much of the time, they get straight-on requests, subpoenas that demand EarthLink identify somebody who sent or received an email with relevance to a particular case. Other times, they have to actively watch a person. That means sucking in and storing the content of emails, an individual's Web browsing, and so on. Seagraves said he's never told why the company is tracking someone, but he acknowledged there's no question that in some cases it has to do with national security.

"We get the entire gamut of law enforcement tools, including FISA orders and national security letters," he said one moment, only to correct himself later. "I can't tell you about the particulars of any. And I really can't tell you if we've ever gotten any."

He explained: "The federal law says that it's a criminal act if I tell you anything about a FISA order that I've gotten. I would probably go to jail. In fact, I've been told by the FBI that I would go to jail."

Seagraves described how the company uses a mix of hardware and software to isolate an individual under suspicion. That way, he said, they can protect their innocent customers' privacy while complying with the government's request. "We have to balance the needs of our customers and the needs for us to attract customers and make money," he said, "with being responsible and doing our part in providing information to the government.

"We have to balance those two," he stressed, "in order to survive."

ELIZABETH BARKER, an investigator at Fifth Third Bank in Cincinnati, typed a password into a desktop PC. She clicked her mouse on one of the tabs that appeared on the screen and then worked her way through a long list of names and confidential account information. Each one of the people on her screen had been deemed suspicious by a surveillance system the bank installed in July 2003.

Barker clicked on a free checking account in a branch hundreds of miles away. The software had noticed it was strange in a variety of ways: No employer was listed for the customer. The balance on average was far higher than normal for a free checking account, and the transactions usually involved a lot of cash. The surveillance system, produced by a company called Searchspace, had picked it out of millions of other transactions screened for odd patterns. She pulled up a graphic display of the account history. It illustrated how the customer had gone, in just a few days, from having $100,000 to being overdrawn. The same pattern had occurred a few months earlier. "I would consider this very suspicious," she said.

Page after page of refined reports showed a variety of problems with other customers, individuals and businesses alike. After installing the software, the bank made hundreds of reports of suspicious activity that might have been overlooked. Some of them involved suspected terrorists. Two businesses opened by "owners of middle Eastern descent" got tagged for wiring money to counterparts in the United Arab Emirates and trying to hide the ultimate destination of the cash, according to a confidential document provided by the bank. Another "group of Arab men" was reported after the software determined they had all used the same birth date and apartment address for a plethora of check and cash transactions. They had wired the money to China. A doctor was targeted for "reverse money laundering." He had sent his legally gotten pay to firms in the Middle East and Ukraine, evidently taking care to keep the amounts below what he thought would draw attention. For two years, Barker had been looking into the data for criminals and terrorists, more than half of that time without the help of Searchspace. She broke into a smile when asked about the difference. "You can't even make a comparison," she said.

THERE'S NO OVERSTATING the value government investigators place on financial activity. It's considered almost like a fuel for their intelligence engine. Bank transfers; the ties among customers; the use of automated teller machines. Such records also contain a wealth of identity information. The FBI, particularly data-savvy agents like those in the Proactive Exploitation Group, believe that these details, coupled with data mining, amount to a new kind of weapon in the amorphous war on terrorism. One of the first changes at the FBI after the attacks was the creation of a financial intelligence unit.

Driven by provisions of the USA Patriot Act, banks, securities firms, insurers, casinos, and other companies must aggressively seek out signs of threatening activity. It could be money laundering, financial backing for conspiracies, identity theft, or terrorism. Under the Patriot Act, financial institutions must try to find it and then report any suspicious activity electronically to a virtually unknown Treasury Department agency called FinCEN. "The Patriot Act is imposing a citizen-soldier burden on the gatekeepers of the financial institutions," David Aufhauser, the former general counsel at Treasury, said not long after the law was signed by President Bush. "In many respects, they are in the best position to police attempts by people who would do ill to us in the U.S., to penetrate the financial systems."

Given how sensitive Americans are about their financial affairs, that was powerful stuff. Ask a guy on the street and odds are he'll tell you the only personal information he feels more private about are his health records. In 1999, when the government proposed a series of measures requiring close scrutiny of financial information, people went wild. The plan was called "Know Your Customer." It called on banks to better identify customers, establish patterns for their accounts, and watch for deviations that might qualify as suspicious activity. The aim was to curb money laundering. Banks had long been required to report suspicious activity that came to their attention. They also had to give the government information about cash transactions of $10,000 or over. Know Your Customer went much further than many Americans thought was acceptable at the time. When word of the plan became public, hundreds of thousands complained. In March 1999, the Know Your Customer plan was dropped.

Few people said a thing when the Patriot Act not only revived those mandates but expanded them substantially. David Medine, the former financial privacy specialist at the Federal Trade Commission, watched with amazement as Congress slipped provisions into the Patriot Act that trumped the earlier rules. "Sept. 11 obviously made us totally rethink where to draw the line with respect to government access to customer information," he said at the time.

"The question going forward is: Did we draw that line in the right place?" Medine said. "It is really a fundamental civil liberties issue."

As directed by the Patriot Act, Treasury Department regulations required that securities firms, money services businesses, and broker-dealers file reports on suspicious activity, something banks have been doing for several years. Those firms, along with mutual funds, operators of credit card companies, and some other financial companies, also must have anti-money-laundering programs. Congress also said that financial companies must authenticate new customers, check their identities against government watch lists, and maintain records for government scrutiny. The law encourages financial institutions to share information among themselves about customers suspected of being involved with terrorism or money laundering, and it gives them protection from legal liability for doing so. In addition, it gives law enforcement and intelligence agencies greater access to confidential information without a subpoena while also requiring that credit bureaus secretly turn over credit reports to the CIA, the National Security Agency, and other intelligence agencies when presented with a request signed by a senior agency official.

While law enforcement officials said the cooperation of the financial services industry is critical to the war on terrorism, there's no question what it has meant for individuals. They are being asked—actually, forced—to give up some of their privacy. H. Rodgin Cohen, chairman of Sullivan & Cromwell and a leading financial services lawyer in New York, said financial companies will find themselves asking customers about seemingly suspicious but innocent activity that might be embarrassing or involve private matters, such as health care. He predicted that banks also will file more suspicious activity reports, with less evidence, to avoid trouble from the government. "As long as the government can enlist the financial institution as part of the front-line defense against money laundering and terrorism, it has got to be anticipated there will be more in the way of intrusions on privacy," Cohen said. "It is just a different manifestation of whether they can wiretap you."

THE NEW MANDATES have spurred expansion of a cottage surveillance industry. A host of high-tech companies now offer the financial world tools that can track virtually every transaction individuals make. While the banks keep track of how much money we all have, when we write our checks and tap in our personal identity numbers into ATMs, it's not nearly as systematic or probing as the government now requires. That's why banks like Fifth Third have turned to companies like Searchspace, which automates the process of rooting out and reporting suspicious behavior.

Searchspace allows large financial companies to "interrogate their data." Just as an intelligence agent might debrief an informant, bank computers use the artificial intelligence tools provided by Searchspace to ask reservoirs of transaction information questions about customers: Are they behaving normally? Do they have appropriate associates and friends? Does it seem like they're hiding something from the government? Trying to launder ill-gotten cash? Do they fit the profile of terrorists? The system can flag a securities account that never trades stocks. It could draw attention to someone of apparently modest means who receives a $40,000 wire transfer from abroad and then sends out a large check. By sweeping through vast electronic repositories of information, financial institutions using this software can find links among customers that a person would never see. Not long ago, such exploration would have been almost futile, or it would have been considered a huge intrusion into customer privacy. Now this questioning can go on perpetually and become ever more refined, as the computers learn the patterns and predilections of every customer.

A few companies used such tools before September 11, as computer power increased and the government increased efforts to stop the flow of drug and mob money through the U.S. banking system. Many more have embraced this automated monitoring since then. TowerGroup, a Massachusetts research firm that tracks financial services, estimated that banks and other institutions doubled their spending on monitoring systems in 2003, to $120 million. "This is just a sea change in the industry," one analyst said.

Searchspace was founded in 1993. Its system grew out of research done at University College London, a leader in work on artificial intelligence. While artificial intelligence is still in its infancy, it is real and it's becoming a routine if unseen part of our lives, used by the credit, marketing, telecom, and military industries. It is so powerful that a competitor of Searchspace once made the inevitable comparison to George Orwell's prediction of omnipresent watchfulness. ("Sometimes we've referred to our product as the 'Big Brother,'" said Alison Holland, a spokeswoman for NetEconomy, a Dutch competitor that pitches its systems to U.S. firms. "It can monitor so many things.")

Almost half of the top financial institutions in the United States use Searchspace to fulfill their anti-money-laundering obligations, including the Bank of New York, Wells Fargo, UBS, and Fifth Third Bank. In promotional material, Searchspace claims that its software systems create profiles of every customer and are "continually self-updating." "So even if your organization has 30 million accounts," says the company's marketing material, "the solution will continually assimilate and assess information to maintain a unique individual profile for every single account. And because the process is data-driven, there is no need for human intervention.

"By monitoring all business activity within your organization when it occurs, the profiles provide the basis from which the software can rigorously detect, analyze and report on unusual or suspicious activity."

• • •

AT THE HELM OF SEARCHSPACE CORP. in the United States is chief executive Konrad Feldman, a trim, freckled, redhaired Brit who looks like a grown-up version of Harry Potter's best pal, Ron Weasley. Though the claims Searchspace makes for itself seem outsized, one comes away convinced after speaking with Feldman.

Feldman pulls no punches about his company's mission. It helps banks watch and understand individuals better than ever before. He also acknowledges the terror attacks have stimulated great interest in his business. Before the Patriot Act, banks were exceedingly tight about spending money on any technology that didn't directly bolster their bottom lines. Since the law's implementation, those same institutions realize they could be fined or suffer blows to their reputation if they fail to root out money laundering or terrorist customers. Without help from computers, that's a nearly impossible task, even harder for giant operations that routinely handle tens of millions of transactions a day—online, at ATMs, and over the telephone. With his software, the banks don't have to erode customer convenience to meet their expanded anti-terror, anti-money-laundering responsibilities.

Feldman's office is high up on Broad Street in lower Manhattan, not far from the New York Stock Exchange. Through his window, he can see the Statue of Liberty in the harbor. "A lot of it is due to the fact that all industries are focused on making it simpler for customers to interact with the companies, and they've introduced technology-driven mechanisms so that customers do that," he says.

"Internet access to your bank account is an example of that, and other self-service devices. That provides certain efficiencies for the customers and businesses but it also erodes context so it increases the ability to pretend to be someone that you are not."

Feldman doesn't have any illusions about his software being foolproof. Though it can monitor many tens of millions of transactions, it can't catch all the money launderers of the world, let alone the terrorists, whose profiles are dramatically different. People who launder money, like drug dealers or mob bosses, take mountains of ill-gotten gains and try, through a variety of transactions, to cloak the illegality. Sometimes they fob off the money on legitimate businesses so that it looks like perfectly legal profits. Terrorists spend cash, and oftentimes not very much at that. Some counterterrorism officials agree that it is akin to the financial patterns of graduate students who live frugal lives. This is very difficult to detect, because it leaves such a small signature in the vastness of our electronic banking system. The U.S. government estimates that the cost of the 2001 terror attacks was between $300,000 and $500,000—as little as $16,000 per hijacker over more than a year. It takes a lot of scrutiny of a lot of bank accounts to discern any pattern there, which means that banks are going to have to watch more people, more closely. "It is about understanding behavior," Feldman says.

"Understanding behavior" is the same mantra used by Acxiom, Trans Union, ChoicePoint, Seisint, and all the other information and marketing services, so it should come as no surprise that Searchspace also touts an added benefit of its systems: Customer Relationship Management. (In some cases it's the sugarcoating that helps the medicine of having to install costly anti-money-laundering software go down.)

When the artificial intelligence comes to understand a customer, that insight doesn't only have to be applied to criminal activity. It can also be programmed to anticipate when a paycheck is coming in, and whether someone is getting a pay raise. Over time it will learn when an individual's family tends to go on vacation. It can calibrate how much a bachelor typically spends on Friday nights and where. By analyzing changes in his behavior, it could also say when he has tied the knot. That of course could give the marketers a chance to look for signs the honeymooners intend to have a baby.

Officials at Fifth Third seem proud of their partnership with Searchspace, even though it means redefining the meaning of financial privacy, and perhaps alienating people who'd prefer their every transaction were not watched. Michael Matossian, the chief compliance and privacy officer, said that in the war on terror, the bank has no choice. "You can look at that as an opportunity for financial institutions to play a role. You really could save lives," he said. "It's all about no surprises."

He said Fifth Third wants to make a name for itself as being one of the most aggressive, sophisticated watchdogs in the financial industry. He's hoping that reputation will put the bank in good stead with regulators. With $91 billion in total assets in 2004, millions of customers, and twenty thousand employees, it was one of the largest banks in the United States. But it was intent on becoming even larger. That will mean merging with other institutions, and that means getting regulatory approval.

THE PATH OF CUSTOMER INFORMATION from Fifth Third to the FBI is not a long one, and because of mandates in the Patriot Act it is getting shorter. The suspicious activity reports generated by Searchspace software go directly to an unheralded player in the war on terror, the Treasury Department's Financial Crimes Enforcement Network. Better known as FinCEN, it was established in 1990 to help fight money laundering. It served quietly for years as a clearinghouse of information about financial crimes, and thousands of authorities tapped into its data, a huge jumble of details, from banks, criminal files, and public records. By the end of the 1990s, it claimed to use artificial intelligence to analyze everything in its databanks—more than 150 million reports in all. "This technology and the expertise of FinCEN's analysts essentially find the needle in the haystack," one proud official told Congress.

Not many people know about suspicious activity reports, in part because customers are never informed if one has been filed about them. But the reports are routinely tapped by local, state, and federal law enforcement and intelligence officials. FinCEN now sends the FBI its entire database, including many millions of reports about large currency transactions. That file is updated at least every month, sometimes more frequently. FinCEN has made a special place for itself as one of the government's early data miners. The influx of suspicious activity reports— the confidential banking records and raw material for its intelligence analyses—has ballooned from about 52,000 in 1996 to almost 300,000 in 2003. The Patriot Act made FinCEN a central player in the war on terror, and a powerful part of the security-industrial complex. Anticipating a rise in reporting, it began operating a secure online network, where banks and other institutions must fill in more than fifty kinds of information, including addresses, account numbers, Social Security numbers, and phone numbers.

As a measure of FinCEN's growing importance, President Bush paid its suburban Virginia offices a visit on November 7, 2001, just days after signing the Patriot Act. "The United States is pressing the war against terror on every front. From the mountains of Afghanistan to the bank accounts of terrorist organizations. The first strike in the war against terror targeted the terrorists' financial support. We put the world's financial institutions on notice: if you do business with terrorists, if you support them or sponsor them, you will not do business with the United States of America," Bush told the small crowd assembled at FinCEN headquarters.

"Today, we are taking another step in our fight against evil. We are setting down two major elements of the terrorists' international financial network, both at home and abroad. Ours is not a war just of soldiers and aircraft. It's a war fought with diplomacy, by the investigations of law enforcement, by gathering intelligence and by cutting off the terrorists' money."

The FinCEN director at the time was James Sloan, a Secret Service and counterterrorism veteran whose office was filled with memorabilia from a long career. Not long after the president's visit, Sloan explained that the president wasn't the only one visiting FinCEN after the attacks. Another visitor was former General Wesley Clark, who was lobbying for Acxiom at the time. Sloan said Acxiom wanted to join ChoicePoint, LexisNexis, and other public records providers as FinCEN contractors.

Sloan said suspicious activity reports, coupled with commercial records and powerful data-mining tools at FinCEN, have turned up thousands of leads and suspects. "This created an opportunity for dialogue that has never existed before," Sloan said of the Patriot Act. "It has given us an opportunity to work with the industry like never before."

KENNETH RITCHHART WALKED BRISKLY through the bland FBI corridors. The white walls and glossy white floor offered no signs about where he was. It has been that way for a long time in the FBI's Washington, D.C., headquarters. No paintings, few clues to help outsiders find their way around.

Ritchhart made his way to an elevator and punched the button for the seventh floor. The doors opened and he strode through exactly the same kinds of hallways until he came to a small ramp. He walked two feet or so up to a brown door, Room 7712, swiped a security card, and turned the knob. It was cool inside, and humming, like the distant sound of a plane ascending. In autumn 2002, Ritchhart was the man re-sponsible at the FBI for building the tools that the Proactive Exploita-tion Group would use more than a year later. The room he entered was unimpressive, somewhat cluttered, filled with computer equipment. Flowing through those machines, though, were many millions of de-tails about both Americans and foreigners.

Beneath fluorescent lights stood metal racks holding metal boxes about the size of large stereo receivers. Off to one side were rows of PCs used for training. In the other direction stood cabinets that resem-ble large refrigerators, each about two feet wide by six feet tall. They looked exactly like the equipment at companies such as ChoicePoint, LexisNexis, and Acxiom, only much of the gear is tagged with small red labels: "This medium is classified SECRET."

Each machine had more computing power than the entire computer system of the Strategic Air Command just one generation ago. "You're literally talking," Ritchhart said, "about going through billions of docu-ments." While the private sector and most other government agencies embraced technology years ago, the FBI continued using decades-old methods of communication. Before the attacks, hundreds of millions of FBI documents sat in paper files, virtually inaccessible to anyone but the case agents and their close colleagues. To change all that, the FBI was depending almost entirely on private industry. It supplied the engi-neers to build the data warehouses, the thousands of personal comput-ers needed in the field offices, the many intelligence tools to make sense of the information, and, of course, much of the information itself.

As he was gearing up, Ritchhart suggested he had a model in mind: John Poindexter's Total Information Awareness project. "The technol-ogy that he's looking at," Ritchhart said, "is right up our alley."

RITCHHART HAS DARK HAIR going gray at the temples. He speaks rapid-fire technese, almost to the point of a mumble, and often dives deep into the details about his software and computers and process. On the lapel of his double-breasted suit was an FBI button. He drank coffee out of a mug emblazoned with the CIA logo. "The problem is the FBI does not know what it knows," Ritchhart said. "The systems don't talk to each other."

Ritchhart speaks with the restrained intensity of a man who has spent his career in the world of intelligence. A retired Air Force colonel, Ritchhart spent twenty-eight years as an intelligence officer working on computer systems. Now he knew as much as anyone at the FBI about database systems and artificial intelligence. Almost no one outside the bureau knew who he was and few people inside understood what he was trying to do. To use his own words, Ritchhart is "responsible for putting together a comprehensive capability to store, retrieve, and data-mine all the information at the FBI."

Like many government leaders at the time—not to mention data company executives on the make to win government contracts—Ritchhart was relatively unguarded about the government's plan for data. He assumed the public would support whatever the bureau did in the name of improving security. Sitting in his office on the ninth floor of the FBI building, Ritchhart explained how the bureau aimed to become an all-seeing protector that could head off the next attack. He pointed to the bureau's blueprint for this technological future, a document entitled *FBI Data Warehousing, Data Mining & Collaboration*, which spelled out the aims with almost evangelical fervor:

"We Are in a Dynamic New World: The Environment has Changed Radically and *Things Will Be Different!* . . .

"We Must Anticipate What May Happen and Prevent Terrorism Not Just Investigate It After The Fact. . . .

"We Must Accelerate Our Ability To Find and React To Relevant Information."

Another draft of the document showed that the effort relied heavily on technology, intelligence, and computer engineering contractors. These included the Mitre Corp., which was designing the data-mining system, and SAIC, the giant Beltway firm that had also worked on the Total Information Awareness program. Jeff Jonas's SRD, which had worked so closely with Poindexter and the National Security Agency, was helping to build in the Non-Obvious Relationship Awareness system. (To underscore the convergence of companies and techniques, it's worth noting that LexisNexis, which also worked closely with the FBI, and with SAIC, both bought shares in SRD.) Ritchhart's blueprint called for a single system that would handle everything from digital wiretap and surveillance records to "Financial Data: Bank Records,

Credit Card Transactions, Hotel, Airlines, Etc." Where appropriate, it would include blood records, DNA files and fingerprints, motor vehicle registrations, and "open source" information from the World Wide Web. "Law Enforcement is an Information Intensive Business." A secret prototype was also expected to include face recognition.

Ritchhart pointed to a page titled "Data Mining & Exploitation." It showed red and green arrows moving across the page, back and forth, to represent the flow of information. There was a picture of a man on a cell phone, an agent in a suburban neighborhood, an Arabic-looking man in a robe on a computer screen. One large red stream of information flowed toward a "Data Warehouse & Virtual knowledge Base." The stream was labeled: "Collect: Government, Public & Private Data."

FROM THE MOMENT HE WAS HIRED, Ritchhart planned on using what he called off-the-shelf computers, software, and other technology. One afternoon, Ritchhart introduced a man named Mason McDaniel, the chief architect behind the development of the bureau's new computer "tool kit." McDaniel was excited about his mission, to make analysis and intelligence tools available to every FBI agent.

Sitting at a long wooden table behind an unmarked door, McDaniel fired up a powerful laptop and began showing what the agency soon would be able to do. One product called Chiliad Athena enabled him to type in simple queries and see a list of documents showing closely related people, places, and events documented in the bureau files. Another product, "Clear Research—Relationship Spider Program"— took information from newspapers, memos, and any other document with words, and showed the links among individuals. The result was like a colorful spiderweb. Something called "Information Work Space"—a product favored by intelligence agencies—depicted virtual rooms in virtual buildings where agents could meet one another for virtual chats. Another tool was In-Spire, which depicted patterns as clusters of glowing lights like the view of a city at night from an airplane. "Without these tools," McDaniel said, "there's no way to bring it together."

Few Americans have heard about these technologies, let alone used them. In all, some sixty technology contractors supported Ritchhart's effort then, up from just a couple when he joined the bureau. Ritchhart also collaborated with a little known organization called the Intelligence Community Metadata Working Group, which is working on a way to ease the sharing of information from agency to agency inside the government. Members include the CIA, the Defense Intelligence Agency, the National Security Administration, and the Justice Department. "There's more collaboration in the last year," Ritchhart said, than in the last twenty years."

BUT HOW WERE THE FBI and other agencies going to stop authorities from abusing these tools? It is often assumed that police will behave properly. But that can be misleading, even setting aside the history of domestic spying thirty years ago. Police often use their networks and information resources as private databanks, from which they can make withdrawals whenever they please.

Consider the case of a former FBI agent cum private investigator named Mike Levin. Working with a group of people who were assumed to be above reproach, he obtained scores of classified records from an FBI-run system called the National Crime Information Center for $100 each. Levin then sold the reports as fast as he could. At least five of his customers were under investigation by federal authorities, including some New York mobsters. A few were involved in a probe of federal mortgage fraud. At least one was an attorney looking to get an edge for a client who faced federal securities charges. His co-conspirators? He told investigators who caught on to the scheme that they included a communications security specialist in the FBI's Las Vegas office and a woman who worked in the city's courts. Two others were agents in the Nevada state attorney general's office. In 2001, Levin pleaded guilty to selling the documents and became a federal witness.

The great majority of officers and investigators undoubtedly follow the rules; but there seem to be exceptions everywhere. The black market for confidential police records is widespread and thriving. From small-town police departments to the vaunted FBI, data systems seep information that's supposed to be secure and private. Even supposing that a national intelligence network will improve the overall security of the United States, it seems unlikely we will ever be sure the information is secure—unless of course the government decides to take information security more seriously than it has to date.

The security of federal computers has been notoriously lax for many years. The General Accounting Office has repeatedly issued studies documenting this. Cases of abuse show that audit trails are often overlooked. Police and federal authorities have routinely stolen, leaked, or sold records from the classified NCIC system. It seems that law enforcement leaders often look the other way rather than sanction the rulebreakers. In addition, the information in these systems is often wrong. The FBI acknowledged as much in March 2003, when officials successfully sought to exempt the National Crime Information Center and other databases from accuracy requirements in the Privacy Act. An agency spokesman said that it is "impossible to determine in advance what is accurate" because so many officials around the country use the system, some eighty thousand in all.

New systems for collecting, sharing, or analyzing information—including Matrix and the Situation Awareness Space—are being embraced faster than the rules regulating them. As of spring 2004, Manavian said, there were no written, binding guidelines on the use of the Situation Awareness Space, even though scores of agencies were using it to share classified information.

Police lean heavily on their data networks. Every state has computer reservoirs of criminal records, details about missing persons, and a wide array of alerts. One of the most widely used is the National Crime Information Center, a classified national network run by the FBI. That's the system that fueled Levin's black market business. With a name or license plate number, anybody with access can call up information such as arrests, detentions, indictments, even police notations. You can get addresses, birth dates, Social Security numbers, as well as gender, race, and physical attributes. These sensitive details are supposed to be protected under federal and state laws. Investigators and others with access are strictly prohibited from sharing the information with outsiders.

There are long-standing rules restricting the use of the FBI's information system. From the moment it was first approved by Attorney General John Mitchell in 1970, critics warned that it was only a matter of time before it would be misused. In *The Rise of the Computer State,* an important early examination of the impact of computers and networks on society, David Burnham warned about the potential erosion of checks and balances on law enforcement authority. It was that fear that had earlier prompted Congress to approve an amendment to the Omnibus Crime Control and Safe Streets Act of 1968, which stated: "The collection, storage and dissemination of . . . [criminal history] information shall take place under procedures reasonably designed to insure that all such information is kept current therein; the Administration shall assure that the security and privacy of all information shall only be used for law enforcement and criminal justice and other lawful purposes."

Police point to those kinds of policies as the bulwark against abuses. In many instances, though, such policies have had the force of clouds. Police across the country have been caught checking out the backgrounds of attractive women, a practice known as "running plates for dates." They have sold confidential records for bags of cash, and used derogatory files to undermine political opponents. Ari Schwartz, associate director of the Center for Democracy and Technology in Washington, D.C., spent several weeks in 2003 looking for such cases. The center is a privacy and government watchdog group that focuses on information issues. Schwartz expected to find instances of abuse, but the number and scale of the cases stunned him. "When you look at it nationally, it's shocking," he says. "Agents are free to search and look for any data, at any time, for any reason."

These aren't only local cops. In December 2002, former Drug Enforcement Agency investigator Emilio Calatayud was sent to jail for twenty-seven months for selling criminal and law enforcement information to a private investigation firm. Earlier that year, two FBI agents were indicted on charges they employed personal details from the National Crime Information Center to undermine a company executive's reputation. Authorities said they were scheming to hurt the company's stock price as part of a stock scam. Along the way, they also used the agency's data systems to track investigations of other stock schemes.

Some of the cases are even more baroque. In Charles County, Maryland, a lieutenant in the sheriff's department apparently decided to use the department's data system to influence several local political contests. According to county officials, Lieutenant Michael J. Allison generated criminal and motor vehicle reports on a host of candidates in 1997 and 1998. In one case, he deleted an old disorderly conduct arrest of the man he hoped would become the next sheriff. He also released records about colleagues and county leaders. Allison was fired.

Other abuses are chronic. Police, dispatchers, even security guards misused Michigan's Law Enforcement Information Network for more than five years. With almost no oversight, they looked up criminal records, driving histories, home addresses. In one case, a state police detective used the system to track his estranged wife. She was later shot dead. A U.S. Border Patrol Agent looked up a stripper's address for a friend. One local police officer tapped into the network to check out a woman he wanted to take out, while another used it to vet a woman he'd met online.

These are just the cases that became public. Oftentimes police agencies are left to their own designs to oversee the system. Such efforts frequently appear to be halfhearted. While most agencies have clear policies in place, police often don't know them, or they're simply ignored. "It's a question of the training and the auditing and the technology and the priorities," Schwartz said. "We have not seen the priority put toward the stopping of misuses in most cases."

One former sheriff's deputy, who was accused of abusing the Michigan system at least seventeen times, told the *Detroit Free Press:* "There isn't anybody, anywhere in law enforcement, that doesn't check people out. If they say they don't I'd stake you a hundred that they're lying."

These are the kinds of people John Ashcroft and other law enforcement leaders expect to become part of the nation's expanding domestic intelligence system.

ON FEBRUARY 25, 2002, Stephen Nash walked into a hangout for activists called Café Zapatista, also known as The Human Bean, not far from his home in Denver. Terry Apple, the café's owner, said hello and handed over a manila envelope, saying someone had left it for Nash. Nash was a glazier by profession, an activist by inclination. At forty-nine, he is a longtime member of Amnesty International and has been marching and leafleting the Denver area for many years. One of the most outspoken groups he supported was Denver CopWatch, which had criticized the Denver Police Department for allegedly using a heavy hand with minorities. ("They pretty much do what they want," Nash said.)

For all his street experience, Nash was not prepared for what he found when he opened the envelope. Inside were computer printouts from the Denver police. They were dossiers about him and his wife, with their home addresses, driver's license numbers, and the groups they belonged to. What caught his eye, though, was how the police computers had categorized them. Both were labeled "criminal extremist." He suddenly felt very strange. Who else had these mistaken records and what were they going to do with them? "How far can this go?" he asked himself.

The Nashes weren't the only ones concerned. Some days later, Nash got a call from Mark Silverstein of the ACLU of Colorado. Silverstein had received packets of files as well, probably from the same insider. He wanted to have a meeting. Would Nash and his wife, Vicki, join him? On March 11, Silverstein held a press conference, where they disclosed the documents and called on Mayor Wellington E. Webb to intervene.

"These documents also demonstrate that the Denver Police Department has inappropriately smeared the reputations of peaceful advocates of nonviolent social change by falsely labeling their organizations as 'criminal extremist,'" Silverstein wrote in a letter to Webb.

"Although the ACLU has obtained only a small sample of the police files, the few pages I have seen provide an alarming glimpse of the kinds of information the Denver Police Department is recording and the kinds of peaceful protest activity it is monitoring inappropriately."

The result was a flood of revelations, and an unexpected look into the unsettling and weird world of domestic intelligence, at least as it was practiced in Denver. First came the mayor's acknowledgment: A police intelligence unit had been compiling information about law-abiding citizens for decades. It had maintained files on more than 200 organizations and some 3,200 individuals. Then came the details about who was in those files. If not for the seriousness of the situation, the list might have seemed almost farcical. Included was an elderly nun who worked to better the lives of poor Indians in Chiapas. She was thought to support overthrow of the Mexican government. A Denver secretary who rallied for Native Americans and fair trade was cited for having a "direct relationship" with an "outlaw biker" gang. A Colorado University professor made it into the system for speaking out at a rally against police brutality.

As for Nash, he showed up repeatedly. In some cases, he was cited for his "direct relationship" to the American Friends Service Committee. Though one file noted that the group takes its "political stance from the Quaker Religious Movement"—a group known for its pacifism—it nevertheless gave them and Nash the label of "criminal extremist." It was the same for End the Politics of Cruelty, a group that criticized the Denver Police Department.

"We knew that the police attended a lot of our events. But we hadn't realized they were keeping a score card," Nash would say later. "It was like a wake-up call. It was a confirmation of our worst fears about police."

IT TURNS OUT that Denver's criminal intelligence bureau had collected some 100,000 cards on a hodgepodge of subjects over five decades. Some were truly intelligence-related, many were not. In 2000, police decided it was time to become more sophisticated in their operation. They wanted to automate their files. They reached out to Orion Scientific.

Founded in 1989, Orion was built on analytical software first developed by the Defense Advanced Research Projects Agency, the same agency that housed John Poindexter's Total Information Awareness project and also funded Joseph Atick's face recognition research. The company sold itself as a real insider, and a range of law enforcement and intelligence authorities already relied on its software, both in the United States and abroad. That included the Defense Intelligence Agency, the Justice Department, and the FBI. After the terror attacks, new intelligence operations in California and New York City embraced Orion. One of the products used by Ed Manavian's people was OPNet, an Internet surveillance tool that "contains approximately 100 gigabytes of public source terrorism related data dating back to 1944." Orion claims that OPNet enables intelligence analysts to collect and share information much more easily, partly through the use of link diagrams. Orion had made a pitch for a contract in the Total Information Awareness project, but Poindexter and his colleagues dismissed the company's technology as inadequate for their purposes.

On top of all that, company president Jim Stinson burned up considerable energy pitching his expertise and the company's technology might. "Whatever your endeavor, my hope is that we can help you operate more efficiently, respond more quickly, do more with less and for those chosen few—help you make the world a safer place," Stinson wrote in a brochure for one analytical product called OrionMagic.

For all Orion's apparent sophistication, there was one problem. Though the Denver police spent $45,000 to license the company's software at the end of 1999, they didn't pay for enough training. And Orion apparently didn't require it as a condition of using its powerful tools. Instead, the police supervisors made up the rules as they went along, but even those rules were never distributed. A review of the operation after the fact found that it was often up to the officer doing data entry to decide how to categorize someone. Sometimes the most convenient category was "criminal extremist."

In June 2002, a panel appointed by the mayor to review the fiasco concluded the police department had no justification for keeping any of the files it had amassed. The panel softpedaled the consequences. "We see no reason to punish anyone in the police department for retaining improper information," they wrote.

"The inclusion of all sorts of information in criminal intelligence files was a result of transferring information from a Rolodex to a sophisticated computer program. The lack of assistance and training from the software led to most of the problems."

In the push to improve information sharing, what's to stop people like Nash from being forever tarred without their knowledge? Prevented from flying? Treated as a special risk during traffic stops or trips abroad?

"People are often wondering, 'What database am I in? What consequence is going to be visited upon me?'" Silverstein, the ACLU attorney, said. "They don't know what the consequences are in store for them as a result of being labeled 'criminal extremist.'"

Unlike the Denver police, Orion doesn't have to account for its role in the episode. For months in 2003, Stinson rebuffed requests to discuss his business. He was busy arranging the sale of his company to SRA International, a giant government contractor that often works in the intelligence world. In announcing that deal, on January 8, 2004, SRA said Orion represents great profit potential, suggesting that was in part because of its ties to the Defense Department. SRA officials also refused to discuss the company and the products it sells. "It's just something they simply aren't comfortable talking about," said SRA spokeswoman Laura Luke. "There are just too many sensitive areas and so forth."

THE FUTURE OF THE FBI is being charted, in part, in New York, at the largest of the agency's fifty-six field offices. It was there the bureau started its first formal intelligence unit outside of Washington, D.C., and also where Assistant Director Pasquale D'Amuro, head of the New York office, was trying to employ technology to make the most of the bureau's new surveillance powers.

One day in March 2004, D'Amuro took a visitor on a tour of his domain high above downtown Manhattan. He typed in a passcode, opened a plain blue door, and walked a few steps into the room, a part of the FBI's new intelligence unit, a place where few outsiders will ever be permitted to go. D'Amuro pointed to a large, colorful diagram, one of many tacked or taped on the walls. It was a link chart, the product of computer programs that find associations among people, their phone calls, bank transactions, and associates. This chart had red, blue, yellow, and green rays starting at some of the locus points and connecting to others. All the analysts in New York use such computer and surveillance tools now. Before long, so will those in the rest of the country. The charts have become an emblem of a new kind of policing—indeed, of our age.

D'Amuro is an operations guy who spent much of his long career at the agency directly involved in investigations. After September 11, 2001, he was summoned to the J. Edgar Hoover Building in Washington to oversee the bureau's response to the attacks. He soon became chief of counterterrorism and counterintelligence. He helped launch the technology initiatives that eventually led to the instant data-mining operation during the 2003 holiday. He also became a devout believer in technology-enhanced intelligence and in the sharing of that intelligence with other agencies and private companies. "It's absolutely critical," D'Amuro said. "I don't think a human being could process the amount of information that we deal with on a daily basis."

As D'Amuro worked his way through the office, it was clear his new intelligence unit had a long way to go, something he acknowledged. The scene around him looked more like a caricature of a cop shop than one of the nation's newest intelligence operations. There were desktop computers and speedy Internet connections and information analysis tools, but the carpet was dingy and worn. Manila files a foot deep covered entire tables. Paper was strewn everywhere. Was this the old FBI, the agency that couldn't find its own documents, or the new proactive agency, that relied on technology and artificial intelligence for leads? The incongruity was inescapable.

"It's an evolutionary process that is greatly improved from where we were prior to 9/11," D'Amuro said. "The system that's being developed for the bureau is something that's an evolutionary process. It doesn't happen overnight. We needed to revamp our information technology tools.

"Those new tools," he added, "are going to bring a tremendous resource of both software and hardware, and allow a search capability unlike anything we've had before."

Joining D'Amuro was Timothy Herlocker, the assistant special agent in charge of the intelligence operation. Under Herlocker's arm was a set of plans, which he unfurled in a vast open room that some wit named, in a handmade sign posted by the door, THE PICNIC AREA. The room had the same threadbare feel of the other analyst's office. But the plans showed a place that would soon be transformed into a top-secret bunker, an operations center overlooking much of the city. There would be a wall-high set of giant television screens for viewing data, link charts, and surveillance videos. There would be high-speed lines connecting it to every other field office, as well as state and local police. A large portion of the room would be constructed to protect the nation's most precious secrets. And its computers would be linked to others at the CIA, the military, and the nation's other spy operations. This is what Herlocker called the "high side of intelligence."

The room would be the embodiment, in other words, of the post-9/11 ethos of intelligence and information sharing.

D'Amuro expressed satisfaction with Herlocker's plan and the infusion, haltingly, of new technology and commercial information services into the FBI's operation. It's all about making the FBI more efficient. But a question begged to be asked: Can the FBI become too efficient? He dismissed that concern, saying federal agents are well trained to protect civil liberties. And they're watched closely by Congress, inspectors general, and other outsiders to make sure they don't go too far. "Now people can say, 'Why do we need Big Brother looking at all that type of information?'" he said. "The American people in this country have nothing to fear about the information that we're collecting. We don't have time to mess around, taking a look at people that we're not interested in. There's a reason for us to look at the people that we look at."

Standing in the nascent command center, not far from yet another link chart and photos of Arabic men under investigation, he said the ones to watch are the companies, the very same operations that supply his analysts with so much information about Americans. "There are all kinds of oversight and restrictions to the federal government, to Big Brother, going out there and collecting this type of information," D'Amuro said. "Yet there are no restrictions in the private sector to individuals collecting information across this country, which potentially could be a problem for the citizens of this country."

10
NO PLACE TO HIDE

Richard Smith opened the door of the Starbucks near the corner of Amsterdam and 70th Street on Manhattan's Upper West Side. He stepped up to where other customers were ordering their coffee concoctions and pointed to the wall behind the clerk's head. Hanging there was a black cube. It was smaller than a wallet and connected to a narrow cable. Smith smiled knowingly. It was a surveillance camera.

He turned toward a set of tables and upholstered chairs, where young, caffeinated folks typed away at laptop computers or talked on their mobile phones. Some of them were connected to the Internet through a wireless network known as WiFi. Starbucks offers the service as a convenience to attract the digerati who like to get wired while working. It happens also to be an extremely efficient data collection mechanism, forever noting the presence of computers and the times and places of contacts.

Smith walked back out to the street, looked around, and headed toward a subway station. As in many cities, the public transit system in New York no longer allows people to use tokens. To boost efficiency, turnstiles now rely on small cards with magnetic strips. These strips enable straphangers to cut the time it takes to ride by paying for many trips at one time, with a credit card if they choose. All they have to do is swipe the MetroCard to get in. Those cards also record travel activity. As he examined the vending machines, he noticed something else: security cameras behind a one-way mirror.

Over and over, Smith found that someone or something was looking at people electronically, sweeping up information, sending it across digital networks. He went to a Kinko's store and paused at a device that enabled customers to use a credit card to make copies. He stopped in a small deli and found an ATM. There was a "hand reader" at a grocery store that clocked employees in. They're all sensors that record identities and the times and places of transactions.

As he walked on the street, he pointed out people using their mobile phones and cameras hanging over building entrances. Even a new Porsche SUV parked on Broadway served as a sensor: its satellite navigation system was designed to pinpoint and record exactly where the driver was on the planet.

Smith is a former computer programmer, an Internet specialist, a nerd of a very high order. At forty-eight, he has a beard, bushy eyebrows, and a serious demeanor that masks a ready sense of irony and humor. He has devoted years to the study of data collection and surveillance networks. In the late 1990s, it was Smith who uncovered the technical underpinnings of several surreptitious methods of tracking people online, including something dubbed "Web Bugs." He found code in Microsoft Word documents that showed who had handled them. Then as a computer consultant he began tracking the accelerating convergence of many commonplace electronic devices and networks that collect information about us.

In short, he is one of the very best at watching those who watch us, a technical guy who understands the deepest implications of the data revolution and the partnership between government and the information industry. "What has changed is that we might have a thousand times more data for law enforcement to work with," Smith said. "And human beings have never lived in that regime before."

That perspective made him an excellent surveillance tour guide of New York that day, in late summer 2003. It took him no effort: finding sensors on the Upper West Side was as easy as spotting pigeons in the park. They were everywhere, electronic sentinels, absorbing information about so many individuals and sending it to databases, public and private, as the digital fuel for our emerging surveillance society.

SMITH GOT INTO HIS OWN CAR, a Volvo, and pulled out some electronic "goodies" he keeps handy to demonstrate his ideas. One device was a global positioning system, or GPS, receiver that, when connected to a laptop, tells him exactly where he is at any given moment. It was a two-year-old model that cost about $100 when he bought it. It had enough storage to hold the equivalent of about 6 million pieces of paper filled with information. That's relatively small compared with what he could have bought for $100 that day: a new system with four times the storage capacity. Then he showed off a wireless camera. It was smaller than the one he noticed at Starbucks, a cube about as wide across as a postage stamp. Operating on a 9-volt battery, he said, it can broadcast a television signal up to 200 feet.

He started his car and drove south toward the Lincoln Tunnel, not far from the Empire State Building. The global positioning system was on and tracking our every move. But Smith was not as impressed with it as he used to be. New cell phones, he said, can be programmed to transmit their location every few seconds to the mobile network. He steered his way through the tunnel and, on the New Jersey side, went to a tollbooth.

Government agencies have been collecting tolls forever at bridges, some highways, and on ferries. Until the early 1990s, the vast majority accepted only coins and currency. The point was to collect money. Now the role of tollbooths is evolving. More and more, they're also becoming a matter-of-fact part of a security and law enforcement infrastructure as digital checkpoints. Cameras are often pointed at drivers' faces and their license plates. When drivers use an electronic transponder such as E-ZPass to automatically pay the tolls, they're also handing over information about themselves.

That's what happened, with zero fanfare, when Smith drove slowly by the booth. The transponder, held against his windshield, sent out a signal that he was coming. The system knew it was his car, because he had previously registered and shared his bank account number. The technology in the tollbooth took note of the identification number and exact time and location that the car passed by. In the vast majority of these transactions—and there are millions of them every day now in the United States—drivers get what they pay for: convenience. Millions of transponders have been issued since the E-ZPass system was first installed in the New York region in the early nineties. On some days, more than eight of ten cars going into Manhattan use them. They're not just for tolls anymore. Fast-food customers use transponders to charge snacks, while airport parking lots use them to deduct fees. "It has just revolutionized the way our operation is run," a transit authority official said.

The devices are also helping to change the way police think about their work. When an assistant U.S. Attorney in Baltimore named Jonathan Luna went missing in December 2003, one of the first things investigators obtained were the electronic toll credits (in addition, of course, to credit card records and surveillance video). They were able to show that his Honda Accord had wound its way through three states before he ended up drowned, in a Pennsylvania creek, with thirty-six stab wounds to his body. Attorneys also rely on such systems to establish the whereabouts of their clients, or their adversaries' clients.

Smith said the heart of the system, the thing that makes it all work, is something called radio frequency identification, or RFID. In the case of most toll systems like E-ZPass, that's the transponder. The ones most drivers use, as with almost everything digital, are becoming dated. They're clunky, he said, nothing at all impressive compared to the minute identity tags that are about to change our world.

THINK ABOUT YOUR DAILY ROUTINE, and you will begin to understand Smith's idea about convergence and what this means for you. When you wake up and sign on to the Internet and browse the Web, companies record where you go, the pages you access, anything you order or buy. If you go to a newspaper site, it records everything you read, because you have voluntarily registered and they know who are you. Suppose you turn on your TiVo machine? That act is being recorded. So is the fact that you're watching last night's *Daily Show*.

You use your debit card for breakfast on the way to your office. Or you hop in your car and pass through E-ZPass. There are cameras at the parking garage, subway station, and, of course, the bank and Starbucks. Depending on the city you live in, a camera system is monitoring the streets, even at stoplights. If you take money from the ATM at lunch, there's a growing chance that artificial intelligence is probing that transaction for signs you may be a terrorist or money launderer or have ties to unsavory people.

At work, you use a magnetic strip ID card, or an iris scan or a fingerprint or face recognition system to enter the building. The time and date of your arrival are kept, possibly forever, in a computer system. Your exit at lunch is recorded by one computer. The fact you stopped by the pharmacy to pick up your prescription is recorded by others, some of them run by entities across the country known as pharmacy benefit managers. Your computer is a sensor, of course, and chances are the boss is recording the email you typed to your pal and the fact you ogled the swimsuit edition of a sports magazine online. There's a better chance they're recording you the old-fashioned way, with a camera, perhaps when you leave work early or take a cigarette break. Driving home in that new Cadillac? If so, you're probably taking advantage of the global positioning system like Smith's because, after all, it's pretty nifty technology. At home, you can't resist buying that sweater or book or "sensual gift" from a catalogue for your spouse. And when you call the 800 number to order, their computers are recording and taking note of everything: your phone number, name, voice, and key words that you use. That's because the phone, linked to computers, has become a sensor, too.

IT'S NO STRETCH to say the future of data collection—one part of it, anyway—is embedded in the rubber casing of Smith's Volvo key. It's a radio frequency tag built into the key as part of an anti-theft system. Without the key in hand, thieves would have a much tougher time starting the computer-laden car. It's a modest example of a much larger trend. In just a few years, these tags have become cheaper and better, and they're spreading fast. That's in part because they don't need a power source to work. Unlike the transponders used for electronic tolls, the tags need only to be scanned by a low-power device. They echo back the information they contain, extraordinarily long strings of unique numbers and codes. Those codes provide links to files already on computer servers, enabling someone doing the scanning to know precisely what object or person they have encountered. The latest tags can hold 128 bits. That's a very big number—bigger really than you can imagine. It means, Smith said, that virtually *everything* in the universe could be labeled with a tag containing a unique number.

There's no end to the potential use of these things, which means that there is no end to the kinds of product monitoring or personal surveillance by companies, law enforcement, or private investigators. Such thinking has naturally stoked industry expectations. Some observers estimate spending on the tags will jump from $91.5 million in 2003 to $1.3 billion in 2008. Even discounting for hype, that's a lot of tracking. Like 6 million other people, for instance, Smith also has something called Speedpass to automatically pay for his gas at Exxon. Manufacturers are already putting RFID on pallets to ease logistics. Instead of having to read a label and record something in a computer, a worker only has to pass a wand within a few feet to record exactly what's on the pallet, where it came from, where it's supposed to go. (Indeed, when linked to databases, there's literally no end to the information that could be appended to the ID code at the moment a wand apprehends it.) In 2003, retail giant Wal-Mart mandated that suppliers begin using RFID starting in 2005 to improve efficiencies and cut down on costs. The Defense Department followed suit, saying that its own top suppliers had to begin using the technology in January 2005. The Food and Drug Administration, meanwhile, said it is studying the feasibility of putting the devices in drug containers as part of a "track and trace" program to prevent counterfeiting. Casinos are in on the new technology. Gambling chip makers have begun manufacturing chips containing the ID system both to fight fraud and to monitor high rollers.

Radio frequency chips and readers likely will also be components in the "virtual border" to be created as part of the border surveillance program called U.S. Visit. Accenture, the giant consulting firm that won the enormous contract to build the system, used its familiarity with RFID to help distinguish itself from other contractors.

Some companies already are talking about embedding the devices into paper currency. Hitachi produces a chip that appears suited to that task. The Japanese company sent out a vial containing perhaps one hundred of them. At first glance the vial looked empty; only on closer inspection was it apparent the chips were in there, off to one side, black and minute. They looked like fleas.

About the same time, the director of the Enterprise Charter School in Buffalo began using the electronic tags to monitor the movements of students. Every student has to wear an ID card containing the tag. When they arrive at school, the tag triggers a kiosk to record their presence and display their photos. The same technology is used in a Texas jail and on wristbands to track prisoners of war in Iraq. For the school, it's about security and efficiency. "Before, everything was done manually—each teacher would take attendance and send it down to the office," the school's director Gary Stillman told Wired.com. "Now it's automatic, and it saves us a lot of time."

A firm called SAMSys Technologies, meanwhile, uses the tags to create an all-purpose surveillance tool for amusement parks called the SafeTzone System. Everybody at the park would get a SafeTzone Locator, a watch-size tracker. Parents could use it to find their kids on an electronic map, buy goodies for them without pulling out their wallets, and cut down on waiting times for rides. They bill it as a combination of gee-whiz and surveillance, in one tiny package. "The SafeTzone System is making the entertainment park experience more enjoyable and less frustrating for families and groups."

The people promoting the tags are effusive "Try this quick quiz. What tiny technology can help cut credit card fraud, turn a piece of plastic into an intelligent stored value card, improve customer relationship management at banks and retail outlets, and perform countless other valuable tasks? Give up?" Vicki Ward, an IBM executive, wrote in a marketing paper. "The answer is RFID tags. And based on the momentum of their uptake in the first half of 2003, they are about to enter everyone's lives much sooner than many industry observers had expected. RFID—radio frequency identification—is a technology that is rapidly crossing over from being expensive and experimental to universal usefulness."

Ward has seen the future from the inside. IBM is working on a sweeping new approach to customer identity. It wants to put the electronic tags in your credit cards, bank passbooks, and anything else that will enable businesses to automatically "know you" when you arrive. This is another one of those customer relationship management initiatives—the same impulse that fueled the data revolution of the 1990s. The project is named "Margaret," for the mother-in-law of Paul McKeown, a senior executive in charge of "smart card" initiatives. It seems that Margaret went into her local bank one day and no one recognized her. Someone asked for her identification, which she neglected to bring along, and then sent her away. McKeown figured that should never be allowed to happen, particularly not to "high-net-wealth" individuals. So the "Margaret" project was begun.

Other initiatives also are likely to show up in your own wallet—or in your arm—before too long. At the end of 2001, a New Jersey surgeon embedded one about the size of a grain of rice under his skin. (He was among the first to join millions of pet dogs and cats that had the RFID implanted, to enable animal welfare agents to track and identify them.) Later on, a Florida family, quickly dubbed the "Chipsons," had the IDs injected into their arms by a company trying to capitalize on the technology. Now the company, Applied Digital Solutions, is marketing its VeriChip system in Mexico and South America. It claims the embedded tags will improve the security of buildings and children. One company called MetroRisk, a security company, bought 2,100 VeriChips and dozens of scanners at the end of 2003. The next year, Attorney General of Mexico Rafael Macedo de la Concha and dozens of colleagues had the chips implanted as well, enabling them to easily pass through an electronic checkpoint in a new anticrime facility.

THE EMAIL TO KATHERINE ALBRECHT arrived on December 15, 2003. "Ms. Albrecht, I am an employee of Grocery Manufacturers of America, the world's largest association of food, beverage and consumer product companies," it began. "I was wondering if it would be possible for me to attain [sic] a copy of your biography for our sources."

The note struck Albrecht as odd. For several years, she had run an advocacy organization called Consumers Against Supermarket Privacy Invasion and Numbering. Her group initially focused on shopper cards that grocers used to track customer purchases and give them discounts.

The grocery industry was among the leaders in trying to parlay personal information and database profiling into more targeted marketing. That offended Albrecht, who considered such efforts intrusive and argued customers didn't understand the bargain they were making when using the cards. She was savvy about how to create a public stink by publicizing how the efforts work, sending out dispatches on the Internet and questioning the companies relentlessly. When she turned her attention and research to the use of identification tags in products, she threatened to create a public policy flap that could cost the industry a lot of time and money.

Albrecht decided she had better write back and find out a little more from the group. The day after she got the email, she sent her own note: "Per your request I can send you a bio under separate cover. . . . But as your request is a bit unusual, you have me curious. (I am used to being interviewed or invited to speak somewhere before being asked for a bio.)"

Then came a surprise, yet another message evidently not intended for her eyes. "I don't know what to tell this woman! 'Well, actually we're trying to see if you have a juicy past that we could use against you,'" wrote a young woman who worked with the Grocery Manufacturers' public affairs officials. A spokesman dismissed it as an inside joke, a flippant remark by an inexperienced employee. But Albrecht was floored. "I was laughing and horrified. 'You've got to be kidding,'" she recalled thinking to herself. It took a few minutes for the creepiness to set in.

"My thinking was, 'Holy shit. They are out to get me.'"

It was a small exchange in the early struggle over the implications of radio frequency identification. Supporters like IBM, Accenture, and retailers contend the technology offers profound opportunities for efficiencies and improved security and an entirely new level of one-to-one marketing. With enough tag readers, companies could manage their goods and get to know their customers in a completely new way. Skeptics like Albrecht believe the tags will be revolutionary for another reason. As they become smaller, and the readers more powerful, monitoring could become almost ubiquitous. It would be like having real-world "cookies" linked to us, sending back information about everywhere we go.

Albrecht's legwork has documented how far research of the tags already goes: soap packages, aerosol cans, shampoo bottle caps, coffee cans, paper dog-food bags all carry forms of the ID. Tag manufacturers are rushing ahead with new forms. One company embeds metal fibers into paper that can be read as a "signature" that serves as a unique code. Another company called Intellitag builds chips into a plastic "credit card format" that it calls an intelligent identification card. Homeland security, luggage tags, customer loyalty cards? The company is pitching them all. It's already being used by some government officials at border crossings. "For security applications," the company's promotional material said, "the unique write [sic] capability of the Intellitag ID card enables it to act as an 'electronic passport.'"

A couple of organizations, including a federation of research universities, are working on a standard that would enable every manufactured item in the world to be given a unique ID, at least theoretically. "The Internet of Things," they call it; "how intelligent tagging is about to change the world." Researchers discount as shrill the criticism and focus instead on the enormous potential for improving logistics and customer convenience. But the readers could take almost any form—or be built into walls, doorways, cars, or planes. The tags, embedded in shoes or luggage or the seams of trousers—officials are contemplating embedding them in airline tickets—might be just the thing for aviation or building security. Or for the intelligence officials who believe that some form of Total Information Awareness will make us safer. Once again, marketers would be leading the way.

RICHARD SMITH DROVE BACK through the Lincoln Tunnel and headed downtown. He explained one reason why all this has happened: the accurate prediction three decades ago by Intel co-founder Gordon Moore that computer processing power would double roughly every year. That extraordinary trend yielded many of the electronic gizmos and networks that both dazzle and watch us. "Anything that uses chips will get better, smaller, faster, more mobile," Smith said. "Fundamentally, Moore's Law is driving the creation of these surveillance networks. One of the fruits of Moore's Law is the Internet, that unimaginably complex global computer network that was born coincidentally the same year that Moore made his famous observations. It's built on systems, or protocols, that break up information into packets, whip them to the right destination, and put them back together, all in a flash.

Though programmers could not have foreseen the particulars, this system, often known as TCP/IP, has been able to accept an amazing array of other kinds of technology and activities, including the World Wide Web, Internet telephony, video transmission, ATM transaction, mobile phone service. The list goes on and on. Before long, our phones, laptop computers, PalmPilots, watches, pagers, and much more will play parts in the most efficient surveillance network ever made. Forget dropping a coin into a parking meter or using a pay phone discreetly on the street. Those days are slipping by. The most simple, anonymous transactions are now becoming datapoints on the vast and growing matrix of each of our lives. "The fact that you did something at a particular time," Smith said, "will be recorded and will never go away until the last hard drive is destroyed."

As he negotiated the streets of New York, Smith was becoming more philosophical. Behind the technician's mask was someone who cared deeply about American values, autonomy, privacy, and such. "We all like many of these surveillance systems because they provide us with convenience," he said. "Cell phones—they allow us to talk when we aren't at home. We can talk when we are on the road and get information. We can talk to our family. Credit cards help us to buy things easier. We don't have to carry around as much cash. We love fast lanes because it allows us to avoid that twenty-minute line. All of these things, they benefit us. And by and large these systems are being put in to benefit us. The trouble is, there are secondary uses, and it's law enforcement and lawyers. In a legal situation, the more information the better. And that is the disadvantage that we are going to be talking about a lot more."

Why worry if you have nothing to hide? "We have nothing to worry about," he said, tongue in cheek, "until they make a mistake."

THE CONVERGENCE SMITH SEES takes many forms, some of them a strange mix of mundane and extraordinary technology. That's what James Turner learned after renting a Chrysler Voyager. Turner was a box office manager at the Palace Performance Arts Center in New Haven, Connecticut. In October 2000, he rented the minivan from a company called Acme Rent-A-Car. He paid with a debit card and headed south to Virginia, where he was planning to review some shows to stage at his theater. Like many of the drivers around him, Turner zipped down I-95, going more than 80 miles an hour. But unlike most of them, Turner was being watched from above, his every move recorded.

It turns out that Acme had installed a global positioning system in the car. It was called the AirIQ. It included a computer in the vehicle, a transmitter, and a back-end server that enabled Acme to watch Turner's progress on a Web page. Had they wanted, Acme officials could have shut the car down. The rental agreement alluded to all this, but he apparently didn't notice. Turner found out what was happening when he got to Virginia and tried to buy gas with the same debit card he had used to rent the minivan. He was denied. When he called his bank, a clerk told him that Acme had made three withdrawals for a total of $450. That was the penalty assessed for three speeding violations in Connecticut, New Jersey, and Virginia.

In effect, Acme had become a remote traffic enforcer, using satellites, the Web, pint-sized computers, and transmitters as its tools. Turner sued, charging Acme with invading his privacy. Included in the court records were maps that showed the *exact* longitude and latitude of Turner's Voyager, down to six decimal places, and the *exact* time he was speeding, down to the second. "Said surveillance by Defendant seriously interfered with the Plaintiff's solitude, seclusion and in his private affairs," said the papers his attorney filed in Connecticut Superior Court. The trial date was set for the spring of 2004. "The Defendant knew or should have known the use of a 'GPS' system would be offensive to persons of ordinary sensibilities."

Turner also submitted a claim to the state Department of Consumer Protection. After an investigation, the department ordered Acme to stop fining people, and to return the speeding fees. Turner wasn't the only one watched and tagged by the company. "It's horrible. It's like I was some sort of an animal that was tagged by scientists so they could observe my mating habits," another driver told *Wired*. "Like I really want these guys to have a record of exactly where I went with the car I rented from them? A little knowledge can be a dangerous thing."

Such systems are only getting better, as *New York Times* writer John Schwartz showed at the end of 2003. Schwartz focused on a company called OnStar and a personal security system it offers to include in new cars. Many drivers welcome the system as a source of comfort and convenience because it serves as an automated guide and enables drivers to call directly to OnStar operators. It can unlock doors, and even helps police track down thieves. But Schwartz, who has written about privacy and civil liberties issues for years, knew there was more to the story. If OnStar could listen in as a convenience, it could also listen in to eavesdrop. "OnStar is one of a growing number of automated eyes and ears that enhance driving safety and convenience but that also increase the potential for surveillance," Schwartz wrote. "Privacy advocates say that the rise of the automotive technologies, including electronic toll areas, location-tracking devices, 'black box' data recorders like those found on airplanes and even tiny radio ID tags in tires, are changing the nature of Americans' relationship with their cars."

Two years earlier, FBI agents in Las Vegas got a court order giving them the right to listen in on a system much like OnStar (though the company was not identified in court papers). The agents had access to the conversation in one suspect's car for thirty days before the company got cold feet and asked a federal court to block the eavesdropping. Another company called Networkcar promises to track a vehicle and monitor its performance for $1,000. The service offers remote sensors that automatically send the information to a tailored page on the Web. Among other things, it uses a GPS system to record the history of the vehicle activity. Parents use the system to watch where their children go. Some Marine Corps officials are using it to track their own drivers.

Another tracking system is in the works by the company called TransCore. They're the company that operates the electronic E-ZPass toll systems. Now TransCore wants to use paper-thin transponders—RFID tags affixed to the windshield—that would enable government agencies to electronically track whether motorists have proper insurance coverage, registration, or unpaid traffic tickets. Not surprisingly, the company promotes the service as a convenience to drivers. It came up with a snappy acronym—EVR, short for electronic vehicle registration—to underscore the idea. "Motorists can take advantage of increased speed, convenience, and accuracy as a result of EVR at inspection centers. Using EVR, vehicle information such as VIN, make, model, and license plate number is automatically transmitted to a database for inspector to validate data and perform inspection. After inspection, updated information is loaded to a DMV database for inter-agency use."

In selling the idea to government agencies, TransCore stresses the potential efficiencies—and homeland security benefits. "Government agencies lose millions of dollars each year due to an estimated 7 to 15 percent of vehicles not compliant with annual registration requirements, which trickles down to tax payers and law-abiding citizens who foot the bill," the company's promotional material says. "Increase the level of coverage without significantly increasing the number of agents and ensure public safety using spontaneous monitoring in the face of AMBER Alerts, Homeland Security Threat Level Advisories, or special events that cause traffic congestion."

ONE OF THE GREAT MOVIES about surveillance begins with a view of a sun-splashed park. A man high above on the roof of a building with a telescope is watching a couple on an afternoon stroll. It looks like the scope is mounted on a gun, but it's really a high-powered listening device. We hear a dog bark, an emergency siren, the sound of singing and clapping, all of it coming in and out of focus. We see one of the man's colleagues in another building, who is listening to the couple's conversation with other kinds of eavesdropping gear. A third man follows them on the ground, a tape machine concealed in a shopping bag. A fourth monitors all of them from a van made to look like a glass installation service.

This is the opening scene of *The Conversation*. At its center is actor Gene Hackman, who plays an obsessive surveillance specialist named Harry Caul. He is running the operation and frets incessantly about the recording quality. One of his colleagues happens to be a cop moonlighting for extra cash, and there's a suggestion they may be working as contractors for the Justice Department or Internal Revenue Service. But when one member of the team wonders aloud who is paying them and why and what the conversations they are recording mean, Hackman says it doesn't matter. He just wants to do a good job. "I don't care what they're talking about," he says, sitting inside the van behind a one-way mirror. "All I want is a nice fat recording."

Directed by Francis Ford Coppola, the movie came out in 1974, coincidentally the same year the Privacy Act took effect. It captured the brooding angst and paranoia of the day. It also signaled just how far surveillance technology had come—the kind of technology that made Senator Church so uneasy during his study of domestic surveillance by the government. As spooky as it seems, that eavesdropping equipment seems as dated now as a mainframe computer. Gone are the days when tape recorders were used. Now almost everything is digital and all-purpose. The same computer programs can collect and analyze the fruit of all sorts of eavesdropping and surveillance. Mug shots. Telephone calls. Email. Video. Face prints. It doesn't matter, as Smith pointed out, because it's all just data.

The government doesn't have to go to covert contractors like Harry Caul these days to get the best surveillance gear. Intelligence and law enforcement agencies now can order it directly, sometimes off the shelf. One government contractor is Verint Systems, the marketing and eavesdropping specialist on Long Island that attended the International Association of Chiefs of Police technology conference in Philadelphia in late 2003. Verint is short for "Verifiable intelligence." And "Powering Actionable Intelligence" is its motto.

Verint is a prime example of the merging of public and private surveillance, a company accelerating the tendency of all kinds of data to flow together. Its marketing claims at times seem almost like parodies of the security-industrial complex: "Verint solutions transform raw VOICE, VIDEO, AND DATA into ACTIONABLE INTELLIGENCE—mission critical analyses to enhance security and increase enterprise profitability."

Though it markets its equipment to spies and snoops, Verint is a public company based in a modest building in Melville, New York. It has some nine hundred employees around the world, two thirds of whom have technical or engineering backgrounds. Because of its ties to the government and the war on terror, its stock has soared since 9/11, quadrupling from a low of about $6 in August 2002 to more than $25 in early 2004. The company earned $150 million in the year after the terror attacks. By early 2004, it had recorded eight quarters of growth.

But Verint is much more than a government contractor. There's a chance you have come into contact with Verint without knowing it. Home Depot's 1,600 stores are beginning to deploy Verint's video computer surveillance gear. So are Dulles Airport outside Washington, the Capitol Building downtown, and casinos around the country. Verint software not only takes in digital images, it watches the movement of people for signs of trouble or shoplifting. Face recognition can be added. So can programs that help companies like Home Depot analyze customer movement to improve sales. Home Depot officials call this a "multi-dimensional retail tool." The systems at Dulles and the Capitol allow authorities to watch people remotely, say from a secure bunker command post. Or they can revisit the recordings long after the fact, using face recognition to find people who passed through the buildings. The Department of Homeland Security's Bureau of Citizenship and Immigration Services is using Verint's systems to screen travelers. The company claims it combines computer software and surveillance cameras in a way that predicts when an individual poses a threat. Its "BehaviorTrack" service automatically searches the video for suspicious activity—or a sales opportunity. "By providing real-time alarming, BehaviorTrack allows the appropriate proactive action to be taken. This proactive action may include addressing a security breach or a customer service need."

Verint also improves commercial eavesdropping. A service called ULTRA Customer Intelligence Analytics relies on data mining to listen in on customer voices, search for key words, and prompt salespeople to take action. This is useful to call centers and telemarketers who want to give customers good service on the fly and press the right buttons of people's personalities. Here's how Verint puts it: "Detects subtle, often counter-intuitive patterns and cause/effect relationships from recorded interactions to generate revenue opportunities." One of the newest ULTRA customers is the Internal Revenue Service. The IRS has some 18,000 agents at 46 call centers who handle some 42 million questions every year. Some of those centers began embracing ULTRA in the fall of 2003, to provide what the company called "world-class customer service." The financially adventurous might take care, though, because each call could be recorded and, one assumes, analyzed automatically for signs of tax cheating.

An anchor of Verint business remains government wiretapping, and its customers include the Justice Department, Army Intelligence, and an array of law enforcement and government agencies the company declines to identify. The tools they sell to these agencies provide "an end-to-end solution for live monitoring of intercepted target communications and evidence collection management," according to a stock prospectus. The company describes this as "lawful communications interception, historically referred to as wiretapping."

Verint maintains close ties to the law enforcement and intelligence worlds, here and abroad. The company, founded in 1994, is a subsidiary of Comverse Technology. Sitting on the board are former police and intelligence officials. David Worthley, president of subsidiary Verint Technology Inc., previously worked as chief of the FBI's telecommunications industry liaison unit. That unit was responsible for wiretapping. Director Kenneth A. Minihan is a former lieutenant general who served as director of the National Security Agency. Another director, Howard Safir, was police commissioner for New York City and a former executive in the DEA and U.S. Marshals Service. (He is also a consultant to Choice-Point and personally advises its president, Derek Smith.) In addition, Verint maintains close ties to the Israeli military and intelligence communities. The company is funded in part through grants from the Israeli government.

The Patriot Act had a salutory effect on Verint's business because, the company said, it "significantly expanded federal wiretap capability and eased the process for acquiring wiretapping warrants for intelligence gathering purposes." The company is predicting even brisker business going forward. The threat of terrorism has made wiretapping a good business to be in these days.

ON SEPTEMBER 16, 2003, Charles McQueary paid a visit to the National Defense Industry Association. McQueary was the homeland undersecretary in charge of the new Directorate of Science and Technology. He was there to cultivate the association's 950 member companies, and to stoke their inclination to cash in on the historic push to create a homeland security infrastructure.

McQueary praised his audience for being so focused on protecting the United States, for protecting their way of life. Then he encouraged them to think big, far-out ideas about the kinds of research and development they can do to create new brands of sensors and other technology to detect and intercept attacks before they occur. Some of what he's aiming for goes into territory that John Poindexter was exploring. His plans include trying to replicate what he called the "sixth sense" that criminal investigators, border agents, and law enforcement authorities develop after years in the field. "It has been well known for years that experienced agents have developed almost a sixth sense—an ability to pick up on ineffable cues from an individual that indicate deception or otherwise 'raise the antennae' of suspicion," he told the contractors. "Today, we are exploring sensors that capture some of these indicators. There are also other indicators that these agents cannot detect, and for which we are developing capabilities to provide that information. We are working on: infrared detectors that register the heat signals around the eyes that are indicative of an autonomic 'fight or flight' response; and remote sensors for heart rate, or skin galvanic response."

It was another case of reality supplanting science fiction. In 2003, McQueary's people also began supporting the study of ways to enable border patrol to examine the protein fragments on a visitor's skin. They would monitor whether a person has been handling chemicals or other materials that might be used in a weapon of mass destruction. Presumably, the test could also be calibrated to show whether an individual has been handling cocaine, marijuana, or other drugs.

None of this will be easy, but it could be lucrative for those who try. "Let me assure you, we will support you as you support us. So what do we want from you?" McQueary asked the contractors.

"We want you to recognize the economic opportunity that homeland security presents. It is important for all Americans to remember that when the terrorists struck on September 11, 2001, one of their goals was to cripple the U.S. economy. We must remember this and change our mindset to make protecting the homeland a mission that moves our economy forward."

One of the driving forces behind this research is the new Homeland Security Advanced Research Projects Agency (HSARPA), which is modeled on the Defense Department's DARPA. The folks at HSARPA budgeted almost $1 billion on research in 2004, more than $300 million focusing on the development of sensors and other cutting-edge technology. One initiative called "determination of intent" would try to profile the planning activity of suicide bombers and their associates, and then use computer surveillance to seek them out. It was another strong echo of Poindexter's work.

One kind of sensor that's already getting a lot of attention and financial support from the government is called "smart dust." Leading the way on smart dust is a company called, appropriately enough, Dust Networks. Founded in 2002 by engineers from the University of California at Berkeley, Dust builds battery-powered sensors called "motes" that keep getting smaller and smarter. By early 2005, they expect to have a version about the size of a bottle cap that can sense chemicals or the presence of vehicles and maybe take photographs. If several handfuls of these motes are dropped in a nine-square-mile area, they can communicate to one another and then transmit their collective assessment to a main computer, or even a PalmPilot. The company is selling dust as a way to monitor almost anything: the efficiency of refrigerators, the strength of a military convoy, and the activities of people. Eventually smart dust could be as small as a grain of sand and operate for years at a time without new batteries.

David Bolka, the director of HSARPA, said he believes the government's support will accelerate the process of making sensors better, faster, smaller, and cheaper. At the same time Bolka acknowledged his agency's research is going to make some people uneasy. That's why government is already planning to help make people more comfortable with cameras, detection devices, and surveillance systems of all kinds. Otherwise, some are going to become very anxious. "It's the fear of the unknown," he said. "We'll have a backlash from the populace and privacy advocates, and rightly so."

Bolka said he'll leave the task of striking the balance between security surveillance and privacy to others. His job is to speed the creation of the technology, not make the policy to guide its use.

RICHARD SMITH'S TOUR was drawing to a close. He was downtown now, still ticking off surveillance devices. Not far away, one of his clients was installing a new ID system in an office building. There were plenty of cameras around us, some obvious, some not. He said even hotels collect new kinds of information when customers use those new card keys instead of the old metal ones. In Florida, two airline pilots were accused of flying their commercial jet while still drunk from a binge the night before. Prosecutors not only had the bar bill, they obtained records from the electronic locks, which recorded the instant when the card slipped in. The records showed the men returned to their rooms early in the morning, only a few hours before their flight.

Smith shook his head at the idea of so much scrutiny, but as he stood on the street, not far from where almost three thousand people died in the terror attacks two years before, it was clear he had no illusions. The more computer storage space we have, he said, the more likely it is we will fill it up. That's the nature of things. Just as likely is the government's increasing reliance on the many details we leave behind in the routine course of our lives. Law enforcement and intelligence services don't need to design their own surveillance systems from scratch. They only have to reach out to the companies that already track us so well, while promising better service, security, efficiency, and, perhaps most of all, convenience. It takes less and less effort each year to know what each of us is about. When we were at the coffeeshop and where we went in our cars. What we wrote online, who we spoke to on the phone, the names of our friends and their friends and all the people they know. When we rode the subway, the candidates we supported, the books we read, the drugs we took, what we had for dinner, how we like our sex.

More than ever before, the details about our lives are no longer our own. They belong to the companies that collect them, and the government agencies that buy or demand them in the name of keeping us safe. "Our lives are being recorded," Smith said, spelling out a simple truth of life after 9/11. "It is like all of these electronic diaries are being kept by different people."

Only we have no control over the diaries, and we can't even know what they say about us. And there's no place to hide.

NOTES

INTRODUCTION: NO PLACE TO HIDE
I visited the 110th Annual Conference of the International Association of Chiefs of Police, entitled "A Law Enforcement Education and Technology Exposition," in late October 2003. It was a revelation. The introduction and other sections of this book draw on taped interviews with entrepreneurs and police, as well as documents and promotional brochures collected from the conference. As at most marketing events, the people there were in general more than happy to talk about their products and strategies. Exceptions included officials from Verint and Seisint, who only discussed their plans in a limited way. The Orion booth was unmanned during my visit but some brochures were available for the taking. Many conversations with Peter Swire, the chief privacy counselor in the Clinton administration, proved valuable. Scores of interviews with business, law enforcement, and intelligence officials, along with civil liberties advocates of many political stripes, informed the introduction and indeed the entire book.

2   the company's brochure said: Orion Scientific Systems brochure, *Automated Information Processing Features of Orion Software Products.*
3   "a phone call—a quarter": Accurint brochure, *Seisint Arms Law Enforcement with Accurint Intelligence.*
4   "pictures of your neighbors": Phil Ramer, special agent in charge of statewide intelligence at Florida Department of Law Enforcement, for *Washington Post* story in August 2003.
9   "liberty may prosper together": President Dwight D. Eisenhower, farewell address, The Avalon Project at Yale Law School, 1961; http://www.yale.edu/lawweb/avalon/presiden/speeches/eisenhower001.htm
9   "under constant surveillance?": One of several interviews with Peter Swire in 2003 and again in the spring of 2004.

10   "There would be no place to hide": The scene and quote from President George W. Bush on March 15, 2002, come from a transcript provided by the U.S. Government Printing Office via the Gale Group. The quote from Church is from a recording of *Meet the Press*, Aug. 17, 1975, provided by the Library of Congress.

CHAPTER 1. SIX WEEKS IN AUTUMN

In the summer of 2002, I began a series of interviews with the aim of writing a book or creating a documentary that would explore the meaning and domestic impact of the government's declared war on terror. I spent many hours recording conversations with Viet Dinh, the assistant attorney general charged with crafting the important legislation now known as the USA Patriot Act; Jim Dempsey, now the director of the Center for Democracy and Technology; and Senator Patrick Leahy. In addition, I conducted extensive interviews with congressional staffers, legal experts, and civil liberties activists, including Laura Murphy of the American Civil Liberties Union and Marc Rotenberg of the Electronic Privacy Information Center. I am indebted to Beryl Howell, the former general counsel of the Senate Judiciary Committee and a close adviser to Leahy, for her clear briefings on the swirl of political and legislative activity accompanying the creation of the USA Patriot Act. All of the people mentioned above and many others too numerous to name gave me informed and measured insight on legal and social issues that have often been overwhelmed by partisan or ideological rhetoric. The result was a cover story in the October 27, 2002, edition of the *Washington Post Magazine*, edited by my colleague Lynda Robinson, that charted several of the most compelling events leading up to the law's approval. Please note that, as with any endeavor of this sort, much detail from those hectic days had to be left on the cutting-room floor. I have added and updated the material for the book, including extensive interviews conducted in collaboration with John Biewen of American RadioWorks for a public radio documentary.

I learned much about the recent history of domestic surveillance from two men who were directly involved. One was Ralph Stein, a law professor at Pace University who served as an Army Intelligence officer in charge of domestic counterintelligence analysis. After leaving the Army in 1968, Stein helped organize congressional hearings that exposed domestic surveillance abuses. The other was Christopher Pyle, a professor at Mount Holyoke College, who taught law at the Army's intelligence school at Fort Holabird, Maryland. Pyle later wrote pathbreaking articles that helped spur those congressional hearings.

12   legal hand against terrorists: Interviews with Viet Dinh in the summer of 2002. Most of the material in this chapter appeared in Robert O'Harrow, Jr., "Six Weeks in Autumn," *Washington Post Magazine*, Oct. 27, 2002.
12   "they should have caught these guys": Interviews with Jim Dempsey in the summer of 2002.
13   more tools to stop future attacks: Interviews with Patrick Leahy in the summer of 2002.
17   "We should not wait": Interviews with Morton Halperin in the summer of 2002.
18   remembers those days well: Curriculum vitae of Christopher H. Pyle, 2003.
18   at Fort Holabird, Maryland: Interviews with Chris Pyle, including one at his home conducted with John Biewen of American RadioWorks, Dec. 2, 2003.
19   "What can you tell me?": Pyle interview.
19   The top card was about Arlo Tatum: Ibid.
20   won a Polk Award in 1971: Ibid.
20   "political activity within the United States": "CONUS Intelligence: The Army Watches Civilian Politics," *Washington Monthly* (January 1970).

20   was collecting and sharing about them: *The Privacy Law Sourcebook 2000*, Marc Rotenberg, Electronic Privacy Information Center.

21   "a recipe for government overreaching": Interviews with Laura Murphy in the summer of 2002.

22   "our shock didn't turn into panic" and the quotes that follow: Leahy interviews.

30   targeted by those FISA warrants: Dan Eggen and Sudan Schmidt, "Data Show Different Spy Game Since 9/11," *Washington Post*, May 1, 2004.

30   suspects on computer watch lists: See the stories of the David Nelsons and Johnnie Lockett Thomas in chapter 8, The Government's Eyes and Ears.

30   associating with certain campus seminars: Interview with Jessica Biddle, a student at the University of Texas School of Law and LBJ School of Public Affairs, who was approached by an Army Intelligence officer about a campus forum on Islam and the law. See also "Army's Look at Muslim Conference Irks Some," *Austin American-Statesman*, Feb. 14, 2004, and "Presence of Army Agents Stirs Furor," *Houston Chronicle*, Feb. 14, 2004.

30   initially on immigration charges: U.S. Court of Appeals for the District of Columbia Circuit, No. 02-5254 and No. 02-5300, *Center for National Security Studies et al. v. U.S. Department of Justice*, argued on Nov. 18, 2002, decided on June 17, 2003.

31   Ashcroft appeared at Federal Hall: Transcript of speech I attended and taped, Sept. 9, 2003.

32   "put to good or bad use": Interview with Viet Dinh, Dec. 11, 2003.

32   "Now it can be done electronically and constantly": Interview with Jim Dempsey, Dec. 11, 2003.

33   "came up on someone's computer screen": Interview with Patrick Leahy, Dec. 10, 2003.

CHAPTER 2. DATA REVOLUTION

I became acquainted with Acxiom in 1997 and 1998, during the early stage of reporting on data marketing and privacy issues for the *Washington Post*. I have written a few stories about the company since then and draw on that work for this chapter. I traveled to Little Rock and Conway in 2003 to visit with officials, including Jennifer Barrett, and tour the company's data facilities. At the time, Charles Morgan declined to meet with me. I can't say for sure why, but I suspect it had something to do with the fact that retired General Wes Clark, an Acxiom director and lobbyist, was contemplating a run for the White House.

In the fall of 2003, Morgan changed his mind. I conducted an extensive taped telephone interview with him on Nov. 13, 2003, and found him responsive. Unless otherwise noted, the majority of quotes and ideas from Morgan come from that interview. I also relied on other company officials, who patiently explained how the company works and listened to follow-up questions about its operations. I have turned to the company's marketing and financial documents as well, including proxy statements and annual reports.

As noted below, I have drawn on other journalism about the company to round out the chapter. I am indebted to a fine piece in *Success* magazine by David Carnay for the core of the racing anecdote about Morgan. Two books proved especially useful for the section about the history of automated data collection: *The Naked Society*, by Vance Packard (New York: David McKay Co., 1964); and *The Assault on Privacy*, by Arthur Miller (Ann Arbor: University of Michigan Press, 1971). Also illuminating and helpful was David Burnham's *The Rise of the Computer State* (New York: Random House, 1980).

34   With just days to go: David Carnay, "Speed Racer: Charles Morgan used to

come to Sebring as a spectator. Now he's a driver on a top team," *Success*, June 1, 1997.

34   at close to 200 miles per hour: Taped telephone interview with Charles Morgan, Nov. 13, 2003.

34   the word AXCIOM in bold letters: Ibid.

35   high-tech packaging of personal information: Ibid.

35   in the business as "gentlemen drivers": Interview with Ken Breslauer, author of *Sebring: The Official History of America's Great Sports Car Race*, Sept. 2, 2003.

35   and breaks his right hand: Carnay, "Speed Racer."

35   "you'd probably wet your pants": Ibid.

36   one of the nation's poorly educated states: Arkansas has long lagged behind most other states in education spending and student achievement. One recent analysis by Morgan Quitno, *State and City Ranking Publications*, put Arkansas thirty-eighth in the nation for 2002–3. See http://www.morgan quitno.com/edrank.htm

36   low-slung brick buildings: Tour of Acxiom facilities, June 2003.

36   "purchase behavior and lifestyle data": Acxiom annual report, 2003.

37   what's called a petabyte of information: Interviews with Acxiom officials, June 2003.

37   stack of King James Bibles: This is based on rough assumptions, including the fact the Bible contains about one megabyte of information. The math was confirmed by a senior Acxiom official, who said the estimated height of the stack is conservative.

37   Something Axciom calls "grid computing": Morgan interview.

37   his hands would be black with grease: Ibid., and interview with another Acxiom official.

38   engineering degree from the University of Arkansas: Fleming Meeks, "Keep Your Eye on the Track; Acxiom Corp. Chief Executive Charles Morgan, Jr.," *Forbes*, Jan. 6, 1992.

38   he'd just met as "buddy": Deposition of Charles Morgan, May 8, 2001, Hendrix Reporting Service, *Progressive Business Publications vs. Acxiom Direct Media Inc. et al.*

38   "I'm really in a hurt here": Ibid.

38   Demographics occasionally couldn't meet its payroll: Morgan interview.

38   "executives on half salary": Carnay, "Speed Racer."

39   the American Bible Society: Interviews with Morgan and Jennifer Barrett.

39   single largest individual shareholder: According to Acxiom proxy statement for the annual meeting on Aug. 6, 2003. His worth was based on a $15 share price at the time. By April 2004, the price went as high as $24.75.

39   such as the Church League: See Miller, *The Assault on Privacy: Computers, Data Banks, and Dossiers*, p. 70.

40   newlyweds, 500,000 in all: Packard, *The Naked Society*, p. 183.

40   lists of 400,000 car owners: Ibid.

40   "we are very attractive": Ibid.

41   report before passing judgment: Miller, *Assault on Privacy*, p. 69.

41   "wasn't considered a well-adjusted person": Ibid., p. 71.

41   reports to credit granting: Ibid.

41   "commodity and a source of power": Ibid., p. 23.

42   "the ultra-intelligent machine": Cited in ibid., p. 10.

43   than the first Apollo lunar module: Interview with Paul Saffo, Sept. 4, 2003.

43   equals all the words ever spoken: Peter Lyman, Hal R. Varian, et al., *How Much Information 2000*, study produced by School of Information Management and Systems, University of California at Berkeley. Web page, www.sims .berkeley.edu/research/projects/how-much-info/datapowers.html

44 "to convince customers this is good for them": October 1997 interview with Charles Morgan.

44 to some 52 million households: Pamela Klein, "ADVO Signs Deal to Refine Direct Marketing," *Hartford Courant,* Jan. 8, 1991.

44 bought half of InfoBase: Larry Sullivan, "Acxiom Joins Forces with Direct Mailer; Better Days Predicted," *Arkansas Democrat-Gazette,* Aug. 1, 1991.

44 agreement to manage Polk's data: R. L. Polk & Co. Web site, www.polk .com/about/index.asp

44 hundreds of millions of pieces a year: See Acxiom press release, May 1, 1996: "Acxiom Corporation (Nasdaq: ACXM) announced today that it has completed the acquisition of the assets of Direct Media/DMI, Inc. ('DMI') for $25 million. The purchase price is payable in three years and may, at DMI's option, be paid in 1,000,000 shares of Acxiom stock in lieu of cash."

44 American Data Resources, I Rent America: "Acxiom Rolls Out Major Enhancements to (IB) Consumer Infobase for Direct Marketers," *PR Newswire,* June 5, 1996.

45 "jointly marketed data products": Multex.com Report on Abacus Corporation, May 12, 1999.

45 "products to its clients": Multex.com Report on Abacus Corporation, April 20, 1999.

45 "the lives of every American": Denison Hatch, "Privacy: How Much Data Do We Really Need?" *Target Marketing,* Jan. 2, 1994.

46 partner in developing new technology: Interview with Charles Morgan, who added: "Believe it or not, Trans Union approached us first . . . Trans Union exec who was charged with development in the direct marketing and credit card acquisition approached us. It must have been around 1990. And they started dialoguing with us and improving their capability to serve the large financial institutions. Also wanted to build some more advanced data products and felt like Acxiom might be a partner, and we latched on as a way to gain a partner and to gain ways to get into what has become our fastest growing segment—financial services. It looked like a win-win situation."

47 up from $50.6 million the year before: Acxiom annual report, 2003.

47 "responsible for the computer infrastructure": Morgan interview.

47 The bible of mailing lists: According to a clerk who answered a toll-free number provided by *SRDS Direct Marketing List Source,* August 2003.

48 almost double the sales a decade before: Interview with Christina Duffney of the Direct Marketing Association, Sept. 11, 2003.

48 breaking the law by selling its lists: See Supreme Court denial of certiorari, June 10, 2002.

48 Trans Union fought hard: Interviews with David Medine, former associate director for financial practices at the Federal Trade Commission, in 2003 and 2004.

48 "trading privacy for profits": Ibid.

49 ended the case in June 2002: See Supreme Court denial of certiorari, June 10, 2002.

49 "purchase behavior and lifestyle data": Acxiom annual report, 2003.

49 details about the credit cards you own: Internal documents obtained from a contractor working with Acxiom on a government project and confirmed by Acxiom officials.

50 to shop or make an inquiry: Robert O'Harrow, Jr., "Unlisted Numbers Not Protected from Marketers," *Washington Post,* Dec. 19, 1999. Other details for this section came from helpful Acxiom officials.

52 "tagging your phone number" . . . "very nervous" . . . and "'collecting your info.' Nobody knows": Ibid.

53 to automatically provide warranties: Background interviews with an Acxiom
     official who declined to be named.
53 survey for a new marketing initiative: Robert O'Harrow, Jr., "Survey Asks
     Readers to Get Personal, and 400,000 Do," *Washington Post,* Dec. 16, 1998.
53 its subscribers better. Much better: Ibid.
54 intimate details about their lives: Ibid.
54 "want to let something out": Quoted in ibid.
55 "it's a benefit to the subscriber": Quoted in ibid.
55 to surreptitiously identify every respondent: Robert O'Harrow, Jr., "Survey
     Says: You're Not Anonymous; A GE Investments Canvass of Shareholders
     Contained Coding That Allowed the Firm to Identify the Respondents,"
     Washington Post, June 9, 1999.
56 "not to pull a fast one on our customers": Ibid.
56 September 11 attacks abruptly changed: Morgan interview: "Quite candidly, I
     had decided many years ago that we would not do business with government.
     We had done work with political parties and our experience with that was
     just not outstanding. And we decided we weren't going to do work with the
     government. Activities in and around 9/11 caused us to rethink that."
56 One of them was Bill Clinton: Telephone interview with William Jefferson
     Clinton, Oct. 31, 2003. Clinton agreed to discuss Acxiom after many requests
     to his office in New York. Speaking on a cell phone, he was engaging and can-
     did about events after September 11, 2001. I rely on his remarks throughout
     this section.
57 training executive at Acxiom: Morgan interview.
57 driver's licenses and phony telephone numbers: Ibid. *Morgan:* "We had gotten
     that early on, and we just found current and former addresses of the hijack-
     ers, and we stopped shortly thereafter not knowing what to do. But we even-
     tually contacted the FBI and the Department of Justice and offered our
     assistance." See also Clinton interview.
57 "might have been associated with": Morgan interview.
57 rallying on their behalf in the state: [From CRP: Charles Morgan himself do-
     nated $4,000 to Bill Clinton's campaigns over the course of several years. He
     is only on record as having given Hillary $250. Acxiom as a company, though,
     has given well over $80,000 in soft money to the Democratic Congressional
     Campaign Committee, the National Republican Senatorial Committee, etc.]
57 and Ashcroft agreed: Clinton interview.
58 "we could help work on that balance": Morgan interview.
59 "on every air carrier passenger, airport and flight": Clark refused repeated re-
     quests for interviews. I relied on internal documents, lobby registration re-
     ports filed with the clerk of the U.S. House of Representatives, and accounts
     of his activity from business associates and government officials, including
     Michael Jackson, former undersecretary of the Department of Transportation.
59 received nearly half a million dollars: Acxiom officials and company proxy
     statements.
59 called the Office of Information Awareness: Poindexter conversation, Febru-
     ary 2004.
61 "It's straight up": I attended this event in New York and watched David
     Harris's performance. On September 12, 2003, I interviewed him by tele-
     phone to clarify details about his "close-up magic" act.
61 The economy would suffer: From testimony given by Jennifer Barrett, Chief
     Privacy Officer for Acxiom, on H.R. 4678, the Consumer Privacy Protection
     Act of 2002, before the House Subcommittee on Commerce, Trade and Con-
     sumer Protection, Sept. 24, 2002. (She also spoke on behalf of Experian and
     Trilegiant.)

61 "I work for Big Brother": Robert O'Harrow, Jr., "Data Firms Getting Too Personal?" *Washington Post*, March 8, 1998.

62 the company's access to personal information: For this section of the story, I rely heavily on a taped interview with Jennifer Barrett on June 26, 2003, in Little Rock.

63 "mutually exclusive? Absolutely not": "Beyond Consumer Privacy to Consumer Advocacy," March 2002, Charles Morgan, Company Leader; Jennifer Barrett, Fair Information Practices Leader.

64 "smarter, faster, and at a lower cost": Testimony given by Jennifer Barrett on H.R. 4678, Sept. 24, 2002.

65 "could build this mega-scale database": Internal Information Awareness office email to John Poindexter, May 2, 2001.

66 a series of privacy storms: For this and everything below, see Robert O'Harrow, Jr., "Posing a Privacy Problem? Driver's-License Photos Used in Anti-Fraud Database," *Washington Post*, Jan. 22, 1999. See also Robert O'Harrow, Jr., and Liz Leyden, "U.S. Helped Fund Photo Database of Driver IDs; Firm's Plan Seen as Way to Fight Identity Crimes," *Washington Post*, Feb. 18, 1999.

69 all there at the request of Charles Morgan and Jennifer Barrett: This section relies heavily on "Privacy at Stake," *Chief Executive*, Nov. 1, 2000, which contains a transcription of the conversation among participants, including Morgan and several chief executives and privacy officers from other companies and organizations.

69 to apologize to customers: See Robert O'Harrow, Jr., "CVS Also Cuts Ties to Marketing Service; Like Giant, Firm Cites Privacy on Prescriptions," *Washington Post*, Feb. 19, 1998.

70 "we're going to suffer a lot": "Privacy at Stake," *Chief Executive*, Nov. 1, 2000.

71 called Market Intelligence Group: I relied on documents filed by federal prosecutors in the U.S. District Court for the Southern District of Ohio, Western Division at Cincinnati. Thse included a statement of facts by U.S. Attorney Robert A. Behlen, Jr., on Dec. 2, 2003. In March 2004, I also interviewed Behlen about the case and Baas's attorney, Tim Smith, for details about Baas. For context, I called Kevin Poulsen, a computer security specialist and journalist who wrote about the incident at SecurityFocus.com.

73 "the level of comfort that they need": Morgan interview.

CHAPTER 3. WHO AM I?

Michael Berry's story captures the angst of identity uneasiness, and Berry tells his own story well. This chapter relies heavily on a mix of his recollections, financial documents, and interviews with business and government officials. Follow-up interviews with his friends and associates, along with company and law enforcement officials, confirmed the numerous details of his account. I spent many hours speaking to Berry, on the telephone and in person, starting in the spring of 2003 and continuing through the summer of 2004. For the section on the changing nature of identity, I am indebted to Deirdre Mulligan, director of the Samuelson Law, Technology and Public Policy Clinic at the Boalt School of Law, University of California at Berkeley, and to Bob Blakley, chief scientist for security and privacy at IBM Tivoli Systems. A report by Barbara Span of Star Systems called *Identity Theft in the United States: An Update* spelled out the complexity and urgency of the identity theft problem. Evan Hendricks, an identity theft expert and editor and publisher of *Privacy Times* newsletter, provided much-needed context of a consumer advocate, while Dennis Lormel, a former FBI agent who specialized in financial crimes, provided valuable insights from a law enforcement point of view, both before and after he left the FBI.

Synovate, formerly known as BAI Global, provided details about credit cards, as did David Robinson of the *Nilson Report*. To learn more about the investigation of

Demorris Hunter, I turned to Orlando homicide detectives Roy Filippucci and Barbara Bergin, who graciously shared as much as they could about their case. For the section about *America's Most Wanted*, I relied on a videotape of the program provided by the television show and printouts of pages from their Web site provided by Berry. Material about James Rinaldo Jackson came from court records, conversations with his attorney, and from a story I wrote for the *Washington Post*. An early version of this chapter ran as a cover story in the *Washington Post Magazine* entitled "A Case of Stolen Identity," edited and improved by my able colleague Lynda Robinson.

78   almost 10 million in the previous year: See "FTC Releases Survey of Identity Theft in U.S.," Federal Trade Commission press release, Sept. 3, 2003.
80   "complicated to sort out who's who": Several interviews with Bob Blakley, beginning June 18, 2003, for *Washington Post Magazine* story.
81   a man named Michael Berry: Interviews with Roy Filippucci, for *Washington Post Magazine* story.
83   "this year is going to be worse": Interview with Dave Harned, for *Washington Post Magazine* story.
85   a genial con artist from Memphis, Tennessee: For this section of the chapter, I relied heavily on a transcript of Jackson's appearance before U.S. District Court Judge Deborah A. Batts on Sept. 26, 2000.
89   "identity theft and identity fraud vulnerabilities": Interviews with Dennis M. Lormel, former chief of the FBI's Terrorist Financial Review Group, for *Washington Post Magazine* story.
90   had been set up to process credit card transactions: Complaint filed with the U.S. Southern District of New York Court in the case of *United States of America v. Ali Saleh Kahlah al-Marri*, aka Abdullakareem A. Almuslam, Violations of 18 Nos. 1001, 1014, and 1028.
92   to create an ID system: Taped face-to-face interview with Steven Brill, at his office, Nov. 19, 2003.
93   "recognized in more than one place": Ibid.
93   "identifying and tracking American citizens": ChoicePoint press release, "Brill, ChoicePoint and Partners to Launch 'Verified Identity Card,'" Oct. 23, 2003.
93   "they are who they say they are": Brill interview.
95   "careful, accountable privacy policy": Ibid.
95   "identity thieves more likely to be caught": "Fact Sheet: President Bush Signs the Fair and Accurate Credit Transactions Act of 2003," Dec. 4, 2003.
95   "with this new law, we're taking action": Office of the Press Secretary release, "President's Remarks: President Bush Signs Identity Theft Legislation," Dec. 4, 2003. http://www.whitehouse.gov/news/releases/2003/12/20031204-2.html
96   "Congress was hearing about this": Telephone interview with Kate Ennis, April 2004.
96   "there's no there there": Ibid.

CHAPTER 4. THE MATRIX

I began looking at Seisint and the system known as Matrix in the spring of 2003. For months, Seisint officials did not return phone calls. A woman designated as spokesperson stoked my interest by declaring the company would share details about the system only with law enforcement officials. I made headway with state intelligence officials in Florida, as well as with associates of Matrix inventor Hank Asher. I also obtained a variety of documents through Freedom of Information requests.

Though I was on book leave, I wrote a news story about Matrix for the *Washing-*

ton Post in August 2003. In October 2003, I visited Hank Asher at his home and on his boat in Boca Raton, Florida. Those hours of taped conversations, along with many telephone conversations and a meeting in New York, are the source of numerous details about his work and life. Equally important are dozens of pages of confidential police reports I secured from the Florida Department of Law Enforcement (FDLE) through that state's Freedom of Information law. Those documents, including internal memos, investigative reports, and Seisint records, were essential in spelling out details of Asher's past and his work on Matrix. I relied as well on a deposition by Asher, conducted as part of a civil case in May 1999.

Seisint chief executive Paul Cameron helped clarify matters along the way and provided valuable details about the visit to the White House. In addition, I spoke to current and former law enforcement officials at the local, state, and federal levels for this chapter. I won't name them all, but among the most helpful were: Phil Ramer, an intelligence official at the FDLE; James T. (Tim) Moore, former commissioner of the FDLE; Bill Shrewsbury, a former FDLE agent who later worked for Asher; Michael Mullaney, a federal prosecutor in Florida who later became the principal deputy chief for counterterrorism at the U.S. Department of Justice; and Bill Berger, the North Miami Beach police chief and a friend of Asher.

For the section about the White House visit, I also spoke to a former associate of Asher's from the early 1980s, who corroborated police reports and offered fresh details. For the section of the chapter touching on the Washington, D.C., area sniper, I am indebted to my colleagues Sari Horwitz and Michael E. Ruane. I drew on their fine writing and reporting for *Sniper: Inside the Hunt for the Killers Who Terrorized the Nation* (New York: Random House, 2003), which was excerpted by the *Washington Post* in October 2003. I am further indebted to others in the law enforcement and intelligence communities who declined to be named.

98 service that delivered billions of dossiers: Taped interview with Hank Asher at his home in Boca Raton, Florida, Oct. 3, 2003.

99 "I think I can find these fuckers": Asher interview, confirmed in a telephone interview with Bill Shrewsbury, Oct. 17, 2003.

99 "that looked pretty interesting": Asher interview.

99 potential threat was Marwan al-Shehhi: Ibid., with elaboration in subsequent telephone conversations. *Asher:* "September 14, that was Friday. I sent 419 names to the Florida Department of Law Enforcement, the Secret Service, and the FBI. Now, this was just from watching the news. No names had been released, no anything had been done. But out of my database of over 450 million people that either have lived in this country or passed through this country, I got down to a list of 419 through an artificial intelligence algorithm that I had written."

99 information about handicap parking stickers: Deposition given by Hank Asher before the U.S. District Court, Southern District of Florida, Miami Division, in the case of *Database Technologies, Inc. v. High Tech Data Services, Inc. and Data Tracks Technology, Inc., Kevin Elwood, and Marcella Elwood,* May 19, 1999, p. 43.

100 "we can catch these guys": Asher interview, confirmed by James Moore.

101 other agencies across the country, and even competitors: Asher interview. *Asher:* "We had . . . between four and six FBI, either Special Agents or analysts, either one or two Secret Service people, anywhere from two to four INS people, and then probably about ten of my scientists, technologists, programmers, and myself. Customs would float in and out, other agencies would float in and out."

101 "pictures of your neighbors": Telephone interview with Phil Ramer, June 9, 2003.

102   give them whatever they need: Asher interview. *Asher:* "I was [in my office].
       And a guy called me on the phone and said, 'You won't believe what hap-
       pened.' So I turned on my TV and about forty people came into my office and
       we all stood there and watched the second plane crash into the building.
       . . . And in a state of shock, as we all were, I instructed every salesperson and
       every employee in the company to start calling law enforcement, and telling
       them that they had unlimited free access to Accurint to investigate what was
       going on."

102   "plants in the corners": Shrewsbury telephone interview. Asher said: "I was
       scared to death that I couldn't support my children. The years before I started
       being successful as a programmer, my mother actually helped me pay child
       support. I had friends help me pay child support. I had been broke for so
       long. While I built DBT, I was living in a four-hundred-square-foot apartment
       that was on top of a twenty-two-story building. It was a beautiful view and
       the whole roof was like my patio, but it was four hundred dollars a month. I
       had one of those little refrigerators like people have in their office."

102   a "High Terrorist Factor" score: ACLU Brief #2, *New Documents Obtained by
       ACLU Raise Troubling Questions About Matrix Program,* May 20, 2004.

102   planes crashed on September 11: Interview with Asher, May 20, 2004.

102   "we're going to make a lot of money": Asher interview, Oct. 3, 2003.

103   private investigators, lawyers, and newspapers: Ibid.

103   "I find 'em, you fuck 'em": Telephone interview with Hank Asher, Oct. 19,
       2003, confirmed by Shrewsbury.

103   Asher took away between $117 million and $147 million: Wyatt Olson, *New
       Times Broward–Palm Beach,* Sept. 11, 2003. According to this account, Asher
       was forced out of the company by other directors, who considered him impul-
       sive and erratic.

103   "when I built DBT, not make $150 million": Asher interview, Oct. 3, 2003.

104   better known as Matrix: Ibid.

104   thought the allusion would be amusing: Ramer telephone interview.

104   before it was called Seisint: Interview with Ole Poulsen, Oct. 17, 2003.

105   "customers 150 years ago": Don Peppers and Martha Rogers, *The One to One
       Future: Building Relationships One Customer at a Time* (New York: Doubleday,
       1996), p. xiii.

105   "change, but a revolutionary one": Ibid., p. xxviii.

105   "redefined what computers can do": Interview with Hank Asher, Oct. 17,
       2003.

105   the companies said in a press release: Seisint and Equifax press release,
       "Equifax and Seisint to Deliver Breakthrough Advantage for Credit Marketing
       Industry: New Technology for Credit Marketing Solutions Will Enable
       Equifax to Reduce Delivery Time by Up to 70 Percent," June 11, 2001.

105   Accenture, another partner and investor: Seisint Web site, www.seisint
       .com/aboutus/index.html: "Mr. [Joel P.] Friedman is a partner at Accenture.
       During his 29 years with the firm, Mr. Friedman has held many leadership
       roles. . . . He is a member . . . of the Accenture Worldwide Board of Partners.
       . . . Mr. [Paul S.] Cameron joined Seisint in the spring of 2000, following a
       14-year career with Accenture. As a Partner in the firm, Mr. Cameron built a
       reputation for leading large, highly complex operations engagements. . . ."

106   the company was forced to back down: See EPIC Alert, Jan. 10, 1997, at
       http://www.epic.org/alert/EPIC_Alert_4.01.html

106   to make life easier for marketers: Robert O'Harrow, Jr., and Elizabeth Corco-
       ran, "Intel Drops Plans to Activate Chip IDs," *Washington Post,* Jan. 26, 1999.

107   "is already linked together": Poulsen interview.

107   "But they did": Asher interview, Oct. 17, 2003.

108 "the invisible become visible": Matrix brochure, *Multi-State Anti-Terrorism Information Exchange: "Where risks appear immediately, law enforcement must repond instantly."*

108 "identified in advance as suspicious": Jeffrey Rosen, *The Naked Crowd: Reclaiming Security and Freedom in an Anxious Age* (New York: Random House, 2004), p. 20.

108 "because there's a threat out there": Poulsen interview.

108 "just blows me away": Asher interview, Oct. 3, 2003.

109 at Bethlehem Steel, which paid much more: Deposition given by Hank Asher in *Database Technologies, Inc. . . . .*, p. 8.

109 "had things my friends didn't have": Asher interview, Oct. 3, 2003.

109 "it was pretty sophisticated": Ibid.

109 A self-described adrenaline junkie: Ibid.
   Asher: "What started out to seem like an adventure and something exciting to do, the realization of the harm it could cause was blatantly ignored by an adrenaline junkie."
   O'Harrow: "That's what you were."
   Asher: "I still am."

109 company "went into liquidation": Deposition given by Hank Asher, *Database Technologies, Inc. . . . .*, p. 12.

110 Chicago, New York, and San Diego: Ibid., p. 15.

110 "to further business causes": Ibid., p. 14.

110 "I loved the adrenaline": Asher interview, Oct. 3, 2003.

110 "they were classy and everything else": Ibid. Asher's account in this section and the following one is backed up by detailed confidential police reports and memos obtained under the Freedom of Information Act, as well as by interviews with current and former law enforcement officials.

110 "were really of the rascal nature": Ibid. As with other parts of this chapter, Asher's remarks are supported by documents and interviews with knowledgeable people, including one former friend of his who was often with Asher during this time. I relied heavily on such information when preparing for my interview with him. There's no way to know for certain that Asher's description of limited involvement in the drug-smuggling enterprises is entirely forthcoming. A cautious reader also will remain skeptical about his claims here and elsewhere in the chapter. For example, he claims never to have worked as a police informant, but that claim was cast into doubt by his friend Tim Moore, who told me: "We were aware of his informant activity, but we were also aware he had never been arrested or charged."

110 even more remote airports in Oklahoma: Interview with a companion who declined to be named, Oct. 13, 2003.

111 "I was a criminal": Asher interview, Oct. 3, 2003.

111 he has never broken the law since then: Ibid.
   Asher: "I can tell you since June of 1982 I have never broken the law. . . . I have never committed a criminal offense. Speeding, whatever . . . I don't know about that."
   O'Harrow: "Seven days spread over what period of time?"
   Asher: "Six in six weeks, and one probably a couple months before that."

111 "a drug smuggler in the early 1980s": Memorandum by Special Agent Supervisor Bill Butler entitled "Henry Asher Background (Confidential Information)," Sept. 10, 2003.

112 their contracts for AutoTrack: David Kidwell, "DEA, FBI Suspend Online Contracts," *Miami Herald,* July 3, 1999.

112 promoted Matrix to state and federal officials: Telephone interview with James T. (Tim) Moore, October 2003. "He's a genius," Moore said. "It's good technology. It supports a national versus federal solution. . . . I believe in the project."

112 "I didn't feel good about it": Asher interview, Oct. 3, 2003.
112 The confidential police report . . . according to the police document: Bill Butler memorandum. See also FDLE memorandum written by IRCA Richard
Lawrence to ASACE. Wayne Dickey, Investigative Services Bureau, regarding
"Autotrack Data Base," Oct. 4, 1993.
113 "continued to meet afterwards": Asher interview, Oct. 3, 2003.
113 "that any plan was actually implemented": Confidential FDLE memo. The
Oct. 4, 1993, memo discussed a plan to charge Asher in relation to "one load
of cocaine around 1979–1980. A federal indictment was being prepared in
about 1985 or 1986 on several people involved with ASHER in smuggling,
and they were short on witnesses. Therefore instead of indicting ASHER,
they subpoenaed him to testify as a witness in the case. Although the statute
of limitations had run out on the actual smuggling charge, a federal conspiracy charge could have still been made on ASHER. ASHER 'was not pleased'
and tried to get out of testifying," said a section of the memo. "Attorney F.
LEE BAILEY called and tried to get ASHER out of the subpoena as well. BAI-
LEY claimed ASHER was working for the federal government in some national security capacity."
113 "the mind of a scientist": Telephone interview with Ira Siegel, Oct. 24, 2003.
114 "about what he has created": Telephone interview with Martha Barnett, undated.
114 "He was never charged or indicted": Interview with John Walsh, Sept. 2,
2003.
114 "hollow eyes and a hollow soul": Asher interview, Oct. 3, 2003.
114 "It was done very quietly": Telephone interview with Hal Robbins, May 29,
2003.
115 Secret Service had people at Seisint: Interview with U.S. Secret Service Public
Affairs Office spokesman, June 10, 2003. "We were part of that," the
spokesman said.
115 Stafford went to work: Ibid.
115 required a change to the state constitution: Email from Paul Anderson to
Robert O'Harrow, Oct. 22, 2003.
116 "important here is the product": Telephone interview with Richard Ward III
at his office in northern Virginia, October 2003.
117 "responding to terrorist threats": *Congressional Record* Colloquy, copy provided
by Paul Anderson from office of Senator Graham, July 23, 2003.
117 "PS, your children are not safe": Transcript of opening statement by Assistant
Commonwealth's Attorney James A. Willett, compiled by court reporters
Ronald Graham & Associates, Oct. 21, 2003.
117 "You don't go where you don't know": Asher interview, Oct. 3, 2003.
118 "I thought I had caught him": Ibid.
118 "Next Tuesday he's ours": Ibid.
118 left the Seisint office for the day: Telephone interview with Bill Shrewsbury,
Jan. 9, 2004.
119 the likely one came from Tacoma, Washington: Ibid.
119 "we could have saved some lives": Ibid. Shrewsbury noted correctly that other
information services were also deeply involved in the hunt for the snipers, including competitors ChoicePoint and LexisNexis.
119 " 'Part of this reward money should be ours' ": Asher interview, Oct. 3, 2003.
119 The Roosevelt Room: I relied on several interviews for the section about the
demonstration of the Matrix at the White House, including Asher, James
Moore, Seisint chief executive Paul Cameron, and press officials in the offices
of Vice President Dick Cheney and Governor Jeb Bush. While confirming the
meeting, Cheney's press office declined to provide any details about it. Katie

Hinson, a research assistant in the office of the curator of the White House Historical Association, provided a useful description of and background for the Roosevelt Room.

120 "it's a national project": Telephone interview with Paul Cameron, Nov. 6, 2003.

121 "didn't know about this past": Telephone interview with Charles Lewis. Lewis was commenting in response to my request for his reaction. When asked whether it was appropriate for Asher to be in the meeting, Moore said: "That wasn't an issue. With me, the man's past was his past. I was focusing on his technology." In explaining Cheney's reluctance to discuss the meeting, his spokeswoman said: "They're private meetings. . . . If they were public meetings, they'd be held in public." She had no comment about Asher's past.

121 "disqualifying technology by the author": Interview with Attorney General John Ashcroft, July 22, 2004, in his Justice Department office.

122 "to see it in real time": Telephone interview with Vernon Keenan, Nov. 7, 2003.

122 "display after display after display": Ibid.

124 "Lexis will see that that happens": Robert O'Harrow, Jr., "LexisNexis to Buy Seisint for $775 Million," *Washington Post*, July 15, 2004.

CHAPTER 5. LOOK ME UP SOMETIME

A starting point for Look Me Up Sometime was ChoicePoint's own press releases, annual reports, and other financial statements. They tell an amazing story about the company's relentless focus on growth through acquisition. They also show the company officials' tireless push to frame their efforts as a public service. Visits with officials at facilities in Alpharetta, Georgia, and Boca Raton, Florida, along with numerous follow-up interviews, provided much-needed context and detail, as well as quotes used throughout the chapter. I also relied on numerous interviews with senior ChoicePoint managers and employees, law enforcement officials who work with the company, and some competitors and people whose lives have been affected by ChoicePoint activities. A long taped interview with chief executive Derek Smith was especially helpful in the section about ChoicePoint's stated aims and his own motivation for growing the company so quickly.

For the section on how data is gathered, the company arranged an interview with Carolyn Lucas. I also relied on the excellent reporting of my colleague John Biewen of American RadioWorks, who accompanied and recorded Lucas on her rounds of courthouses one day in 2003. Chris Hoofnagle of the Electronic Privacy Information Center graciously shared his views in the course of several interviews. Hoofnagle also gave me a copy of a paper that appeared in the *University of North Carolina Journal of International Law and Commercial Regulation* 29 (3) (Spring 2004), which cogently examines ChoicePoint's impact on society. It is titled: "Big Brother's Little Helpers: How ChoicePoint and Other Commercial Data Brokers Collect, Process, and Package Your Data for Law Enforcement."

Jeff Jonas contributed to the chapter and the book by hosting me and Biewen in Las Vegas. He described how his Non-Obvious Relationship Awareness system works, and gave us a tour of one of his casinos. I interviewed Matthew Frost twice about his experience in the 2000 election. I also relied on some very good journalism in the *Palm Beach Post* and *Washington Post*, as well as on the U.S. Commission for Civil Rights report, *Voting Irregularities in Florida During the 2000 Presidential Election* (June 2001). For the section about Mary L. Boris, I relied on interviews with her and Bernard Leachman (her brother and lawyer), as well as on court documents, including a March 14, 2003, ruling by John G. Heyburn II, chief judge of the U.S. District Court in Louisville. ChoicePoint vice president James Zimbardi and company spokesman James Lee took time to explain some new homeland security services, as well as ChoicePoint's push into the world of intelligence.

126 to hide his sense of shame: Telephone interviews with Matthew Frost, Nov. 13 and 24, 2003.
126 a fast-growing data giant called ChoicePoint: See Global Securities Information, ChoicePoint Inc., custom report, Nov. 18, 2003.
126 a new law . . . mandated such arrangements: U.S. Commission for Civil Rights Report, *Voting Irregularities in Florida During the 2000 Presidential Election* (June 2001): "The statutory requirement to hire a private agency to assist in purging the voter files was enacted after the incidents of voter fraud in the 1997 Miami mayoral election that included votes cast in the names of deceased persons. At the Commission hearing in Tallahassee, L. Clayton Roberts, director of the Division of Elections, described the history of chapter 98.0975 of the Florida statutes: 'This section of the statute was passed in response to a 1997 Miami mayoral election where it was challenged in court and went up through the court system in the state of Florida. The gentleman who originally won that mayor's race was turned out of office. There was a grand jury investigation. There was a Senate select committee appointed to investigate that election. There was [an] allegation and it was eventually proven that a large number of people who were deceased cast ballots—well, someone cast ballots in the name of some people who were deceased in that election. People who were convicted felons who had lost their right to vote under the Florida Constitution cast ballots in that election, and people who were also registered in another municipality or another county within that area cast ballots in the city of Miami mayor's race.'"
126 against lists of known felons: Ibid., chapter 5: "The amount paid to DBT Online for its performance of the contract with the Division of Elections was $3,221,8000. DBT representatives offered vague testimony about the actual costs of the services rendered under the contract, insisting that the payment encompassed hours of work, in addition to its 'intellectual property, existing databases, and [our] experience.'"

Reports attribute information to a March 16, 2001, letter written by DBT vice president George Bruder to Mary Frances Berry, commission chairperson. Had the contract been renewed as planned, the total tally would have reached $4,365,800, according to note 170 of the report: "The contract allowed a total payment of $4,365,800 for completion of four phases of the contract, including renewal through 2001. Because the Division of Elections did not renew its option with DBT Online through 2001, DBT Online was not paid the full contract price. Exhibit A, 'Data Processing Services Agreement,' Nov. 28, 1998."

See also George Bruder, Vice President Public Records Group, ChoicePoint, Statement before the U.S. Commission on Civil Rights, Miami, Feb. 16, 2001: "In May 1998, the Division issued an Invitation to Bid with the stated purpose of 'the comparison of various databases with the voter registration information contained in the Central Voter File.' DBT, then an independent company, was among the companies that bid. However, the award went to Professional Analysis, a local Tallahassee company. That company was apparently unable to perform satisfactorily and, in July 1998, the DOE issued a new Request for Proposal. DBT submitted a second unsuccessful bid to process the Central Voter File. In this second RFP process no award was made to any company.

"In September 1998, the DOE issued an Invitation to Negotiate to two companies, Computer Business Service and DBT, and on November 24, 1998, the Florida Department of State, DOE, under Secretary of State Sandra Mortham, entered into a Data Processing Services Agreement with DBT for services to be performed during calendar year 1999. The Agreement provided that DBT was to compare the Division's Central Voter File with a number of public record databases, including some provided by various Florida agencies, other states, and federal agencies, to help the Division determine whether disqualified persons appeared in the Central Voter File."

127   66,000 people identified as felons: U.S. Commission for Civil Rights Report, *Voting Irregularities in Florida During the 2000 Presidential Election* (June 2001), chapter 5.

127   restored voting rights to felons: Robert E. Pierre, "Florida Revisited; Botched Name Purge Denied Some the Right to Vote," *Washington Post*, May 31, 2001.

127   "Their [sic] the customer": Email from George A. Bruder to Malene Thorogood, April 30, 2000. The note was one of several contained in court records discussing the process of reviewing the eligibility of voters and the training of election officials.

127   "have had your civil rights restored": U.S. Commission for Civil Rights Report, *Voting Irregularities in Florida During the 2000 Presidential Election* (June 2001), chapter 5.

128   "It could destroy a life": Interview with Linda Howell, summer 2003.

128   prohibited inappropriately from voting that day: Scott Hiaasen, Gary Kane, and Elliot Jaspin, "Felon Purge Sacrificed Innocent Voters," *Palm Beach Post*, May 27, 2001. They reached this conclusion by comparing the "state's 'felon's list' with a list of all the voters in Florida registered by Election Day. The Post first identified all the purged voters by finding people named on the felon list that did not appear on the November voter rolls. The Post then searched among the purged voters for those that did not match perfectly with a felon— that is, they had a different name or race or birth date—and for voters with convictions in states that automatically restored voting rights to felons."

128   Others put the figure much higher: See Ted B. Kissell, "Felon Follies: A problem that marred the 2000 ballot is back," *New Times–Broward Palm Beach*, Oct. 31, 2002. Elliott Mincberg of People for the American Way claimed to have an expert who was "prepared to testify at trial that 70,000 of those 94,000 names were inaccurate—roughly a 74% rate of false-positives."

129   "I was cheated out of voting": Pierre, "Florida Revisited," *Washington Post*, May 31, 2001.

129   in 2002, in state and local elections: Hiaasen, Kane, and Jaspin, "Felon Purge Sacrificed Innocent Voters," *Palm Beach Post*, May 27, 2001.

129   paying $75,000 to the NAACP: Kissell, "Felon Follies," *New Times–Broward Palm Beach*, Oct. 31, 2002. See also "NAACP Settles Dispute with Felons List Compiler," *St. Petersburg Times*, July 3, 2002.

129   into the lives of regular Americans: See undated *Homeland Security White Paper: The Right Information at the Right Time in the Right Place*, p. 3, put out by ChoicePoint and several business partners.

129   more than 50,000 by 2004: See undated ChoicePoint press release, "Creating a Safer and More Secure Society Through the Responsible Use of Information," in a company marketing folder called *Smarter Decisions, Safer World*.

130   background screening, and identification companies: "In Depth: Tech Biz; Technology's Most Valuable Companies," *American City Business Journals*, July 21, 2003.

130   "conspiracy in entertainment communications": Packard, *The Naked Society*, p. 242.

131   "rights and privileges": Telephone interview with Derek Smith, Nov. 21, 2003.

131   "customer acquisition and retention programs": See ChoicePoint press re-

lease, "ChoicePoint Acquires DATEQ Information Network, Inc.," Jan. 5, 1998, which also discusses the Customer Development Corporation acquisition.

131 examine the background of would-be tenants: See the following ChoicePoint press releases: "ChoicePoint Acquisition Expands One-Stop Shop Services to the Pre-Employment Screening Market," Feb. 1, 2000; "ChoicePoint Acquires Pinkerton's Employee Screening; Business Deal Includes Five-Year Services and Reseller Agreement," July 2, 2001; and "ChoicePoint Acquires ASAP; Expands Capability in Tenant-Screening," Oct. 13, 2003.

132 "counterproductive activities at work": See "Frequently Asked Questions," Esteem: The Power of Trust, http://www.esteemnet.com/faq.html

132 "failing to adequately re-investigate it": Ibid.

132 the highest proportion of those hits: See 2003 WPS Criminal Record Statistics, a report generated by ChoicePoint at my request.

132 38 murderers and 67 sex offenders: See data from ChoicePoint's Volunteer Select service, a report generated at my request.

132 DNA identification effort ever: "Bode Technology Group to Identify Victims at World Trade Center; Country's Largest Private Forensic DNA Lab Contracts with New York," PR Newswire, Oct. 2, 2001. 'This is the largest mass disaster DNA identification effort ever undertaken,' explained Mitchell Holland, Ph.D., the lab director at Bode, who was involved in the DNA identification efforts for TWA Flight 800, Alaska Air, and Egypt Air airline disasters. 'The magnitude of this disaster just cannot be compared.'"

133 "the ultimate identifier": Derek Smith, "Hiding from the Light: Book Proposal," June 23, 2003, p. 5.

133 "you are who you say you are": ChoicePoint press release, "ChoicePoint Acquires VitalCheck," Dec. 2, 2002.

134 "And I love that": Interview with Derek Smith, Nov. 21, 2003.

134 stock was worth about $3.2 billion: Some of the core details come from ChoicePoint: A Look Inside, a presentation by Doug Curling, the company's president and chief operating officer, on Sept. 23, 2003.

134 against us, our businesses, and our nation: Smith interview. He added that " . . . we have to deploy knowledge, information, and technology so that we can better understand what the risks are and deal with them—if not beforehand, very quickly, in order to mitigate the consequences of what has taken place . . . laws are important and necessary, but people can break laws and fences. So one of the only things we are able to do . . . and one of the things we have to know is if people pose a threat. And again dealing with that fairly and responsibly before the last line of security really kicks in."

135 "that doesn't screen their drivers?": Vincent Coppola, "PROFILE: Derek Smith's Brave New World," Georgia Trend, Aug. 1, 2002.

135 the world's largest retailer: ChoicePoint press release, "ChoicePoint, #1 Warehouse Club Offer Powerful Tools to Small Businesses," Nov. 18, 2003.

135 specified when that would be: Mary Lou Pickel, "ID Software for Sale to the Public," Atlanta Journal-Constitution, Nov. 20, 2003.

136 "it has come together so well": Smith interview.

136 over 50 percent more than the year before: Meredith Jordan, "Top Atlanta CEO's Pay up 17% in '02," Atlanta Business Chronicle, June 2, 2003: "Derek V. Smith of ChoicePoint Inc. . . . made $20.3 million in total direct compensation in 2002. Smith's total direct compensation increased 54 percent, up from $13.1 million in 2001. His contract was renegotiated in 2002. The increase can be linked primarily to an increase in options granted from 375,000 in 2001 to 732,000 in 2002 under the new contract. Meanwhile, ChoicePoint's total shareholder return was 4 percent in 2002. The company's net income was up 79 percent over 2001."

137 "by the misuse of certain information systems" Interview with Chris Jay
     Hoofnagle, Nov. 17, 2003. See *The Privacy Law Sourcebook 2000* (Washington,
     D.C.: Electronic Privacy Information Center, 2000), p. 38.

137 foreign intelligence are becoming more interlinked: For a good briefing on
     this, see the testimony of James X. Dempsey, executive director for the Cen-
     ter for Democracy and Technology, before the House Judiciary Committee's
     Subcommittee on Commercial and Administrative law and Subcommittee on
     the Constitution, July 22, 2003.

137 wrote in a paper about ChoicePoint in 2004: Hoofnagle, "Big Brother's Little
     Helpers: How ChoicePoint and Other Commercial Data Brokers Collect,
     Process, and Package Your Data for Law Enforcement" [see p. 313 above, sec-
     ond paragraph for Chapter 5].

138 a "scarlet letter society": Hoofnagle interview.

138 "which ultimately benefit consumers": Hoofnagle, "Big Brother's Little
     Helpers," referring to a letter from Gina Moore at ChoicePoint to Chris Hoof-
     nagle, EPIC, Feb. 21, 2003.

139 "an equal opportunity dossier builder": Hoofnagle interview.

139 about credit and background reports: Ann Davis, "Zero Tolerance: Employers
     Dig Deep into Workers' Pasts, Citing Terrorism Fears—Lilly Bans Contract
     Staffers for Old Petty Crimes; The $60 Bounced Check—A Case of Mistaken
     Identity," *Wall Street Journal,* March 12, 2002.

139 Hikes Point section of Louisville: Interviews with Mary Boris and Bernard
     Leachman, Jr., Dec. 3, 2003.

140 ChoicePoint said in its promotional material: See ChoicePoint annual report,
     2002, p. 8.

141 "even nightmarish, to get them out": Leachman interview.

141 enough about CLUE to complain: Leslie Berestein, "Some Wildfire Claimants
     Told Insurance Premiums Will Rise," *Copley News Service,* Nov. 30, 2003.

142 "perform services for Lilly effective immediately": Davis, "Zero Tolerance,"
     Wall Street Journal, March 12, 2002.

142 "bound by our contractual provisions": Ibid.

143 "But you can't hide from this stuff": Interviews with Det. Glenn Kerns, Seat-
     tle Police Department, assigned to the Joint Terrorism Task Force, in the fall
     of 2003 and spring of 2004.

144 bankruptcies, civil judgments, and liens: ChoicePoint press release, "Choice-
     Point Acquires National Data Retrieval, Expands Presence in Public Records
     Field," Jan. 2, 2003.

144 Terminix extermination company $3,500: John Biewen interview with Caro-
     lyn Lucas for National Public Radio documentary, Nov. 18, 2003.

144 from about 130 million people: Interview with Darryl Lemecha, chief infor-
     mation officer, during visit to ChoicePoint facility in Alpharetta, Georgia, June
     16, 2003.

145 of about 220 million adults: Ibid.

145 "77 round trips to the moon": Estimates prepared at my request by Choice-
     Point, July 18, 2003, for visit to the company's Boca Raton, Florida, facility.

145 "That's just how I look at it": Lucas interview with Biewen.

146 Systems Research & Development: Interview with Jeff Jonas, Sept. 10, 2003.

146 "a supercharger on a V-12 Ferrari": Vincent Coppola, "Killer App," *Men's Jour-
     nal* (April 2003).

146 private investment arm of the Central Intelligence Agency: See SRD press re-
     lease, "Systems Research & Development Receives New Funding from In-Q-
     Tel," July 18, 2002.

147 "Arrest him": Coppola, "Killer App."

148 known as the Griffin Book: Jonas interview.

148   "who otherwise would have gotten in": Thomas E. Weber, "Firm Seeks Obscure Links in Data for Security Risks," *Wall Street Journal*, Jan. 14, 2002.
148   "about what has changed": Jonas interview.
149   in the gray market online: Robert O'Harrow, Jr., "A Deadly Collection of Information; Killer Paid Online Data Broker for Material Obtained Through Trickery," *Washington Post*, Jan. 4, 2002.
150   a LexisNexis service called P-Trak: A story in CNet and postings by the Electronic Privacy Information Center created a privacy firestorm in 1996.
150   acting in the best interests of society: See Robert Pitofsky, Federal Trade Commission Chairman and Others, "Individual Reference Services: A Report to Congress" (December 1997).
150   Boyer's stepfather . . . backed away: Robert O'Harrow, Jr., "Net Privacy Bill Called 'Trojan Horse,'" *Washington Post*, Oct. 25, 2000.
151   "decisions without appropriate tools": Derek Smith, "Privacy and the Workplace: The Latest Trends," *The Link Newsletter (ChoicePoint)* (Summer 2002).
151   welcomed more background screening: See Labor Policy Association press release, "Survey Shows Strong Employee Support for Employer Efforts to Bolster Workplace Security," June 3, 2003.
152   "inappropriate people out of workplaces": ChoicePoint press release, "Post-9/11 Shift Seen in Employee Attitudes About Privacy, Security at Work," April 16, 2002.
152   to the government that day: ChoicePoint International Data Access Statement of Work, U.S. Immigration and Naturalization Service, Sept. 12, 2001.
153   "has been made publicly available": Memo from the FBI Office of the General Counsel National Security Law Unit, "Guidance Regarding the Use of ChoicePoint for Foreign Intelligence Collection or Foreign Counterterrorism Investigations," addressed to National Security Counterterrorism Information Resources, Sept. 17, 2001.
153   contractors to collect the information: Hugh Dellios, "U.S. Data Mining Investigated; 'Information Trafficking' Riles Latin Americans," *Chicago Tribune*, Oct. 12, 2003.
153   "people than the Nicaraguan government": Ibid.
153   invited ChoicePoint executives to Mexico City: Jim Krane, "U.S. Drug and Immigration Probes Suffer After Vendor Stops Selling Latin American Citizen Data," Associated Press, Aug. 28, 2003.
153   was considering charging them with treason: Susana Hayward, "Mexico Arrests Database Officials: They Allegedly Collected Voter Data That Was Resold to the U.S. Government," *San Jose Mercury News*, Nov. 27, 2003.
154   "of the people of Mexico and ChoicePoint": Dellios, "U.S. Data Mining Investigated," *Chicago Tribune*, Oct. 12, 2003.
154   in the months after the attacks: Davis, "Zero Tolerance," *Wall Street Journal*, March 12, 2002.
154   bottom line was only going to grow: Adelia Cellini Linecker, "Tigher Security Focus Boosts Prospects Here," *Investor's Business Daily*, July 10, 2002.
154   the year before the attacks: These estimates are based on fiscal 2002 report of $791 million and fiscal 2000 report of $603 million. See ChoicePoint annual report, 2002.
154   anti-terrorism units across the country: Amendment of Solicitation/Modification of Contract, U.S. Department of Justice Procurement Services Staff, April 11, 2002.
154   criminal backgrounds were hired inappropriately: Sara Kehaulani Goo, "TSA Hiring Practices to Be Probed: Homeland Security Office to Question Background Checks," *Washington Post*, May 28, 2003.
155   there were already eighteen installations: These details come from interviews

I conducted with ChoicePoint vice president James Zimbardi and company spokesman James Lee on March 22, 2004. Zimbardi referred to "Choice-Point's distributed public records database." He said the system has a "query manager" that reaches out to different databases, controlled by different police and government agencies, and pulls back the necessary information about people. They claim this happens instantaneously, hence the idea of a Matrix redux. They said this approach improves privacy protections, because it does not compile personal information in one large system.

156 that most people would believe them: Zimbardi and Lee agreed with the idea of ChoicePoint working as an intelligence service. "It's a fair characterization," Zimbardi said, after hearing the end of the chapter described and, in several cases, read to him. "We do act as an intelligence agency, gathering data, applying analytics."

During the conversation, Lee suggested that people would think Choice-Point was exaggerating if it made those claims itself. "Frankly," Lee said, "it's not a story we should be telling."

CHAPTER 6. THE IMMUTABLE ME

I relied heavily on occasional interviews with Joseph Atick over more than two years. These were lively conversations over meals and on the telephone. One interview, at the trade show, was conducted with radio reporter and producer John Biewen for possible inclusion in a documentary for National Public Radio. For the history of biometrics, I drew on Simson Garfinkel's fine *Database Nation: The Death of Privacy in the 21st Century* (Sebastopol, CA: O'Reilly & Associates, 2000) and Jeffrey Rosen's incisive book, *The Naked Crowd*. William Rogers, publisher of *Biometric Digest*, shared his knowledge about the industry's growth. Professor Jim Wyman at San Jose State University also helped outline the biometrics world, and I am indebted to his paper, "Biometrics and How They Work." For the section on the use of iris scans at New Egypt Elementary School in Plumsted, N.J., I am grateful for the help of Raymond L. Bolling III, a security consultant who gave me a tour and patiently explained how the system worked.

158 "No problem": Interview with Joseph Atick, Dec. 30, 2003.

158 out of hotels in Washington, D.C.: Atick interview, Sept. 22, 2003. "It was an amazing period after 9/11," Atick said. "The industry was called upon as a partner from Washington. I camped here for three months. Like other heads of industry called on to help shape some of the early mandates, there was a barrage of six mandates that changed the landscape of security, etc. Some of it encapsulates the vision you have, some do not."

159 "as a personal crusade": Rick Montgomery, "Don't Look Now, But They're Capturing Your Face," *Kansas City Star*–Knight Ridder/Tribune News Service, Dec. 6, 2001.

159 about his products: Atick interview, Dec. 30, 2003.

160 "to prove your identity": Atick interview, Sept. 22, 2003.

160 in mathematical physics in 1987: Identix Web site, www.identix.com/company/comp_team_jatick.html, and Atick interview, Sept. 22, 2003.

161 "knowledge and actionable items": Atick interview, Sept. 22, 2003.

161 "like the birth of a child": Interview with Joseph Atick, Aug. 16, 2001.

162 the real mother: Garfinkel, *Database Nation: The Death of Privacy in the 21st Century*, pp. 37–38.

162 who had killed her two sons: Scottish Criminal Record Office Web site, www.scro.police.uk/fingerprint_history.htm

163 on files from some 40 million people: Phone interview with FBI spokesman Paul Bresson, Dec. 8, 2003.

163 "these fingerprint cards is difficult!": FBI For the Family Web site, www.fbi.gov/kids/k5th/whatwedo2.htm

164 "or that of society at large": Garfinkel, *Database Nation,* pp 40–41.

164 who he claims to be: Jim Wyman, "Biometrics and How They Work" (course outline), San Jose State University, p. 10.

165 "it would be ten years away": Atick interview, Sept. 22, 2003.

165 "change the world in the next twenty years.": Ibid.

165 "user or operator action required": Visionics Corp., "Federal Government Adopting Face Recognition," PR Newswire, July 7, 1997.

166 "that we had dummy cameras": Rosen, *The Naked Crowd,* p. 43.

168 "We're very bad at it": Robert O'Harrow, "Password Stress Means Memory Overload," *Washington Post,* Sept. 3, 1995.

168 "This is ground zero": Interview with William Rogers, Jan. 2, 2004.

170 even if there were no guards present: Jeremy Bentham, *The Panopticon Writings,* ed. Miran Bozovic (London: Verso, 1995).

170 "I find it chilling": "Should People Who Are Criminals Be Under Surveillance?" *CNN Talkback Live,* transcript, Feb. 1, 2001.

170 right to privacy in public places: Alexander T. Nguyen, "Here's Looking at You, Kid: Has Face-Recognition Technology Completely Outflanked the Fourth Amendment?" *Virginia Journal of Law and Technology* 7 (2)(2002), p. 12: "Courts have held that there is no expectation of privacy in what an individual knowingly exposes to the public."

171 after the protests in Tiananmen Square: Ibid., p. 17.

171 reader eight of ten times: Bruce Schneier, "Fun with Fingerprint Readers," *Crypto-Gram Newsletter,* May 15, 2002; www.schneier.com/crypto-gram-0205 .html#5—"Matsumoto tried these attacks against eleven commercially available fingerprint biometric systems, and was able to reliably fool all of them."

171 "believing claims from security companies": Bruce Schneier, *Beyond Fear: Thinking Sensibly About Security in an Uncertain World* (New York: Copernicus Books, 2003).

172 an accounting and computer business: Avis Thomas-Lester, "Questions Linger for Loved Ones of Woman Killed in Lake Arbor Home," *Washington Post, Prince George's Extra,* Jan. 16, 2003.

173 submitted to the court by police: Ruben Castaneda, "Mistaken Arrests Leave Pr. George's Murder Unsolved," *Washington Post,* June 22, 2003.

173 "shoot me for not telling the truth": Ibid.

174 "starting not to shake": Ibid.

174 electronic fingerprint reader to identify customers: Melinda Fulmer, "Grocery Stores Checking Out Fingerprints: Small shops are using biometric technology that retrieves customers' data to cut losses from fraud," *Los Angeles Times,* Nov. 25, 2003.

174 in order to cash paychecks: Will Wade, "Using Fingerprints to Make Payments at POS Slowly Gaining Popularity," *Credit Union Journal,* April 21, 2003.

175 to deploy a similar system: BioPay LLC press release, "BI-LO Extends Agreement with BioPay, Creating the Nation's Largest Retail Implementation of Biometric Identification Systems," Nov. 10, 2003, www.biopay.com

175 and BioPay LLC of Herndon, Virginia: Wade, "Using Fingerprints to Make Payments at POS Slowly Gaining Popularity," *Credit Union Journal,* April 21, 2003.

175 Every machine costs about $10,000: Fulmer, "Grocery Stores Checking Out Fingerprints," *Los Angeles Times,* Nov. 25, 2002.

175 "already given away all your privacy": Ibid.

176 create its own biometric-sharing network: Interview with Bob Schmidt, Dec. 30, 2003.

176 through its own facilities: Atick interview, Dec. 30, 2003.

176 long after when they were taken: Identix Incorporated, Form 10-K, Securities and Exchange Commission, Washington, D.C., 20549.

176 members to do business remotely: Rogers interview.

176 "where identity theft breeds": ChoicePoint press release, "ChoicePoint Selects BIO-key to Help the Fight Against Fraud and Identity Theft," Nov. 18, 2003.

177 faces of the 72,000 spectators: Lev Grossman, "Welcome to the Snooper Bowl." *Time magazine,* Dec. 12, 2001.

178 who have more than one license: Viisage Technology, "Viisage Awarded $8 Million Contract by Kentucky; New System Will Improve Licensing Security and Convenience," *Business Wire,* April 6, 2001.

178 Viisage's Face Trac software: Grossman, "Welcome to the Snooper Bowl," *Time* magazine, Dec. 12, 2001.

178 "we caught nineteen, that's astounding!": Ibid.

178 "doing it for any other reason": Bobbie Battista, "Should People Who Are Criminals Be Under Surveillance?" *CNN Talkback Live,* transcript, Feb. 1, 2001.

179 "it didn't have any impact": Interview with Bob Guidara by my researcher Deborah Popowski, Jan. 8, 2004.
     Question: "Is there any information indicating that the face recognition software had any deterrent effect on crime?"
     Guidara: "Not at all. It didn't have any impact, it didn't touch one person, [and since] you can't measure the deterrent effect, it served no measurable purpose. That's why we stopped using it."

179 to follow women on the street: See Rosen, *The Naked Crowd:* "When you put a group of bored, unsupervised men in front of live video screens and allow them to zoom in on whatever happens to catch their eye, they tend to spend a fair amount of time leering at women. . . . A control room in the Midlands, for example, took close-up shots of women with large breasts and taped them up on the walls," p. 48.

180 "looking in public places": Interview with Det. Bill Todd, Tampa Police Department, July 14, 2003.

180 "until the law takes that burden from me": Atick interview, Aug. 16, 2003.

181 variable lighting and other factors: P. Jonathon Phillips, Patrick Grother, et al., "Face Recognition Vendor Test 2002: Overview and Summary," www.frvt .org/frvt2004/default.htm (March 2003), p. 4.

181 completely undermine the point of the system: Ibid., p. 6.

181 to approach a suspect: Todd interview.
     Det. Todd: "A false positive would come up here as well."
     Int: "How many of those have you had?"
     Todd: "I can't tell an exact number. We've had a very small percentile in terms of overall captures."
     Int: "A couple hundred?"
     Todd: "At least a couple hundred over time. Unlike an access control system, we haven't taken the human element out of this. I want an officer to make a judgment call."

182 "as far as we could": Interview with Raymond L. Bolling III, May 7, 2003.

183 assistance than they were entitled to: Iridian Technologies Web site, www.iridiantech.com/products.php

183 "I'll get one for my home": Interview with Lauren Lindsay, May 7, 2003.

183 "to preserve my security": Interview with Lina Page, May 7, 2003.

183 There was no obvious problem with crime: Pat Kossan, "Phoenix School First to Install Face Scanners," *Arizona Republic,* Dec. 11, 2003.

184 "guests at the country club": Reelect Joe Arpaio Web site, www.reelectjoe .com/index2.cfm

184 "I feel it's worth it": Michelle Rushlo, "Ariz. School Installs Facial Scan System," Associated Press, Dec. 12, 2003.

184 a familiar figure of the industry: Identix Web site, www.identix.com/company/comp_team_jatick.html

184 captured by Identix machines: Atick interview, Dec. 30, 2003.

185 fingerprints to demographic data: Identix Incorporated, Form 10-K 2002, Securities and Exchange Commission.

185 "reaffirms Identix' leadership position": Identix press release, "Identix Awarded BPA from U.S. Department of Homeland Security to Provide Biometric Livescan Systems, Services to Citizenship and Immigration Services and Other Departments Within DHS," Oct. 3, 2003.

185 "no longer a rogue technology": Atick interview, Dec. 30, 2003.

185 documents that can be read by a machine: Fred Barbash and Sara Kehaulani Goo, "U.S. Begins Tracking Foreign Arrivals: Fingerprint-Matching System Deployed at Airports and Seaports," *Washington Post,* Jan. 5, 2004.

186 "customer information processing": Acxiom press release, Dec. 17, 2003, www.acxiom.com/default.aspx

186 once they enter the country: Ibid. "There'll be no monitoring of their activity once they're here," Homeland Security secretary Tom Ridge said on the NBC *Today Show* on Jan. 5, 2004.

186 "It can even tell twins apart": Atick interview, April 16, 2004.

187 police, and biometric products: Atick interview, Sept. 22, 2003.

187 main source of technical information about biometrics: See the Biometrics Consortium Web site, www.biometrics.org/REPORTS/CTST96/

189 "Those are important factors": Atick interview, Sept. 22, 2003.

CHAPTER 7. TOTAL INFORMATION AWARENESS

This chapter could have not been written in the same way without the cooperation of John Poindexter and J. Brian Sharkey, who described their efforts and aims at length. On one occasion, John and Linda Poindexter invited me to their home in suburban Washington, D.C., served me a delicious lunch, and gave me a tour of Poindexter's office and the photographs and other memorabilia from his time in government. With few exceptions, usually involving what he declared to be national security matters, Poindexter answered my most pointed questions, despite his professed distaste for journalists. For his part, Sharkey welcomed me to his office at SAIC in Arlington, Virginia, not far from Poindexter's former office at DARPA. In addition, I derived great insight about Poindexter's complex character and history from Robert Timberg's wonderful book, *The Nightingale's Song* (New York: Simon & Schuster, 1995).

I have relied heavily on an array of documents, some dating back to the late 1990s, when the concept of Total Information Awareness—the systematic collection and analysis of massive amounts of information to find terrorists before they struck—was first shaped. These documents include public presentations, reports to Congress, and email correspondence with Poindexter and others involved in the program. I also turned to email first obtained through the Freedom of Information Act by the Electronic Privacy Information Center.

For background on the Iran-Contra scandal, I turned to William S. Cohen and George J. Mitchell's *Men of Zeal: A Candid Inside Story of the Iran-Contra Hearings* (New York: Viking, 1988), and to *The Iran-Contra Affair: The Making of a Scandal,* a detailed study by researchers and writers at the National Security Archive, found at http://nsarchive.chadwyck.com/icacknow.htm; the authors include Malcolm Byrne and Peter Kornbluh. One of the most helpful papers is the very good overview titled "The Iran-Contra Scandal in Perspective," Jan. 26, 1990, by Byrne and Kornbluh. The Supreme Court brief, "United States of America v. John M. Poindexter, October

Term, 1992," also provided helpful background, as did a document produced by Poindexter called "Report to Congress Regarding the Terrorism Information Awareness Program," May 20, 2003. I turned to a fine investigative book, James Bamford's *Body of Secrets* (New York: Doubleday, 2001), for details about the National Security Agency.

192   to the greatest degree possible: J. Brian Sharkey, slides for "Total Information Awareness," Presentation given at DARPA Tech '99 in Denver, Colorado. June 3–7, 1999; http://www.darpa.mil/darpatech99/presentations.htm

193   "'I can make it worth your while'": Interview with J. Brian Sharkey, Feb. 6, 2004.

194   "building relationships and moving fast": Ibid.

195   "their transition to operational users": "Report to Congress Regarding the Terrorism Information Awareness Program" (in response to Consolidated Appropriations Resolution, 2003; cited hereafter as Report to Congress), May 20, 2003, p. 1.

196   "domestic intelligence and counterintelligence information": Appendix C of the Report to Congress.

196   as the Advanced Research Projects Agency: See Defense Advanced Research Projects Agency, "Technology Transition," p. 8. This document was undated; it can be accessed via the Web at www.darpa.mil/body/pdf/transition.pdf.

196   it made the Internet possible: See ibid., pp. 12, 19, and 40–41.

197   thrived on DARPA-funded discoveries: Ibid., pp. 14, 32–33, and 42–43.

197   "to that greater level of detail": Interview with John Poindexter, accompanied by John Biewen, Dec. 11, 2003.

198   to know where it's stored: Report to Congress, p. 4.

198   "organizations, places, and things" and "legitimate activities": Report to Congress, pp. 7–8.

198   by the way he or she walked: Ibid., p. 10.

199   King of the Fall Festival: Timberg, *The Nightingale's Song*, p. 35.

199   "He was born an old man": Ibid.

200   "what King Henry wanted": Interview with John Poindexter, April 10, 2004; Timberg, *The Nightingale's Song*, p. 105.

200   "with the system from the start": Timberg, *The Nightingale's Song*, p. 106.

200   "I had in my Caltech experience": Ibid., p. 105.

201   with wounds to his chest: Tom Matthews, "The Shooting of the President: Reagan's Close Call," *Newsweek*, April 13, 1981.

201   "at the time was a typewriter": Poindexter interview, Dec. 11, 2003.

201   $14 million crisis management center: Timberg, *The Nightingale's Song*, p. 295.

202   "some of the first to use laptops": Poindexter interview, Dec. 11, 2003.

202   traveled to Iran to arrange arms sales: See Cohen and Mitchell, *Men of Zeal: A Candid Inside Story of the Iran-Contra Hearings;* see also "The Iran-Contra Affair: The Making of a Scandal," at http://nsarchive.chadwyck.com/icacknow.htm

203   "to Poindexter's testimony": Cohen and Mitchell, *Men of Zeal.*

203   "and the end result is what's important": Poindexter interview, March 21, 2003.

204   "even more scandalous than Iran-Contra": William Safire, "You Are a Suspect," *New York Times*, Nov. 14, 2002.

204   "How many terrorists are going to slip through?": Robert O'Harrow. "U.S. Hopes to Check Computers Globally: System Would Be Used to Hunt Terrorists," *Washington Post*, Nov. 12, 2002.

204   "if I've ever heard one": Ibid.

205   "unconstitutional system of public surveillance": Public letter signed by Marc Rotenberg and others, addressed to Senators Tom Daschle and Trent Lott, Nov. 18, 2002.

205   "dollars to be sent down the drain": Office of Senator Chuck Grassley, press

release, "Grassley Requests Information on Defense Total Information Awareness Program," Nov. 22, 2002.

206 an analog for the O in Office: Poindexter interview, March 21, 2003. During an interview on Dec. 12, 2003, Poindexter offered more detail: "It is traditional for offices in DARPA and programs to have logos. It helps build up a team spirit and a feeling of identity, and it is a useful mechanism. I asked my deputy to think about some ideas for logos and in that process, I had earlier pointed out . . . the great seal of the United States. It consists of a pyramid which has thirteen bricks in the base . . . represent[ing] the thirteen original colonies. And at the top is an eye and you can find on the Internet there is an eye. And I've forgotten at this point the Latin around the logo but it has to do with knowledge and a better world and [a colleague] liked that and so he wanted to come up with the initials of the office, and he recognized that the great seal of the U.S. had the eye to represent the I and the pyramid was roughly in the shape of the A and then the earth was the O for office. The logo was meant to express the idea about knowledge and having Total Information Awareness about what is going on in the world and it also represents the initials of the office."

206 "the rights of millions of Americans": Sen. Ron Wyden, transcript of floor statement on Jan. 14, 2003, provided by Wyden's office.

207 to allow "traders" to bet on terrorism: Wyden and Sen. Byron L. Dorgan, letter to John Poindexter, July 28, 2003.

207 "time to end it once and for all": Wyden and Dorgan transcript of press conference, July 28, 2003.

208 "and the basis for its freedoms": John Poindexter, undated draft of letter to DARPA director Anthony Tether. See also Bradley Graham, "Poindexter Resigns But Defends Programs: Anti-Terrorism, Data Scanning Efforts at Pentagon Called Victims of Ignorance," *Washington Post,* Aug. 13, 2003.

208 "so powerful it's scary": Bill Powell, "How George Tenet Brought the CIA Back from the Dead," *Fortune,* Oct. 13, 2003.

209 "attempting to cross the border": U.S. Department of Homeland Security, Office of the Press Secretary, Fact Sheet, "Science and Technology Accomplishments," undated.

209 to assess risks in crowds: Interview with David Bolka, director of Homeland Security Advanced Research Projects Agency, March 24, 2004.

209 intelligence units across the county: See Department of Homeland Security press release, Feb. 24, 2004, http://www.dhs.gov/dhspublic/interapp/press _release/press_release_0354.xml

210 "processes into their programs": Sharkey interview.

211 "operations every second": Bamford, *Body of Secrets,* p. 4.

211 "all the human languages" and "analytic tools will emerge": See Advanced Research Development Activity, undated documents, http://www.ic-arda .org/InfoExploit/ and http://www.ic-arda.org/Novel_Intelligence/index.html

213 "will continue, one way or another": Poindexter interview, Dec. 11, 2003.

CHAPTER 8. THE GOVERNMENT'S EYES AND EARS

My starting point here was an ongoing look at the aviation screening system conducted for the *Washington Post,* including interviews with key officials whose remarks sometimes appeared without attribution in stories on the front page. I am indebted to Michael Jackson, who agreed to be identified and speak for the record at great length about his hopes and aims for the project. Ben Bell III and Admiral James Loy also provided much-needed context and ideas in a series of conversations over about two years. David Sobel and his colleagues at the Electronic Privacy Information Center deserve much credit for successfully pressing secrecy-minded government officials for details about aviation screening, through Freedom of Information lawsuits. James Madison would surely applaud their work; I am grateful to have had the fruit of their efforts. Jerry Berlin provided important background about past and current screening efforts, and he helped to underscore important ideas about the potential impact of such surveillance efforts on American society. For the concrete stories about what can go wrong, I am indebted to Johnnie Lockett Thomas, David Nelson, Aquil Abdullah, and others who shared their experiences with me.

216 "We just saw the future": Interview with Michael Jackson, April 10, 2003.
217 "'not a universal law enforcement tool'": Robert O'Harrow, Jr., "Air Security Focusing on Flier Screening," *Washington Post*, Sept. 4, 2002. For this story, Jackson spoke on condition that his name not be used. He agreed to speak on record for this book and permitted me to use his name.
218 almost 700 million passengers: U.S. General Accounting Office report, *Air Traffic Control*, GAO-02-591, June 2002, executive summary, p. 2.
218 the Center for Public Integrity: Charles Lewis and the Center for Public Integrity, *The Buying of Congress* (New York: Avon Books, 1998), p. 3.
218 aircraft more than a hundred times: Statement of Gerald L. Dillingham, director of Physical Infrastructure Issues, U.S. General Accounting Office, given before the Committee on Governmental Affairs and its Subcommittee on Oversight of Governmental Management, Restructuring, and the District of Columbia, U.S. Senate. "Aviation Security: Vulnerabilities In, and Alternatives For, Preboard Screening Security Operations," Sept. 25, 2001, p. 5.
218 shortly before the attacks: Dillingham statement, p. 6.
219 burgers and fries for lunch: Ibid., p. 7.
219 the timing was not coincidental: *The Buying of Congress*, p. 191.
219 "knew the ins and outs of our systems": John Solomon, "FBI Suspects Hijackers Took About a Dozen Test Runs," Associated Press, May 28, 2002.
220 closer scrutiny because of those lapses: Dan Eggen, "Airports Screened Nine of Sept. 11 Hijackers," *Washington Post*, March 2, 2002.
220 quickly disavowed the project: Frank J. Murray, "NASA Plans to Read Minds at Airports," *Washington Times*, Aug. 17, 2002. The documents behind the story were obtained by EPIC through a Freedom of Information lawsuit. See http://www.epic.org/privacy/airtravel/foia/foia1.html, and ftp://ftp.hq .nasa.gov/pub/pao/pressrel/2002/02-160.txt
221 "for the patriotic impulse as well": Jackson interview.
222 indications of fraud and deceit: This is a set of undated documents bearing the words: "HNC Software Inc. Proprietary & Confidential For Review and Evaluation by the US Dept. of Transportation Only."
222 "passenger, airport and flight": Part of a document labeled "Integrating Data and Protecting Privacy" prepared by Acxiom and presented to government officials, provided to me by officials at Acxiom. It is a familiar pitch from Acxiom: use data exensively and define the terms of "privacy" in a fashion that does not get in the way of doing business. "Is integrated data a privacy concern? Not if it is done properly," the paper asserts.
223 "I need help": Interview with James H. Vaules, Oct. 7, 2003, following a visit to LexisNexis offices in Ohio on Aug. 13, 2003.
224 to generate a score for them: For a history of the company, I turned to "The LexisNexis Timeline: Celebrating Innovation . . . and 30 years of online legal research," provided by the company.
224 7 million searchable documents every week: These details come from a briefing paper called "Risk Management," prepared for my visit to the company on Aug. 13, 2003.
226 "just really on a larger scale": Vaules interview.

227 "quick fix that won't fix anything": Letter to Vice President Al Gore from David Banisar, staff counsel to EPIC, and several other representatives of privacy and civil liberties organizations, Feb. 11, 1997.

228 "'Give me your driver's license'": Interview with David Nelson of Salem, Oregon, undated.

228 having trouble even booking flights: Letter to Congressman Joseph M. Hoeffel from Dr. Enrique Hernandez, Oct. 14, 2002.

229 "have been futile": Letter to Congressman Jay Inslee from Jim Thompson, Sept. 25, 2002.

229 "You feel guilty": Interview with Aquil Abdullah.

230 "'Who is this creep?'": Nelson interview.

230 detained her for forty minutes: Interviews with Johnnie Lockett Thomas, including Aug. 14, 2003, as well as follow-up letters, chronology, and other documents provided by Thomas.

230 "every time you fly": Thomas interview.

231 "I must be guilty of something": Thomas letter, Aug. 18, 2003.

231 "We're playing with dynamite": Interviews with Jerry Berlin, including April 1 and Oct. 1, 2003.

232 including types of meals ordered: Berlin interview.

233 "the FAA commenced the development": Berlin interview and undated memo to me in early summer 2003 regarding his work on the development of CAPPS1.

233 It created the Commission on Aviation Safety and Security: See White House Commission on Aviation Safety and Security, *Final Report to President Clinton*, Feb. 12, 1997. The report can be read at http://www.fas.org/irp/threat/212fin~1.html

234 "change in American culture": Berlin interview.

234 that indicates a potential threat: O'Harrow, "Air Security Focusing on Flier Screening," *Washington Post*, Sept. 4, 2002.

236 "a significantly more powerful tool": O'Harrow, "Air Security Focusing on Flier Screening," *Washington Post*, Sept. 4, 2002.

236 "We don't have a thinking system": Ibid.

237 "to secret action by the government": Interview with David Sobel, June 3, 2003. I have spoken to Sobel many times during the course of this book.

239 telling him. "Do it": Interview with Ben Bell III, June 4, 2003. I have spoken to Bell many times during the course of this book.

239 "risk assessment in the U.S.": Ibid.

241 but he was determined to try: I have relied on workshop documents dated March 16, 2003, and interviews with participants, including James Loy and Ben Bell III. During one interview on Oct. 6, 2003, Loy said: "We worked oh so hard to reach the privacy world."

241 "all the things I hold dear": Loy interview, Oct. 6, 2003.

242 "our very limited goal at the moment": Testimony by James L. Loy, director of the Transportation Security Administration, before the Census Subcommittee of the House Government Reform Committee, May 6, 2003.

243 "struggling to do the right thing": Jackson interview, Sept. 11, 2003.

245 "Where do you draw the line?": Ibid.

245 privately he was angry: Ben Bell interview, April 1, 2004. Bell had just left the government. He spoke, on tape, for more than ninety minutes.

246 "It is not a police state": Ibid.

CHAPTER 9. GOOD GUYS, BAD GUYS

Much of this chapter is built around interviews with Ken Ritchhart, who was given the responsibility for updating the FBI's computer technology infrastructure and electronic intelligence network. A spokesman in the FBI's financial intelligence unit provided details for the opening sections. Paul Bresson helped to arrange the interviews and find answers to follow-up questions. Ed Manavian, whom I interviewed at a doughnut shop in Brooklyn, provided useful background on the Joint Regional Information Exchange Systems, elaborating on documents that sketched in the plan. For details about the FBI's long-standing troubles with computer technology and records, I turned to some very good journalism, including stories in the *New York Times*. Les Seagraves, an assistant general counsel at EarthLink, served as a fine host when I visited the Internet service provider in Atlanta. Michael Matossian, the chief compliance and privacy officer at Fifth Third Bank in Cincinnati, gave a good overview of how the financial services industry is trying to meet new mandates to monitor customers. Konrad Feldman, the Searchspace chief executive in the United States, patiently translated into layman's terms the sophisticated software systems that Fifth Third and other financial institutions use to track so many transactions.

Denver activist Stephen Nash provided documents and clear descriptions of his experience with the city's police department. It's probably worth noting that Orion Scientific was most unhelpful and never returned phone calls to answer even basic questions about the company's role in domestic intelligence. In contrast was the coopration of Pasquale D'Amuro, the FBI assistant director in charge of the agency's New York field office. He took me on a tour of the FBI's intelligence center in New York and explained why he believes that personal data and computer tools are critical to the war on terror, and why the country also has to maintain proper oversight on such tools, both in and out of the government. I should note that after the terror attacks, D'Amuro served as executive assistant director in charge of counterterrorism and counterintelligence.

247 actual targets and rough timelines: John H. Cushman, Jr., "Terror Alert Is Raised to 'High,' Increasing Scrutiny of Travelers," *New York Times*, Dec. 22, 2003. See also transcript of Carol Lin and Mike Brooks, "Ridge Speaks on Raising Threat Level," *CNN Live Event/Special 10:00*, Dec. 22, 2003; and Curt Anderson, "Security Around United States Enhanced Amid Intelligence Showing Al-Qaida Wants Big Strike Soon," Associated Press, Dec. 22, 2003. Details confirmed by interview with James Loy.
248 to create an instant data-mining operation: Interviews with director of the FBI's Proactive Exploitation Group, Feb. 5 and April 8, 2004.
248 United, and other carriers: Ibid.
249 some five thousand pages an hour: Ibid.
249 news servers, software, and the like: Interview with FBI spokesman Paul Bresson, March 8, 2004.
250 "future events or behaviors": Colleen McCue, Emily S. Stone, and Teresa P. Gooch, "Data Mining and Value-Added Analysis," *FBI Law Enforcement Bulletin* (November 2003), http://www.fbi.gov/publications/leb/2003/nov2003/nov03leb.htm#page_2
250 wrote by hand on the document: Routing slip, document obtained from the Federal Bureau of Investigation, Sept. 16, 2001, available at http://epic.org/privacy/choicepoint/cpfbic.pdf. See also Chris Jay Hoofnagle, "Big Brother's Little Helpers" [see Chapter 5 notes, p. 313 above].
250 "and spit out potential results": Proactive Exploitation Group interview.
251 "that address each of those areas": FBI director Robert Mueller, transcript of Justice Department announcement, Federal News Service, May 29, 2002.
251 misplaced some four thousand documents: Eric Lichtblau and Charles Piller, "War on Terrorism Highlights FBI's Computer Woes," *New York Times*, July 28, 2002.
252 whether he was being watched: Ibid.

252 "the nation's vaunted G-men": Ibid.
252 "a comprehensive intelligence program": Mueller at National Press Club
     Luncheon, Federal News Service, June 20, 2003.
253 perceived as overly chary with information: Interview with Ed Manavian,
     chief of the California Department of Justice, Criminal Intelligence
     Bureau, March 8, 2004. Manavian elaborated at length in a later, taped
     interview.
253 "some of the things we were working on": Interview with John Poindexter,
     March 8, 2004.
255 "and other lawful activities": *National Criminal Intelligence Sharing Plan,* spon-
     sored by the Office of Justice Programs, U.S. Department of Justice, October
     2003, p. 48.
255 "for them to get away with it": Remarks by Secretary Tom Ridge to the Inter-
     national Association of Chiefs of Police Annual Conference, Office of the
     Press Secretary, Department of Homeland Security, Oct. 23, 2003.
257 "that they use to get us to act quickly": Interview with Les Seagraves, Feb.
     11, 2003.
257 "fabric of society in fundamental ways": Robert Corn-Revere, "Testimony on
     Carnivore and the Fourth Amendment," Federal Document Clearing House
     Congressional Testimony, July 24, 2000. Corn-Revere appeared before the
     Constitution Subcommittee of the House Judiciary Committee.
259 "balance those two . . . in order to survive": Seagraves interview.
260 "You can't even make a comparison": O'Harrow, "In Terror War, Privacy vs.
     Security," *Washington Post,* June 3, 2002.
262 "whether they can wiretap you": Ibid.
262 companies to "interrogate their data": Interview with Konrad Feldman, Dec.
     3, 2003.
263 "just a sea change in the industry": Robert O'Harrow, Jr., "In Terror War, Pri-
     vacy vs. Security," *Washington Post,* June 3, 2002.
263 "unusual or suspicious activity": Quoted from *Clearing Your View with Search-
     space and IBM,* a 2002 brochure.
265 $16,000 per hijacker over more than a year: U.S. General Accounting Office,
     GAO-04-163, November 2003, p. 6.
265 "It is about understanding behavior": Feldman interview.
268 "is right up our alley": Interview with Ken Ritchhart, Nov. 4, 2002. Speaking
     about Poindexter and his initiatives on March 20, 2003, Ritchhart said: "It
     was totally misunderstood . . . I personally think he was trying to make a sig-
     nificant contribution to the American government."
269 "and React To Relevant Information": *FBI Data Warehousing, Data Mining &
     Collaboration: An Enterprise View of Data.* In 2004, FBI officials began trying to
     avoid the use of the term "data mining" because of the growing sensitivity of
     the public. The thrust of their efforts remained unchanged.
270 "no way to bring it together": Interview with Mason McDaniel, March 20,
     2003.
271 "than in the last twenty years": Ritchhart interview.
271 and became a federal witness: Ryan Oliver, "Informant Was Key to Stings,"
     Las Vegas Review-Journal, June 29, 2001; and Jeff German, "A Nevada Investiga-
     tor Is Suspected of Taking Hush Money," *Las Vegas Sun,* Aug. 28, 2001.
272 some eighty thousand in all: The Bulletin's Frontrunner, "Concerns Raised
     Over Accuracy of FBI Terrorists Databanks," citing *Government Executive Maga-
     zine* (1/8, Strohm), Jan. 8, 2004.
273 balances on law enforcement authority: Burnham, *The Rise of the Computer
     State,* p. 67.
273 "at any time, for any reason": Interview with Ari Schwartz, spring 2004.

273 to a private investigation firm: "Former DEA Agent Sentenced for Bribery,"
Los Angeles Times, Dec. 19, 2002.

"A former Drug Enforcement Administration agent was sentenced to 27
months in prison this week after pleading guilty to bribery and other felonies
stemming from his sale of sensitive law enforcement information to a private
investigative agency.

"Emilio Calatayud, 36, was arrested in June in Mexico.

"Prosecutors said he received at least $22,500 in bribes in exchange for
giving Triple Check Investigations of San Dimas information obtained from
computer systems operated by the DEA, FBI and state Department of Justice."

See also Kevin Poulsen, "Law Enforcement Computers Allegedly Became a
Treasure Trove for California Info Broker," *SecurityFocus,* Jan. 22, 2001: "The
purloined data allegedly came from three law enforcement computers to
which Calatayud had otherwise lawful access: the FBI's National Crime Information Center (NCIC), which maintains nationwide records on arrest histories, convictions and warrants; the California Law Enforcement
Telecommunications System (CLETS), a state network that gives agents access to California motor vehicle records, rap sheets and fingerprints; and a
DEA database called the Narcotics and Dangerous Drug Information System
(NADDIS)."

274 Allison was fired: Annie Gowen, "Board Recommends Firing Officer in Mis-
conduct Case," *Washington Post,* Oct. 15, 2000.

274 "misuses in most cases": Schwartz interview.

274 "that they're lying": M. L. Elrick, "Information Abuse Has Many Forms," *Detroit Free Press,* Aug. 1, 2001.

275 "do what they want": Interview with Stephen Nash, Feb. 23, 2004.

275 his wife, Vicki, join him?: Interview with Mark Silverstein, undated.

275 wrote in a letter to Webb: See http://www.aclu-co.org/spyfiles/
chronology.htm

276 a rally against police brutality: Details come from dozens of police reports, including some under the title "Denver Police Department Intelligence Bureau
Information Summary," obtained by the ACLU of Colorado.

276 "our worst fears about police": Nash interview.

277 "led to most of the problems": Orion Scientific Systems license agreement
with the Denver Police Department, Nov. 2, 1999. Though the document
mentions training, officials have said the Police Department did not pay for
instruction that was sufficient.

277 "of being labeled 'criminal extremist' ": Silverstein interview.

278 "sensitive areas and so forth": Text of voice mail from Laura Luke, retrieved
Feb. 23, 2004.

278 high above downtown Manhattan: Pasquale J. D'Amuro, assistant director
in charge of the New York field office, took me through his offices on April
5, 2004. I taped virtually all of the interview with D'Amuro and his colleagues.

279 "unlike anything we've had before": D'Amuro interview.

280 "for the citizens of this country": Ibid. "Officers are trained in civil rights,
how to do it without violating rights—oversight from several different
groups," D'Amuro added. "The info we're collecting is public info—that the
country has the ability to collect. If other info requires authorization from
the courts—e.g., a federal grand jury subpoena, then we go that process.
The benefit for the people of this country is that the FBI is trained in doing
that. We want to make sure in doing these investigations that we don't go too
far."

CHAPTER 10. NO PLACE TO HIDE

I am indebted to Richard Smith, who agreed to combine an extensive interview about sensors and surveillance with a walking and driving tour of of real-life examples in New York. With balance and a quiet passion, Smith gave new insight into the convergence of so many different kinds of sensors, many of them machines that we take for granted. Katherine Albrecht provided useful information about RFID and an activist's perspective about what it could mean.

I relied on some very good journalism about GPS devices, and received help on the section about James Turner from his attorney, Bernadette Keyes. I happily reviewed *The Conversation,* the film directed by Francis Ford Coppola, and found it both illuminating and unsettling. The quotes come directly from the movie. When I write about Verint, I am obliged to company spokesman Alan Roden, who arranged for a visit and graciously gave me financial documents about the company.

283 our emerging surveillance society: Interview and tour of New York with Richard Smith, Sept. 5, 2003.

284 "the way our operation is run": Joie Tyrrell, "Speeding into Our Hearts; E-ZPass Comes of Age After a Decade," *Newsday,* July 13, 2003.

284 thirty-six stab wounds to his body: Matt Apuzzo, "Prosecutor's Route Adds to Mystery About His Bloody Slaying," Associated Press, Dec. 15, 2003.

286 that's a lot of tracking: "Retail Spending on RFID Systems to Surpass $1 Billion by 2007, According to IDC," *Business Wire,* Jan. 7, 2004.

286 automatically pay for his gas at Exxon: "Speedpass Donates $10,000 to Chicago Ronald McDonald's Houses," *VNU Business Media,* March 11, 2004.

286 and cut down on costs: Beth Bacheldor, "Defense Department Mandates RFID Use by Suppliers," *Information Week,* Oct. 13, 2003.

286 program to prevent counterfeiting: U.S. Department of Health and Human Services, FDA, *Combating Counterfeit Drugs: A Report of the Food and Drug Administration: February 2004.*

286 to fight fraud and to monitor high rollers: Jeff Hecht, "Casinos Lead the Chip Revolution," *New Scientist,* Jan. 10, 2004.

287 "and it saves us a lot of time": Julia Scheres, "The Three R's: Reading, Writing, RFID," *Wired.com,* Oct. 24, 2003.

287 less frustrating for families and groups: "SAMSys Technologies and SafeTzone Technologies Make Life More Amusing with an RFID Enabled System That Includes Location Services and Cashless Spending," *Canada Newswire,* March 16, 2004.

287 "experimental to universal usefulness": Vicki Ward, "Coming everywhere near you: RFID," IBM.com, http://www-1.ibm.com/industries/financial services/doc/content/landing/884118103.html

288 trying to capitalize on the technology: David LaGesse, "An ID Card That You Can Never Lose," *U.S. News & World Report,* Sept. 8, 2003.

288 "your biography for our sources": Email to Katherine Albrecht from Grocery Manufacturers of America employee, Dec. 15, 2003.

289 "They are out to get me": Interview with Katherine Albrecht, Jan. 9, 2004.

289 that serves as a unique code: Katherine Albrecht, Consumers Against Supermarket Privacy Invasion and Numbering (CASPIAN), *Privacy and Societal Implications of RFID,* pp. 20–21.

290 "to act as an 'electronic passport'": Intellitag 915 Mhz ID card, Intermec, http://www.intermec.com/eprise/main/Intermec/Content/Products/ Products_ShowDetail?section=Products&Product=RFIDI_05

290 "about to change the world": *Privacy and Societal Implications of RFID,* p. 23.

291 "until they make a mistake": Smith interview.

291 after renting a Chrysler Voyager: Colleen Van Tassell, "GPS: Gotta Pay for

Speeding. Coming to small claims court: Roadrunner vs. Acme Rent-a-Car," *New Haven Advocate,* June 14, 2001.

291 some shows to stage at his theater: Interview with Turner's lawyer, Bernadette Keyes, March 22, 2004.

292 "persons of ordinary sensibilities": Legal complaint filed in state Superior Court J.D. of New Haven, Oct. 23, 2001.

292 "can be a dangerous thing": Acme customer Jen Stewart, quoted in Michelle Delio's "Rent-a-car Motto: Speed Bills," *Wired News,* July 21, 2001.

293 "relationship with their cars": John Schwartz, "This Car Can Talk; What It Says May Cause Concern," *New York Times,* Dec. 29, 2003.

293 to block the eavesdropping: Kevin Poulsen, "Court Limits In-Car FBI Spying," *SecurityFocus,* Nov. 20, 2003.

293 to a tailored page on the Web: Ralph Vartabedian, "Car-Monitoring System Allows You to Be Your Own Big Brother," *Los Angeles Times,* Dec. 31, 2003.

294 "that cause traffic congestion": TransCore promotional material; see http://www.transcore.com/EVR/why_evr.html

295 short for "Verifiable intelligence": Interview with Verint spokesman Alan Roden, during a visit to the company's headquarters in Melville, New York, June 19, 2003.

295 "and increase enterprise profitability": See Verint annual report, fiscal 2002, p. 1.

296 a "multi-dimensional retail tool": Verint Systems press release, "Home Depot Selects Verint's Digital Solution," Sept. 16, 2003.

296 passed through the buildings: Verint Systems press release, "Metropolitan Washington Airports Authority Upgrades Verint's Networked Video Security Solution at Dulles International Airport," March 25, 2003.

296 "or a customer service need": Verint promotional material for Loronix Video solutions, http://www.verint.com/video_solutions/gen_ar2a_view.cfm?article level2_category_id=22&article_level2a_id=82

296 "to generate revenue opportunities": Verint promotional material for ULTRA, http://www.verint.com/contact_center/gen_ar2a_view.cfm?article_level2 _category_id=6

296 for signs of tax cheating: Verint Systems press release, "Verint Systems Selected to Deliver Multi-Million Dollar Intelligent Recording Solution for the U.S. Internal Revenue Service," Sept. 4, 2003.

296 Justice Department, Army Intelligence: This information comes in part from a Department of Defense response to my request on June 9, 2003, under the federal Freedom of Information law.

297 "referred to as wiretapping": Verint stock prospectus for 5 million shares, June 12, 2003, pp. 45, 39.

297 was responsible for wiretapping: Edward Warner, "FBI Shakes Up Staff: Bureau Reassigns Its Liaison Chief," *Reed Business Information,* June 16, 1997. See also Verint Web site, www.verint.com

297 from the Israeli government: Verint annual report, fiscal 2003, p. 27.

297 "for intelligence gathering purposes": Verint stock prospectus 2003, p. 40.

298 "or skin galvanic response": "Remarks by Under Secretary Dr. Charles Mc-Queary to the National Defense Industry Association," Directorate of Science and Technology, Sept. 16, 2003.

298 fragments on a visitor's skin: U.S. Department of Homeland Security, Fact Sheet, "Science and Technology Accomplishments," www.dhs.gov

298 "that moves our economy forward": "Remarks by Under Secretary Dr. Charles McQueary," Sept. 16, 2003.

298 and other cutting-edge technology: Rick Merritt, "Homeland Security Agency Focuses R&D on Sensor Nets," *Electronic Engineering Times,* Jan. 5, 2004.

299   without new batteries: Chris Taylor, "What Dust Can Tell You," *Berkeley/Time*
        magazine, Jan. 12, 2004. See also Thomas Hoffman, "Mighty Motes for Medi-
        cine, Manufacturing, the Military and More," *Future Watch*, March 24, 2003.
299   "privacy advocates, and rightly so": Interview with David Bolka, March 24,
        2004.
300   "being kept by different people": Smith interview.

ACKNOWLEDGMENTS

THE ROOTS OF THIS BOOK go deep into my work for the *Washington Post*. I owe a special thanks to Jill Dutt, financial editor and colleague, who gave me great latitude to explore and explain the data revolution. My colleague Glenn Kessler, now a reporter, as an editor helped me develop what we called the privacy beat early on. The editors on the *Post*'s North Wall consistently gave the stories good play. When I mentioned writing a book, they immediately offered encouragement. Thanks all.

I received help on the project from many quarters. One of my most important collaborators was John Biewen, a veteran radio reporter and producer for American RadioWorks, the documentary arm of American Public Media. Biewen signed on to transform the book's ideas and details into radio. He ended up an indispensable colleague who improved the book and documentary with his own legwork and tart observations. The documentary, also called *No Place to Hide*, stands on its own as an examination of the impact of computers, database marketing, surveillance, and all the rest.

Deborah Popowski, who is destined for great things, performed yeoman duty as my researcher. She spent a great many hours making calls, writing crisp memos, checking facts, and challenging my assumptions. The interns at American RadioWorks—you know who you are—chipped in enormously by transcribing interviews.

The essence of two chapters in the book appeared first as stories in the *Washington Post Magazine*. They were well received thanks in part to my *Post* colleague Lynda Robinson, an editor who pressed relentlessly and cheerfully to emphasize the narrative pull of the stories. Robinson eventually read every chapter of the book, and her suggestions improved every one of them.

There's no way I can thank all the many scores of people I interviewed or consulted for the book, or indeed over the years. I'd like to point out a few who provided something extra or helped me understand what lay behind the complexity: Mary Culnan, James Dempsey and his colleagues, Viet Dinh, Robert Douglas, Beryl Howell, Deirdre Mulligan, Christopher Pyle, David Sobel and his colleagues, and Ralph Stein. Special thanks to David Medine and Peter Swire for reading through the relevant chapters and offering smart advice and criticism.

I'm grateful for the sound advice of my agent, Amy Rennert, who gave me a wonderful introduction to the world of publishing.

I'm indebted to Liz Stein, my editor at Free Press. At every stage she expressed unwavering confidence in my reporting and writing. She listened, made suggestions, and listened some more. Then she improved every page, saving me from myself in many instances by asking for more detail or by making so many thoughtful cuts. Thanks also to Maris Kreizman, her able colleague, and all the others at Free Press who made the book, my first, better in both obvious and subtle ways.

Finally, thanks to my family. I should note that Ana, age eleven, and Cormac, age three, helped me in one crucial way: They rarely complained about all those weekends when Dad wasn't around to see films, wrestle, or play ball. Most of all, a kiss for Christina. It is her support that in the end made this book possible.

INDEX

ABOUT THE AUTHOR

ROBERT O'HARROW, JR., is a reporter at *The Washington Post* and an associate of the Center for Investigative Reporting. He was a Pulitzer Prize finalist for articles on privacy and technology and a recipient of the 2003 Carnegie Mellon Cybersecurity Reporting Award. He lives in Arlington, Virginia.